OUTSPOKEN

a decade of transgender activism & trans feminism

-julia serano

switch hitter press

OUTSPOKEN
A Decade of Transgender Activism and Trans Feminism
Copyright © 2016 Julia Serano

Published by
Switch Hitter Press
PO Box 11133
Oakland, CA 94611-1133
www.switchhitter.net

2003 performance poetry photo on left side of front cover by David Huang
2009 APA protest photo on right side of front cover by lore m. dickey, PhD
cover design and book layout by Julia Serano

Publisher's Cataloging-in-Publication

Serano, Julia, author.
    Outspoken : a decade of transgender activism and
trans feminism / Julia Serano.
    pages cm
    Includes bibliographical references.
    LCCN 2016916191
    ISBN 978-0-9968810-0-5 (print)
    ISBN 978-0-9968810-2-9 (eBook)

    1. Serano, Julia--Literary collections.
2. Transgenderism--Literary collections. 3. Transgender
people--Literary collections. 4. Feminism--Literary
collections.   I. Title.

HQ77.9.S469 2016   306.76'8
                          QBI16-900051

9 8 7 6 5 4 3 2 1 BLAST OFF!!!

Dedication

This book is dedicated to the countless gender-variant people in the past who paved the way to make it possible for me to live as an outspoken trans woman around the turn of the millennium.

And to the many trans folks of my own generational cohort, with whom I engaged, debated, collaborated, and/or performed, and whose writings, art, performances, and activism influenced much of the work in this collection.

And to the next wave(s) of transgender people who will no doubt explore new paths, pioneer new forms of art and activism, and make even greater inroads into garnering respect and appreciation for trans lives and perspectives.

table of contents

Introduction

My original idea for this book was relatively straightforward: Since 2002, I have written extensively about transgender experiences, issues, and activism. These writings have taken many forms: performance poetry and spoken word, personal stories, blog posts and essays, speeches and keynotes, academic articles, and magazine and webzine pieces. While much of this work has already appeared in my first two books—*Whipping Girl: A Transsexual Woman on Sexism and the Scapegoating of Femininity* and *Excluded: Making Feminist and Queer Movements More Inclusive*[1]—many other pieces (including some of my personal favorites!) have not been readily available up until now. Much of my earliest work first appeared in various zines and my own self-made chapbooks, which are no longer in print. Other pieces were published online, but may be difficult to find given the Internet's relentless prioritization of new content over old. Still others were written for a one-time performance or event, and have not seen the light of day since. So in 2014, I began digging through my old computer files, searching for these previously unpublished or difficult-to-find pieces, with the intention of compiling and publishing them together for readers who are interested in my writings and/or in trans activism more generally.

As I pored over these older texts, I was struck by how much trans communities and activism have changed over such a relatively short time period. While many pieces in this collection are as relevant now as they were at the time that I wrote them, others felt like rediscovering something that had been buried in a time capsule. Some of the earliest pieces espouse notions and language that were popular in the wake of 1990s–era transgender activism, but which have since fallen somewhat out of fashion. A few of the chapters describe community dynamics and debates that have subsequently receded or which now take on different forms. Even the pieces that I wrote about trans-specific psychiatric diagnoses during the latest *DSM* revision (during 2009–2012), while still quite pertinent, feel as if they are from a previous era, as much of the trans community has since turned its focus onto other concerns.

The speed at which trans activism has evolved is at least partly due to the cyclical nature of trans communities: Often the people who are most active and involved (especially in online settings) tend to be relatively new to the community, such as people who have recently "come out" as trans and/or who are transitioning (or have recently transitioned). And after a several year period of being passionate about, and absorbed in, conversations about trans identities, experiences, and activism, many trans people disengage to some degree, or move onto other interests or concerns. As a result, we (the community as a whole) tend to have a somewhat short memory span, even when it comes to fairly recent events in trans history. So rather than present this book as simply a collection of writings, I additionally set out to reconsider this recent past and to contextualize it for those who were not there to personally witness it.

In addition to providing glimpses into recent trans history, the pieces in this collection also chronicle my own personal transformation from a gender-queer musician who was relatively new to writing and trans activism when I first began, to a trans feminist author who is (in some circles, at least) taken seriously as a "gender theorist" (a designation that still sounds somewhat surreal to me). I have never been inclined to write a memoir or an autobiography, as the minutia of my daily life never seemed particularly interesting to me. But I am a huge fan of "behind the scenes" stories and documentaries that reveal the life events and thought processes that ultimately led some person(s) to produce a particular creation or endeavor. I am often asked about how I first became involved in trans activism, or how I came to write *Whipping Girl*, and so on, so I thought that it might be fun for me (and potentially interesting to readers) to share some of these backstories. More importantly, I found that these backstories significantly helped with my previously stated goal of historically contextualizing many of these writings.

For all of the aforementioned reasons, I have decided to format this book like a reader. The chapters cover a time span from 2002 through 2014. This is admittedly a little bit longer than a decade—my apologies to literalists out there. The chapters are organized (roughly chronologically) into five parts: "Performance and Poetry," "Articulating Trans-misogyny," "Pathological Science Revisited," "Communities and Disparities," and "Differences of Opinion in Trans Activism." Each of these sections represents an evolution in my perspectives and interests, and each begins with an introduction that provides the necessary backdrop to understand the matters at hand. Additionally, each chapter includes a brief introductory sentence or paragraph detailing when (and sometimes why) it was written, where it was originally published or performed, and other potentially noteworthy information. Other supplementary details and commentary are provided via the Notes section at the end of the book.

While some of the pieces have been edited for clarity, to reduce redundancy, or to include additional relevant information, for the most part they adhere to their original form. As a result, some of the language and opinions that I express in earlier chapters may differ somewhat from those that I forward in later chapters or have stated elsewhere. Since such differences are germane to my aim of illustrating how trans activism has evolved over time, I have tried to keep the pieces relatively intact rather than smoothing over these inconsistencies. To help readers navigate the shifts in language, and to aid readers who are relatively new to transgender identities and issues, I have created an online glossary called "There Is No Perfect Word: A Transgender Glossary of Sorts" (which can be found at **http://juliaserano.com/terminology.html**) that provides not only definitions, but commentary and resources regarding history and differing opinions about said terms.

The title of this book, *Outspoken*, comes from a line from "Cocky" (Chapter 10) in which I describe performing "my out-spoken word pieces"—a purposeful play on words, given that I was primarily an out-as-trans spoken word performer when I began my forays into trans activism. "Outspoken" also accurately depicts my activist and writing style circa 2003–2007, which (in retrospect) I would characterize as forceful and, at times, in-your-face (in contrast to my subsequent work, where I have strived to be a little more diplomatic and circumspect). In the subtitle, the reference to "A Decade of Transgender Activism and Trans Feminism" is meant to highlight the fact that this collection represents a snapshot in time: Some of the ideas and language forwarded in this collection would likely seem unnecessary or a complete overreach to trans activists from previous decades, and they will also likely be regarded as quaint or outdated by trans activists in the future. And this is perfectly fine, as all activism is necessarily situated within a particular place and time.

This book is not intended to recap all facets of trans activism that have occurred over the previous decade. Many crucial trans issues and noteworthy events are not covered at all here. Rather, being a collection of my writings, it is often highly personal and disproportionately concerned with matters that were on my mind or that directly impacted me. There were countless other gender-variant people during this same period of time who were creating amazing art and facilitating positive change for trans people in the world, some of whom espoused ideas and perspectives that differed (sometimes significantly) from my own. For readers seeking a more comprehensive overview of trans activism as it existed during the early twenty-first century, I encourage you to consult the works of these additional trans artists and activists.

I should also clarify that this book does not contain all of my trans-related writings from this time period. Numerous pieces were left on the proverbial "cutting-room floor"—these include writings that were not of the highest quality; slam poems that in retrospect were a little too gimmicky; essays about topics that I have been especially prolific about (e.g., trans woman-exclusion, psychiatric depictions of trans people[2]) and which would only add further redundancy to this collection; and blog posts that were immediate reactions to current events in society or within trans communities, which may once have been relevant and timely, but which would not likely hold up today as stand-alone chapters. While not included here, many of these disregarded pieces can still be found on my blog and website.[3]

A content note for those interested: Instances of transphobia and other forms of marginalization are discussed in depth throughout this text. While there are no graphic discussions about physical or sexual assault, those issues are touched upon in passing in several of the chapters (e.g., 4, 10, 16, 26). Desire to self-harm and/or suicidal ideation are discussed (to varying degrees) in Chapters 4, 9, 10, 11, 15, and 17.

Finally, since this book represents my own personal take(s) on trans activism over the last decade or so, it seems fitting to briefly describe my relationship with trans communities and activism prior to the events described in the book. What follows is not meant to be a stereotypical "trans narrative," but rather a brief retrospective regarding where I am personally situated as a trans person within the course of transgender history.

I was born in the late 1960s, just outside of Philadelphia, which is where I grew up for the most part. I spent my formative childhood years in the 1970s, and went to junior high, high school, and college during the 1980s. In other words, I am a product of the pre-Internet age. Nowadays, young trans people who are trying to make sense of their gender can gain insight into their circumstances by seeking out information on various websites and social media. This does not in any way make being trans easy, but it does allow contemporary gender-variant folks to readily seek out community support and resources as they navigate the many obstacles in their lives. In contrast, when I was growing up, the trans experience was especially dominated by two factors: invisibility and isolation.

For instance, I figured out that I was trans in 1979 when I was in sixth grade. I say, "figured out that I was trans," but that is sort of a misnomer, as I didn't have the word "trans" to identify with. I didn't have any label, really. I just thought of myself as a boy who desperately wanted to be a girl for some inexplicable reason. I remember wondering whether there were other kids who felt the same way that I did, but there was really no way to find out without revealing how I felt, and I couldn't imagine doing that.

Occasionally, I considered telling my parents about my dilemma, but I was pretty sure that they didn't know anything more about this whole wanting-to-be-a-girl-thing than I did. In retrospect, it was probably best that I didn't tell them, because they probably would have brought me to a psychiatrist. And given the prehistoric state of trans-related psychiatric theories and therapies back then, I would likely have been subjected to gender reparative therapy, and perhaps even electroshock therapy, as many trans children of my generation had to endure.[4] Anyway, I kept all my trans feelings to myself and did my best to persevere as a boy. I was sad that there didn't seem to be any way for me to be a girl, but honestly, I was just as sad to be so isolated and alone.

This isolation went hand in hand with invisibility. The only trans public figure that I was aware of during my childhood was Renée Richards, although when people talked about her they often insinuated that she transitioned in order to gain an unfair advantage in women's tennis, so I wasn't sure how much relevance that had on my life. When I was in high school, I went to my town's local public library to look up the words "transsexual" and "transvestite"—these were words that I would occasionally overhear, and which seemed like they might be relevant to me, although I wasn't quite sure what either of them meant. I searched through the now old-fashioned library card catalogue but couldn't find a single book or article on either subject.

It wasn't until a few years later, in the late '80s when I was in college, that I was first able to hear or read trans people speaking in their own voices about their own identities and lives. This came in the form of a documentary called *What Sex Am I?* (which aired on cable TV) and Jan Morris's 1974 memoir *Conundrum*, which I found in my college library.[5] Granted, it wasn't much, but at least it was something. Over the years that followed, I would occasionally come across movies or books that had trans characters, although they were usually the creation of trans-unaware media producers. Today we would likely describe many of those books and films as "problematic," as the trans characters were usually two-dimensional stereotypes that took the form of surprising plot-twists or the butt of jokes. As bad as these depictions often were, many trans folks (including myself) purposefully sought them out and even appreciated them to a certain extent. After all, as flawed as they were, at least they offered a little bit of visibility. At least they acknowledged that we existed.

In 1989, I moved to New York City for graduate school. While I was aware that the city had a significant trans population, I was unable to find community there. This was partly of my own doing. I was working about sixty hours a week (as people sometimes do in grad school), which didn't really leave me with much time to find myself trans-wise. I had seen advertisements in *The Village Voice* for places like Club Edelweiss (a NYC trans bar/club), but at the time, I was really closeted and couldn't possibly imagine going out in public dressed for fear that people I knew might see me. I suppose that a basic trans support group where I could meet and get to know other trans folks in a private setting would have been perfect for me at that time in my life, but I was not aware of any such groups, nor did there seem to be any obvious way to find them if they did exist. In lieu of finding actual community, I was at least able to find resources and reading materials by and about trans people via Lee Brewster's bookstore (which I describe in Chapter 8).

In 1993, I moved to Lawrence, Kansas—a college town just outside of Kansas City. And it was there that I finally got to meet and befriend actual trans people, almost fifteen years after I first became conscious that I was trans. It happened at a trans social and support group called "Crossdressers and Friends." The group consisted predominantly of trans female/feminine-spectrum folks, mostly crossdresser-identified, but there were a few trans women and trans male/masculine-spectrum folks who would attend. Partners were also welcome. Most people there identified within the gender binary—as male crossdressers, or as transsexual women or men. There were a few of us who admitted to not being exactly sure what we were, but there wasn't really any language for us then. The broad umbrella term "transgender" hadn't quite come into vogue (at least not in Kansas), and it would be at least five years before I would first hear the word "genderqueer."

I joined Crossdressers and Friends in 1994, which happens to be the year

Kate Bornstein's influential book *Gender Outlaw: On Men, Women and the Rest of Us* was first published.[6] Remarkably, I don't recall anyone in the group ever mentioning it. Honestly, I wouldn't be surprised if none of us even knew that it existed, as it was extremely difficult to find out about anything that wasn't mainstream back in those days. While the Internet existed in 1994, it was not yet in widespread use.

The only reason that I knew Crossdressers and Friends even existed was from a small ad on the back page of a Kansas City alternative weekly paper. During this particular time and place, if you were discovered to be trans, you would almost certainly be fired from your job and ostracized by your local community. I know this still happens, but back then, there were virtually no legal protections for trans people, and almost no trans-focused organizations to act as a support system when this would occur. Anyway, to ensure everyone's safety, newcomers were not allowed to attend any meetings until they had been vetted, first by phone, and then subsequently in a face-to-face interview. I remember meeting Gina, the first trans person who I ever had a sustained conversation with, at a discreet location—a quiet Mexican restaurant on the outskirts of town. The clandestine nature of the encounter felt like something out of a spy novel. We talked, and she reported back to the group that I seemed legitimate, after which the group invited me to their bi-monthly meet ups.

When I think back to that time, what strikes me most is that I was convinced that my life would always be that way: one giant secret. I would always be either a closeted crossdresser or—if I ever did transition—a trans woman who was living "stealth."[7] That's just how circumstances seemed to force trans people to live their lives during that time. If you would have told me back then that one day I would be an out trans author whose books are often carried in mainstream bookstores, and who is often invited to give talks about trans issues and activism at colleges and conferences, I never would have believed you.

But things slowly changed. I wasn't aware of it back when I was in Kansas, but during that time, gender-variant people were starting to come out and take to the streets in groups such as Transexual Menace, Hermaphrodites with Attitude, and Transgender Nation.[8] Back then—when there was virtually no media coverage of trans people and issues (outside of occasional and purposefully sensationalistic talk shows), the simple act of a dozen or more gender-variant folks gathering together in a public space and speaking truth to power was a revolutionary act of trans visibility. And along with Kate Bornstein's book, the '90s saw the publication of other important trans activist books by Leslie Feinberg, Riki Wilchins, Patrick Califia, and others.[9] These books often encouraged trans folks to stop hiding or playing down our gender difference, and to be out about being trans. While I do not believe that trans people need to be out if they do not wish to be, it seems clear that the increasing numbers of people who have since decided to be out as trans have greatly helped challenge the invisibility that we long experienced.

I first read some of the aforementioned books around 1999–2001. By this point, I was living in the San Francisco Bay Area, and was in the midst of a five-year transformative period in which I went from identifying as a cross-dresser, to identifying as bigender/genderqueer, to ultimately identifying as a woman.[10] I am not sure how those years of my life might have played out if I did not have access to those books and the revolutionary ideas contained therein. And by the time that I made the decision to transition to female in late 2000, the Internet had already taken off and was becoming widely accessible. For the first time, trans folks could type words like "transsexual," "transgender," "sex change," "not sure of my gender," etc., into a rudimentary search engine and find resources and people who shared the same experience. I soon joined several trans-focused email lists—they were mostly transition-focused (which was information I was seeking out at the time), but other trans-related topics and issues were routinely discussed. While online communities are old hat nowadays, at the time it seemed unbelievable that I could regularly interact with scores of other trans people on a daily basis. Those groups basically became my community until after my transition, at which point I began to participate in the Bay Area's queer and trans performance scenes (which is where Part 1 of this book commences).

It is now over a decade later, and things have changed far more rapidly and extensively than I ever could have possibly imagined. Trans people still face isolation and invisibility, although these aspects of the trans experience are no longer quite as predominant as they used to be. While we still make up a relatively small percentage of the population, we can fairly readily find one another and organize online via social media and other community forums. With regards to visibility, it used to be that I could go months on end without seeing or hearing anything about transgender people in the media or in my personal life (outside of trans circles, of course). Nowadays, I regularly read articles written by trans writers for relatively mainstream media outlets, stumble upon television interviews with trans actors and artists about their latest projects, watch serious news reports covering transgender issues in a non-sensationalistic way, and so on. And looking beyond the mainstream (which is remarkably easy to do these days given the Internet), I can find more books, articles, music, films, art, and activism—all created by and/or for trans people—than I could ever possibly consume. There was a time in the early 2000s when I felt like I had read or viewed almost all of the trans-themed content that was accessible to me; nowadays, I feel like I cannot possibly keep up.

These are all promising trends, but there are still many obstacles to overcome. We still are often denied basic rights that others take for granted, and we routinely encounter difficulties accessing health care and navigating our way through various social and legal institutions. Trans people, and especially trans people of color, disproportionately experience high levels of harassment and physical assault, workplace discrimination, unemployment, poverty, and homelessness.[11] While the increase in trans visibility over the last decade has been mostly a positive development, it has to some extent made us more obvious targets and sparked a backlash from conservative political forces (as seen in the recent rash of proposed "bathroom bills" that would make it either illegal or dangerous for trans people to use public restrooms[12]).

What especially strikes me is that, while trans people have made many gains over the last decade or so, binary gender norms have barely budged at all. A foundational premise of the transgender movement that garnered momentum in the 1990s was that we needed to convince the rest of the world that binary gender norms are oppressive and negatively impact everybody. It seems that on this point, we have not found much success, as gender-non-conforming bodies and behaviors are still regularly disparaged and discouraged in most strands of society. Instead, where we have made progress is in convincing a growing swath of the population to recognize that some people (i.e., trans folks) do defy binary gender conventions—we exist and deserve to be treated humanely. But this disparity in progress creates a dilemma for us: How can we ever be seen as anything other than second-class citizens if most people continue to look down upon gender non-conformity in others? Nowadays, people increasingly oppose blatant acts of anti-trans discrimination, yet most of these same people would likely balk at the notion that trans people's gender identities, bodies, and experiences are just as valid as their own.

It is my hope that this retrospective collection will not only offer glimpses into recent trans history, but also provide insights into how to challenge the many double standards that transgender people (and countless other people) face. While many of the early chapters describe on my own personal experiences as a trans person, or focus on issues more specifically faced by trans women or transsexuals, toward the end of the book (especially in Part 5, "Differences of Opinion in Trans Activism") I share my thoughts on how to make transgender activism (and social justice movements more generally) more robust, flexible, and accommodating of difference. Transgender people vary from one another in our identities, personal histories, life trajectories, ages, sexualities, geographies, how we are socially situated, and in every other imaginable way. It is my hope that, moving forward, we don't fall into the traps that have undermined or derailed other past activist movements—specifically, the misguided notions that all members must meet certain ideals or norms in order to be seriously considered; the tendency to create or perpetuate binaries and hierarchies rather than striving to eliminate them; and the selfish tendency to focus on the concerns of a supposedly special few rather than striving for gender equity and social justice for everybody.

Part One

Performance and Poetry

Prior to my transition in 2001, my primary creative outlet had always been music. For many years, I was the vocalist/guitarist/primary songwriter for the indie-rock/noise-pop band Bitesize. We were a fixture in the San Francisco Bay Area music scene from 1997–2005: We released a pair of albums (1999's *The Best of Bitesize* and 2001's *Sophomore Slump*), garnered some college radio airplay, and toured up and down the West coast numerous times. It was through music that I first expressed my trans identity, even if I was not quite sure what exactly my identity was at the time. One of the first songs I wrote for Bitesize was "I Forgot My Mantra," which was basically about me being a crossdresser without ever explicitly stating so. It was full of coy lyrics like "I do secret things when I'm alone in my room, but exactly what I will not say/There are things that I often do in public, but they're embarrassing/I do secret things when I'm alone in my room, because I'm into that thing." And the chorus was a single flippant line: "I'm a hermaphrodite, but that's beside the point." For the record, I was not trying to claim an intersex identity with that lyric—I'm not sure I even knew exactly what intersex was back then. I was just trying to express that I saw myself as harboring some combination of maleness/masculinity and femaleness/femininity within me.

Other early Bitesize songs were about my personal experiences as a trans person. "In the Know" was about the first time that I went out in public presenting as female at the age of twenty-one. And the song "Switch Hitter" was an embellished story about how I first decided to change my sex while watching my baseball league's all-star game. The chorus of the song was: "A year from now I'll be the center of attention/After I have had my sex change operation." Other songs I wrote around this time were fictional trans-themed tales. The song "Surprise Ending" was about a trans woman who accidentally runs into the bully who picked on her as a child, and "Understudy" (my personal favorite Bitesize song) is about a transgender teenage thespian who gets to play the role of Ophelia in a Catholic boys school rendition of *Hamlet*. (For those interested, these songs are available for your listening pleasure at Bitesize.net)

I cannot tell you how freeing and empowering it was for me to get up on stage with Bitesize and belt out those lyrics. I felt sure that I was outing myself with all these trans-themed songs, although most friends and fans never seemed to connect the dots, at least not until I publicly came out as trans in December 2001.[1] Since Bitesize was well known in our local music scene, it ended up being a rather public coming out during a time when there was very little trans awareness in the general public. At the time, I was aware of a handful of trans-fronted bands scattered across the country (a few were even local), but it still felt like we (i.e., Bitesize) were in relatively uncharted territory. Thankfully, our audience and others in the local music scene were generally accepting. It probably helped that people already tended to view me as eccentric and gender unconventional, so my transition was probably not as much of a mental stretch for people as it may have been otherwise.

In any case, given our band's previous history (e.g., several records, articles, and interviews in which I was identified by my male name and with masculine pronouns), and our desire to continue playing together, it seemed inevitable that I would remain out about being transgender post-transition as our band moved forward. While that created numerous obstacles and awkward moments along the way, I mostly welcomed it, because I was tired of keeping my trans identity secret. On top of that, having grown up during a time when there were hardly any readily available transgender-themed art or role models, I embraced the idea of remaining visible as a trans performer.

In addition to simply being out, I also wanted to talk about my experiences and perspectives as a trans person. While I continued to do this through music (via Bitesize and, more recently, my current music project Soft Vowel Sounds), I eventually found the "pop song" format to be rather limiting for what I was hoping to accomplish. After all, song lyrics are usually only about one or two hundred words, and thus not as well suited for the expression of more complex stories or ideas. Somewhat by accident, I gravitated toward spoken word as an outlet for these expressions. My partner at the time (who is mentioned by name in some of these chapters) was the co-host of the Berkeley Poetry Slam, and I had been attending slams[2] and other performance poetry events for years, although solely as an audience member. Then one day in 2001, I experienced a long-forgotten memory of a brief friendship that I shared with another trans person back when I lived in Kansas. Inexplicably, the piece just flowed out of me in the form and cadence of a slam poem, eventually becoming the first chapter, "Vice Versa."

While I never imagined myself as a poet or spoken word performer, I was very comfortable being on stage and speaking in public, so I figured I would give it a shot. Since you need to have as many as three previously prepared pieces to compete in a poetry slam, I decided to write several more poems before taking the stage—those initial pieces became "Ophelia Revisited," "Either Or," and "Small Blue Thing" (all collected here), plus "Barrette Manifesto" (which later became a chapter of *Whipping Girl*).[3] While it took me a while to get the hang of performing on stage without a guitar strapped around my shoulder and my bandmates by my side, I eventually became fairly decent at it.

Over the next three years, I self-published two chapbooks (i.e., small hand-made books) of slam poetry: *Either/Or* (2002) and *Draw Blood* (2004).[4] These collections were somewhat different in content and tone.

While it contained a number of serious pieces, *Either/Or* was often pur-posefully playful and humorous. Part of the reason for this was because I was genderqueer-identified at the time (which is why I avoided explicitly referring to myself as a "woman" in those poems, opting instead to use less-loaded terms like "girl" and "boy"). Like many genderqueer individuals of that era, I was profoundly influenced by Kate Bornstein and Riki Wilchins, trans writers and activists who often used humor and played up their own gender ambiguity and non-conformity in order to challenge readers' binary notions of gender, and I attempted to do the same in some of my early writings. On top of that, *Either/ Or* was written during my first year post-transition, as I was still coming out to people and managing other people's reactions to my transness on a regular basis. One approach that helped me make it through that period was utilizing humor—poking fun at gender conventions, making irreverent comments about my own transness, and so on. So it is not surprising that such tactics may have seeped into my writings during that time.

While a few of the pieces collected in *Draw Blood* were playful in tone, the overall feel of the chapbook was more dark and intense. This was partly because I was experiencing a lot of emotional pain at the time, as I explain in the chapter "Introduction to *Draw Blood*." But it was also because I was becoming more immersed in activism during this time period. While I had called myself a trans activist prior to this point, it was mostly because I was an out transgender artist who put on trans-themed performances and events. However, it was my experience at Camp Trans in August 2003 (which I have described elsewhere[5]) that really evangelized me as an activist. I was becoming increasingly absorbed in feminism and gender theory, and more outspoken and unapologetic about voicing my opinions as a trans woman. This personal evolution—from being an artist who dabbled in activism, to primarily seeing myself as an activist who used art to challenge the status quo—is chronicled in the last chapter of this section: "San Francisco Bay Area Trans Performance and Activism."

This section includes all the spoken word pieces from this particular period of my life that I remain proud of, and which were not previously included in my previous books *Whipping Girl* and *Excluded*.[6] I have found that readers who are more familiar with my subsequent gender- and activism-themed books and essays often have certain misconceptions about these earlier poems that are worth mentioning here. When writing solely for the page (or computer screen) about issues that are important to diverse people, I work hard to be as objective as possible, and to reasonably consider alternative points of view. In contrast, these early slam poems are highly personal in nature and meant to represent a singular point of view (i.e., my thoughts and feelings at the time of writing). For example, what I say about my own experience with religion in "Sleeping Sickness," or my own experiences with sexuality in "Book Worm" or "Mix and Match," should definitely *not* be viewed as the-singular-trans-perspective on these matters, nor as my definitive takes on religion or sexuality more generally. Rather, they should be viewed as highly personal reactions and ruminations, which is how they were originally intended.

Furthermore, I believe that (as with music) performance poetry is an excellent medium for conveying emotion more so than mere words or information. For this reason, many of my early spoken word pieces are purposefully dramatic or even bombastic at points, as I was trying to affect audiences on a gut level, in addition to an intellectual one. Along similar lines, I am fairly liberal with my use of profanity in spoken word pieces. This is not because I am trying to be "provocative" or "edgy," but because the sounds of those words when vocalized tend to impact people on a visceral level that is not comparable with how they are experienced when being read off the page.

Many of the pieces in this section differ from their original form in a number of ways. For starters, in my *Either/Or* and *Draw Blood* chapbooks, I visually presented these spoken word pieces as poems, whereas here they are formatted in prose in order to keep them stylistically consistent with the rest of the book. Furthermore, as I continued to perform these spoken word pieces in subsequent years, the specific wording often evolved, sometimes accidentally, but often purposefully (and hopefully for the better). Finally, as the oldest pieces in this collection, they are also the ones most likely to appear dated as the result of ongoing shifts in trans-related language, so I did make a few edits regarding terminology in this section.[7]

What follows is who I was, and what I was thinking, in the first few years immediately following my transition.

1

Vice Versa

This was my first spoken word poem, written in 2001. It was first published in Either/Or *(2002) and subsequently appeared on the webzine* Big Ugly Review.[1]

I almost forgot about her, buried alive in the back of my mind. At the time, I was a twenty-six year-old closet case, a self-described occasional cross-dresser. And she was just like me only vice versa.

I met her in Kansas City at my first transgender support group meeting. The chairs were set up in a circle and most of the seats were filled with cross-dressers[2] in their forties and fifties. They were painstakingly dressed, wearing Sunday's best, floral prints and muted pinks with just a hint of five o'clock shadow. Looking strangely sweet, almost equal parts aunt and uncle.[3] And she seemed so out of place there, the only one in T-shirt and jeans. And genetically speaking, she was the only girl in the room.[4] And chronologically, we were the only two in our twenties.

After the meeting's minutes, and a guest speaker from Mary Kay offering makeup tips, she introduced herself to me. She told me her name was Joan; I told her mine was Tom.[5] And after a bit of random chitchat, she asked if I wanted to hang out some time. I said "sure," and a week later we did.

I drove to Topeka where she lived. I remember the two of us were sitting on her bed listening to Tom Lehrer on her portable cassette player when I asked her what her deal was. She said she wasn't sure what to call herself exactly. She was attracted to men, but when she masturbated, she imagined herself with a penis topping them. And I could tell that she was embarrassed until I told her that I knew exactly what she meant. Because I was just like her, only lesbian.

And so I told her—the first time told anyone—about back when I was in the seventh grade and had the biggest crush on a girl named Kathy. And every pre-teen fantasy that I had about her began with me being turned into a girl somehow. And only afterwards would we run away together.

Then Joan told me about her high school boyfriend who told her he was gay. And she replied that she wasn't surprised and that she liked him that way.

We told our gender histories like we were swapping war stories. Experiences we couldn't share with our families or friends, because they were never there and they would never understand. But that night, sitting on Joan's bed, for the first time in my life, I didn't feel quite so much like an alien.

The last time I saw her was a Saturday evening we spent watching a *Star Trek: Next Generation* rerun—the episode where Beverly Crusher falls in love with a Trill.[6] And we both sat still on her couch next to one another. And when our bodies touched, it was the first human contact that either of us had in a while. At one point, I put my arm around her, and she leaned into me, and it felt like we were pretending that I was the he and she was the she.

And for a moment, I thought one thing might lead to another. Maybe we would make out on her sofa and wake up naked next to one another. And somehow it almost made sense, like we were each other's long lost complement, the way that two odd numbers add up to make an even. But the problem was, we weren't really a perfect match, we were more like exact replicas—the same, only vice versa. And while there was definitely some mutual attraction, nothing ever happened, because after all, I wasn't a gay man, and she wasn't a lesbian.

Now it's eight years later, and I'm not in Kansas anymore. I'm a woman living in Oakland. And that bedroom in Topeka literally feels like a lifetime ago. And every now and again, when I find myself feeling alone, I think about Joan, and wonder how he's doing.

2

Ophelia Revisited

I wrote this spoken word poem in 2002 after reading the book Reviving Ophelia: Saving the Selves of Adolescent Girls.[1] *The female character in this piece is a composite of several girls I knew during my childhood and adolescence. It was first published in* Either/Or *(2002) and subsequently appeared in the anthology* She's Shameless: Women Write About Growing Up, Rocking Out and Fighting Back.[2]

We were more than just neighbors, we were practically best friends. And we would spend endless summer days together exploring the nearby woods, finding secret paths that led to landmarks only we knew about. And in the late afternoons, we would hijack the playground two blocks away, and we'd turn seesaws into pirate planks, swings into trapezes, and monkey bars into towering infernos.

Some days we would both be wearing baseball caps, and adults would joke that you couldn't tell us apart except for your ponytail. That was the only way to tell that I was the boy and you the girl. That was when we were ten.

Three years later, we were avoiding one another in junior high school hallways, our friendship shut off like a faucet as we sought the approval of different cliques. And I saw you kiss your boyfriend hello at his locker each morning. No longer sporting baseball caps, you wore Capri pants and spaghetti-strap tops, and I watched you speak "I love you" to him in secret codes made up of hair twirls and perfectly timed eye blinks. And I got the distinct impression that he didn't speak your language.

But I did. I knew too much for my own good. And I never told anyone this then, but I spent many sleepless nights wishing I was you. But junior high was no place for this transgender tomboy to try to find herself, what with everyone acting out scenes from *Lord of the Flies*, and unwritten rules like boys hold their notebooks at their side while girls cradle theirs against their chests. So I learned to settle for something less, like simply making it through the day without having anyone figure me out.

That's why I wore oversized flannel shirts to distort my slender body, practiced making stone-cold don't-fuck-with-me faces to convince even the biggest pricks to leave the small kid alone. And in school, I excelled at science and math, because I knew that numbers and facts could never betray me the way that my own emotions could. I used logic as a shield, wielding my opinions like battle axes at anyone who dared to get close to me. In other words, I turned into the cocky teenage boy that I was supposed to be. But I would have traded it all to spend one day in your shoes.

And now, years later, I wonder if you felt the same way about me back then. Not that you wished you were a boy *per se*, but did you miss the part of yourself that would have liked to play stick ball or taken your rage out on my drum kit?

And I'm starting to think that the same thing happened to both of us: At the age of twelve we split ourselves down the middle, allowed only to take half into adolescence. You took the feminine, I the masculine, but we both sacrificed half a human being to the gods of fitting in. We both learned to say all the right things while biting our tongues; we swallowed our pride, trying not to vomit up disgust. And we both hated our bodies for choosing our fates for us.

It took me twenty years to put the pieces of myself back together. And I'm still learning how to be both the giggling girl and the scientist. And I'm not sure what happened to you, but I'd like to imagine that you've managed to put yourself back together too.

3

Either Or

This piece was an expression of my genderqueer identity at the time that I wrote it in 2002. It was first published in Either/Or *(2002) and subsequently appeared in the magazine* Transgender Tapestry.[1]

It should have been no big deal really. Just another Saturday night in a bar, some guy flirting with some girl. And she wasn't even interested in him, and it should have been no big deal. Except that I was the girl. And the guy was the first straight boy who ever took an interest in me. In the past, other men had hit on me, but only the ones who like their girls to be boy underneath. But months of hormone replacement therapy erased away most visible traces of my maleness. So much so, that this straight boy didn't think twice before flirting with me.

And it took me by surprise. We talked for a while before he gently touched the side of my arm and smiled. And my brain went wild with a million thoughts set off like fireworks, like my life flashing before my eyes: years of potions and spells, crossdressing rituals designed to conjure up the girl in me, just so I could catch a glimpse of her reflection in a bathroom mirror or store front window.

And I wasn't even into this boy, but he made me blush. His flirts felt like hard won accomplishments—years of suffering and sacrifice finally paid off when this guy saw a real girl when he looked into my eyes. Our language doesn't have the words to describe this. It's the sort of thing that ordinarily gets taken for granted. From the moment the doctor announces, "it's a girl" or "it's a boy," most people's gender is written in granite. But my gender is more like a carrot on a stick; it's always dangling right in front of me.

Because I may pass as a woman,[2] but I have a male past that runs thirty-some years deep. And it's full of memories that I don't regret, secrets that

I shouldn't have to keep. And every time I meet a stranger who turns into a friend, it's only a matter of time before I find myself telling them. And I've seen that look a hundred times, when what I am changes in their eyes. And they can act nonchalant and polite, but from that point on they can't help but see the boy in me, and I'm no longer quite the girl that I used to be.

My gender is a boulder that I roll up a hill each day only to have it come crashing back down on me.

And that's why it's so tempting for me to just lose myself in those rare moments of absolute authenticity, like when that straight boy flirted with me. Because a part of me wants desperately to be seen as 100 percent female. But somehow the burden of a million sins of omission seems like too high of a price to pay for the privilege of merely blending in.

Because the real problem is that gender is exclusive—it's always either/or. And I guess that makes my gender none of the above. Because my gender is the answer to a trick question. It's like that optical illusion where you see either a vase or two faces, but you can't see them both at once. My gender is more than the sum of my anatomical parts. And you can choose to see me as either female or male, that's up to you to decide. And if you still don't get what I'm trying to say, well that's okay. My gender takes more than three minutes to describe.

4

Scared to Death

I first performed this piece at the Berkeley Poetry Slam on November 20, 2002, the date of the fourth annual Transgender Day of Remembrance. It also appeared in Either/Or *(2002), and in 2003 I repurposed the fourth paragraph of this piece for Chapter 10, "Cocky." While I currently have some mixed feelings about this chapter (which are contextualized in Note #2), I decided to include it in this collection because quite a number of people have expressed to me that this piece was important to them.*

Few people make it through high school without having at least one classmate commit suicide. For me, it was Tony Newman. In eleventh grade, he locked himself in the garage with the car running. The act seemed so unlike him. He was one of the few popular kids who everyone genuinely liked. And every time I saw him, he was either laughing or making someone else laugh. Apparently, he never spoke about being depressed and he didn't leave a note, so the reason why he took his own life remained a mystery. It lingered like a lump in people's throats.

I had a theory that I never shared with anyone. I wondered whether Tony felt like I did. I was transgender, although at the time I didn't have a word for it. But I was good enough at math to know that, statistically, there had to be at least a few other people keeping the same secret. And I put two and two together, because I knew that suicide had crossed my mind a few hundred times. And I knew that I'd rather be dead than be seen dressed as a girl. And I knew how much it hurt to have thoughts that you don't want, but you can't turn off.

And now I know that this is nothing new. There are statistics that suggest that up to 50 percent of transgender people try to end their life, if not by suicide, then indirectly through substance abuse.[1] And every day I consider myself lucky to have made it this far.

Although sometimes, I still feel like I'm one step away from the grave. Because once every two weeks, someone is murdered for being transgender.[2] These are no unfortunate accidents, no victims of circumstance. These victims are often beaten beyond recognition; these are attempts at total obliteration. And sometimes, I can't help but wonder whether I might be next. Because at least once a week, I get up on stage and out myself in songs and spoken word pieces. Sometimes I worry that I'm making myself a target, because all it takes is one asshole in the audience who feels that his manhood is threatened by my mere existence.

But I remind myself that there are many ways to die, and the slowest, most torturous one of all is being scared to death. Because being intimidated into silence is like being suffocated—in both cases someone else is taking your last breath. So tonight I speak on behalf of an entire endangered species,[3] because I know that silence really does equal death. And I know the only thing that stops injustice is protest. And my words are meant to pay tribute to every transgender voice that has been silenced, whether by suicide, or homicide, or those who are still alive, but have been frightened into keeping quiet. And I hope that this piece will be but one of a million small acts, that together add up to fighting back.

5

Small Blue Thing

This piece was first published in Either/Or *(2002) and it subsequently appeared in* the anthology Take Me There: Trans and Genderqueer Erotica.[1]

Writers and poets are notorious for having the guts (or perhaps lack of good judgment) to share their deep dark secrets with us. Making public their embarrassments and abuses, amusing or moving us with personal insights into issues that too often go unspoken.

But there is one topic that I have yet to hear any self-confessionals about: impotence.

So leave it to the transsexual woman to be the only one with the proverbial balls to admit that, way back when, on many an occasion, I would get aroused, even to the point of orgasm, without my penis ever getting hard enough to properly perform penetration.

And back when I considered myself a straight boy, I was embarrassed by this. And the women I dated, twenty-something het girls, trained since birth to burden male shame tried to take the blame for my flaccidness, despite my assurances that I was intensely attracted to them, that my lack of erection was not a reflection of them.

But by my late twenties, I had moved well beyond missionary position vanilla sex, and I found myself with bisexual women who were into topping me while I played the femme role. And when their hands hiked up my skirt and began to flirt with the space between my legs, they didn't really care how hard I got, just so long as I was hot, squirming, and breathing heavy.

But I did have one last fling with the whole penetration thing, and I shared it with the most kick-ass girl in the universe. For most of her adult life, she considered herself a dyke—eight straight years of exclusively sleeping with women. And ironically, I first met her shortly after she had rediscovered her appreciation for men. She was trying the word "bisexual" on for size and, much to my surprise, I found myself ready, willing, and able to rise to the occasion!

For about a month or two.

Eventually, pretending to be a boy lost its novelty, and I found myself once again imagining how wet my vagina was getting, when I should have been entering her instead. And like I said, this girl was kick-ass, and I didn't want to disappoint. So I did what any self-respecting semblance of a man would do: I set out to score some Viagra.[2]

It was so easy to get! I just went to my doctor, told him I was impotent, and voilà, he wrote me a prescription, no questions asked. He didn't even take my temperature. But designer drugs don't come without a price, as I spent thirty bucks for three blue pills.

I wasted the first one on a necessary test run, and it seemed to work just fine. So the second time, I tried it with the kick-ass girl. After our date, we went back to her place and began to suck face, and before I knew it I had circled second base, and that's when the pills kicked in. And unlike most drugs I've taken, there was no buzz really, no giddiness or disorientation. Just a reliable hard on.

And afterwards, I let the kick-ass girl in on my little secret and she thought it was hilarious. And my little blue pills became our little inside joke that no one else knew about. Although I only refilled that prescription twice before we both got bored with straightforward sex and began to explore more sordid details.

So here comes the happy ending: I married the kick-ass girl, transitioned to female, and we were together for ten years, living as lesbians. And on the rare occasion when one of us had a hankering for penetration sex, I no longer needed Viagra. I just used my strap on.

6

Class Dismissed

When a spoken word performer first steps onto the stage, the audience will tend to make all sorts of assumptions about them based on their (real or imagined) gender, race, ethnicity, age, size, style of dress, and so on, before they even utter a single word. In my case, this audience assessment additionally included the mistaken presumption that I was assigned a female sex at birth. As a result, I found that many in the audience would become surprised or disconcerted at the moment in the piece when I first explicitly mentioned being trans—this was especially true back in 2002, when there was very little transgender awareness in the general public. In this piece (which appeared in print in Either/Or*), I purposefully wielded the so-called "reveal moment" to confront and challenge the audience's binary perception of gender.*

I am not here to read a poem. I am here to fuck with your mind. And maybe you think that's a pretty catchy opening line, and you're waiting to see what happens next. Well, what if I told you that I use to be a man. As recently as a year ago. And like many guys in the audience, I grew up dating girls, playing tackle football, and pissing in urinals. And by now you're probably picking up on the clues, and the boy I use to be is starting to come into view. And if any of you thought the blonde-haired freckled girl was kind of cute a minute ago, well I doubt you still do.

So tell me, do I look any different to you? If so, then why? My appearance hasn't changed since I first stepped onto this stage. In fact, the only thing that's changed is *you*. And I would like you to keep that in mind as we move past *The Crying Game* moment[1] and onto the real question: Why does my sex even matter to you?

See, I am not the only person here with a gender issue. Every single one of us is obsessed with it. We read gender into every human act: We project it onto people's driving skills, their willingness to make a commitment, even their TV remote control habits. And just glance around this room right now and notice how your mind subconsciously assigns a gender to every person the split second you see them, some so far away that you can't even make out their faces.

We think this way because we've been brainwashed. Before we could speak in complete sentences, we were duped into believing that male and female are opposites.[2] But we're not. The truth is, we are practically identical, 99.9 percent the same on a genetic level.[3] We've just been trained to exaggerate that fraction of difference into a chasm, into two mutually-exclusive classes.

And gender is not about biological sex.[4] When you first saw me, you didn't see my chromosomes or reproductive capabilities. Rather, you read my *class* as female. Because gender is first and foremost a class system. And it is held together by the myth that it arises from our organs, our instincts. But for every gender generalization you can make, I can find a thousand exceptions. And natural laws are not supposed to have exceptions! If gender was natural, little boys wouldn't have to be told not to cry, and little girls wouldn't have to be taught that certain ways of sitting aren't ladylike. If gender was natural, it wouldn't need to be so highly regulated.

And besides, you're smart enough to know how slight biological differences can be distorted by pseudoscientific spin. Similar arguments have been used to justify eugenics and books like *The Bell Curve*.[5] And would you want to live in a world that used different pronouns based on people's race, or size, or income level?

Anyone who has studied class knows that the system seems invisible when you have a stake in its existence. And when we buy into distinct gender differences, we're exercising an entitlement. And I gave up the privilege of being seen as a "real woman" tonight so that I could share this bit of truth with you. And it will be worth it if it helps even a handful of you to realize that my gender is all in your mind.

7

Super Hero

This spoken word piece was first published in Either/Or *(2002). All of the super hero and doll references are explained in the Notes section.*[1]

When I was a young boy, I played with dolls. And no, I'm not talking about Barbie, although my sister had one of those, but I wouldn't touch that doll's sorry ass with a ten-foot pole. And my uncle once gave me a G.I. Joe, but that doll never saw a day of service, he just rested in peace in his unopened box like he came with toe-tags included.

No, when I was a young boy, I played with super hero dolls!

And my parents didn't mind. After all, super heroes are practically perfect boyhood role models. Sure their outfits are a bit flamboyant: capes, tights, and masks in color schemes that would even make drag queens green with envy. And while super heroes are sensitive enough to rescue cats out of trees, or help elderly ladies cross streets, they are man enough to kick their archenemies' asses and send them packing back to the radioactive planets they came from. And when you are a young boy, you're taught that that is what's really important.

And some of my boyhood friends were also into super heroes, but only because they dreamt of being faster than a speeding bullet, more powerful than a locomotive. But what they didn't notice is that all super powers come with a built-in Achilles' heel—like Kryptonite, if you will. And that super heroes are vulnerable in ways that mere mortals can't understand. And if you twist a super hero's arm a bit too much, you might snap their rubber-band spines, and their limbs will go limp in their body suits. I would accidentally do this from time to time—I didn't know my own strength back then.

And unlike my friends, I didn't play with super heroes because I was jealous of their super-human powers. I played with super heroes because I felt sorry for them. Because I understood that super heroes are not just admired, but they are also despised. And they have to spend most of their lives in disguise. And as a young transgender child, I didn't dream about growing up to be a super hero someday. Instead, I identified with them. Because I knew what it was like to pretend, to hide my true identity and special powers behind pseudonyms and mild manners.

And even at the age of seven, I understood why Superman chose to love Lois Lane from afar. That's just the sick sort of thing that you do when you don't want anyone to find out who you really are.

That's why I always imagined the Hall of Justice as one big support group meeting, where super heroes could console one another other, and talk about how all the super powers in the world couldn't give them the one thing they wanted most: to be a normal.

That's why I made sure to play with my super heroes every single day, so that they knew they were loved. And when I wasn't around, I put them all in one big shoebox. That way, they could look after one another.

And sometimes I still imagine myself as a super hero. But these days, I refuse to be mild mannered. Because I've lived in the closet long enough to know that phone booths are few and far between. And after spending most of my life feeling helpless, I've learned that every single minute is an emergency.

8

Book Worm

During the 1980s and 1990s, queer/trans pioneer Lee Brewster owned two stores in New York City: a more renowned clothing boutique that catered to crossdressers and drag performers, and the lesser-known bookstore that I describe in this spoken word piece (which first appeared in Either/Or*).[1] Some trans people of different generations, backgrounds, or sexualities may take issue with certain aspects of this piece—I have tried to contextualize these matters in the Notes section for this chapter.[2]*

It was just off of Forty-second Street, but not where you'd expect it to be. Not in Times Square, by the porn shops and signs advertising "Live Nude Girls," in the ex-Triple-X district that's now home to the Disney Store.

No, this place was way west of Broadway, out where the avenues reach the double digits, just before Manhattan falls off into the Hudson. And from the outside, it didn't look like a store, just an ordinary second floor apartment. This was on purpose. The only way to find out about this place was from a small ad on the back page of *The Village Voice*.

And the first few times I walked through the door, I couldn't help but hold my breath for a few seconds. I felt like a pickpocket, like I had just gotten away with something. And once inside, I'd head toward the stacks of books and magazines—hundreds of them laid out in flea market fashion on rows of foldable tables. And most of it was pulp fiction: rough-cut and card stock covers, cheesy illustrations and typos galore. And every single item was about boys who were turned into girls.

And I was like a kid in a candy store. Once a month, I'd buy more than I could afford on my grad-student-living-in-New-York-City budget. Because back then, I was a twenty-one year old boy who wanted the unthinkable. And this place made my most embarrassing thoughts and unspeakable desires seem possible.

My favorites were the novelettes about men forced into femininity.[3] They offered guilt-free scenarios, as I imagined myself turned into a housemaid or secretary against my will. Then there were the magazines featuring photos of so-called "she-males," and I spent hours staring at their seemingly "in between" bodies. Most people are either disturbed or turned on by the sight of a woman with a penis, but for me, all I felt was jealousy, because the girl in the picture was one step closer to female than me.[4]

And maybe this store sounds pretty creepy to you, but for me, it was the safest place on the planet. Because when I was there, I was no longer a freak, just an ordinary customer. And you should have seen the place during weekday lunch hours, as the store filled up with businessmen in three-piece suits, all of them closeted trans people or admirers, all with healthy desires that had been shamed into secrets.[5] And we all came to this place to reclaim a lost part of ourselves.

And simply to be in a room full of people who were somewhat like me, felt like taking part in a ceremony. And reading the mangled prose of those X-rated books felt like breaking bread with far away strangers who shared the same sins as me. And admittedly, many of the story lines were blatantly offensive or degrading, but they were way more liberating than anything that I had read in my honors English class. Because those books gave me something that I never had before: permission to exist.

Because back then, I was a twenty-one year old boy who wanted the unthinkable. And I had planned to take my secret to the grave with me, until that dirty bookstore literally saved me.

9

Introduction to Draw Blood

As the title suggests, this was the introduction to my second chapbook Draw Blood, *written in 2004.*

Stoic is one of the most fucked-up words in the English language. We have all been taught to revere those who remain silent about the obstacles they face, the pain they endure. We honor people who choose to keep their own personal tragedies and traumas to themselves, so that the rest of us need not confront the horrors that they have faced. But stoicism is just a fancy word for shame. Secrets kill people every day.

Stoicism was the virtue that I lived by most of my life. The secret that I kept from the world was that I was a boy who wanted to be a girl. I never told anyone close to me about this until my late twenties. For most of that time, it seemed like I didn't have much of a choice in the matter. I didn't want to devastate my family, to freak out my friends, to distance strangers. I didn't want to make anybody else feel uncomfortable on my behalf, so I kept it all to myself. I didn't tell anyone about how much I hurt on the inside. I never spoke up when I heard somebody say something ignorant or hateful about other gender-variant folks. Instead, I let all of that pain and shame build up inside of me until it literally consumed me.

In my early thirties, I took the first step towards relieving myself of that pain: I transitioned from male to female. When I came out, many people reacted much as if I had a death in my family. After hearing the news, they gave me their support and condolences. They respectfully began referring to me as Julia and as she/her, but they never brought up the subject of my transition again. I'm sure they were just trying to be polite, avoiding a potentially sensitive subject. But for me, after having kept a huge part of myself hidden for so long, the silence was deafening. I wasn't about to let my life turn back into a secret again.

The need to break this silence led to me writing and performing spoken word in the first year after my transition. In my early pieces, collected in the chapbook *Either/Or*, I set out to communicate some of my observations and experiences being transgender. In retrospect, while those pieces were sincere, they also were very controlled. I tried to make important intellectual points about gender without ever getting too emotional, without ever acknowledging my pain. This became more and more obvious to me as I performed those pieces at poetry slams and open mics. I would often have people come up to me afterwards to tell me how courageous I was for speaking openly about being transgender. Then, the next day, I would spend an hour talking to my therapist about how much I hated myself, how difficult it was living with all of the ugly connotations and assumptions that plague the word transsexual, how I often thought about hurting myself as a way to let out all of the ancient pain that I had kept buried within me since I was a child.

I named this collection *Draw Blood* because many of these poems are my attempts to bring that pain to the surface, to acknowledge it so that I might be able to finally move beyond it. In the title piece, I describe this process as being "like cutting into a snake bite in order to work the poison out of me."[1] But this pain didn't arise in a vacuum. Many people fail to realize that it is their own issues and uneasiness with gender and sexuality that create an atmosphere in which trans people are routinely ridiculed and demonized. In the opening piece "Cocky," I put it this way: "I've been made to feel shame and self-loathing so that everyone else can take comfort in what their bodies mean."[2]

It is no coincidence that "Draw Blood" is also a fighting reference. One of the most frustrating aspects of being an out trans person is that we are always being put on the defensive, forced to explain ourselves to other folks who are arrogant enough to believe that their own personal definitions of what it means to be a woman or a man apply to everyone, people who have the audacity to believe that viewing a Discovery Channel documentary or an *Oprah* special on transsexuals gives them any insight into our lives and experiences.[3] I have found that it is simply not enough to convince the world to tolerate trans people. If we really want to be taken seriously, we must go on the offensive and challenge the naive yet commonly held theories about sex and gender that are prevalent in both the straight and queer communities, for these misguided beliefs form the very framework that allows others to place us at the bottom of their pecking orders.

One of the main reasons why I spend so much time writing and performing spoken word pieces about my trans experiences is that I am trying to fill a void that has been present for as long as I can remember. For decades, trans people have been methodically marginalized, our voices silenced, our existence reduced to the status of laughingstock and pop psychology caricature. As I say in the closing piece "Fighting Words": "everyone needs to stop talking about transsexuals and listen to what we have to say for once!"[4] I know for a fact that I would not have felt so scared and alone during my childhood if I had the chance to hear songs, stories, and spoken word pieces by other trans musicians and writers. That's why it has been so inspiring for me to be a part of the San Francisco Bay Area trans-performance scene, and to see it grow so much in such a short time. For this reason, I dedicate this book to all of the trans, intersex, and genderqueer artists, writers, performers, activists, and organizers who I have had the pleasure of meeting and working with over the last few years. Hopefully, the work that we are all doing will help ensure that today's sex/gender-variant children do not have to face the isolation and shame that we had to endure.

10

Cocky

In November 2002, as I was trying to make sense of what it meant for me to be an out trans female performer, a transgender teenager named Gwen Araujo was murdered. While most mainstream news outlets ignore incidents of anti-trans violence (especially back then), Gwen's murder garnered national attention.[1] Like most reasonable people, I was appalled by her murder, but the incident struck me on a far more visceral level than that. She was from Newark, CA, a mere thirty minute drive from my home. According to accounts, the incident that precipitated her murder occurred when the girlfriend of one of Gwen's eventual killers nonconsensually groped Gwen to discover that she had a penis—a bodily attribute that I shared at the time. I wanted to write a piece that both captured the fear that my gender incongruity seemed to evoke in other people, and the corresponding fear that I experience knowing that my body might be a lightning rod for other people's gender and sexual insecurities. The result was "Cocky"—it was written in early 2003 and would eventually become my signature spoken word piece. The piece was published in Draw Blood, *and has been excerpted numerous other places.[2]*

We are often told that we are living in a man's world, and in this culture no image represents power more than the phallic symbol. And if the penis equals power, then I am illegally armed. My body, full of freckles and feminine curves, is like a stealth bomber. I fly just under everyone's radar, but only because they choose not to see me. Only because nobody wants to believe that a sweet, petite green-eyed girl like me could ever possibly be packing heat.

They say that it's not the size of the wand, but the magic that it does. Well, after many months on estrogen, my penis is pretty darn small, but she has supernatural powers! She's like some pissed off ancient Greek goddess—my penis changes the meaning of everything. Because of her, every single one of my heterosexual ex-girlfriends has slept with a lesbian. And every guy who hits on me these days could be accused of being gay. My penis bends everyone who's straight. She can make the most entitled cat callers and womanizers scurry away with their tails between their legs, all because of six small words: "I used to be a man."

Being a transsexual, I realize that most people see my femaleness as a facade, as an elaborate hoax. But I am more real than any of them could ever hope to be. I am real because, unlike them, my gender is not based upon what other people think of me. That may make me an object of ridicule, but I am not the butt of anyone's jokes, because I know that people make fun of trans folks because we are the one thing that they fear the most. I am more badass than any gangster, more dangerous than an entire marine corps. My penis is more powerful than the cocks of a million alpha males all put together. Because when a man is defined as that which is not female, and a woman is defined as that which is not male, then I am the loose thread that unravels the gender of everyone around me.

They say it's not the size of the boat, but the motion of the ocean. Well, my penis gives most people seasickness. She makes them dizzy, because most people are not secure enough in their own masculinity or femininity to survive a night in the sack with me! My penis turns simple sexual pleasures into political acts. She turns biological impossibilities into cold hard facts. My penis is the curiosity that you've been told will kill your cat.

See, my penis can be deadly.

Especially to me.

I've heard almost every true crime story about what frightened macho boys do to trans women. Every bludgeoning and mutilation, bodies beaten beyond recognition. And I've imagined it all happening to me in first person. And every time I get up in front of a crowd to perform one of my out-spoken word pieces, I can feel myself morph into a slow moving target. And after the show, when I walk back to my car in the dark, I'll be holding my breath, half-expecting that inevitable blow to the back of the head. And sometimes, I wonder why it hasn't happened yet. And sometimes, I wonder why they don't just get it over with. And sometimes I just wish I was dead.

See, I never wanted to be dangerous. And I spent most of my life wishing that I didn't have a penis. I used to hate my body for not making any sense to me, and these days, I often hate it for being so in between. Some mornings I can barely get up out of bed because my body is so weighed down with ugly meanings that my culture has dumped all over me. See, I've been made to feel shame and self-loathing so that everyone else can take comfort in what their bodies mean.

So, if I seem a bit cocky, that's because I refuse to make apologies for my body anymore. I am through being the human sacrifice offered up to appease other people's gender issues.

Some women have a penis. Some men don't. And the rest of the world is just going to have to get the fuck over it!

And if I am destined to be the loose thread that unravels the gender of everyone around me, then I am going to pull, and pull, and pull, until everyone is exposed, until they all finally see that all along they were merely wearing the emperor's new clothes.

I know that people don't like it when I turn the tables on them, but what the hell else am I supposed to do? Play a hand that was dealt from a deck of cards that's been stacked against me?

If I seem a bit cocky, that's because I've spent my entire life being backed into a corner. And like a frightened animal, pumped full of adrenaline and sick of hunger and hiding, I am finally desperate enough to come out fighting.

11

Sleeping Sickness

This spoken word piece was written in 2003, first appeared in print in Clamor Magazine, *and was later included in* Draw Blood.[1]

In the name of the Father, the Son, and the Holy Spirit, Amen. That's how it begins. My nights are spent composing insomniac open letters to you, two-hour long monologues that end in exhaustion. And sometimes, in the middle of my day, I'll remember that I fell asleep before ending my previous night's prayer with an proper Amen, and I'll wonder whether my channel to you is still open, my every word an invocation, the sounds of my Atari games, little league practice, and eighth grade history class becoming the annoying background noise of heaven.

And maybe forgetting to say amen makes my life one long continuous prayer. If so, then you were there that afternoon when I tucked my penis tightly behind my legs just to see what I'd look like without it. When I wrapped bedroom curtains around my body like a prom dress, and turned tattered shoelaces into necklaces and bracelets. And you were there later that same night when I began another prayer within a prayer to once again beg for your forgiveness.

Wanting to be a girl never came up in CCD[2] or Sunday mass, and it's not covered in the Ten Commandments, but from everything the nuns and priests have taught me about you, I know that you do not approve. And when I turn to your holy words to look for anything that might shed some light onto whatever this is that I'm going through, I find myself returning to the same story: The one about Abraham and how you commanded him to sacrifice his son to you, stopping the blade only seconds before he went actually went through with it. And forgive me Father, for I can't help but think that that was a fucked up thing to do.

And perhaps I'm like Abraham and this is just another one of your tests. Maybe you put girl thoughts into the heads of twelve-year-old boys just to see how they'll react. Maybe I'm an experiment and you're up in heaven looking down on me, taking notes as I tear myself apart in self-hatred, tossing and turning in bed as if acting out my inevitable burning in hell.

And at first, my sins made me even more devout. I'd lie awake each night clutching the glow in the dark rosary beads my grandmother gave me, repeating the words that I once heard her say: "Blessed are those who have not seen yet believe."

And I want to believe, but more and more it just feels like you're torturing me. And I'm doing the best that I can to plug up all of the holes in this disintegrating dam, as my brain bleeds rivers of bad thoughts that pour out of my mouth and hands like wounds that won't clot. And I can't understand why you won't help, when I've asked you over and over again to please, either turn me into a girl, or else make these thoughts stop!

The nuns say that you answer all prayers, it's just that sometimes the answer is no. Well, I am tired of praying to a god who only offers me "thou shalt nots." I'm tired from lack of sleep, from keeping secrets that burn so much they hollow me out. I am tired of hurting so much that sometimes I pray that I don't wake up. So forgive me Father, for I have sinned. I have dared to share all of myself with you, forcing you to watch one long sacrilegious prayer within a prayer within a prayer within a prayer, like a serpent swallowing its own soul, like a serpent swallowing itself whole.

And maybe tonight I'll finally be cured of this sleeping sickness. Because the last few years of living in absolute shame and unbelievable pain has made me fearless enough to finally say Amen.

12

Mix and Match

This spoken word piece was written in 2003, first appeared in print in Larry-bob Robert's zine Holy Titclamps, *and was later included in* Draw Blood.[1]

We are quite a pair. A year and a half ago, we were pronounced husband and wife. And you're still my wife, only now I'm your "was-band." And when we first met five years ago, I was a pre-transition transsexual and you were calling yourself bisexual, and we gallivanted around Berkeley and Oakland disguised as a straight couple. We had so much fun with the roles of boy and girl; we gave Oscar-winning performances! I wore the condoms and you wore the diaphragm, and we'd ham it up in the sack. No one else has ever made me laugh so much during sex.

And afterwards, we would lay on the bed in that cliché post-coital pose: You'd curl your body along my side and press your head against my chest, and I'd wrap my arm around you as if I was protecting you from something. And these days, when we strike the same pose, your head rests on my developing breasts, and when I cradle your sleeping body, I feel almost maternal.

And if sometimes it's like I'm your mother, then other times it's like you're my obnoxious younger brother. Who knew that you, a radical-feminist[2] dyke, could get such eighth-grader amusement from snapping the backs of my bra straps, or giving my breasts a quick squeeze the way Harpo Marx honks his horn. And forgive the pun, but it really does make me horny.

And if sometimes you act like my younger brother, then other times you're like my big sister, guiding me with advice, sharing all of the things that you learned having reached womanhood before me. And if anyone were to ask this ex-boy what it's like to be in a lesbian relationship, I would say that it feels like being sisters, best friends, and lovers simultaneously.

I know that when a lot of people see a same-sex couple, they often try to figure out who's the butch and who's the femme, as if all queer people were latent heterosexuals. More often than not, they base their impressions on hairstyle. But we keep them second-guessing: Your short hair is dyed a fabulous bright red, and often accessorized with barrettes too cute for most preschoolers. And my long curly hair is often tied back in a practical ponytail. I guess I'm the femme tomboy and you're the butch girlie-girl.

And when most people think of lesbian sex, they probably imagine lots and lots of cuddling. And we do some of that, in between the wrestling, and tickling, and biting, and coming, and let's not forget all of the musical numbers, comedy routines, and sex toys. And sometimes, I wrap a strap-on over my "real McCoy," and I fuck you with all of the sweetness of a girl and the aggression of a boy. And sometimes you like it when you're on top, and sometimes you ask me to tie you up, and I'll never forget the time that you turned bondage into a magic act. While I stepped out of the room for a minute, you undid your knots, and sprung to your feet like Houdini shouting "Ta-da!" Like I said, when we have sex, you crack me up.

Our love is like one long list of seemingly contradictory anecdotes. Before I transitioned, our names were posted next to our apartment doorbell: my first name listed as "Tom" and yours as "Dani." But our landlord misspelled your name "D-A-N-N-Y" and we joked about how we were secretly two gay boys. Our love transcends all categories, all orientations, and all identities. Our relationship is not about me being this and you being that; we are not merely each other's better half. No, we are *everything* to one another.

They say opposites attract, but I'm not so sure about that. I'm no longer impressed with boy versus girl, or butch versus femme—I've learned that I can be any of those things depending upon what mood I'm in. And I use to be really into the idea of tops and bottoms, dominants and submissives, but these days I get off on the fact that both of us are such perfect switches. And no matter how you serve it, our love is always delicious, because we mix and match.

13

Endgame

This spoken word piece was written in 2003, and only ever appeared in print in Draw Blood *(2004). I wrote it in one sitting, crying throughout most of it.*

I **can't wait to** get home from school and retreat to my bedroom, where it's safe to step outside of my eleven year old body and become someone else for an hour or two. To take on new shapes and new names, explore imaginary landscapes that seem to stretch to infinity.

I am too young to understand that the possibilities are not really endless, that there is such a thing as playing with fire. If one is not careful, even innocent play can take you over the edge of the world.

This has become my favorite game—I've played it many times before. It begins when the bad guy turns me into a girl. And my bedroom becomes a mountain range, a desert, the bottom of the ocean, as I search to the ends of the earth for my nemesis in order to capture him, so that he can turn me back into a boy.

But lately, I've been improvising, trying out new plot twists, exploring uncharted story lines. Sometimes after being turned into a girl, our hero ignores her archenemy and goes off on her own adventure. With each day she becomes more self-confident, and her costumes become more elaborate. And sometimes she looks at herself in the bedroom mirror, impressed with the girl she sees staring back, while trying not to reflect on the fact that she was a boy just before this story's first act.

One day, I dare to ask myself the one question that I have been avoiding: Why is this my favorite game?

Sitting on the edge of my bed, with a blanket wrapped around my torso, my fingers wrestling with one another. I have just solved a riddle. I had no idea that my life was a puzzle until I put the pieces together.

The truth is, this game has never been a game.

Suddenly, I feel foolish. And scared. And very much alone.

14

Period Piece

While I enjoy poetry slams, a drawback of the genre (in my humble opinion) is that it often rewards gimmicky poems, especially ones performed in a highly exaggerated manner. This is one such poem.[1] I am not sure if it holds up well on the page, but I am including it here because it is one of my earliest trans feminist (rather than simply trans-themed) pieces. It was written in 2003, and was first published in Draw Blood. *For a more serious and nuanced account of this same subject matter, please consult Chapter 4 of* Whipping Girl.[2]

I swear to God that I am not on drugs! It's a prescription, for a legitimate medical condition, that is, if you consider my gender to be a birth defect. And after spending most of my life on testosterone, I can't tell you how different it feels to finally be on female hormones. I find myself getting upset some times, and my friends will say, "You're so emotional these days." And I'll reply: "This is not a fucking mood swing! I'm just pissed off at the dismissive attitude I've been getting since I started taking estrogen!"

Back when I was a boy, when I would get upset, everyone would take me very seriously. But these days, when I get just as upset about the *exact same thing*, nobody even listens to me! They just try to console me with soothing words and hugs, or they shove bottles of Midol[3] in my face, while completely ignoring the thing that was bugging me in the first place!

And when I decided to cycle my hormones to simulate menstrual hormonal changes,[4] I had friends who were flabbergasted. "Why would you ever want to do that?" they'd ask. And when my doctor reluctantly gave me my progesterone prescription, it came with a warning label that read: "May cause drowsiness or dizziness." I swear, I am not making this up. This is obviously the work of the same male supremacist medical specialist who derived the word "hysterical" from the Greek root for uterus.

But I have news for you: Female hormones are not drugs. They don't have side effects. Plenty of women operate heavy machinery, and some of us study molecular biology, post-modern theory, and write kick-ass slam poetry. And since when did men corner the market on the "practical department?" Fuck, I've met plenty of guys who are best described as emotionally repressed time bombs set to go off at a moment's notice.

So, being one of the relatively few people who have been on both sides of the fence, allow me to put my two cents in. In my experience, testosterone felt like a thick curtain that draped over my emotions. It deadened their intensity, made all of my feelings pale and vague, as if they were ghosts that would haunt me. But on estrogen, I have *all of the same emotions,* only now they come in crystal clear.[5] I'm more aware of my surroundings, more sensitive to smells, tastes, and touch, and of course, the orgasms are much much better. In fact, as far as I can tell, the only thing that sucks about being female is that now people treat me like I'm a little baby girl.

But I'm not taking it anymore! The next time I get legitimately angry or upset, and some guy has the nerve to say, "Damn, girl, you must be on the rag," I'll remind him that menstruation is when a woman's testosterone levels are at their highest.[6] Then I'll give him a kick to the groin and shout out, "Now our cycles are in sync!"

Because I am sick of having my opinions dismissed as mere symptoms of my body chemistry. If you don't like what I have to say, then fine, I double-dog dare you to debate me. Just leave my hormones out of it!

15

Draw Blood

Written in 2004, this piece became the title poem of Draw Blood.

I don't know what's worse: listening to Billy Ocean singing, "Get out of my dreams, get into my car" or having a root canal. Unfortunately, I get to experience both simultaneously, reliving minor soft-rock pop hits from the '80s as the oral surgeon hovers over me. For those of you who have never had a root canal, it's the only way to save teeth so badly damaged that they feel pain incessantly. The doctor drills a hole in the tooth down to the roots, removes all the nerve endings and fills it up with rubber cement, so that the tooth no longer hurts, it just sits in your mouth like a mannequin.

The sound of the drill filling my skull stops for a second and the oral surgeon checks in with me. "Let me know if this hurts and I'll give you more Novocain." I nod my head up and down. And as he resumes his chiseling away at me, I allow myself one of those awful thoughts that sometimes slip their way into my brain: "I wish I could feel the pain." And I'm reminded of all the marks on my body that no one can see. On my arms. On my stomach. Temporary scars drawn in blue and black ink. My body is covered in self-inflicted Rorschach blots and I'm not quite sure what all of them mean. Because when I press the pen to my skin, I don't picture anything at all. I just imagine that I'm drawing blood.

These are the new secrets that I keep: visions of placing my palms face down on hot stove burners; walks where I imagine the world turned ninety degrees so that my forward motion becomes free falling. I think about physical pain as a release, as a way to turn off all the thoughts that bombard my brain— words like "hate" and "dumb" and "dead," which drip through my head like a second-grader name-calling water torture from the inside out.

And the only way I've found to silence these desperate thoughts is to write about what it was like to grow up transgender: To feel betrayed by my own body; to survive by splitting myself up into secrets; to later become the tornado that turned my family's lives upside down; to be placed in the position of having to explain myself over and over again to absolute strangers; to feel obligated to smile when others make insensitive comments or try to make light of my situation.

I used to make a really good punching bag. I was a sponge capable of soaking up everyone else's uneasiness. But these days, I feel the need to get up on stage and wring myself out in public, so that my pain might finally have some witnesses.

And when words are not enough to alleviate these chronic aches, then I place the pen on my skin and pretend that it's a razor blade. I am drawing blood, like cutting into a snakebite in order to work the poison out of me. With black sharpie, I draw black holes all over my body because I am trying to draw all my demons out of me. I use pens instead of needles or knives because I'm desperately trying to write myself some kind of happy ending.

And as the oral surgeon finishes up, I think about my tooth, which is now filled up with rubber cement. It sits in my mouth, sturdy and permanently numb, like a mannequin.

16

Open Letter to Lisa Vogel

In 2003, I attended Camp Trans, which was the annual protest of the Michigan Womyn's Music Festival's "womyn-born-womyn"-only policy, which excluded trans women from attending. (Note: "womyn" is an alternative spelling of "woman" preferred by some feminists.) This festival (often referred to as "Michfest" or simply "Michigan") and its trans woman-exclusion policy are also alluded to (to varying degrees) in Chapters 19, 20, 21, 27, and 28, as it was a focal point for much of my early activism.[1] During and immediately after my 2003 experience at Camp Trans, I scribbled a several-page rant into my writing journal, in an attempt to vent all of the intense emotions I was feeling. Two spoken word pieces emerged from that rant: This piece and the following chapter "Fighting Words," both of which were only ever published in Draw Blood. *Lisa Vogel is the sole proprietor of Michfest. Reportedly, 2015 was the festival's final year—they never did welcome trans women to attend.[2]*

You call your festival a "celebration of everything female." Well, as one of the tens of thousands of trans women who are excluded from your event, I am writing to challenge your sense of entitlement. How dare you tell me that I am not a woman! You draw lines in the sand to mark where you believe woman begins and ends, but your definitions are distorted with contradictions, as they were designed specifically to draw me out of the picture. Tell me, how do you expect woman to grow beyond her old boundaries and into new roles when you are so set on patrolling her borders?

As you know, feminist critiques of Western science describe masculine perspectives as being reductionist and feminist approaches as being holistic.[3] So tell me, why do you revert to man-made labels and define me based on my organs and chromosomes? You, who no doubt cringes every time a woman is objectified, every time a man fixates on her specific body parts, how easily you turn around and reduce me to my genitals!

Every time you fixate on my male past, or what's underneath my pants, you deny every other aspect of my person. I am a woman every time I walk down the street, dealing with catcalls and jerks trying to railroad me off the sidewalk. I am a woman every time my opinions are dismissed, and every time I fight back to make sure that somebody doesn't get away with it. And I am a woman every time my lesbian life partner and I dare to hold hands and kiss in public.

You insist that all trans women still have male energy, but nobody ever senses it in me. You falsely believe that you know the difference between woman and man, but as someone who has transitioned from one to the other, I can tell you first hand that when it comes to gender, most people only ever see what they want to see.

So the question is: Why do you choose to see me as a man? What feminist goal is served by lumping me into the same category as the alpha males that you call your oppressors? Doesn't the fact that I've risked so much demonstrate that I believe woman is something worth fighting for? Have you ever considered embracing me as living proof that a woman's fate is determined not by the limitations of her body, but rather the expansiveness of her mind? And if most straight men are scared to death about what I represent, then tell me, as a feminist, doesn't that mean that I'm doing something right?

We could be allies, but instead of acceptance, you only offer me excuses. When I say I want to participate in women's space, you announce that I've come to destroy it. When I insist that I am a woman, you play word games and declare that the Michigan Womyn's Music Festival is all about "girlhood." You say that I will bring violence onto the land, but the truth is that trans women aren't any more violent than other women. You worry about me flaunting my penis, but the sad truth is that most of us trans women feel such societal stigma regarding our bodies that it is often difficult for us to undress in front of others.

And the most insulting excuse that you use to exclude me from the festival is that my body might trigger abuse survivors. When you make this callous claim, you erase the fact that trans women are verbally and physically abused for being women too. I have had men force themselves upon me. And you seem oblivious to the countless additional ways in which trans women have been violated and abused by male culture. Every trans woman is a survivor and we have our own triggers. They come in sets of two, like pronouns and public restrooms, designed to remind us of every time someone else has had the audacity to define our genders for us. And "womyn-born-womyn" is one of my triggers too.

"Womyn-born-womyn" is your attempt to normalize yourself in opposition to me. It is the same strategy that heterosexuals use when calling themselves "straight" and everyone else "queer." "Womyn-born-womyn" is your attempt to create another hierarchy, another class system, between "born" versus trans women. Well, I refuse to be a second-class citizen. And as far as I'm concerned, this debate is no longer about my body—it is about your bigotry, your gender issues, your contradictions, your tired-ass thirty-year-old dogma.

This debate is no longer about my male privilege—I gave that up years ago. This debate is about your birth privilege[4] and how you devalue woman by taking for granted the fact that people view you as female both inside and out. It is your birth privilege that allows you to consider "don't ask, don't tell" to be a reasonable festival policy. It is your birth privilege that entitles you to hurl epithets at me without ever considering what it might be like to be in my shoes, without ever imagining how angry you would be if someone thought they had the right to tell you that you are not a woman, how frustrating it would be if every time you acted feminine it was dismissed as parody and every time you acted butch it was seen as a sign of your true male identity.

I cannot understand how any lesbian, who has struggled against patriarchal ideals about what makes a "real" woman, can turn around and use the word "real" against me. That is not feminism, it is merely hypocrisy.

I hear many women say that they are "tired of this debate." Well, unlike them, I don't have the luxury of being bored with this issue because it is me who is being discriminated against. And since practically all of the discussions they've had about Michigan's "womyn-born-womyn"-only policy have taken place in the absence of trans women, their claims that they have participated in a true debate are clearly illegitimate.

Some of my queer woman friends make apologies on your behalf. They say they feel torn between respecting my identity as a woman and understanding your protectiveness of women's space. But I tell my friends that they are not the ones who are torn. I am the one who is being torn, in half, stripped of my identity and all of my life experiences, stripped of the person that I am and reduced to just my penis and male past.

I tell my friends that they don't feel torn, they just feel uncomfortable about the decision that every single one of them has to make. They can either support a transphobic policy or call other women out on their prejudices. Because it is not feminist to ignore discrimination within your own community. And no place can ever truly be called "women's space" until all self-identified women are included.

17

Fighting Words

Like the last chapter, this was written during and shortly after Camp Trans 2003, and was subsequently included in Draw Blood. *The writing and performance of this piece was inspired by Carolyn Connelly's performance of her poem "Fuck You (A Poem for Monty)," which I also reference in my essay "On the Outside Looking In."[1] While it was a very cathartic piece to perform, it tended to go over like a lead balloon at poetry slams. It became increasingly clear to me that, while slam audiences were often open to poems that seemed to fit the "transsexual overcomes adversity" mold, they were averse to poems wherein I pointed out that their own assumptions about gender and trans people are largely responsible for creating the very obstacles that we are forced to overcome.*

Transsexual. Transsexual, transsexual, transsexual, transsexual, transsexual, transsexual, transsexual. I can say it over and over again, but I can't change how that word sounds. Transsexual is one of the most maligned words in the dictionary. It's the ten-thousand-ton ugly assumption that the world has dropped on top of me. Because as far as most people are concerned, transsexual is just a triple-X-spam email advertising the one type of porn that no one they know will admit to whacking off to. Transsexual is a sure-fire one-liner in a Jay Leno monologue. It's Howard Stern's second favorite word (after lesbian). I even heard that transsexual women will be coming out to their boyfriends again on this week's *Jerry Springer*. Even psychobabble hacks like Doctor Laura and Doctor Phil want in on the "hot tranny action."[2]

Well, fuck all of them! I want my fucking word back! It's mine and they can't have it!

Like the vast majority of transsexuals, I grew up closeted, but not by choice. I was intimidated into silence. As a child, I took every dumb-ass joke and ignorant hateful comment that I heard about transsexuals and turned them all in on myself. It felt like death by a million cuts. My developing brain bathed in self-hatred, as I learned at a young age that the only way I'd be allowed to survive was if I buried myself alive. I kept a twenty-seven year long secret.[3] And for most of that time, I honestly would have killed myself if I thought that there was any chance of my family and friends finding out.

And that's exactly how the world wanted me to feel. Because most people are like powder kegs, so full of insecurities about their own gender and sexualities that they've become scared to death of me, for simply being a spark that they're afraid might set them off. So instead, they engage in an unspoken strategy, redirecting their fear back at me. Because they realize that if they can bully me into keeping quiet, then they will be free to appropriate my identity and say whatever the fuck they want about me, thus turning their worst nightmare into a laughingstock.

But that's all about to stop. Because I'm out now, and I'm ready to go toe-to-toe with every non-transsexual person who is arrogant enough to assume that they have even the slightest clue of what I'm all about. I am calling the whole fucking world out!

I'm calling out every person who thinks they've never met a transsexual before. Because chances are you've met scores of us. You're just naive enough to believe that we'd be so different from you that you would be able to notice us.

I'm calling out every person who assumes that transsexuals must be delusional because we don't conform to common sense. Well, fuck that! Common sense is what tells us the world is flat.

I'm calling out every paranoid straight boy who assumes that transsexual women are out to deceive him. The fact that you are homophobic and conceited doesn't give you the right to take your fears of inadequacy out on me!

I'm calling out every woman who believes that being born female makes her more of a woman than me. Fuck, after spending most of your life never quite measuring up to our society's unrealistic expectations about what a "real woman" should be, you have the nerve to turn around and use that same bullshit on me?

I'm calling out every person who has ever complained about how difficult it is to use the right pronouns with me. Here's a helpful hint: Why not try thinking before you speak?

I'm calling out every person who has ever called me courageous. Because, after hearing that a hundred times, it just sounds like the nicest possible way of saying: "I'm glad I'm not in your shoes."

I'm calling out every person who has offered me backhanded compliments like, "Wow, I never would have guessed," or "You're so lucky you're able to pass." Oh, so I should be grateful that I don't *look* like a transsexual?[4] Well fuck that, I am a transsexual!

And while I'm at it, I'm calling myself out: for every time I pretended that being a transsexual was no big deal; for every time that I played it down so that somebody else wouldn't feel so uncomfortable around me.

Fuck everyone who has ever felt uncomfortable around me!

And fuck me, for every time that I tried to make the best of the role of circus freak, jumping through everyone's hoops and juggling their false impressions of me. Fuck me, for not having the guts to just be a bulldozer and run all their expectations right the fuck over.

Fuck me, for every time I worried about what others might think, when all along I should have been shouting out, "Shut the fuck up!" at the top of my lungs. Because the whole fucking world doesn't know what the fuck they're talking about. Everyone needs to stop talking about transsexuals and listen to what we have to say for once.

So shut the fuck up! Because transsexual is our word. And you can't fucking have it anymore.

18

Cherry Picking

In 2004, I was invited to perform in a reading entitled CHERRY: Queering Virginity, First Encounters of the Queer Kind. The show was curated by Gina de Vries as part of Sara Moore's ongoing spoken word series San Francisco in Exile. This is the piece that I wrote for that show. It later appeared in the anthologies Trans/Love: Radical Sex, Love & Relationships Beyond the Gender Binary *and* Best Sex Writing 2013: The State of Today's Sexual Culture.[1]

The first time that I learned about sex was in fifth grade. It wasn't by way of a sex education class or a Mom and Dad birds-and-the-bees speech, but rather a joke. One of those completely unfunny dirty jokes that little kids tell as a way to pass along important information. I think the punch line was, "Mommy, Mommy, turn on your headlights, Daddy's snake is about to go into your cave!" Now granted, before hearing the joke, I already had a strange relationship with my penis. I used to draw pictures of myself naked with a needle going into my penis, imagining that it contained special medicine that would make the thing disappear. And every time I used the urinal in the little boy's room, I had a sneaky suspicion that something wasn't quite right. But that night, after hearing the joke, I remember looking down at my penis, knowing what it was supposedly for, and I felt absolutely detached and dumbfounded.

The first time that I dressed as a girl was in sixth grade. I had insomnia and one night I felt compelled to wrap a pair of white lacy curtains around my body. I stared at my reflection in my bedroom mirror for hours. I looked like a girl. Perhaps it should have been no surprise. I was pre-pubescent and had one of those longish late-'70s boy haircuts. But it completely blew my mind. I looked like a girl. And the scariest part about this revelation was that it somehow made perfect sense to me.[2]

The first time that I had a crush on someone was in seventh grade. Her name was Kathy and I thought she was cute. Nancy told me that Kathy liked me, but I was too chickenshit to ask her out. So instead I fantasized about her. I imagined that some bad guy had captured us both and, as part of his evil scheme, he would offer me two choices: He would either kill Kathy or turn me into a girl. He left it up to me to decide and I would always gallantly choose the latter. And Kathy would be so impressed that I had sacrificed my maleness to save her life that she would ask me out on a date. I always said yes, and the rest of the fantasy involved different permutations of the two of us sucking face. All of this happened before I ever heard the word "lesbian."

The first time that I decided to change my sex was in tenth grade. It happened at my baseball league's all-star game. I wasn't playing in the game, but I went with a few friends who also didn't make the team. While we were sitting in the bleachers, a group of neighborhood girls walked by, and some of my flirtier guy friends started teasing them in that teenage-boy "I like you" sort of way. Both groups struck up a conversation, but I just sort of sat there and stared. It seemed so obvious to me that I should be one of those girls rather than one of these boys. It was so sad because nobody could see it but me. So I decided to get a sex change operation. I didn't really know what that was or what it involved; I had only heard about it on TV. Later, I realized that if I wanted to pursue such a thing, I would have to let all of my friends and family know that I wanted to be a girl, and I couldn't think of anything more frightening. So instead, I tucked the memory of my all-star game epiphany into the dark recesses of my brain. Like a time capsule, I wouldn't come across it again for another fifteen years.[3]

The first time that I had a girlfriend was in twelfth grade. She was smart and quirky and interesting and cute and completely kick-ass. I totally fell for her; she was my first true love. After dates, we would park on a quiet, dark street and make out with one another. Her lips were the first that I kissed, her body the first that I intimately touched. She was one year younger than me but way more mature. When I left to go to college, she suggested that we see other people. I was devastated, but she said that we were both still really young and had our whole lives ahead of us. She was right.

My first supposed sexual peak came when I was eighteen. It was my first year of college and I didn't really have any freshman sexual experiences to speak of. Some years are just like that. But don't feel bad for me: I made up for it by having a second sexual peak as a woman at the age of thirty-five.

The first time that I masturbated to orgasm was when I was nineteen. Nobody ever believes me that it happened so late, but it's true. Before then, when I'd play with myself, I would push down on my penis and rock my hand back and forth. I've since been told that that's how a lot of girls first do it. I think I just did it that way instinctually. It felt really good, but I never orgasmed. Then, my college girlfriend gave me my first hand job and I learned the power of the stroke. Granted, I knew about the stroke from watching porn and listening to that Billy Squier song,[4] but it never occurred to me to try it out on myself. It worked like a charm. It's amazing how you can have a body all of your life, yet there's always something new that you can learn about it.

Strangely enough, I don't really remember the first time that I had penetration sex—that supposedly landmark day when I officially lost my virginity. It's true. I know that it happened when I was nineteen with my girlfriend throughout most of college. I've lost the particular night that we "popped each other's cherries" in a blur of dorm room sex scenes the two of us shared over a three-year period. Eventually, she went on the pill, and since we were each other's first, we stopped using condoms. I could never get over how amazing it felt to be inside her, to feel my genitals inside her genitals. To this day, that feeling is the only part about being physically male that I fondly reminisce about.

The first time that I ever went out in public dressed as a woman was when I was twenty-one. I came home from college for Easter weekend while the rest of my family was away on a trip. I shaved off the silly looking beard I had grown over the semester. I put on my sister's black cotton knit dress. It had long sleeves, so no one could see my arm hair, and I wore opaque tights to hide my leg hair. I'm sure that I put way too much makeup on my face and way too much product in my hair, but nobody seemed to care because it was the eighties. I drove to a mall about an hour away from my parents' house so that I wouldn't run into anyone who knew me. As I approached the entrance, an older man held the door open for me and called me "sweetie." I felt flattered and insulted at the same time, but mostly, I was just amazed to be getting away with this. After walking around the mall for about ten minutes, I realized that I was hungry and hadn't eaten all morning. I drove to a Burger King for a shake and fries. The woman at the drive-thru window said, "Thank you ma'am," as she handed me my change and receipt. I can't begin to tell you how beautiful those three simple words sounded to me.

The first time that I told someone that I crossdressed was when I was twenty-three. He was a friend of a friend, and we were hanging out at a party.

Out of the blue, he told me he was bisexual and he thought I was cute. I told him that I wasn't into boys, but I did like dressing up as a girl. We talked about it all for a couple of hours. When I woke up the following morning, I practically died of embarrassment.

The first time that I kissed a boy was when I was twenty-four. It happened in the Bronx. I was coming to terms with my submissive fantasies and met a dominant guy through a personal ad he had placed in *The Village Voice*. Now in my fantasies I was always female, but I was afraid to go to his place cross-dressed, so instead I went in drab ("tranny talk" for "dressed as a boy"). When I got there, he was dressed head-to-toe in leather and reeked of patchouli. His stereo was blasting Depeche Mode, which seemed really cliché to me.[5] He tied me up to his bed, blindfolded me, and began kissing and groping me. It was extra-weird because he had a moustache and I kept imagining that his mouth was some strange combination of a porcupine and a leech. It wasn't a lot of fun for me. I'm sure he didn't enjoy himself much either, what with me being a confused and inexperienced bottom who just sort of lay there doing nothing. Afterwards we both talked about our favorite Woody Allen films. I never saw him again.

The first time that I had sex with someone while in "femme mode" was when I was twenty-eight. She was a bisexual friend who I dated on and off for a bit. First we went to the SF MoMA to see a Frida Kahlo exhibit. Then we went back to her place and shared a bottle of wine. We kissed. She fondled my foam breast through my shirt and told me how much she missed being with a woman. Afterwards she lent me some clothes that were less dorky than the ones I had on, and she took it upon herself to redo my makeup and hair. She made me look way better than I did earlier that day. We left her house to go to The Chameleon, a local dive bar. She laughed when the Latino boys in her neighborhood made the snake sounds at me. We had a few beers and talked. It was like two girls talking, she even said so. We both cried at one point; I'm not exactly sure why, but in retrospect I think it was because we both realized how sad it was that I had to keep this part of me hidden most of the time. Afterwards we went back to her place and made sloppy sex. She wanted me to penetrate her, but I couldn't keep it up. How could I after all of that? The next morning, I woke up and realized that I didn't bring any boy clothes along because I wasn't planning on spending the night. She lent me a pair of her pants and a hockey jersey for me to wear on the return trip to my apartment. She was a lot bigger than me, so when I put on the shirt it felt like I was wearing a tent.

I seemed so small. I can't remember ever feeling less like a boy than I did sitting on the BART train wearing that hockey jersey.

When I was thirty, I met Dani, who would eventually become my wife. We shared lots of firsts together. She was the first dyke activist that I ever dated, the first partner I ever moved in with, the first person I shared a checking account with. We even merged our CD collections. She was the first person to take me with a strap-on dildo, the first to give me a purely anal orgasm, the first person who truly understood how to make love to my physically male body while relating to me as a woman. Dani was by my side the day that I first called myself queer and the day I first dared to refer to myself as transgender. She was the first person that I ever asked to marry me. On a rainy night, during that brief period when we were calling each other fiancé, the two of us were lying in our bed. I told her that I was thinking about transitioning. We held hands and talked about it through the night. In the morning she took me out to breakfast by Lake Merritt. She made me laugh. Somehow she made the scariest day of my life seem really, really beautiful.

The first time that I took female hormones was when I was thirty-three. It was the day after our honeymoon. I washed the pills down with water then sat on the balcony of our apartment waiting for the buzz to hit.

The first time that I had a female orgasm was about two months after that. I was masturbating, and for the first time in my life "the stroke" just wasn't doing it for me. I just needed . . . more. So I grabbed Dani's Hitachi Magic Wand. A few years back I had tried out her vibrators, but they were way too much stimulation for my male organ. But now, after two months of being on female hormones, I could place her vibrator directly onto the tip of my penis and wow! Suddenly I found myself writhing for ten or fifteen minutes straight at a sexual state at least twenty times more intense than any boy orgasm I ever had. I decided right then and there that I was never going back.

The first day that I lived as a woman was a day that Dani and I planned to celebrate. On our honeymoon, she bought an expensive bottle of wine for us to share on that special occasion. However, some firsts don't happen in a very clear-cut fashion. There was no first day of being female for me. Instead, I just gradually changed over a five-month period and, before I knew it, strangers were referring to me as she even though I was still dressing in drab. We ended up drinking that bottle of wine on our wedding anniversary instead.

Some people have asked me, when I eventually have bottom surgery, if I will become a virgin again. You know, a "vaginal virgin" of sorts. I just laugh.

The whole idea of virginity is utterly ridiculous, as if every person's life can be divided up neatly into an innocent, childlike half and the impure, adult half. People who believe that must have excruciatingly boring and simplistic sex lives. For me, there have been many first times, and each has given me a rare opportunity to see myself a bit differently. My life has no singular defining point, because each first time is dependent upon all of the other ones that came previously. And while having surgery may mark the end of my physical transition to female, I don't see my sexual evolution as reaching some sort of conclusion. If there is one thing that I've learned, it's that there are always more first times for me to look forward to in my future.

19

San Francisco Bay Area
Trans Performance and Activism

At the time that I first started performing spoken word, I knew a small handful of other trans writers and artists. And I had attended a few transgender-themed shows in the Bay Area, but these were fairly rare events. Then suddenly in 2003, the confluence of numerous individual artists, organizers, and performance series blossomed into a thriving Bay Area trans performance scene. It was a "scene" in the best sense of the word: Many of us got to know one another, we inspired each other, and we went out and supported each other's events. It was one of the most amazing things that I have ever been a part of. But like all scenes, it eventually fizzled out after a couple of years, the inevitable result of individual organizers experiencing burn out and participating artists going off in various directions.

As I was compiling my past writings for this book, I stumbled upon this essay. I initially wrote it in March 2005 when I was asked to contribute a piece to an anthology of stories and advice about organizing queer events and festivals. Sadly, the anthology never came to be, but in retrospect I'm glad that I wrote this piece, as all of the details of how that scene came together were still relatively fresh in my mind. While this essay is not an especially exciting read—it is mostly the chronicling of people and events, and is largely meant to share my thoughts about queer/trans performance scenes and organizing, I have included it here because it is a small piece of trans history that I would like to see preserved. I have no way of fact-checking most of the details in this piece, so please consider this to be merely one individual's recollections from a scene that involved numerous other artists, organizers, and participants. Many of the events and performance/literary series listed here (specifically, the ones that I either performed in or organized myself) can also be found on my Events webpage and the GenderEnders website.[1]

Sometimes being a part of a wonderful, groundbreaking event is a matter of being at the right place at the right time. Other times, you have to start from scratch, lay the foundation, and do most of the work yourself. I have experienced both types of situations in my work organizing transgender-related performance and activism in the San Francisco Bay Area.

My interest in organizing trans events grew out of my own artistic endeavors as a musician and spoken word artist. In the years just before I came out as transgender and transitioned from male to female, my main creative outlet was my band Bitesize. When the band first formed, I was still fairly closeted, so I naturally channeled much of my gender-questioning self into lyrics for some of our songs. It was through those songs that I first spoke (or more accurately sung) openly about wanting to change my sex, identifying as female, and being transgender.

In the year 2002, just after I transitioned, I also began performing spoken word at poetry slams and open mics. Unlike my band's lyrics, which occasionally included transgender themes or references, all of my performance poetry pieces were about gender and my experiences being trans. Transitioning was an amazing experience, not only because it offered me the chance to finally become comfortable with myself, but because it also gave me the opportunity to speak openly about who I am for the first time, and to share what I have learned about gender with other people. I finally had a voice and I wasn't about to throw it away by going back into the closet. And I felt driven to correct what I felt was a grave injustice: that as both a child and as an adult, I was made to feel such shame and self-loathing about who I was due to other people's irrational fears and ignorance about gender difference.

Even though I was performing music and spoken word regularly in the San Francisco Bay Area, I rarely crossed paths with other trans performers. Since finding my own voice was so important for me as a trans person, I was eager to seek out other trans artists. To this end, I set out to get more involved in queer and trans performance. One of the best ways I found to do that was to attend queer open mics, as they offered me a chance not only to listen to other artists, but to introduce them to my work as well. When I first started out, my favorite two open mics to attend were the long-running K'vetch, hosted by Lynnee Breedlove and Tara Jepsen, and Hubbub, hosted by Larry-bob Roberts of *Holy Titclamps* and *Queer Things To Do in the San Francisco Bay Area* fame. At these events, I finally had the opportunity to meet other trans artists and writers.

My continuing desire to connect with trans artists led to me coming up with the idea for GenderEnders in early 2003. The name is obviously a play on "gender bender," a phrase that I never especially liked, because it seems to describe a sort of playful and temporary toying with gender (the implication being that one may "bend" gender but they cannot "break" it). I thought that GenderEnders better captured the mood of the day, as many of us in the trans community, including me at the time, were defining ourselves outside of the binary gender/sex system. The name also refers to the fact that we gender/sex-variant folks are invariably tacked onto the back-ends of queer acronyms.

My initial vision for GenderEnders was a transgender, intersex, and genderqueer-focused open mic event; the motto I came up with was "dotting the *i*'s and crossing the *t*'s in the LGBTIQ performance community!" Before I got around to putting together the first GenderEnders show, I was contacted by Kight Fetish, an organizer of Kithology, a trans/queer resource and website that threw regular events that allowed folks to socialize outside of the bar scene. Kight had heard about me through Larry-bob and asked if I wanted to perform at and/or help out with organizing a community picnic that was in the works.

From what I've been told, the idea for the picnic grew out of a discussion that Kight had with Sam Davis from United Genders of the Universe, a trans/genderqueer support group open to everyone who views gender as having more than two options. The idea was to have an event that would bring together the many various gender-related communities in the San Francisco Bay Area. Having the event be a picnic was appealing for several reasons. First of all, it could be free and open to anyone who showed up. It would also allow other people to add their own creativity and ideas to the event. The eventual location for the picnic, Dolores Park in the Mission District of San Francisco, allowed plenty of space for folks to set up their own booths, table, games, etcetera.

The event was eventually given the somewhat unwieldy title: The Trans/Intersex/Genderqueer & Buddies Community Picnic. Besides Kight, Sam, and me, the other folks I remember being primarily involved in organizing the event included Cian Dawson from the Transgender Steering Committee, and Larry-bob. Evan Bee and Molly Straylight also helped out a lot with providing DJ equipment and electricity needs.

My role was to manage the performances for the event. Most of the artists had already signed onto the event by the time I became involved. It was my job to get them the details for the event, find out what sound or equipment needs they had, and to provide sound equipment for the show (I borrowed my band's PA, microphones, and stands). Another crucial aspect of the job was mapping out a precise schedule of what time each artist would go on, and for how long. This is important, not only to keep the flow of the show entertaining for audiences, but to ensure that no artist goes overtime. I have found that this is crucial for any show that involves more than a few acts, because if each of the performers toward the beginning of the show goes over time, the artists scheduled toward the end of the bill will end up having to drastically shorten their sets, or even worse, be cut from the show entirely.

The Picnic took place on Sunday, May 18, 2003, from 12–5 p.m. The performers included a mix of music, drag and burlesque, and spoken word: Shawna Virago, solidad decosta (and her musical duo Two Tricks), Larry-bob, Transformers, OTHER (Thea Hillman and Storm Florez), Daphne Gottlieb, Burlesque-esque, Transcendence Gospel Choir, Katastrophe, Disposable Boy Toys, and me.[2] There were also a couple of last minute impromptu performers towards the end of the event. The show was emceed by Fairy Butch, with Rocco Kayiatos (a.k.a., Katastrophe) and me filling in during the very beginning.

While I was mostly concerned with the performance aspect (after all, that was my job), that was only a part of the event as a whole. We had a DJ table set up in the middle of the park, and DJ Sam, DJ Beet, DJ Molly S, and DJ Spike took turns spinning records. The "Tranny Clothing Swap" provided an opportunity for folks to patch, sew, stud, and trade clothing on the barter system. Hiccup Queer & Genderfuck Playground brought all of their gear for people to play volleyball, wrestling, and kickball. Other picnic activities included face painting, a dance space, and a genderfuck beauty salon.

All in all, the Picnic was an amazing success. It was estimated that somewhere between 300–500 people turned out for the event. Even more important than the sheer number of people was the good feeling and sense of community that many folks came away with. While the Bay Area is believed to have one of the largest transgender populations per capita of anywhere in the world, it was still very rare during that period in time to have a trans-majority event of that size. While the event was geared towards transgender, intersex, and genderqueer (TIG)-identified folks, we worked hard to make sure that non-TIG people felt welcome as well. Part of the impetus for this came from us having learned the harsh lessons of exclusionary policies which have particularly marginalized trans people, preventing us from participating in many gay, lesbian, and women's events and spaces. We also felt that it was important to include our partners, family, friends, and allies who have stood by our sides over the years. After all, they are a part of our community too.[3]

Perhaps the most amazing part about the Picnic was that it turned out to be a galvanizing moment that opened the doors to a new wave of regular TIG-focused events in the Bay Area. Gender Pirates, which had previously been a dance party put on by United Genders of the Universe, began to have monthly music, drag, and spoken word performance benefits at the club El Rio. Other regular trans/queer cabarets took to the stage at El Rio, including Wicked Messenger, hosted by Sherilyn Connelly and Frankie Tenderloin, and Karma, organized by Nafis and Garcia. My own show, GenderEnders, also got off the ground later that year, starting out at the Cherry Bar, but later finding a permanent home at Femina Potens, a women- and transgender-focused art gallery and performance space. In addition to these regular events, a number of trans-focused benefit shows took place in during the fall of 2003, raising money for organizations such as Pronoun Schmonoun (which addresses gender-variant healthcare issues), Camp Trans, and San Francisco mayoral candidates Tom Ammiano and Matt Gonzalez.

This new crop of TIG-focused events joined the ranks of other regular trans-hosted events that were already taking place in San Francisco, including In Bed With Fairy Butch, a cabaret and dance party for queer women and trans folks, and Writers with Drinks, hosted by Charlie Jane Anders, which showcases writers spanning different literary genres. Other earlier TIG-focused events had been organized by groups such as Transgender San Francisco (TGSF), or individuals like Thea Hillman, who put together Intercourse: A Sex and Gender Recipe for Revolution, and Rated XXXY: An Evening of Erotica and Education Benefitting the Intersex Society of North America. The annual trans and queer cabaret extravaganza Fresh Meat, organized by Sean Dorsey as part of the National Queer Arts Festival, was also already in the works when the Picnic took place.

Clearly, the Trans/Intersex/Genderqueer & Buddies Community Picnic did not create the TIG performance scene. Rather, we rode a wave energy that was borne out of two decades of TIG activism and the gradual acceptance of our communities. If anything, the Picnic simply added to that momentum, by making it clear to future organizers that there was a large potential audience for TIG performance and events.

One possible backlash that can happen after any large and successful event is that the different organizers involved might try to claim all the success for themselves, or squabble over competing visions for the future. Luckily, this has not happened with the Picnic. The following year, we threw the Second Annual Trans/Genderqueer/Intersex/Drag & Buddies Picnic, but rather than making it another performance-focused event (which requires a lot of top–down organizing), we decided that it should be a democratic shindig. There was no central organizing committee—instead, everyone who attended was encouraged to take ownership by adding themselves, and their creativity and effort, to the event. Once again, we had a great turn out and people brought their own interests, information, and activities to the occasion.

Another new aspect to the Picnic in 2004 was that it became a part of the first ever TIG Week, a series of performance and community-building events taking place during the last week of May. The idea for TIG Week came together in an impromptu sort of fashion, when the organizers of the Picnic, Gender Pirates, TGSF Unity, and GenderEnders decided to combine forces with events that we already had planned for that week. We thought that since gender/sex-variant folks tend to make up the last few letters of the LGBTIGQ acronym, it was only fitting that TIG Week take place during the last week of May, thus ushering in Queer Pride Month.[4]

Some people might assume that having so many similarly-themed events in such a short period of time would result in competition between individual shows over a limited pool of potential audience members. While that may be the way things work in the business world, in my years of experience as a performer and organizer, I have found that the opposite is true for the arts: The more similarly-themed shows there are, the faster that scene grows and the more attention it garners. As the number of TIG-focused shows increased, it generated even more excitement and momentum from audience members, organizers, and performers alike. This resulted in media coverage (which was rare for trans-themed events back then), both in alternative weekly papers as well as mainstream daily papers like *The San Francisco Chronicle*, which ran a large article on the Bay Area's TIG-performance scene in late December 2003.[5] This media coverage helped reach even more TIG people who might have previously been unaware of the scene. The entire community benefits when organizers and performers support, rather than compete, with one another.

Another benefit of having so many different TIG-focused events is that it can inspire individual shows to take somewhat different approaches. Because the scene already had a number of cabaret-style trans and queer shows, which usually feature a multitude of performers each doing relatively short sets, I have worked on making GenderEnders different by only having two features per night, but allowing them up to thirty minutes a piece for their sets. This allows the artists the rare opportunity to stretch out and perform pieces that they might not be able to pull off in the shorter sets that occurred in other shows. Over the last year and a half, we have been able to feature Lynnee Breedlove's new band Stop Looking At My Boyfriend, Storm Florez, Katastrophe, Thea Hillman, Charlie Jane Anders, Shawna Virago, Matthue Roth, The Urban Hermitt, Jaycub Perez, Max Wolf Valerio, Butch Greenblatt, Sherilyn Connelly, Seely Quest, solidad decosta, Johnny Pratt, MK, and Lipstick Conspiracy. We have also had a few special-themed shows, my favorite being our "Tranny Lovers Show!"[6] in May 2004, featuring Michelle Tea, Meliza Bañales, Annalee Newitz, Clare Lewis, Rhiannon Argo, and Ricky Leyva.

Another aspect that distinguishes GenderEnders from the other regular TIG events is that we have an open mic at the show to provide a space for members of our community to perform their music, spoken word, or other types of performance in front of an audience for perhaps the first time. I believe this is crucial for keeping the scene fresh and to allow new and unique voices to find a home in the community. I am happy to say that we have a new TIG open mic in the Bay Area: the trans youth-focused Translate, hosted by Brooklynne Thomas. Since both Translate and GenderEnders take place outside of the traditional bar and club scene, our shows allow TIG folks of all ages to participate.

Thus far, most of the events that I have been involved in, including GenderEnders and the Picnic, have been focused on bringing together voices and performers from different, and often disparate, TIG communities. In a sense, this is a continuation of the work by many activists over the last decade and a half, who have made a concerted effort to unite folks under umbrella words like "transgender" or "TIG." This has been done in an attempt to encourage us all to work together, gaining strength in numbers, so that we may achieve rights and respect in the world. Such a strategy has been extraordinarily effective in accomplishing this goal, as the acceptance of TIG folks in the Bay Area (and even the nation as a whole) has reached levels that many of us have never dreamed of before.

Having said that, there is always a potential problem with the umbrella strategy, in that certain subgroups within the collective will inevitably have their voices heard over others. This can happen when one subgroup is better organized, exists in larger numbers, and/or possesses certain forms of privilege that other subgroups do not. One can see this phenomenon in the queer community at large, where many LGBT organizations and media outlets focus almost exclusively on gay and lesbian issues, with bisexual and transgender issues receiving only minimal attention. And while lesbians and gay men share common goals, such as fighting homophobia or working for same-sex marriage, these two communities often face very different sets of problems. For example, the lesbian community struggles more with issues of sexism and classism as a result of lesbian women not having access to the benefits of male privilege that gay men experience.

In a similar manner, it has been my experience that trans women face certain issues that are not shared by the rest of transgender community. My understanding of this grew out of my work with Camp Trans, the annual protest against Michigan Womyn's Music Festival's trans women-exclusion policy.

I first became involved with Camp Trans when I helped put on a benefit show for the organization in the summer of 2003, shortly after the first Picnic. I was later invited to perform at that year's Camp Trans. I was initially under the impression that I could go there and intellectually fight for trans woman-inclusion. But being right there at Michigan, in the midst of the largest annual women-only festival in the world, and knowing that I was not welcomed because the festival organizers did not respect my female identity, had a profound effect on me. Having my body be the actual battleground upon which the trans revolution was being fought upon struck me on a deep emotional level and drove me to become even more involved in helping to organize the following year's Camp Trans.

In my work on this issue, I have found that the exclusion of trans women from women's and lesbian spaces does not take place in a vacuum. Rather, it happens in the context of a dyke community that has grown increasingly accepting of trans men and other folks on the female-to-male (FTM) spectrum. While Michigan's official policy is that the festival is for women only, a significant number of attendees are male-identified trans people and female-assigned genderqueers, who identify outside of the male/female gender binary. Musicians who have publically stated that they answer to male pronouns are regularly invited to perform at the festival, while trans women who identify fully as women and are treated by the world as female are routinely turned away. This discrepancy—being open to trans men but not trans women—mirrors trends that exist throughout much of the lesbian community as a whole.

The premise that trans women should be singled out for exclusion because we "used to be men" (by a community that welcomes people who are men *now*) is highly suspect. Rather, I believe that the preference for trans men over trans women in the lesbian community reflects the differing values we place on maleness and femaleness, and on masculinity and femininity, in society at large. In a recent article I penned,[7] I discuss how traditional sexism results in trans women being regularly ridiculed, sensationalized, and sexualized by the media, whereas trans men often remain invisible.

Currently, I am working on a couple of related projects designed to challenge the anti-trans woman sentiments that are prevalent in both mainstream society and queer communities. To increase awareness of these issues, I have been working on publishing essays, articles, and poems that combine my personal experiences as a trans woman with certain relevant concepts from the feminist and trans activist movements. I eventually plan to publish these pieces together in a collection, tentatively titled *Hot Tranny Action*. My hope is that this body of work will effectively communicate how traditional sexism shapes popular stereotypes of trans women and provide new strategies and insights towards fighting both misogyny and transphobia. Since this book project will take some time to finish, I have begun work on a corresponding website that will be home to many of these writings in the meantime.[8]

Even though I have taken on this trans woman activism project, I still continue to be heavily involved in TIG performance events and activist causes. After all, queer activism often requires us to fight on many different fronts. As a trans woman, I cannot pretend that there is only one single issue from which I suffer. Not only am I transgender, but as someone whose life partner is female, I am a dyke as well. And because I have the privilege of being able to pass in my identified gender, on a day-to-day basis I am more often discriminated against for being a woman than I am for being transgender or lesbian. For me, feminist, queer, and trans activism are all interrelated, all necessary tools to use towards reaching the eventual goal of ending discrimination based on gender, sex, and sexuality.

Part Two

Articulating Trans-Misogyny

At the end of the previous chapter, I mentioned a series of trans wom-an-centric writings that I was beginning to work on, one that would draw connections between the various forms of sexism that I personally faced as a queer-identified transsexual woman. While I assumed that this book project would "take some time to finish," a serendipitous turn of events resulted in that collection (which ultimately became *Whipping Girl: A Transsexual Woman on Sexism and the Scapegoating of Femininity*) coming to fruition far sooner than I had expected. Since all the chapters in this section were either written concurrently with, or are related in some way to, *Whipping Girl*, I figured that I would briefly describe how that book (and some of the ideas contained therein) came to be.

In December 2004, I was invited to read at Michelle Tea's Radar Reading Series in San Francisco. After the event, Brooke Warner introduced herself to me and mentioned that she was an editor at Seal Press. She said that she missed my reading (a set of performance poetry), but liked what I had to say during the question and answer session. I thanked her and gave her a copy of my chapbook *Draw Blood*. I didn't think too much about it at the time, as Seal

Press was not actively publishing poetry. But then a few months later, in April 2005, Brooke contacted me out of the blue and asked if I had ever considered writing a book of personal essays. And it turns out that I was already in the early stages of working on one.

While performance poetry is a powerful medium for expressing personal stories and opinions, its time constraints often make it too limiting for taking on more complex topics or rolling out long and involved arguments, which is what I now wanted to do. While in my poetry, I regularly described the transphobia that I faced as a trans person and the misogyny that I faced since transitioning to female, I now wanted to explore how these phenomena intersected in my life, and for others on the trans female/feminine spectrum. The first of such essays was "Skirt Chasers: Why the Media Depicts the Trans Revolution in Lipstick and Heels," which first appeared in *Bitch Magazine* in the Fall of 2004.[1] Then in June 2005, I released a chapbook entitled *On the Outside Looking In: a trans woman's perspective on feminism and the exclusion of trans women from lesbian and women-only spaces*, which included three additional essays on this topic (which were later re-worked for *Whipping Girl* and *Excluded*).[2]

To the best of my knowledge, *On the Outside Looking In* was the first publication to contain the word "trans-misogyny"—a term I used to refer to the intersection of transphobia and misogyny, and which has since caught on, at least within transgender and activist circles. I believe that I coined the term, although I cannot rule out the possibility that it arose elsewhere independently, as during that time I had had conversations with a number of trans women about how much of the transphobia we face might be better described as expressions of misogyny.

In the years since *Whipping Girl* was published, the term "trans-misogyny" has taken on a life of its own, and people now use it in ways that I never intended. Specifically, I used the term to describe how the existence of societal misogyny/traditional sexism greatly informs how people perceive, interpret, or treat gender-variant people who seemingly "want to be female" or "want to be feminine" (regardless of their actual identity). However, many people nowadays use the word "trans-misogyny" in an identity-based manner to refer to any and all forms of discrimination targeting trans women. According to this latter usage, some would argue that people who identify as men, or male crossdressers, or drag queens, cannot possibly experience trans-misogyny—a close reading of *Whipping Girl* will reveal that I very much disagree with this premise. (See Chapter 48 of this book for a detailed explanation regarding why identity-based views of marginalization tend to be inaccurate and exclusive.)

Along similar lines, I have observed people using "trans-misogyny" as shorthand to suggest that "trans men are privileged, and trans women oppressed, end of story." I reject such oversimplifications for the very same reasons that I rejected earlier reciprocal claims (which were quite prevalent back when I was writing *Whipping Girl*) that "trans women experience male privilege, whereas trans men do not." Male and masculine privileges can provide very real advantages to those who are granted them. But this does not mean that those who experience said privileges automatically have it easy, are fully accepted by society, and/or are immune from other forms of marginalization (e.g., transphobia).

It should also be said that trans-misogyny (in my original conceptualization of the term) was not intended to suggest that trans female/feminine folks experience misogyny whereas trans male/masculine folks do not. Obviously, trans male/masculine individuals may experience misogyny at various points throughout their lives, including post-transition (e.g., if their trans status is discovered). Once again, what I was trying to convey with "trans-misogyny" is how the widespread presumption that femaleness and femininity are inferior to, or less legitimate than, maleness and masculinity, creates assumptions, stereotypes, and obstacles for trans female/feminine people that are not generally experienced by those on the trans male/masculine spectrum (unless, of course, post-transition they are read by others as a man who wants, or is trying, to be female and/or feminine).

I was interested in articulating trans-misogyny because it both accounted for how people on the trans female/feminine spectrum tend to face the lion's share of sensationalization, consternation, and demonization in mainstream considerations of trans people, and also helped to make sense of the disparities in acceptance of trans men versus trans women that existed within my own queer women's community during the time (as I alluded to at the end of the last chapter). To be clear, I don't think that this disparity was solely due to trans-misogyny, but it most certainly was a contributing factor.[3]

Over the years, I have occasionally come across people who will protest that lesbians in their community don't accept trans men at all, or that trans women are accepted in their own queer women's community to the same extent as (or perhaps even more so than) trans men. I don't doubt that these configurations exist—in fact, in my mind they seem to form a continuum over time, with the former being extremely common during the '80s and '90s, and the latter resembling where we may slowly be heading. But throughout most of the '00s, especially in U.S. urban queer women's communities, the disparity that I describe in these pieces was extremely commonplace, if not ubiquitous.

I am perfectly fine with the idea of trans male/masculine people participating in (what are ostensibly) queer women's communities. What I was primarily objecting to in some of the chapters that follow is how that participation tended to be *practiced*—for instance, how some trans men's emphasis of their former status (e.g., as "girls" or "lesbians") encouraged others to continue using trans women's former "male" status against us; or how lesbians who excluded trans women would so frequently point to trans men in the space in order to make the claim that they couldn't possibly be "transphobic." It is this latter claim (which I heard scores upon scores of times back then) that seemed to necessitate the coining of an entirely new trans female/feminine-specific term. To be honest, I am not sure that I would have gravitated toward the neologism "trans-misogyny" if it were not for my activist work challenging this particular disparity.

Anyway, once my *On the Outside Looking In* chapbook was complete, I passed it along to Seal Press, and they liked it. So I followed that up with a book proposal, which they accepted. I was thrilled by the possibility of having a book published, especially with Seal Press, as their history of publishing books "by women, for women" would likely help the book garner some legitimacy and attention among feminists who might not be especially familiar with transgender people and issues.

I was also highly aware of how lucky I was: While Bitesize had been playing out for eight years, and many people had expressed excitement and appreciation for our music, none of them worked for a record company that had the means to release our music to a wider audience. And yet, here I was—a relatively unknown writer with three chapbooks and a handful of magazine articles to my name—who just so happened to be at the right place at the right time to get noticed by someone who expressed interest in publishing my book.

While I was excited about the opportunity, I was also naturally quite nervous, never having written a full-length book before. I had a handful of essays and spoken word pieces in hand, but I still needed to write the bulk of the book. Seal Press gave me a year and a half to work on it before the entire manuscript would be due. And that was pretty much all I did for that year and a half of my life. I was working full-time as a biologist at UC Berkeley, so I got up every morning and wrote from 5 to 8 a.m. And when I got home from work,

I read voraciously for my book research.

I have learned a lot about writing from reading authors of various genres and styles. But during the time that I was working on *Whipping Girl*, I remember being influenced by four authors in particular: Audre Lorde, Riki Wilchins, Patrick Califia, and bell hooks. While these writers are admittedly quite different from one another in content and style, all four had penned collections of essays that I found to be powerful and uncompromising, yet simultaneously accessible, easily discernable, and highly persuasive. These authors seemed to use fierce combinations of logic, passion, personal experience, and humor to win over readers to their point of view—and this is precisely what I was striving to do in my book. Audre Lorde's style of poetic prose especially resonated with me as a "recovering slam poet" (as I sometimes half-jokingly refer to myself now). While I am incapable of writing prose as beautiful as hers, I try (in my own way) to incorporate some of what I've learned from writing performance poetry and song lyrics into my essays. Rather than just stringing words together, I am always thinking about the cadence of a sentence or paragraph, and I often purposefully try to arrange words and phrases so that they internally rhyme and/or flow into one another. Even when I am writing for the page, I am always considering how the piece in question would sound if it were to be spoken aloud. I'm sure that most readers never consciously pick up on this, but I'm inclined to believe that it likely makes the book a more pleasant and compelling read.

The most difficult decision that I faced while working on the book was whether or not to use the then relatively unknown "cis terminology" (in which the prefix "cis" is used to refer to the non-trans majority); I discuss my reasons for choosing to do so in Chapter 25. I had discovered this language online, but it was not yet widely in use within trans communities (or at least the ones that I was involved in), and I had never before seen it in print.[4] So I very much worried that including this new language—in addition to several other new terms that I was introducing (e.g., trans-misogyny, effemimania, subversivism, subconscious sex, gender entitlement)—might make the book seem alien or unintelligible for some readers. But thankfully, rather than driving readers away, cis terminology eventually caught on, and is probably one of the main concepts (along with trans-misogyny) that people most commonly associate with *Whipping Girl*.

The book underwent a number of title changes while it was a work in progress. The tentative title in my book proposal was *Hot Tranny Action*, but as I discuss in Chapter 45, we decided that that would create too many mis-conceptions about what the book was about. In the book contract, the ten-tative title was listed as *Feminine Wiles,* which I liked, but it ultimately was deemed too old-fashioned sounding. My publisher and I went back and forth with alternate titles for quite a while. In an interview I gave in August 2006, I referred to the tentative title as *Who's Deceiving Who?: Transsexual Women, Sexism and the Future of Feminism* (which I had completely forgotten about until I stumbled upon that article last year).[5] Then one day, after Brooke had emailed me a list of potential titles, we were talking on the phone and she asked me what I thought about her suggestion of "Whipping Girl." I replied that I was confused by that one (honestly, the first thing that popped into my head upon seeing that title was BDSM!), until she pointed out that the phrase was intended to be the feminine version of "whipping boy"—this seemed to fit perfectly with the book's discussions of the societal scapegoating of femininity, so we eventually settled on it.

While the book touches upon a number of topics related to gender and gender-variant people, it is primarily focused on challenging societal critiques of three particular subgroups—transsexuals, trans female/feminine-spectrum individuals, and people who are feminine in gender expression—as I found that these three aspects of my own person were rarely defended at the time, both in mainstream society and within many strands of feminism, queer, and trans-gender activism. Since these three subgroups were routinely maligned within activism and academia, I spent a significant chunk of the book debunking or re-thinking certain entrenched beliefs within feminism, gender studies, queer theory, and transgender activism. This (unsurprisingly, I suppose) led to a few sensationalistic synopses of the book (such as a *San Francisco Chronicle* book review headlined "Transsexual finds sexism in feminism"[6]), and I have since encountered a few claims that I was somehow disproportionately blaming feminists and queer activists for the marginalization of these three subgroups. That was not my intention—I was simply working to make these movements more aware and inclusive of transsexuals, trans women, and feminine people, as I believe that we have a stake in these movements as well.

Upon its completion, I was pretty sure that the book would be well re-ceived among trans women and other trans-spectrum people, as I was writing from that particular standpoint. I also hoped that it would resonate with many femmes, and perhaps even garner some attention within queer and feminist circles more generally. So I was really excited to find that, soon after the book was released in June 2007, it seemed to make an impact outside of the trans and femme bubbles. But I had no idea that, in subsequent years, some would consider it to be an important feminist text, or that it would eventually be used as teaching materials in gender and queer studies, sociology, psychology, and other college courses. While I was writing it, I very much saw myself as an outsider challenging the feminist and academic orthodoxy, so it was somewhat surreal to witness the book become accepted in many (albeit most certainly not all) corners of activism and academia.

Whipping Girl was originally intended to be a book of personal essays, and as such, it is replete with my own personal stories and perspectives on the world. Of course, these particular anecdotes and interpretations stem in part from me being socially situated as a white, middle-class, able-bodied, "generation X," out, queer-identified transsexual woman living in a major city in the U.S in the early 2000s. But now that it is often presented in classrooms and other settings as an "authoritative" or "definitive" book about trans people and issues, its rather specific focus unfortunately results in a number of other important topics getting relatively less consideration. *Whipping Girl* offers little discussion about the issues and experiences of non-binary-identified people, intersex people, trans male/masculine-spectrum people, straight-identified trans people, trans people of color and other cultures, and so forth. Over the years, numerous people have expressed to me their disappointment in these omissions. Had I known at the time that the book would one day be viewed as an authoritative or definitive "transgender book," I probably would have written it very differently: less personal and transsexual-focused, and more general and intersectional. But, for better or worse, it is what it is: the perspective of one individual trans woman situated in a particular time and place.

I'd like to think that *Whipping Girl* makes numerous points that remain insightful or useful. But I will be the first to admit that it is far from the whole story, and I am grateful for the many other gender-variant writers of various identities, backgrounds, generations, and geographies that are filling in the many gaps that the book overlooks.

Postscript added June 2016: A Second Edition of *Whipping Girl* was recently published—it is pretty much the same book, albeit with a new Preface that places the book in historical context, clarifies several arguments I made over the course of the book, and discusses the many changes in transgender activism since the book's initial release.[7] I further expound on some of the ideas that I first presented in *Whipping Girl* (e.g., gender entitlement, subversivism and the "reinforcing" trope, subconscious sex and my "intrinsic inclinations" model) throughout *Excluded*. On my blog, I penned several responses to frequently asked questions about the book regarding terminology, the original book cover (which depicts a woman putting on a necklace), and the chapter "Submissive Streak."[8] Finally, I update my thoughts about media depictions of trans people in the recent article "Expanding Trans Media Representation: Why Transgender Actors Should Be Cast in Cisgender Roles."[9]

20

Her Own Femme

As I was writing Whipping Girl, *I was invited to perform as part of the 2006 Femme Conference in San Francisco. For the event, I co-wrote and performed a spoken word piece with Meliza Bañales and Celestina Pearl called "Her Own Femme." What follows is my part of that piece, which touches on many of the themes (e.g., trans woman-exclusion, the scapegoating of femininity) that I was concerned with in* Whipping Girl. *My experiences at this conference and event are cited in the subsequent chapter and discussed in detail in my essay "Reclaiming Femininity" (which appears in* Excluded*).*[1]

I

For many queer women, femininity is something that others foist upon them: an unwanted burden, an expectation that they are unable or unwilling to meet. But for me, a young trans girl forced against my will into boyhood, I was taught to see femininity as foreign, forbidden, taboo. During my childhood and teenage years, I found myself quite capable of keeping my desire to be female to myself, because that was invisible, like an alternative reality that only I was privy to. And while the fact that I was attracted to women confused me given my dreams of being a girl, it was taken for granted by everyone else around me. But the one aspect of my queerness that was most difficult for me to manage was my femininity. It was like ether or air, always there, just waiting for the chance to leak out of me.

In a world where boys are ostracized for throwing like a girl, using their hands when they speak, or non-sarcastically using the word "cute," I survived by censoring myself, by butching it up a bit. And despite the fact that masculinity hung on me like an ill-fitted suit, I learned to rely on the safety it offered me. It stopped others from questioning me. It encouraged them to take me seriously. People often mistake masculinity for strength, when in reality it is merely a shield that deflects the negative connotations, sexual innuendos, and accusations of inferiority aimed at those who are feminine. Growing up in a society that is fueled by male homophobic hysteria, it took me many years to figure out that there is no act more brave than proudly embracing one's femme self.

II

In the mid–1990s, I moved out to the Bay Area. Within six short years I went from calling myself a crossdresser, to bigender, to transsexual woman. Somewhere in the middle of that period of self-discovery, I met my eventual wife Dani. On one of our early dates, she told me about her early experiences coming out as a dyke in the early '90s. She too had tried to butch it up a bit. She shaved her head, wore Doc Martens boots and motorcycle jackets. When she told me this, she was wearing a polka dot blouse and barrettes that had butterflies on them.

These days, people who know we're a couple often seem confused by the fact that both of us are unafraid to be feminine. They will ask, "So who wears the pants in the relationship?" as if no coupling is complete unless one of the partners takes on the boy role. It angers me how people assume that femme cannot exist without a masculine counterpart. My femme expression is not meant for any man, any boy, or any butch. It is not a performance, or an artificial construct designed to entice, allure, or appease anybody. I am femme solely for me.

III

The more time that I spend in the greater queer community, the more I come to realize that, for all of our fabulous fashions, outrageous sex, and acts of gender rebellion, we tend to have pretty conservative views regarding gender expression. In gay male culture, masculinity is praised while femininity remains suspect. In the dyke community, masculinity is praised while femininity remains suspect.

Many argue that trans women like myself shouldn't be allowed to participate in lesbian events and women-only spaces like the Michigan Womyn's Music Festival. They pretend to be most disturbed by our "male energy" or "male" genitals—a hypocritical stance for a community so infatuated with drag kings and strap-on dildos. The real reason why many dykes feel threatened by trans women is because of our femininity. A friend of mine from Camp Trans who worked the line at Michigan, trying to convince attendees that the festival should open its doors to trans women, had a lesbian mockingly reply, "I'm surprised that an MTF would want to go camping. Aren't they afraid they might break a nail?" Trans male and queer female friends of mine tell me all of the time about dykes they know who openly lust after trans guys, yet deride trans women for being "creepy" and "effeminate."

When I first started performing at queer women's events, aware of these trans-misogynistic stereotypes, I (once again) purposely censored my femininity and played up the parts of myself that are more tomboy rather than girly-girl. Eventually it struck me how fucked up it was that in my day-to-day life, I am an out and proud transsexual and dyke, yet whenever I entered supposedly "safe" queer spaces, I felt that I had to hide my femme side. I know that I am not the only queer woman who has felt this way. At a recent event I was at, a performer asked the hundred or so queer women and trans folks in the audience, "How many of you love femmes?" and the crowd bursted into applause. During my set, I asked the audience, "How many of you *are* femmes?" and a mere eight people begin to cheer. And many of those who remained silent looked at least as femme as me.

It saddens me that my community is not afraid of shouting, "We're here, we're queer, get used to it!" Not ashamed of creating queer porn, burlesque and erotica, nor speaking openly about embracing BDSM, androgyny, polyamory, and fat pride. Yet we are so desperately embarrassed about our femininity.

21

Frustration

In August 2006, one of my local LGBTQ papers published an article called "Michigan Or Bust: CampTrans Flourishes for Another Year."[1] It included quotes from two male-pronoun-using trans male/masculine-spectrum people who regularly attended the Michigan Womyn's Music Festival, and who talked about "changing the festival from within" with regard to the festival's longstanding trans woman-exclusion policy. Having grown wearisome of that meme (which I had heard countless times during the three previous years that I was doing activism around changing that policy), I was compelled to write this palpably angry post, which sort of went "viral" in a pre-social-media sense (i.e., it was heavily re-posted in various trans- and queer-themed email groups).

Here is a scenario that I hope will spark some long overdue dialogue: Say a woman you know is the victim of sexist discrimination, and her discriminators were unapologetic about it. If you were a righteous male ally, would you: 1) hold the discriminators accountable by calling them on their shit, boycotting their business, etc., or 2) assure the woman that you will meet privately with her discriminators, behind closed doors, and try to show them the error of their ways?

If you chose #2, and the discriminators refused to change their ways, would you: 1) hold the discriminators accountable by calling them on their shit, boycotting their business, etc., or 2) instead, continue to meet with the discriminators in private to try to change their mind, because you have worked with them before on other issues, and you know they are good people deep down?

If at this point you still would chose #2, would you continue with that strategy for years on end? Would you continue even if some people used the fact that the discriminators were willing to meet with you as evidence that they aren't really sexist?

If you were the woman in this scenario, how would you feel? Angry? Frustrated? If every time you spoke with the "male ally" about the issue, he simply told you to be patient, that these things take time, wouldn't that sound condescending and patronizing to you? Would you even consider that man an ally?

As a trans woman, this is how I feel right now about many FTM-spectrum folks (as well as many non-trans queer women) in my community. While some trans guys and queer women I know are righteous allies in the fight against trans woman-exclusion policies in lesbian and queer women's communities, others choose to enjoy the privilege they have being accepted in queer women's spaces, even if it comes at the expense of trans women's identities. Often this is couched in the language of fighting to change such policies.[2] What is typically overlooked is how this enables anti-trans woman sentiment in queer/trans spaces.

People pretend that specific events like Michigan are merely isolated incidents, but this is not the case. Many trans women—even ones who are dyke or bisexual-identified—do not feel comfortable in queer women's spaces (even the ones that explicitly include us) because of the anti-trans woman sentiment that often exists in those spaces. All it takes is a handful of dykes to make trans misogynistic comments that are not called out by others in the community (whether they be queer women or FTM-spectrum folks) to drive trans women away.

I find it sad that no one (FTM or non-trans queer woman) has ever asked me why more trans women don't come out to shows that occur at the intersection of the trans and queer women's communities (while scores of trans guys attend these events, typically there are a mere handful of trans women). If they did ask me, I would tell them about all the times that I've had trans women ask me when I'm performing next, and when I tell them that it's at a queer women's event or a queer/trans event, they have told me that they'd rather not go because they do not feel comfortable or safe in those spaces, because they have been harassed or belittled at such events before.

At the Femme Conference this past weekend, there was a significant turn out of FTM-spectrum folks but hardly any trans women—even though it was a *femme* conference. When Shawna Virago and I (the only two trans women there who I was personally aware of) brought up issues that made us feel unsafe and uncomfortable in that space (specifically, the spoofing of trans identities in the film *Female-to-Femme* and several anti-trans woman comments made by one of the keynote speakers) we were described by some as being "divisive."³ I have heard similar complaints about "divisiveness" from queer women and FTM-spectrum folks regarding Michigan, Osento,⁴ etc. We are not being divisive! We simply want to be fully respected in our own community!

I am not comfortable about the way that people who play Michigan or make trans-misogynistic comments are coddled by other queer women and FTM-spectrum folks in my community. When folks who play Michigan or who are Michigan-apologists take the stage at trans events, it says to me that trans women are second-class citizens in our community. I am all for fighting under the transgender umbrella so long as all of our concerns are being addressed. But if "transgender" means that trans women's concerns and representation is going to take a back seat to trans men's concerns (just as lesbians' concerns often take a back seat to gay men's within queer activism), then maybe this isn't really my community after all.

22

Questionable

The following piece was written in 2006 and initially intended for inclusion in Whipping Girl. *Looking through my notes from that time, it appears that I originally planned for this to be the first chapter of Part 1 of the book. I really liked how the piece forcefully challenged commonly held assumptions that many readers would likely have—much like "Fighting Words," albeit with significantly less profanity. But as the book took shape, I had already decided to lead with a headstrong Introduction followed by a manifesto, so I was concerned that following those chapters with another "in your face" piece might run the risk of alienating some readers. For these reasons, I ultimately decided to commence Part 1 of the book with a chapter on terminology and two chapters on media depictions (which I thought were more likely to win over non-trans feminist-minded readers) before delving into ideas that they might find more challenging. While I believe I made the right decision, it left this chapter without a home, as the piece was somewhat redundant with points I had already made in other chapters. So it sat in a proverbial "desk drawer" (i.e., a file on my computer) until now.*

People always ask me what I was like as a little boy. Did I play with dolls? Did I want to wear dresses or have long hair like my sisters? Did the fact that I had three sisters and no brothers have anything to do with why I became a transsexual? Did I think that I would get more attention from my parents if I had been born a girl? Was my mother domineering and my father passive, just like Sigmund Freud used to say?

People always ask me about my family. How did they take it? Did they disown me? Have they gotten over it yet? How did my wife react? Was she surprised? Did she know that I was a transsexual before we got married? Did she stay with me? If so, why? Do we still have sex? How do we have sex? Does this mean that I am a lesbian now? Did I become a woman so that I could become a lesbian? If I'm attracted to women, wouldn't it have made much more sense for me to stay a man? Have I ever considered the possibility that maybe I am just a gay man in denial? How do I know that this isn't just a phase I am going through?

People often ask me about public restrooms. Is it weird for me to go into the women's room now? Do I ever go into the men's room by mistake? Do I miss the short lines to the men's room? Do I stand up or sit down when I urinate now?

People always ask me about my body. What did I look like when I was a man? Do I have any "before" pictures that they can see? Did I have electrolysis to remove my beard? My body hair? If so, did it hurt? Did I have surgery to become a woman? If not, do I plan on having surgery eventually? Why would I possibly want to get rid of my penis? How can I possibly call myself a woman if I still have a penis? Does my penis still get erect? Can I still get my wife pregnant?

People always ask me about the hormones. What kinds of hormones do I take? Do they make me emotional? Ditzy? Angry? Irrational? Forgetful? Do I get PMS now? Did the hormones make my breasts grow? Or do I wear falsies? Or perhaps they are implants? What does it feel like to have breasts? Since I am attracted to women, does that mean that my own breasts turn me on? Do I ever worry that I'll get breast cancer from all of the hormones?

When they mention breast cancer, I find myself wondering whether these same people interrogate cancer survivors this vigorously. Did you have surgery? If so, did they remove just the lump or did you have to have a mastectomy? I have never met a person who had only one breast before. What's it like to be missing a breast? What kind of chemotherapy did they give you? Did it make your hair fall out? Did it make you ditzy? Angry? Irrational? Forgetful?[1]

I understand that people have lots of questions regarding me being a transsexual. I honestly wouldn't mind answering them if their questions weren't always so cliché, so predictable. Why do they want me to rehash all of the same superficial aspects of being a transsexual that have already beaten to death by Geraldo, Oprah, Maury, Sally, and Jerry?[2] Instead, why don't they ask me something that actually has bearing on their own lives? Why don't they ask me what it is like to be treated as a man? And how it compares to the way I am now treated as a woman? Or better yet, why don't they ask themselves if the fact that they are surprised to find out that I was born and raised male brings into question any of the assumptions they make about gender day in and day out.

People keep asking me what it's like to be a transsexual, but they don't really want to know the answer. If they did, they would stop asking all of those ridiculous surgery, sexuality, and restroom questions and instead ask me how it all feels on the inside. They would ask me how much it hurt to have to hide myself for over thirty years, how much shame and self-loathing I had to overcome before I could proudly call myself a trans woman. They would ask me how much it stings when people accidentally address me with the wrong pronouns, or when I'm watching TV or a movie and I'm blindsided by a transsexual or man-in-a-dress joke: "Dude, that lady is no lady." They would ask me if I ever get scared performing spoken word, of never knowing whether some random person in the audience might become offended or upset about my transsexuality and want to do something violent about it. If they really wanted to know what it's like to be a transsexual, they wouldn't ask me about my body at all. Instead, they would ask me about my frustration, my anger, and my fears.

If people really wanted to know what it's like to be a transsexual, they would ask me how annoying it is to constantly be cast in a role that I never auditioned for, to be placed into a situation where, for some reason unbeknownst to me, I am supposed to obediently answer any and all questions that other people have about transsexuality.

I wish that, instead of impulsively asking me question after question, people stopped for a moment to ask themselves why they have so many questions in the first place. After all, if they find transsexuality so fascinating, why is it that they haven't done any research on the subject until now? And do they really and truly believe that they are curious simply because I am supposedly the first transsexual they've ever met? Personally, I have never to my knowledge met a stamp collector, or a Norwegian, or a Christian Scientist before, but if I did, I doubt that I would barrage them with questions.

I wish that people would ask themselves where their fascination about transsexuality comes from. Doesn't it come from the fact that transsexuals are considered to be taboo? And aren't we taboo because other people hate and fear us? And doesn't that hatred and fear force trans people into the closet? Isolate us? Silence our voices? I wish people would ask themselves if their fascination with transsexuals, and the eagerness with which they ask so many questions, contributes to the way in which I am marginalized by society.

Since transitioning, I have spent an inordinate amount of time trying to answer everybody else's questions in the hopes that I might finally be able to shatter their misconceptions, their stereotypes, their prejudices about me. But after six years of taking that approach, I have come to the conclusion that that strategy will never succeed. Because people usually barrage me with questions, not to better understand me, but rather in an unconscious attempt to frame my gender as "questionable," so that their gender can remain "unquestionable" in comparison. It is clear to me now that if I really want to change other people's opinions about me, then I must first turn the tables on them and begin to ask them questions of my own.

23

Finally

Like the previous chapter, this piece was written in 2006 for possible inclusion in Whipping Girl, *but I decided to omit it from the final manuscript that I submitted to my publisher. According to my notes, it was originally intended to be the fourth chapter of Part 2, sandwiched in between "Bending Over Backwards" and "Self-Deception." In the end, I decided not to include this piece because I felt that I had already repeatedly discussed how many feminists have harbored derisive attitudes toward trans women and called for our exclusion from feminism, so I didn't feel the need to belabor the point.*

After reading at a literary event, a woman approached me to let me know that she appreciated the piece that I read. I thanked her. Then, just before walking off, she added, "It's refreshing to finally hear a transsexual woman who is a feminist."

Finally. With that one word, this woman had unknowingly invisibilized the countless feminist trans women who have existed since the early days of second-wave feminism and gay liberation. And she revealed her ignorance of the fact that the supposed lack-of-feminist-trans-women she perceived was the result of institutionalized silencing and the active purging of trans women's voices from feminism, which began over thirty years ago.[1]

Sylvia Rivera was at the Stonewall Riots, and is considered to be a queer and trans icon. Yet in 1973, lesbian feminist Jean O'Leary forced Rivera off the stage of New York City's Gay Pride march, and denounced her and other trans folks for being "men who impersonate women for entertainment and profit."[2] In that same year, Beth Elliott, who had been vice president of the San Francisco chapter of Daughters of Bilitis, was removed from her position and publicly vilified from the stage of the West Coast Lesbian Conference, for the sole reason that she was a trans woman.[3] In 1977, many feminists threatened to boycott the first ever all-woman-owned and operated record company, Olivia Records, unless they fired their trans female recording engineer Sandy Stone.[4] After some initial reluctance, they eventually gave in, and Stone left the collective.

In response to this and similar incidents, trans woman and early gay liberation activist Angela Douglas wrote a satirical letter to the feminist journal *Sister* to highlight the irrational anti-transsexual attitude that was gripping the lesbian and feminist movements. Douglas's letter, which in part said, "Genetic women are becoming obsolete, which is obvious, and the future belongs to transsexual women," was quoted out of context by Janice Raymond to fan the flames of anti-trans woman fervor in her book *The Transsexual Empire*.[5] As if writing an entire book trashing transsexuality in general, and trans women in particular, wasn't enough, Raymond went on to author a study for the U.S. government that lead to the elimination of aid for poor and imprisoned transsexuals, and resulted in most health insurance companies refusing to cover any procedures associated with transsexuality.[6]

Raymond's anti-trans woman rhetoric was so rabid and irrational that it tends to overshadow the fact that her views were largely accepted among other feminists at the time. Adrienne Rich provided Raymond with "resources, creative criticism, and constant encouragement" according to the book's acknowledgements.[7] Andrea Dworkin wrote a blurb for Raymond's book, calling it: "Crucial reading."[8] Renowned feminist author Mary Daly—who also happened to be Raymond's thesis adviser—similarly described transsexual women as the products of "phallocratic technology" that contribute to the "necrophilic invasion/elimination" of women.[9] Founder of *Ms. Magazine*, Gloria Steinem, positively cited Raymond's views on trans women in an article where she suggested that we were a part of the backlash against feminism, and Robin Morgan (who eventually became editor-in-chief for *Ms.*) famously described trans women who wanted to participate in feminism as "leeching off women" and having the "mentality of a rapist."[10]

So when *this* book comes out, I sure as hell hope that nobody naively says, "Finally, a transsexual woman who is a feminist." Because we have always existed, we've just been systematically shut out of past feminist movements.[11] If people wish to apply the word "finally" to this book, let's hope that they say, "Finally, a woman-centric press has published a book by a transsexual feminist. Finally, trans women are being allowed to have a voice in the movement."

24

Trans-misogyny Primer

As I briefly discussed in the introduction to this section, a major focus of Whipping Girl *was to articulate trans-misogyny, which was a new concept to most people at the time (at least outside of certain trans women's circles). In 2009, I quickly put together this "Trans-misogyny Primer" to be used as a handout at a panel I participated in for that year's Women, Action, & the Media conference. It is not intended to be comprehensive, but rather just the briefest of introductions to the concept.*[1]

The words *transgender* and *gender variant* are typically used as catch-all terms to denote all people who defy cultural ideals, expectations, assumptions, and norms regarding gender. While all people who fall under the transgender umbrella potentially face social stigma for transgressing gender norms, those on the *male-to-female (MTF) or trans female/feminine (TF) spectrum* generally receive the overwhelming majority of societal fascination, consternation, and demonization. In contrast, those on the *female-to-male (FTM) or trans male/ masculine (TM) spectrum* have until very recently remained largely invisible and under-theorized. This disparity in attention suggests that individuals on the trans female/feminine spectrum are culturally marked, not for failing to conform to gender norms *per se*, but because of the specific direction of their gender transgression—that is, because of their feminine gender expression and/ or their female gender identities. Thus, the marginalization of trans female/ feminine spectrum people is not merely a result of *transphobia*, but is better described as *trans-misogyny*.

Trans-misogyny is steeped in the assumption that femaleness and femininity are inferior to, and exist primarily for the benefit of, maleness and masculinity. This phenomenon manifests itself in numerous ways:

- Studies have shown that feminine boys are viewed far more negatively, and brought in for psychotherapy far more often, than masculine girls.

- Psychiatric diagnoses directed against the transgender population often either focus solely on trans female/feminine individuals, or are written in such a way that trans female/feminine people are more easily and frequently pathologized than their trans male/masculine counterparts.

- The majority of violence committed against gender-variant individuals targets individuals on the trans female/feminine spectrum.

- In the media, jokes and demeaning depictions of gender-variant people primarily focus on trans female/feminine-spectrum individuals. Often in these cases, it is their desire to be female or to be feminine that is especially ridiculed. While trans male/masculine individuals are often subjects of derision, their desire to be male and/or masculine is generally not ridiculed—to do so would bring the supposed supremacy of maleness/masculinity into question.

Perhaps the most visible example of trans-misogyny is the way in which trans women and others on the trans female/feminine spectrum are routinely sexualized in the media, within psychological, social science and feminist discourses, and in society at large. For example, the media not only regularly depict trans women's bodies and experiences in a titillating and lurid fashion, but they also sexualize trans women's motives for transitioning—e.g., by portraying them as either sex workers,[2] sexual deceivers who prey on unsuspecting heterosexual men, or as male "perverts" who transition to female in order to fulfill some kind of bizarre sexual fantasy. While trans men may face a certain degree of media objectification, their motives for transitioning are not typically sexualized in the same manner. If anything, those who project ulterior motives onto trans men generally presume that they transition in order to obtain male privilege rather than for sexual reasons. Thus, the presumption that trans women (but not trans men) are sexually motivated in their transitions appears to reflect the cultural assumption that a woman's power and worth stems primarily from her ability to be sexualized by others.

25

Whipping Girl FAQ on Cissexual, Cisgender, and Cis Privilege

In addition to introducing the world to the term trans-misogyny, Whipping Girl *also helped to popularize "cis terminology"—that is, language that uses the prefix "cis" to refer to people who are not trans as a means to better articulate the ways in which trans people are marginalized. While this language has since caught on (a testament to its usefulness, I would argue), there has been some backlash against it. Additionally, some people have subsequently used cis terminology in ways that I feel are unproductive or dismissive of other people's experiences. So this book includes three (count 'em, three!) follow up essays—this one (penned in 2009), plus Chapters 47 and 48—intended to explain and clarify the rationale behind this terminology, debunk common misconceptions, and to consider the differing ways in which this language is often used (or misused).*

I have come across people who have assumed that I invented the terms cissexual and cisgender, but this is not the case. As I discuss in the Notes for *Whipping Girl,* I began using the term "cissexual" after reading one of Emi Koyama's Interchange entries from 2002—in that piece, she mentions that the related term "cisgender" was first coined in 1995 by a transsexual man named Carl Buijs.[1]

I don't know much about Carl Buijs or why he coined the term "cisgender." But as a scientist (where the prefixes "trans" and "cis" are routinely used), this terminology seems fairly obvious in retrospect. "Trans" means "across" or "on the opposite side of," whereas "cis" means "on the same side of." So if someone who was assigned one sex at birth, but comes to identify and live as a member of the other sex, is called a "transsexual" (because they have crossed from one sex to the other), then the someone who lives and identifies as the sex they were assigned at birth is called a "cissexual."

As someone who was assigned a male sex at birth, but who lives and identifies as female, I may be described as a transsexual woman, a transgender woman, or a trans woman. Those women who (unlike me) were assigned a female sex at birth may be similarly described as cissexual women, cisgender women, or cis women.

Why Use the Term Cis?

I suppose different people might give different answers to this question, so it is probably best for me to explain why I started using this terminology, and why I chose to include it in the book.

I began writing *Whipping Girl* in 2005, before I had heard of "cis" terminology. A major focus of the book was to debunk many of the myths and misconceptions people have about transsexuals. Initially, I was kind of scattershot in my approach: In one chapter, I would critique the way the term "passing" is used in reference to transsexuals. In another chapter, I would critique the use of the terms "bio boy" and "genetic girl" to describe non-trans men and women. In yet another chapter, I would critique the way that transsexuals are always depicted as imitating or impersonating "real" (read: non-trans) women and men. And so on. After a while, it became obvious to me that all of these phenomena were stemming from the same presumption: that transsexual gender identities and sex embodiments are inherently less natural and less legitimate than those of non-transsexual people.

I realized that it would make a lot more sense to write a chapter for the book that thoroughly exposes this double standard and describes the many ways it is employed in order to marginalize transsexuals. As I was contemplating this, I stumbled onto the aforementioned Emi Koyama post, where she discusses the usefulness of the terms cissexual, cisgender, and cissexism. She said: ". . . they de-centralize the dominant group, exposing it as merely one possible alternative rather than the 'norm' against which trans people are defined. I don't expect the word to come into common usage anytime soon, but I felt it was an interesting concept—a feminist one, in fact—which is why I am using it."[2]

It was then that I realized that the double standard that I was writing about already had a name: cissexism. And the chapter of *Whipping Girl* dedicated to debunking cissexism eventually took on the title: "Dismantling Cissexual Privilege."

People sometimes freak out a bit when confronted with new terms or language. So when doing presentations, I often offer the following analogy to help people understand the usefulness of this terminology:

> *Fifty years ago, homosexuality was almost universally seen as unnatural, immoral, illegitimate, etc. Back then, people regularly talked about "homosexuals," but nobody ever talked about "heterosexuals." In a sense, there were no "heterosexuals"—everyone who wasn't engaged in same-sex behavior was simply considered "normal." Their sexualities were unmarked and taken for granted.*
>
> *If you were lesbian, gay, or bisexual (LGB) during this time period, there was almost no way for you to convince the rest of society that you were unfairly marginalized. In society's eyes, nobody was oppressing you, it was simply your fault or problem that you were "abnormal." In fact, it was quite common for LGB people to buy into this presumption of abnormality themselves, as there was simply no other obvious way to view their predicament.*
>
> *But then gay rights activists began challenging this notion. They pointed out that all people have sexualities (not just homosexuals). The so-called "normal" people weren't really "normal" per se, but rather they were "heterosexual." And the activists pointed out that heterosexuals weren't necessarily any better or more righteous than homosexuals. It was just that heterosexism—the belief that same-sex attraction and relationships are less natural and legitimate than heterosexual ones—is institutionalized within society and functions to unfairly marginalize those who engage in same-sex relationships.*

Once one recognizes that heterosexism is a double standard, then it becomes clear that (whether they realize it or not) heterosexuals are privileged in our society. They can legally marry, engage in public displays of affection with their significant other without fear of being assaulted, their relationships are typically approved of, and even celebrated, by others, and so on. Like all forms of privilege, heterosexual privilege is invisible to those who experience it—they simply take it for granted. By describing and discussing heterosexism and heterosexual privilege, LGB activists have made great gains over time toward leveling the playing field with regards to sexual orientation in our culture.

One can easily understand the potential power of cis/trans terminology by simply replacing "heterosexual" with "cissexual," "heterosexism" with "cissexism," and "heterosexual privilege" with "cissexual privilege" in the above analogy.

Critiques of Cis/Trans Terminology

While cissexism and cissexual privilege are useful concepts, I have met many people (both cis and trans) who don't like the cis/trans distinction. Here are my thoughts on some of the more common criticisms:

1) It sounds too academic/jargony; why can't we speak in plain, simple English?

First, "cis" is not an academic term; it is an activist one.[3] And it sounds like jargon simply because most people are unfamiliar with it. To be honest, when people make the can't-we-speak-in-plain-simple-English complaint, I just want to bonk them over the head with a stack of George Orwell books. Our ideas, thoughts, and beliefs are very much constrained by the words available (or not available) to us. If we didn't have the terms heterosexual, heterosexism, and heterosexual privilege, those of us who are LGB wouldn't have the language to describe (and thus challenge) the marginalization we face because of who we partner with. If we all just spoke in "plain English" circa the 1950s, where do you think we'd be these days with regards to sexual orientation-based discrimination?

2) Comment often made by cis people: "but I don't identify with the term cis."

Cis is not meant to be an identity. Rather, it simply describes the way that one is perceived by others.

An analogy: I don't strongly *identify* with the terms "white" and "able-bodied," even though I am both of those things. After all, I have been able to navigate my way through the world without ever having to give much thought to those aspects of my person. And that's the point: It is my white privilege and able-bodied privilege that enables me *not* to have to deal with racism and ableism on a daily basis.

In general, we only identify with those aspects of ourselves that are marked.[4] For example, I identify as bisexual, and as a trans woman, because those are issues that I have to deal with all of the time (because of other people's prejudices). While I may not strongly identify as white or able-bodied, it would be entitled for me to completely disavow those labels, as it would deny the white privilege and able-bodied privilege I regularly experience.

3) Comment often made by trans people: "I don't like the distinction between cis/ trans because I don't think that I am any different from a cis woman (or man)."

I can relate to this sentiment. After all, I don't believe that I (as a trans woman) am inherently different from cis women. Such a view point would be essentialist and universalist, as it would assume that all cis women are the "same" as each other and entirely distinct from trans women. This ignores the large amount of variation amongst, and overlap between, cis and trans women.

When I use the terms cis/trans, it is not to talk about *actual* differences between cis and trans bodies, identities, genders, or people, but rather *perceived* differences. In other words, while I don't think that my gender is inherently different from that of a cis woman, I am aware that most people tend to *view* and *treat* my gender differently (i.e., as less natural, valid, and authentic) than cis women's genders. That is why this language is so useful, because it allows us to articulate these societal double standards.

The Limitations of Cis Privilege

While cis terminology is extremely useful, like all language, it can be misused. For instance, a friend recently told me of a trans woman she knew who complained that other women were exercising cis privilege over her whenever they complained about experiencing their periods. This is what I told my friend:

I understand where the person is coming from, but I would be hesitant to call that cissexual privilege. I try to only use the term with regards to social and legal legitimacy (e.g., that cis people's legal sex and gender identities are taken for granted and considered valid in a way that trans people's are not). In those cases, there is a blatant societal double standard at work, and cis folks should be made aware that they are taking something for granted that others cannot.

But once we get into issues of biology or bodies (rather than the rights and entitlements associated with them), things become more fraught. For example, I have white privilege, not because my skin has less pigment than people of color, but because my whiteness enables me to not have to face racism on a day-to-day basis. I have able-bodied privilege, not because I can see or walk "just fine", but because (in a society that presumes that everyone can see signs or walk up a flight of stairs if necessary) I don't face the same obstacles or barriers in my day-to-day life that differently-abled people do.

Sometimes, when other women I know are complaining about their periods or pregnancies, I get really sad. While I certainly don't doubt that those experiences are painful and difficult, I feel a sense of loss about not having the opportunity to choose to bear a child if I wished. (I'm not sure that I would want to do that if I was able, but it would be nice to have that option available to me). I have a cis female friend who had very irregular periods her whole life and who was distraught to find out as a young adult that she couldn't bear children (she and her husband eventually adopted after years of infertility treatment attempts). While we've never talked about it, I'm sure we both relate to our similar situations in very different ways. For me, it's wrapped up in my sadness about not having been born female. For her (being socialized female), it's more likely tied to her having imagined since she was a child that someday she'd become pregnant and have her own children.

Both of us are biologically unable to have regular periods or get pregnant. Both of us experience sadness and loss at the fact that we have been denied something that other women take for granted. But to say that people who properly menstruate have cis privilege, or "menstruation privilege," plays into a kind of pathologizing mentality. It plays into the idea that my (and her) body is intrinsically "wrong" while other bodies are "right." I know some trans people see things that way, but I find that disempowering. I wish I had been born female and that I could menstruate, just like I wish that I didn't have skin cancer two years ago, or that I wasn't hypothyroid, or that I wasn't on the verge of needing bifocals, etc. But I don't feel like I was denied any privileges because my body isn't the way that I wish it were. It only becomes about privilege when I am deemed inferior or less legitimate than other people because of my body and situation.

My friend and I share some similarities, but also some differences. She was able to qualify for adoption despite being infertile. It is very likely that if I applied for adoption (on the grounds that I am infertile because I am transsexual) that I would be denied because of my trans status. If I were denied for that reason, that would be a clear case of cis privilege. And while I don't consider it cis privilege when other women are complaining about their periods, I have had cis women tell me that I am "lucky" that I don't have periods. I know for a fact that they would never tell someone like my friend (an infertile cis woman) that she is lucky for the same reason. In that case, I would definitely say cis privilege is at work (because of the double standard).

I am glad that *Whipping Girl* helped to popularize the usage of cissexism and cis privilege. But it is important to keep in mind that all of us are privileged in some ways and marginalized in others. As a trans person, I am very sensitive to cis privilege, but not so attuned to my own white privilege or able-bodied privilege. In the past, I have presumed that someone was exercising cis privilege over me only to find out later that they didn't even know that I was trans. And I have had people (rightly) call me out when I have inadvertently said something that was steeped in my own white privilege or able-bodied privilege without being conscious of it.

This is especially important to keep in mind in feminist settings, where both cis and trans women are marginalized in largely overlapping, albeit sometimes different ways. Being forced against my will into boyhood overall really sucked for me, but I would be lying if I said that I didn't experience *some* advantages as a result. For instance, I was given more freedom in many ways than my sisters growing up. And I honestly can't say whether or not I would have become a scientist if I was raised female. Similarly, I have no doubt that there are a lot of aspects about being raised as a cis girl that are really limiting or disempowering. But there are also advantages (e.g., having people take your gender identity seriously, not being forced against your will into boyhood, etc.).[5]

I want to be a part of a feminist community where we can talk about cis woman-specific issues *and* trans woman-specific issues without the former group being automatically called out for exercising cis privilege and the latter group automatically being called out for supposed male privilege. To achieve this, it is important for us to challenge oppression and discuss privilege. But it is also important for us to listen to what others have to say, and to give people the benefit of doubt whenever possible. Some people are stubbornly prejudiced and repeat offenders, and they of course should be taken to task for that. But most of us (I hope) genuinely want to both understand *and* to be understood. Discussions of "privilege" should be about teaching (and learning) how we each see and experience the world differently; how we each have blind spots in our activism; how we each make incorrect and undermining assumptions about other people. Discussions of "privilege" should serve as a teaching tool, not a weapon to wield.

26

96 Percent

In 2007, I received a small grant from San Francisco's Queer Cultural Center to curate a spoken word event called The "Penis" Issue: Trans and Intersex Women Speak Their Minds for that year's National Queer Arts Festival. The word "penis" appears in quotes because many trans women choose not to use that label to describe their genitals, but also because that aspect of our anatomy is often deemed questionable, suspect, or threatening in both straight and queer spaces. In promotional material, I described the show this way: "It is commonly presumed that all men have penises and all women do not. In this groundbreaking spoken word event, trans and intersex women share their perspectives and experiences living as women who do not conform to this assumption." [1] Elsewhere, I wrote this: "For too long, women with 'penises' have only existed in the public consciousness as the occasional punch-lines of jokes, as movie plot twists, or as an underground niche in the sex industry. We have been commodified, objectified, sexualized, sensationalized, marginalized, demonized, and victimized, but we have never before been given the opportunity to speak in our own voices. Here we speak for ourselves, about our lives, and on our own terms." This is the piece that I performed that evening—it was meant to capture both my many personal and political views on the issue, as well as to serve as an introduction to the rest of the show. It has never appeared in print before.

It's 2004, and once again I'm on stage in another bar doing another spoken word set. I introduce my next piece: "Here's another poem about my penis!"[2]

The audience laughs, a couple people hoot and holler.

I've been performing spoken word for a couple of years now. Half of the shows that I do are queer-themed events, the other half poetry slams where the majority of the audience is straight. Often these audiences will react very differently to specific poems or passages, a sign of their different perspectives and sensibilities. But both queer and straight audiences always enthusiastically laugh at my penis one-liner—apparently amusement over my bodily incongruity appeals to some kind of lowest common denominator. Many people view sexuality as a continuum, with straight folks on one end and queer folks on the other, but that's not how things look to me. I exist at a bizarre nexus of the universe where both ends of that spectrum come around to meet. After all, the only thing that your average twenty-something frat boy has in common with your average middle-aged lesbian feminist is a mutual fear of falling for someone like me: A woman who just so happens to have a penis.

Part of the reason why people laugh when I say, "Here's another poem about my penis," is the seemingly non-self-conscious, almost flippant, way that I say it, as if to give the impression: "Whatever, no big deal." But that's not how I feel on the inside. In my mind, whenever I deliver that line, I feel like I'm defusing a bomb. I conjure up images of a movie or TV protagonist, with wire cutters in hand, fumbling with the red and the green wires, unsure of which one to cut. Just as it looks like they are going to slice the red wire, they make an impulsive decision with only a few seconds left to cut the green wire instead and suddenly everything is quiet. Nothing explodes. It's a triumph of intuition over conscious thinking; gut feelings over endless mind wringing.

When I make quips about my penis in public, that's usually what it is—a gut feeling—instinctual, reflexive. It's most certainly not the smartest or safest thing for me to say, but I'm not trying to be smart. My intention is simply to defuse an explosive situation.

Whenever I perform spoken word, or any time I come out to someone as transsexual, the "penis issue" is always present. For a while, I thought that perhaps I was imagining it, that it was simply a product of my own paranoia or insecurity. But that hypothesis flew completely out the window when I began to do Transgender 101 workshops for college and high school students. As soon as I would finish my opening spiel and announce that I'd be happy to answer any of their questions, I would immediately be barraged by genitalia-themed inquiries: Have you had surgery? Do you plan to have it someday? Why would you ever want to get rid of your penis? If you're attracted to women, wouldn't it make more sense to keep it? Does your penis still get erect? Can you still get a girl pregnant? How can you possibly call yourself a woman if you still have a penis?

The "penis issue" is also in play (only slightly less blatantly) in the way people tend to attach the adjectives "pre-op" or "post-op" to descriptions of trans women, even in contexts where one's genitals are irrelevant. Whenever I catch someone doing this, I'll often nonchalantly begin to refer to all men as either circumcised or uncircumcised, and to all women as either pre- or post-menopausal, just to make a point of how demeaning and objectifying unnecessary information can be sometimes.

The "penis issue" is the elephant that awaits me in nearly every room I enter; I can either pretend to ignore it or acknowledge its existence. That's probably why I came up with the here's-another-poem-about-my-penis one-liner in the first place. Initially, it felt freeing and empowering to take on that taboo, to break that silence, until I realized that that approach was probably backfiring. After all, I was simply inviting people to laugh at the fact that I was a woman with a penis without bringing into question their assumptions and prejudices. Much like the fat standup comic who makes self-deprecating jokes about their own eating habits without ever challenging societal-wide anti-fat sentiment, I was merely reaffirming the belief shared by most in the audience: That the very notion of a woman with a penis is inherently ludicrous.

I realized then that gender-variant women will continue to have to deal with other people's "penis issues" until we turn the tables and ask the world this question: Why do so many people—even those who are otherwise well-meaning, open-minded, progressive, pro-trans, and anti-sexist—continue to get so hung up over the status of our genitals?

In the 1970s, sociologists Suzanne Kessler and Wendy McKenna carried out an experiment to determine how we see gender.[3] They showed participants a series of drawings of people who had a mix of typically male and female attributes: short or long hair, flat chest or breasts, narrow or wide hips, body hair or not, and of course, either male or female genitals. They found that male cues always tended to trump female cues—in other words, figures with a mix of masculine and feminine attributes tended to be read as men rather than women. This disparity was particularly acute for genitals. If the figure with mixed gender attributes had a vagina, people only saw it as female 64 percent of the time—in other words, 36 percent of the time other male cues trumped the presence of a vagina. The reverse was not true: If the figure had a penis, it was read as male 96 percent of the time, often even when all of the other gender attributes were feminine.

So while I relate to my trans male friends who have transitioned in the other direction, I would suggest that the deck is somewhat stacked in their favor. Trans men tend to "pass" better and to freak people out less because of the way we've all been trained to see gender.

And while I empathize with my non-trans sisters when they say they are often accused of not being "real" women because they aren't stereotypically feminine or because they are bisexual or lesbian, I don't think that it's quite accurate to say that we are in the exact same boat. As a trans woman, my issue is not merely that people see me as being inadequately or insufficiently female, it's that as soon as they discover that I have a penis, there is a 96 percent chance that they will see me as a man.

That statistic—96 percent—leaves a deep imprint on the lives of many gender-variant women. A couple of years ago, I was invited to participate in a panel on MTF transitioning at a transgender-themed conference. Each panelist was asked to give the moderator a handful of potential questions that we felt might be useful for the audience. One of the questions I offered was, "How does one manage the difficulties associated with navigating one's way through the world as a woman with a penis?" At the panel, when the moderator raised my question, the other three trans female panelists, who had been quite chatty up until that point, suddenly went silent. Their bodies sat eerily still as if all of the body language had been leeched from them. This had nothing to do with being embarrassed about being transsexual—after all, they were all enthusiastically taking part in this panel. The reason why they kept silent was because they knew better than to answer that question. They knew that the mere mention of having had a penis, past or present tense, would lead 96 percent of those in attendance to lump them in the "man" category.

As someone who is regularly presumed to be a non-transsexual woman, and whose body these days appears female in pretty much every way except one, I find it bizarre that 96 percent of the population will throw all of that evidence out the window—dismissing my female identity, body and lived experiences—and consider me a "man" solely based on my genitals. (And they try to convince me that I'm the one who is mentally disordered?)[4]

Look, this has nothing to do with logic, nothing to do with biology. The problem here is symbolism. In this male-centered world, nothing symbolizes male and masculine power more that the penis. And unfortunately, many of the folks who are most vocal about challenging male domination—feminists and lesbians—often hypocritically buy into this very same phallocentrism when they describe the penis as a tool of rape and oppression.

In the trans community, people often talk about the male/female gender binary as though it were the cause of all of our marginalization. But frankly, as a trans woman, sometimes I struggle more with a different (and often unarticulated) binary, one in which the penis is either glorified or demonized, nothing in between. One can see this dichotomy at work in popular depictions of transsexual women: the psychiatric stereotype of the trans woman who absolutely despises her "penis" on one extreme, and the "she-male" porn image of a trans woman grasping her engorged cock on the other.

Some might find this surprising, but I've found that the people who are least attached to such symbolism tend to be trans and intersex women. We know our own bodies to be mere flesh and blood, and therefore rightly recognize this glorifying and demonizing imagery as something that is projected onto us, a framework that enables other people to objectify us, either as abominations or as androgyne fuck fantasies. Many of us develop far more complex, nuanced, and varied views about our own genitals, recognizing them as a part of our physical bodies and a source of sexual pleasure, albeit one that is often at odds with our own mental self-image and/or societal assumptions regarding gender.

If I had to pick one word that best describes how I feel about my own penis, it would be "ambivalence." This is not to be confused with apathy—after all, I have lots of really intense memories and emotions regarding my penis, it's just that they often exist in contradiction to one another:

As a child, wishing desperately that I could make my penis disappear. As a young adult, recoiling from the word transsexual, in part, because I couldn't imagine parting with it.

In my late teens and early twenties, being in absolute awe of penetration sex, of how amazing it was to feel my genitals inside my girlfriend's genitals.

In my early thirties, a few months after being on female hormones, for the first time sporting a strap-on dildo and entering my wife in that manner, blown away by how it all made so much more sense to me than any other penetration experience in my life.

As a crossdresser in my late twenties, as the man I was with non-consensually tried to force himself on me. I'm eventually able to get away, but to this day, I still sometimes deal with the psychological aftermath of that traumatic event. Then, as a trans dyke at Camp Trans seven years later, a woman from the Michigan Womyn's Music Fes-

tival arrogantly lectures me about how I shouldn't be allowed inside women's spaces because my penis might trigger sexual abuse survivors.

Let me say this: I can't think of any act that is more insulting, more condescending, more entitled, or more triggering to me than having a non-trans woman, oblivious of her own non-trans privilege, lump me into the same category as the guy who tried to date rape me.

I don't have the luxury of seeing my penis in black-and-white, cut-and-dried terms. For me, the penis does not represent power or privilege, because I am regularly marginalized for having one. It is both my center of sexual pleasure and a signifier of something that I don't identify with. It is a constant source of cognitive dissonance, something that has always felt somewhat alien to me, yet nevertheless it is a part of my body. Sometimes I'll successfully forget that it's even there, and then other times, I am excruciatingly aware of its existence. As a performer, I regularly take the stage and proudly recite unflinching spoken word pieces about being a woman with a penis, then the next day, I'll be paranoid over whether there's a visible bulge underneath my jeans or dress. Like I said, my penis provokes feelings of ambivalence.

A few years back, an anthology was published called *Dick for a Day*, featuring women writers—many of them feminist—answering the question "What would you do if, by some mysterious means, you had a penis for one day?"[5] Not surprisingly, more than half the women imagined that this also automatically involved them becoming fully male as well (undoubtedly another sign of how our culture views women with penises as inherently oxymoronic and nonsensical). Those writers who did imagine themselves as women with penises invariably took the glorifying route, indulging in adventures like writing their names in the snow, masturbating, receiving blow jobs, and penetrating beautiful women. Some even imagined that their penis gave them more confidence, that it led to promotions at work, and so forth.

What I found most telling was that not a single person imagined what it would *really* be like to be a woman with a penis. No one explored whether or not they would have to hide it, how they might manage that information on dates, or the potential animosity they might face if random strangers discovered its presence. No one raised the issue of what it might be like to be watching a movie or TV show and be blindsided by one of those crass and belittling "she-male" jokes and to know that it is you who is being ridiculed. No one wondered what it would be like to be shut out of certain women's spaces, to be turned away from a rape crisis center or a battered women's shelter because of the size and shape of their genitals. And no one addressed the issue of male homophobic/transphobic hysteria and the violence that is regularly inflicted on women with penises. In fact, one writer even bragged about how she would whip it out if some obnoxious guy tried to make the moves on her, just to see the look of horror on his face. What a fucking farce. As someone who regularly finds herself in that very same situation, I choose not to "whip it out," and do you want to know why? It's because I'd rather not fucking die.

The most offensive thing about that book is the fact that almost every writer presumed that if she were a woman with a penis that she would somehow be more privileged than she currently is without it. Bullshit! By buying into the male-centric belief that the penis is synonymous with power and privilege, these writers invisibilized the very real struggles faced by gender-variant women. They appropriated our situation while leaving behind our very real life circumstances.

The world will not begin to be safe for gender-variant women such as myself until at least three things happen:

First, people have to get it in their heads that *genital assumption*—the common belief that all men have penises and all women do not—is merely an incorrect presumption on their part. Just as it's arrogant to automatically assume that every person you meet is straight, it is similarly entitled to presume that every person is non-trans and has the genitals that you expect them to have.

Second, we need to recognize that being a woman and having a penis are not necessarily in contradiction with one another. And I'm not merely talking about sex toys here—if I had a dollar for every dyke who gets off on girls wearing strap-on cocks, but who would hypocritically balk at the idea of being with a trans woman, I'd be a very rich lady. No, what I'm saying is that we need to move beyond the 96 percent mentality, where male traits always trump female ones, and where a woman's female identity, personality, life experiences, and the rest of her body can be brought into question or outright dismissed because of the mere presence of a penis.

Third, we need get over our compulsion to either glorify or demonize the penis. In other words, we need to dephallocize the penis—to extricate the concepts of male privilege and power from the flesh and blood of our bodies. I'm not saying that we need to completely obliterate all symbolism and view the penis as an amorphous blob of flesh. All I'm asking is that we allow for other possibilities, that we create a little room for ambivalence.

In order for all of this to happen, gender-variant women cannot merely sit on the sidelines and allow others to appropriate and caricature our real life experiences. If we truly wish to move beyond the "penis issue," then we must begin to honestly put forward our own varied and nuanced personal perspectives as women who do not conform to other people's genital assumption. We must speak openly about the countless ways in which we are marginalized because of our genitals, as well as the ways in which we are sometimes empowered by them. We must allow ourselves to say that it's okay to get rid of it if we want, but it is also okay to find it beautiful.

For me, one of the few things scarier than standing up in front of an audience and talking about my penis for fifteen minutes, is the fact that I have invited five other amazing and powerful women writers and performers to do the same.[6] We are each different people and we each have had different life experiences, so no doubt we will each discuss and deal with the "penis issue" differently. What I hope that you, the audience, will come away with is this sense of diversity and difference, and perhaps even a sense of ambivalence.

27

Talking Past One Another
(The Michigan Womyn's Music Festival, Trans Woman-Exclusion, and Three Different Takes on Feminism)

In 2008, the progressive Internet news outlet AlterNet *approached me about writing an essay on the ongoing controversy surrounding Michfest's trans woman-exclusion policy.[1] By this point, I was experiencing severe activist burnout regarding this particular issue, so I almost said no. But then I realized that this could be a fruitful opportunity to discuss how this matter had recently evolved into a three-sided debate (each side being informed by different approaches to feminism), rather than a two-sided "she-said"/"she-said"-style dispute (which is how it was typically portrayed). In addition, in retrospect, one of my biggest regrets about* Whipping Girl *was that, while I focused heavily on the intersection of cissexism and traditional sexism, I did not give adequate attention to the intersection of cissexism with other forms of marginalization. So I set out to address such matters in the last section of this essay.[2]*

"The grudging admiration felt for the tomboy, and the queasiness felt around a sissy boy point to the same thing: the contempt in which women—or those who play the female role—are held."
  -Radicalesbians (1970)[3]

In 1991, Nancy Jean Burkholder was expelled from the *Michigan Womyn's Music Festival* (Michfest), the world's largest annual women-only event, because festival workers suspected that she was a trans woman. That incident sparked protests from a burgeoning transgender movement to challenge what eventually came to be known as the festival's "womyn-born-womyn"-only policy, which effectively bars trans women from attending. The protests evolved into Camp Trans, which continues to take place just down the road from Michfest each year, and which has become a focal point for a much broader push for trans-inclusion within feminist and queer communities. Despite over fifteen years of petitioning, and a growing acceptance of trans identities in both mainstream society and within queer, feminist, and other progressive circles, the festival still officially maintains its "womyn-born-womyn"-only policy, and countless other lesbian- and queer-woman-focused groups and events continue to harbor dismissive, if not downright disdainful, attitudes toward trans women.

The history of the Michfest trans woman-exclusion debate has been retold countless times—often in an overly simplistic, cut-and-dried manner. The controversy is usually depicted in one of two ways: either pitting the supposedly out-of-touch, transphobic lesbian separatists who run the festival against a more politically progressive transgender minority, or portraying transgender activists as bullies who selfishly seek to undermine one of the few remaining vestiges of women-only space with their supposedly masculine bodies and energies. In addition to being obvious caricatures, these sorts of us-versus-them portrayals obscure one of the most important aspects of the story: the fact that there are actually three "sides" to this debate, each driven by a different take on feminism.

Rather than rehash the history or delve into all of the details about the festival and the controversy, I will attempt to describe these three differing feminist perspectives and discuss how they have played out with regard to the issue of trans woman-exclusion at Michfest, as well in lesbian/queer women's communities more generally.

Unilateral Sexism and Lesbian Feminism

Michfest is one of many women-only institutions that grew out of the lesbian feminist movement during the 1970s and 1980s. A dominant ideology within that movement was the belief that sexism constitutes a unilateral form of oppression—that is, men are the oppressors, and women the oppressed, end of story.[4] While more liberal or reform-minded feminists of that time period focused primarily on the most obvious examples of sexism (e.g., wage and workplace discrimination, sexual harassment, reproductive rights, etc.), lesbian (and other radical) feminists extended their critiques of sexism to include many taken for granted aspects of gender and sexuality. They argued, for example, that masculinity is inherently dominating and oppressive and that femininity is necessarily associated with objectification and subjugation,[5] and that both forms of gender expression are merely products of socialization rather than natural aspects of people. According to this perspective, a first step toward overturning sexism is for individuals to distance themselves from ways of being that are associated with male domination and female subjugation, and instead revert to more natural (and presumably androgynous) forms of gender and sexual expression.

Lesbian feminist critiques did not solely take aim at the heterosexual mainstream; they also targeted other sexual minorities whose gender and sexual practices were deemed (in their view) to emulate unilateral sexism. This includes those who engage in consensual BDSM (who were seen as reinforcing dominant/submissive sexual roles), and butch and femme lesbians, drag performers, crossdressers, and transsexuals (who were all seen as reinforcing masculine/feminine gender roles). While lesbian feminists derided many forms of what we would now call transgender expression, the bulk of their contempt was directed squarely at trans women and others on the trans female/feminine spectrum. This attitude stemmed both from the assumption that trans women are "really men" (i.e., oppressors) and that femininity is tantamount to a "slave status." Thus, according to this logic, trans female and trans female/feminine individuals were viewed as oppressors who appropriate the dress and identities of the very people they oppress. For example, feminist Robin Morgan claimed that trans women "parody female oppression and suffering" and Mary Daly equated trans female/feminine expression with "whites playing 'black face'."[6] Many (including Morgan and, most famously, Janice Raymond) even described trans womanhood as a form of rape.[7]

While many lesbian feminists today will concede that such accusations are beyond the pale, their unilateral perspective on sexism still leads them to insist that trans women should not be allowed to enter women-only spaces such as Michfest based on the assumption that trans women have experienced male socialization and privilege in the past, and/or because their bodies, personalities and energies still supposedly remain "male" or "masculine" on some level.

The Gender Binary, Queer Theory, and Transgender Activism

Prior to the mid–1990s, trans women and allies typically responded to trans woman-exclusion by stressing the similarities between trans women (who live as women and thus experience misogyny in their day-to-day lives) and non-trans women. But this strategy of emphasizing similarities became less relevant by the mid-to-late 1990s due to the rise of third-wave feminisms, which challenged universalizing views of womanhood and examined the many differences that exist between women. For example, third-wave feminists embraced the critiques made by women of color over the years that the belief that sexism was the "primary" oppression, or even a unilateral form of oppression, ignores the ways in which sexism intersects with racism and classism in many women's lives. Additionally, many feminists (especially younger ones) around this time began reclaiming expressions of femininity and sexuality that had previously been considered taboo or repressive among lesbian feminists. But perhaps no shift in feminism had as profound of an effect on transgender-inclusion within queer women's communities than the rise of *queer theory*.[8]

Queer theory shares the lesbian feminist belief that many aspects of gender and sexuality are culturally derived (rather than natural), but takes this notion one step further by bringing into question the very categories upon which sexisms are based. This is often accomplished by critiquing, subverting and deconstructing *the gender binary*—that is, the assumption that there are only two legitimate genders: heterosexual feminine women and masculine men. For this reason, many queer theorists became particularly interested in transgender people, who they sometimes hailed for challenging traditional notions about femaleness and maleness. This view is in sharp contrast to lesbian feminist perspectives, which claimed that these same individuals reinforced oppressive sex roles.

Queer theory both influenced, and was influenced by, the rise of transgender activism—a movement to unite previously disparate gender-variant communities around the idea that these groups are all targeted for discrimination because they transgress binary gender norms. Activists such as Kate Bornstein, Leslie Feinberg, Riki Wilchins, and numerous others, mobilized many transgender-spectrum folks and won over many feminist and queer allies by positioning the transgender community as the cutting edge of a much broader movement to shatter the gender binary.[9] In 1999, Wilchins and other transgender activists took this approach to Michfest, where they revived Camp Trans (after a five-year hiatus) and challenged the "womyn-born-womyn"-only policy on the basis that it is rooted in outdated, binary assumptions about gender.[10]

The idea that transgender identities and expression subvert the gender binary did much to increase transgender-inclusion within feminist and queer spaces. However, this approach did not benefit all transgender people equally.

Because transgender-inclusion was explicitly linked to gender transgression and subverting the gender binary, those individuals who do not identify within the gender binary—for example, people who are genderqueer, gender-fluid, or who engage in "genderfuck" (purposefully playing or screwing with gender expression and presentation)—tended to be most celebrated, whereas transsexuals—especially those who identify within the binary and who appear gender-normative and/or heterosexual post-transition—frequently still had their motives and identities questioned.[11]

It is also common for trans female/feminine-spectrum individuals to be called out for "reinforcing the gender binary" more so than their counterparts on the trans male/masculine spectrum. This is due, in part, to the fact that female and feminine appearances are more readily and routinely judged in our society than male and masculine ones. And because concepts like "transgression" and "rebellion" tend to be coded as "masculine" in our culture, whereas "conformity" and "conventionality" are typically coded as "feminine," there is an unspoken bias that leads masculine transgender expression to be seen as more inherently transgressive than feminine transgender expression. Indeed, such unconscious presumptions about masculinity and femininity have surely contributed to the tendency exhibited by many feminists to praise women who engage in traditionally "masculine" endeavors, while expressing anywhere from apathy to antagonism toward men who engage in traditionally "feminine" endeavors. In fact, one could make the case that historically feminism has been predisposed toward *trans-masculinism*—that is, favoring gender transgression in the masculine direction.

Not coincidentally, perhaps the biggest change in lesbian and queer women's communities since the rise of queer theory and transgender activism has been a growing influx of trans men and others on the trans male/masculine spectrum, many of whom date and/or are partnered to non-trans queer women. While trans men are not officially allowed in Michfest, many still attend anyway (as the festival has essentially had a "don't ask, don't tell" policy regarding gender identity for much of the last decade). The significant attendance of trans male/masculine folks led one trans masculine attendee in 2000 to remark that the festival was "the largest female-to-male trans conference I have ever seen in my life."[12] The festival not only accommodates such individuals, but has also invited trans masculine musical artists who go by the pronoun "he" to perform on the festival stage. It has also become increasingly common for Michfest supporters to claim that the festival is a place for those who have grown up female in a patriarchal society, an interpretation that conveniently enables trans men to attend but not trans women.[13] Indeed, this growing inclusion of trans men has not yielded a similar inclusion of trans women; in fact, many feel that it has only served to make trans women more invisible and irrelevant within queer women's communities.

Trans-Misogyny, Intersectionality, and "Second-Wave" Transgender Activism

I personally became involved in the Michfest trans woman-exclusion issue in 2003 when I attended Camp Trans.[14] This was a turning point year for the protest, as organizers began to make a purposeful effort to focus specifically on working toward trans woman-inclusion (rather than "transgender-inclusion" more generally) and to try to shift the dynamics of the protest from one which favored trans men and others on the trans male/masculine spectrum, to one which is equally welcoming of, and empowering for, trans women. It was there that I first had in depth conversations with other trans women about how people on the trans female/feminine spectrum tend to be more routinely derided and demonized—both in mainstream society and within lesbian and queer women's spaces like Michfest—than our trans male/masculine counterparts. It was clear to many of us that this phenomenon was not simply the result of the fact that we "transgress gender norms" (something which both trans male/ masculine and trans female/feminine folks do). Rather, it seemed to be driven more by *traditional sexism*—that is, the presumption that femaleness and femininity are inferior to, or less legitimate than, maleness and masculinity.

Over the last five years, trans female/feminine feminists have begun to articulate a new perspective on feminism and trans activism that better captures our own experiences dealing with sexism. This approach is not so much rooted in queer theory as it is in *intersectionality*—a theory that grew out of the work of feminists of color (as thoroughly chronicled by Patricia Hill Collins) and perhaps first discussed in relation to the Michfest trans woman-exclusion issue by Emi Koyama.[15] Intersectionality states that different forms of oppression do not act independent of one another, but rather they interact synergistically. Unlike queer theory and lesbian feminism, intersectionality focuses primarily on the ways in which people are institutionally marginalized, rather than fixating on whether any given individual's identity or behaviors "reinforce" or "subvert" the gender system.

According to this view, trans women lie at the intersection of (at least) two types of sexism. The first is *cissexism*, which is the societal-wide tendency to view transsexual gender identities and sex embodiments as being less legitimate than those of cissexuals—that is, nontranssexuals. Cissexism functions in a manner analogous to heterosexism: Transsexual gender identities and same-sex orientations are both typically viewed as being inherently questionable, unnatural, morally suspect, and less socially and legally valid than their cissexual and heterosexual counterparts. Not only does cissexism institutionally marginalize transsexual individuals, but it privileges cissexuals, rendering their genders and sexed bodies as unquestionable, unmarked, and taken for granted (similar to how heterosexual attraction and relationships are privileged in our culture).

While all transsexuals face cissexism, trans women experience this form of sexism as being especially exacerbated by traditional sexism. For example, trans women are routinely hyper-sexualized in our society, especially in the media, where we are regularly depicted as fetishists, sexual deceivers, sex workers, and/or in a sexually provocative fashion (trans men, in contrast, are not typically depicted in this way). The common presumption that trans women transition to female for sexual reasons seems to be based on the premise that women as a whole have no worth beyond their ability to be sexualized. Furthermore, most of the societal consternation, ridicule, and violence directed at trans people focuses on individuals on the trans female/feminine spectrum—often specifically targeting our desire to be female and/or our feminine presentation. While trans men experience cissexism, their desire to be male/masculine is typically not mocked or derided in the same way—to do so would bring maleness/masculinity itself into question. Thus, those of us on the trans female/feminine spectrum don't merely experience cissexism or "transphobia," so much as we experience trans-misogyny.

Trans female/feminine perspectives on sexism have shaken up the dynamics of longstanding feminist debates about trans individuals and inclusion. For example, lesbian feminist critiques of queer theory and transgender activism have charged that focusing primarily on transgressing or blurring the distinction between "woman" and "man" does nothing to address the effect that traditional sexism has on women's lives. Trans female/feminine feminists typically agree with this lesbian feminist critique and further extend it to address the many ways in which traditional sexism impacts our own lives, both as women and as trans women.

Trans female/feminine feminists have also taken issue with the ways in which others have defined and positioned us in the Michfest inclusion debate. For example, queer theorists and some transgender activists often argue for inclusion on the basis that transgender people transgress or subvert the gender binary. Trans women have challenged this approach for being both masculine-centric (as it favors trans male/masculine individuals) and cissexist (as the presumption that we blur or subvert the gender binary is the direct result of people viewing us as "fake" and "illegitimate" women in the first place). Lesbian feminists, on the other hand, typically argue that trans women should be denied entrance into women-only spaces such as Michfest because we were born and socialized male. These claims are also masculine-centric (as they emphasize supposedly "male/masculine" aspects of our history over our female identities and lived experiences as women) and cissexist (as they presume that our female identities are less legitimate than those of cissexual women).

Trans female/feminine feminists have also countered the way in which Michfest has increasingly co-opted queer/transgender rhetoric in recent years in its defense of its trans woman-exclusion policy. For example, a 2006 Michfest press release described "womyn-born-womyn" as "a valid and honorable gender identity."[16] This statement seems to take advantage of the transgender activist claim that there are countless possible gender identities, each of which should be equally respected. However, it fails to recognize who is the privileged majority in this case (cissexual women/"womyn-born-womyn") and who is the marginalized minority (transsexual women). Thus, Michfest's statement is analogous to the hypothetical situation of heterosexual women declaring that "straight woman" is a valid gender identity in order justify excluding lesbian and bisexual women from an event in which all other women are welcome. Most Michfest supporters would undoubtedly recognize such an approach as being unquestionably heterosexist; by the same reasoning, Michfest's trans woman-exclusion policy is unquestionably cissexist. In that same press release, Michfest has also asserted that the festival is not "transphobic" because plenty of transgender people attend, or because it is "home to womyn who could be considered gender outlaws" (an apparent reference to Kate Bornstein's binary-shattering book *Gender Outlaw: On Men, Women and the Rest of Us)*. While this strategy gives the appearance of accommodating queer/transgender perspectives, it does not address the concerns of trans female/feminine feminists, who believe that the festival's policy is primarily cissexist and trans-misogynistic/trans-masculinist (as it is excludes trans women while accommodating trans male/masculine folks).

A recognition of trans-misogyny/trans-masculinism—both within queer and feminist settings, and in society at large—has led many trans women and trans male/masculine allies to critique the growing numbers of trans men who, despite their physical transitions and the fact that they now live as men, still feel entitled to inhabit lesbian and women's spaces. Such individuals will often justify their continued presence in such spaces by citing their female history, or claiming that they don't feel "100 percent like a man" (even though they move through the world and are treated as men). Such claims reinforce the popular misconception that transsexual gender identities should not be taken seriously, and thus has had a direct negative impact on trans women's inclusion in these same spaces. In a sense, these trans men seem to want to have it both ways: being men in the male-centered mainstream and then being "not-men" in queer/feminist/women's spaces. This places trans women in no-win situation: We are treated as second-class citizens in the male-centered mainstream because we are women, and then further derided for supposedly being privileged, infiltrating "men" in queer/feminist/women's spaces.

This growing "gender gap" between trans male/masculine and trans female/feminine communities is not unique to the Michfest trans woman-exclusion debate, but can be seen in other areas of transgender activism. While trans men used to be a minority in the trans community, over the last fifteen years their numbers have significantly increased and, in many cities and college campuses, they have come to dominate transgender organizations and activism. This prominence is often enabled by the trans-masculinist leanings of feminist and queer activism (which tend to be suspicious of, or less welcoming toward, trans women both before and after our transitions). Trans men also enjoy significant social advantages over trans women, both because they physically tend to "pass" as cissexual more often and more easily than trans women, and because of the male privilege they experience post-transition. Trans women—especially those who transition at a young age and who thus do not benefit significantly from male privilege pre-transition—have more difficulties finding and maintaining employment, are more susceptible to poverty, and more likely to engage in survival sex work to make ends meet.[17] There is a growing sense among many trans women that previous models of transgender activism have largely ignored these trans female/feminine-specific issues in a manner similar to how progressive movements during the 1960s largely ignored woman-specific issues, and how the gay rights movement of the 1970s and 1980s largely ignored lesbian-specific issues.

Trans female/feminine feminists are not the only group critiquing the "first wave"[18] of transgender activism for ignoring the ways in which transgender issues are often intertwined with, and exacerbated by, other forms of oppression. Since the early 2000s, a number of organizations—such as the Sylvia Rivera Law Project, TransJustice, TGI Justice Project, and others—have begun to focus specifically on the needs of trans people of color, trans people of low income, and those who are incarcerated—all of whom are especially vulnerable to gender regulation and oppression due to living at the intersection of racism, classism, and sexism.[19] As a testament to the importance of intersectionality, a GenderPAC report on violence against gender-non-conforming youth showed that the vast majority of the victims were of color, poor, or on the trans female/feminine spectrum (and very often, all three).[20] Activists like Viviane Namaste and Mirha-Soleil Ross have pointed out that trans sex workers—who are disproportionately poor trans women and trans female/feminine-spectrum individuals—receive little to no attention or support from mainstream transgender organizations, activists, and academics, despite the fact that they are arguably the most marginalized segment of the transgender community.[21] Other activists, such as Monica Roberts—who blogs under the name TransGriot and who is one of the organizers of the annual Transsistahs and Transbrothas Conference—have written extensively about how mainstream transgender organizations routinely fail to acknowledge issues that disproportionally affect trans people of color.[22] Just as universalizing views of womanhood that existed within second-wave feminism were challenged by third-wave feminists, the universalizing view of transgender people forwarded in the 1990s (which tended to ignore differences with regard to race, class, and direction of transition and/or transgender expression) have increasingly been called into question by this "second wave" of transgender activism.

Given the violence and extreme poverty that afflicts many trans people, some have suggested that the Michfest trans woman-exclusion issue has received an undeserved amount of activist attention. And the fact that tickets to this week-long festival cost several hundred dollars—a luxury many trans folks cannot afford—is often cited by those who view Michfest's policy as primarily a middle-class trans issue. While Michfest is admittedly not the most pressing trans-related issue out there, such critiques miss the larger picture. This is not about the desire to simply attend one music festival. Rather, for lesbian and bisexual trans women, this is about us being able to participate in our own queer women's community—a community in which we face anywhere from antagonism to irrelevancy on a regular basis.

Perhaps more importantly, this is about us being able to have a voice within feminism more generally. Michfest is not only the world's largest annual women-only event, but historically it's been a focal point for dialogues and debates on a wide range of feminist issues. As someone who has experienced first-hand the substantial difference between what it's like to be treated as a woman and as a man, and who now experiences both misogyny and trans-misogyny in my day-to-day life, I have found feminism to be an indispensable foundation for me to make sense of my experiences and to articulate the obstacles and issues that I face. For many of us who are trans women, this is about having a voice in a movement that is incommensurably vital to us.

For years, trans women have effectively had no voice in Michfest. During that time, many cissexual women and trans male/masculine attendees have tried to advocate on our behalf inside the festival. While their intentions may have been sincere, the fact that they entered into a space that excludes trans women, and that they claimed to speak for us (despite not having had a trans female/feminine life experience themselves), their actions further contributed to the erasure of our voices and perspectives. While the "womyn-born-womyn"-only policy remains in effect to this day, Michfest stopped formally expelling trans women from the festival in 2006 (although they still insist that any trans woman who attends is "choosing to disrespect the stated intention of this Festival").[23] While the situation is hardly perfect, it does for the first time allow trans women to speak in their own voices within Michfest. And that's a crucial part of any feminist or activist movement: to allow those who have been marginalized, disenfranchised, and excluded to be able to define themselves, and to speak in their own voices about the struggles they face and the way they experience their own lives.

28

Blog-Born-Blog

In 2007, I began to blog on a semi-regular basis. This was my first entry. It is what we in the literary world call "parody."

Okay, after a half-hearted attempt at blogging a couple years ago, this time I am really going to try to make this work. But there is one thing you should know before we start: My blog identifies as a "Blog-Born-Blog." This means that it was born and socialized as a blog, unlike your blog. While your blog may identify as a blog, live as a blog, and may face the same anti-blog discrimination that my blog faces, my blog believes that your blog isn't nearly as oppressed. After all, your blog may call itself a "blog," but it never had a bloghood like mine had.

You should know that this is a "blog-born-blog"-only webspace, which means that my blog doesn't want so-called pseudo-"blogs" like yours around. But rather than say this to your face, my blog will instead insist that this webpage was always meant to be a place for other "blog-born-blogs" to get together and reminisce about our bloghoods—a bloghood that your blog unfortunately was not unfortunate enough to have had. However, don't you dare accuse my blog of being prejudiced against your blog, because if you do, my blog will claim that "blog-born-blog" is a legitimate webpage-identity. That way, if your blog challenges the policy, my blog will accuse your blog of disrespecting its identity, and then it can retaliate by disrespecting your blog's identity as a "blog." Face it, it's a lose-lose situation for your blog . . .

29

Empowering Femininity

In Whipping Girl, *I argued that we (as feminists) should "empower femininity" rather than dismissing or deriding it. Unsurprisingly, some feminists have subsequently mocked or misconstrued this notion. So to clarify what I meant, I wrote this piece for the* Ms. Magazine *blog in July 2014.*[1]

Early on in my first book *Whipping Girl,* while discussing the tendency within some strands of feminism to discourage women from engaging in acts and pursuits that are considered feminine, I argued that "we should instead learn to empower femininity itself."[2] While many people who read the entire book appreciated my stance on femininity, I have found that those who disagree with me often take that particular quote out of context. And admittedly, it is rather easy to twist the phrase "empower femininity" to make it sound like I was simply calling for more Barbie dolls and glitter nail polish for everyone.

Of course, the reason why it is particularly easy to ridicule the idea of empowering femininity is because we (all of us, as a society) already harbor dismissive attitudes toward anything that is considered feminine. And the very point I was trying to make is that we should move beyond this knee-jerk tendency to dismiss and demean feminine gender expression.

So to counter those who wish to smear the notion, here is a brief outline of ideas I forward in *Whipping Girl* (and specifically in the chapter "Putting the Feminine Back into Feminism") that I believe will help us empower femininity.

Recognize That Feminine Traits Are Human Traits

In our culture, a trait is deemed "feminine" if it is often associated with women. Common examples include being verbal and communicative, emotive or effusive, being nurturing, and having an appreciation for beautiful or aesthetically pleasing things. Similarly, other traits are deemed "masculine" solely because they are often associated with men (for instance, being competitive or aggressive, physical exertion or using brute force, being silent and stoic, and being mathematically or technically oriented). What all of these traits share is the fact that they are all human traits that are found to varying degrees in all people regardless of their gender. Most of us express some combination of traits from both the feminine and masculine categories.

I would argue that there is nothing inherently wrong with feminine traits—like all human traits, they are often useful and play important roles. However, in our male- and masculine-centric culture, there are several forces that conspire to undermine feminine traits and the people who express them.

Traits that are viewed as feminine are considered to be inferior to those deemed masculine. This discrepancy is obvious in the adjectives that we commonly associate with gender expression: the assumption that masculinity is strong while femininity is weak, that masculinity is tough while femininity is fragile, that masculinity is rational while femininity is irrational, that masculinity is serious while femininity is frivolous, that masculinity is functional while femininity is ornamental, that masculinity is natural while femininity is artificial, and that masculinity is sincere while femininity is manipulative.

Not coincidentally, many of these stereotypes are identical to those people have historically projected onto men and women, respectively. Over the decades, feminists have fiercely challenged these inferior connotations when they have been used to undermine women, and we should now challenge these same connotations when they are used to undermine people who are feminine (the majority of whom also happen to be women).

Feminine Traits Are Misconstrued as Being Performed for the Benefit of Men

We see this in the way that the quality of being nurturing (a human trait that is coded feminine) often gets distorted into the myth that it's the woman's job to take care of the man in heterosexual relationships. But it's perhaps most evident in the way that people who appreciate beautiful or aesthetically pleasing things (especially with regards to their own manner of dress and self-presentation) are often presumed to be simply trying to attract or please men.

The women I know who dress femininely are also (far more often than not) generally interested in other forms of visual beauty—they often decorate their homes, compliment others on their dress, and comment appreciatively when they see things that look appealing to them (whether it be a particular hue or color combination, a fashion or style, a work of art or architecture, flowers and other natural objects, and so on). So it is difficult for me to see this notion—that when they express this interest with regards to their own style of dress, they must be doing it to attract male attention—as anything other than highly misplaced and entirely sexist. Not to mention the fact that stereotypically masculine men often never even notice when their female partners are wearing a new outfit or have a new hairstyle. And not to mention the fact that there are women who dress femininely but who are certainly not trying to attract the attention of men (e.g., femme dykes), and men who dress femininely even though such gender-non-conforming presentation is not traditionally considered attractive to most straight women and queer men.

This myth—that feminine dress is primarily designed to attract male attention—exists for a single reason: It enables the societal-wide sexualization of women. After all, if we believe that she wore a pretty dress today because she is trying to pique men's interests, then suddenly catcalls, sexual innuendos, and ogling become seemingly legitimate (because she was essentially "asking for" that attention). And if she says that she is not interested in a man's sexual advances, well then she must be sending "mixed messages," because after all, she was clearly trying to "tempt" or "tease" him given the way she was dressed.

I am highly aware that a huge swath of our culture is dedicated to making women feel like their worth as a human being is inexorably tied to how attractive they are to men. While critiquing that system is legitimate, dismissing people who are feminine (under the assumption that they buy into that system) is misplaced and often invalidates their autonomy (e.g., the fact that they may have dressed that way for themselves and not for others). It also overlooks a number of sexist double standards that exist and lead us to perceive feminine dress differently from masculine dress. When a woman gets ready for a date, we often say she gets "all dolled up" (the assumption being that it is an frivolous and artificial process), while when a man does the same we usually call it "grooming" (which sounds so practical and natural, like animals in the wild). And while some feminists may complain about how feminine fashions often "show off women's bodies for male enjoyment," that completely ignores the fact that a man can go completely topless and no one will assume that he is doing it for anyone else (rather, people will likely assume it is a personal choice based on the fact that he is probably overheated!).

Articles of clothing (or the lack thereof) have no inherent meaning. Any symbolism or connotations they seem to have come directly from our culture or personal assumptions. Rather than critiquing feminine styles of dress, we should instead destroy the sexist myth that feminine dress exists solely for the benefit of men.

Girls and Women Are Encouraged, and Often Coerced, into Being Feminine

People who view femininity and masculinity as female- and male-specific traits, respectively (rather than more broadly as human traits), will often encourage so-called "gender appropriate" behaviors in other people. Sometimes this is done unconsciously or subtly (e.g., by simply expressing approval of gender-conforming behavior), and other times consciously and blatantly (e.g., by outright ridiculing or condemning people who are gender non-conforming). This system has many negative ramifications, one of which is that it puts pressure on girls and women to express feminine traits but not masculine ones.

Feminists have understandably been concerned by this system, although sometimes the strategies that have been forwarded to counter it have been misguided. For instance, some have encouraged women to avoid the feminine and instead pursue masculine approaches and endeavors—this strategy seems to presume that things that are coded feminine are inherently weak, irrational, frivolous, artificial, etc., in relation to those coded masculine. In other words, this strategy seems to accept these sexist double standards at face value rather than challenging them.

Other feminists have claimed that we must do away with all gender expression—both the masculine and the feminine. While I am all in favor of jettisoning compulsory femininity for girls/women and compulsory masculinity for boys/men, entirely doing away with all such behaviors seems unwarranted—after all, many of these behaviors (e.g., being nurturing, or competitive, or emotive, or technically oriented, or appreciating beauty, or physical exertion) are simply human traits that are unnecessarily categorized as "feminine" or "masculine" by society. This approach also mistakenly assumes that people have no individual inclinations or tendencies with regard to these traits. In reality, many people find that, regardless of the gender they were assigned at birth or how they were raised, they tend to gravitate toward behaviors that are deemed feminine, or masculine, or some combination thereof.

Most reasonable people these days would agree that demeaning or dismissing someone solely because she is female is socially unacceptable. However, demeaning or dismissing people for expressing feminine qualities is often condoned and even encouraged. Indeed, much of the sexism faced by women today targets their femininity (or assumed femininity) rather than their femaleness. It is high time that we forcefully challenge the negative assumptions that constantly plague feminine traits and the people who express them. That is what I mean when I say we must empower femininity.

Part Three

Pathological Science Revisited

When I was working on *Whipping Girl*, I spent a considerable amount of effort debunking psychiatric/psychological diagnoses and depictions of gender-variant people. Much of this was done in a chapter entitled "Pathological Science."[1] That title was a purposeful double entendre. It might refer to scientific research that pathologizes gender-variant people, but it is also an already-existing term for research that veers away from the scientific method, often due to researchers' subjective beliefs or biases (which is how I would characterize the bulk of twentieth-century research on gender-variant people). I also spent additional chapters debunking psychologist Ray Blanchard's controversial theory of "autogynephilia" (which had recently been popularized and sensationalized in J. Michael Bailey's 2003 book *The Man Who Would Be Queen*) and explaining why it is impossible to understand trans female/feminine sexualities and trajectories without first considering the fact that we live in a culture where femaleness and femininity are highly sexualized.[2]

Upon completing that book, I felt like I had said everything that I needed to say on this topic. But then two events occurred that pulled me back into this subject matter. The first occurred in 2007, when it was announced that Alice

Dreger had written a book-length article about the controversy surrounding J. Michael Bailey's book, and that it was to be published in the research journal *Archives of Sexual Behavior*. Most trans activists and advocates familiar with the controversy felt that this high profile article was extremely one-sided, and I was one of many who wrote critical "peer commentaries" that were published along with Dreger's final article.[3] In subsequent years, Dreger has continued her campaign to exonerate psychiatrists/psychologists who insist on pathologizing and sexualizing trans identities—my critiques of her blatant misrepresentation of these matters have been published elsewhere.[4]

The second (and far more important) event that compelled me to continue writing about these matters was the announcement in 2008 that a new revision of the *Diagnostic and Statistical Manual of Mental Disorders (DSM)* was underway. The *DSM* is often called the "bible of mental illness" because it lists and defines all of the "official" psychiatric diagnoses according to the American Psychiatric Association. In *Whipping Girl*, I had critiqued the trans-related diagnoses "Gender Identity Disorder" (GID) and "Transvestic Fetishism," both of which were included in the then-existing *DSM (DSM-IV-TR)*. Most of us in the trans community hoped that these diagnoses would be either revised to be less invalidating of trans identities, or eliminated entirely from subsequent *DSM* revisions. Given our hopes, many of us were dismayed to learn that Ken Zucker, who had gained notoriety for conducting "reparative therapy" on gender-non-conforming children, was named Chair of the Sexual and Gender Identity Disorders Work Group. In turn, Zucker named Ray Blanchard as Chair of the Paraphilias Subworkgroup, which meant that Blanchard would play a lead role in revising (and potentially expanding) the Transvestic Fetishism diagnosis.

I wrote numerous articles and essays about these issues over the following years, most of which are collected on my webpage "Debunking Psychological Diagnoses and Theories about Transsexual and Transgender People."[5] In this section, I offer six chapters that best chronicle these developments and my thoughts on these topics. "Psychology, Sexualization, and Trans-Invalidations" provides an accessible and thorough overview of why certain psychological depictions of gender variance are both fundamentally flawed and potentially damaging to trans people. "Stop Sexualizing Us!" and "The Beauty In Us" are short speeches that I gave in 2009 protesting the way in which certain psychological concepts and diagnoses unnecessarily sexualize and stigmatize trans people. "Reconceptualizing 'Autogynephilia' as Female/Feminine Embodiment Fantasies" was written specifically for this book, and summarizes my research and opinions on "autogynephilia" and trans sexualities more generally. "Trans People Are Still 'Disordered' According to Latest *DSM*" is my take on the final revisions of trans-related diagnoses as they now appear in the new *DSM-5*. The final chapter of this section, "An Open Letter to *The New Yorker*," details my own personal experience of having the now disproven theory of "autogynephilia" used to slut-shame me in both an academic publication and a national magazine.

One final note: In December 2015, Canada's Centre for Addiction and Mental Health decided to close Ken Zucker's gender clinic, a move that was widely applauded by trans people and many trans health professionals, but which prompted some media backlash in support of Zucker and his methods.[6] My thoughts regarding "gender reparative/conversion" therapies (and revisionist claims that Zucker's clinic did not conduct them) can be found in my blogpost "Placing Ken Zucker's clinic in historical context."[7]

30

Psychology, Sexualization, and Trans-Invalidations

This chapter was originally presented as a keynote talk for the Eighth Annual Phila-delphia Trans-Health Conference in 2009. I was inspired to write it after, on mul-tiple occasions, I had read or heard sexologists and mental health professionals play down or outright dismiss trans people's concerns regarding psychological depictions, diagnoses, terminology, and theories about trans people.[1] With this speech, I set out to explain, in very basic, easy to grasp language, precisely why trans people's concerns regarding these matters are valid and should be taken seriously within the fields of psychology, psychiatry, and sexology. I would later expand upon the concept of "in-validations" in Excluded *(specifically, Chapter 20, "Recognizing Invalidations").*

Thanks, it's an honor to be here. It's rare that one gets to simultaneously speak to trans activists, allies, and trans health providers, so I am truly grateful for this opportunity. Being here is also somewhat surreal for me, as I grew up just outside of Philadelphia, less than ten miles from here. And I was thinking last night that if you would have told my younger, closeted, isolated self that one day, I'd be here in the Pennsylvania Convention Center giving a keynote talk at a trans-health conference . . . well, let's just say that I would have been really, really mortified.

I want to share with you some of my thoughts regarding how gender vari-ance, transgenderism,[2] and transsexuality are depicted and discussed within mainstream psychology,[3] and the impact that this has on trans people's lives. While this has always been an important topic, it has become especially rele-vant in the last few years, as a result of the seemingly never-ending controversy surrounding J. Michael Bailey's book *The Man Who Would Be Queen: The Science of Gender-Bending and Transsexualism*—a book which many trans activists, ad-vocates, and sexologists found to be unapologetically stigmatizing, sexualizing, and a distortion of both trans people's lives and the scientific literature on the subject.[4] Then there was last year's news that Ken Zucker (who conducts reparative therapy on gender-non-conforming children) and Ray Blanchard (who coined the controversial term "autogynephilia") were to play critical lead roles in determining the language of the Sexual and Gender Identity Disorders section for the next revision of the *Diagnostic and Statistical Manual of Mental Disorders (DSM).*[5] In certain sexology circles, the negative reactions expressed by trans activists in response to these incidents have been caricatured as expressions of "narcissistic rage"—a hysterical, irrational, mass overreaction to the supposedly logical, well-reasoned, empirically-based theories and diagnoses forwarded by psychologists.[6] Reciprocally, in trans circles, psychologists are sometimes caricatured as heartless evil-doers who conspire behind the scenes in order to figure out how to further exploit and subjugate trans people via the *DSM, WPATH Standards of Care,*[7] and so on, in order to achieve academic success and/or monetary gain for themselves.

Personally, I am not a big fan of either of these narratives. First, there are some psychologists who do truly trans-positive work. Further, I believe that the majority of psychologists—even ones that I most fervently disagree with—forward the theories they favor because they sincerely believe that they are correct and will benefit trans people in the long run. I also believe that the concern, fear, and outrage expressed by trans people—even those who are the most vehemently defiant and angry at the psychological establishment—comes from a very real and legitimate place. It comes from our understanding that there is a direct connection between mainstream psychological discourses about gender-variant people and the societal marginalization we face in our day-to-day lives due to our gender variance. While some psychologists and trans health providers recognize this connection, too many others seem unconcerned by the problem. Perhaps they haven't been exposed to, or don't feel that it's important for them to familiarize themselves with, trans perspectives. Or maybe they habitually view us as "other" and therefore have difficulties identifying with our plight. Or maybe they so fancy themselves as experts on transgenderism that they can't comprehend that we (as trans people) have profound experiences and insights into gender that they are not privy to, and that frankly they could learn a thing or two by simply listening to us. Whatever the reason, I feel that a major obstacle that we as a trans community face is getting the greater psychological establishment, as well as the general public, to appreciate why our concern is legitimate, and to get them to understand in really concrete terms how certain psychological theories, therapies, terminologies, and diagnoses cause us very real harm and injury, and therefore should be done away with.

To be honest, I think that we (i.e., trans activists) could do a better job articulating this than we have in the past. For instance, in the trans community, most of the complaints that I have heard about mainstream psychology or the *DSM* tend to center around two words. First, psychologists who forward theories and diagnoses that have a negative impact on trans people are often called out as "transphobic." While this is often a valid critique, most lay people have a superficial understanding of the term, reading it literally as "fear of transgender people." Thus, someone like Bailey can simply say "I have trans friends," or "I support trans surgeries," and this will sound like a reasonable response to most people outside of the trans community. The second word that trans activists regularly employ is "pathologize." People will say that Bailey's book is bad because it pathologizes people on the trans female/feminine spectrum. Or they will say that the trans-focused *DSM* diagnoses Gender Identity Disorder (GID) and Transvestic Fetishism pathologize gender-variant people. While I would agree with these statements, I do not believe that they convey the real problem. For one thing, the word pathologize is a very abstract and esoteric word. While many trans activists, psychologists, and academics understand its meaning, it is not likely to resonate with the general public.

Second, we live in a society where all people must be willing to be pathologized (i.e., diagnosed as having a medical or psychiatric condition) in order to access the healthcare system. In recent years, I have been diagnosed for being hypothyroid and for having skin cancer, yet I never felt a sense of outrage over the fact that I had been pathologized in order to access care in these cases. Here is a more pertinent example: I am lucky enough to have therapy mostly covered by my health insurance plan. This isn't transition-related therapy— it's just your run of the mill therapy. My insurance company won't cover my sessions, of course, unless I am diagnosed with something. So, for insurance purposes, my therapist uses Adjustment Disorder as my diagnosis—it refers to a "psychological response to an identifiable stressor," which could include anything from stress at work or relationship issues, to more serious problems.[8] Despite the fact that this is officially a psychiatric diagnosis, it does not evoke strong outrage in me. In contrast, I was very disturbed about the fact that I needed to be diagnosed with GID in order to transition. This suggests that what bothers me about GID is not merely the fact that I have been "pathologized" (as being pathologized in other contexts does not bother me so much).

Similarly, I don't think that the word "pathologize" really captures why, when I read Bailey's book, I was often filled with palpable anger. Or why I was moved to tears upon hearing a recent National Public Radio story that described a cross-gender-identified child who was undergoing Ken Zucker's reparative therapy.[9]

So if the issue is not pathologization *per se,* why is it that we, as trans people, often experience such an intense, visceral, negative reaction to these theories and therapies? I would argue that it is because they *invalidate* us. The definition of the word invalidate is: to discredit; to deprive of legal force or efficacy; to destroy the authority of; to nullify.[10] Whether deliberately or unconsciously, I believe that the theories and diagnoses forwarded by certain mainstream psychologists do just that to us. And with the rest of my talk today, I hope to draw a direct connection between these theories and diagnoses and the invalidations that we, as gender-variant people, experience in our day-to-day lives.

We live in a world where trans people's gender identities, gender expressions, and sex embodiments are deemed less natural and less legitimate than those of cisgender people.[11] This double standard plays out at virtually every level of our lives. For example, I have the privilege of passing as a cisgender woman in my day-to-day life. In the eight years since my transition, I have never once had someone who presumed that I was a cisgender woman accidentally slip up my pronouns and call me "he." It is simply a mistake that people never (or extremely rarely) make with people they believe to be cisgender. However, once I come out to people as trans, or after they discover that I am trans, it is not uncommon for them to accidentally slip up and call me "he." I say accidentally here because, in most cases, people are apologetic after realizing their mistake. While it may not have been conscious or intentional, such incidents clearly indicate that my gender identity as a trans person is viewed as inherently suspect, and less legitimate, than it is when I am read as cis.

I have had cisgender people say to me, "Why is that such a big deal? I wouldn't get upset if someone slipped up my pronouns." My reply to that is, well, of course you wouldn't, because it never happens to you. And if it did happen to you, it would seem anomalous, and therefore harmless. But in my case, people do often slip up my pronouns, and when they do, it is a sign that on an unconscious level they see my gender identity as less authentic than the gender identities of cisgender people.

In addition to these unintentional slip-ups, I occasionally come across people who purposefully call me "he," who deliberately refuse to acknowledge my female gender identity. When this happens, it is generally done with an air of superiority, and the person makes no attempt to hide their indignation and contempt for me. And for every time that this happens to my face, there are hundreds of times when people direct similar trans-invalidations to the cisgender majority rather than me. For example, often I'll be watching a TV show or movie, or I'll be reading a newspaper or magazine, or a gender studies or psychology book, or maybe I'll be in a restaurant or on the subway, minding my own business, and I'll be blind-sided by an invalidating comment or rant about transsexuals: about how confused, or fake, or sick, or dangerous, or gross, or pathetic, or ridiculous we supposedly are. While these remarks may not have been intended for me, how could I possibly not take them personally, when they are so obviously *about* me?

There is a straight line that connects inadvertent pronoun slips, the inability to legally change the gender markers on one's driver's license or passport, Focus on the Family's anti-transgender fear-mongering ads about "men" entering women's bathrooms, trans people who can't find employment because they don't pass as cisgender, incarcerated trans women who get placed in all-male jail cells, and trans people who are beaten, even murdered, while their assailants claim that they are somehow victims of the trans person's "deception." These acts may differ greatly in their severity, but they all communicate the exact same message: that trans people's gender identities, expressions, and sex embodiments are not deserving of the same rights or respect that are regularly extended to our cisgender counterparts. They all revolve around what Talia Bettcher in her writings calls the Basic Denial of Authenticity.[12]

There are myriad ways in which trans-invalidations may occur. Some people will claim that gender-variant identities, expressions, and bodies are unnatural or immoral, often citing some religious text or "Biology 101" soundbite in order to make their point. Or, they might go out of their way to portray trans people as imitators, impersonators, or even caricatures, of cisgender women and men. Others project ulterior motives upon us. Those who wish to invalidate same-sex attraction will claim that lesbian, gay, and bisexual people just haven't met the right person yet, or are merely looking for an alternative lifestyle, or perhaps they've been duped by the homosexual agenda. Similarly, those who wish to invalidate trans people's gender identities will claim that we must transition in order to gain certain gender privileges, or perhaps we're merely trying to satisfy some sexual fetish, or maybe we're really gay people who are trying to assimilate into straight society and/or to seduce unsuspecting straight people.

All of these invalidating strategies are routinely used to delegitimize us.

Perhaps the most widespread method of trans-invalidation occurs when people presume that trans people are mentally confused, incompetent, or ill, and therefore unable to speak with validity about our own experiences, identities, and personal histories.[13] Of course, claiming or insinuating that somebody is mentally incompetent or inferior is one of the most common forms of invalidation more generally. If you and I disagree about something, I can gain the upper hand by suggesting that you are younger than me and therefore naive, or that you are a layperson, whereas I have an advanced degree. I could even insinuate that you are not as smart as me, or that perhaps that you are a little bit crazy. Because it is such an effective a strategy, invalidation based on mental inferiority has been invoked to perpetuate racism: There is a long history, stretching from phrenology to *The Bell Curve*, of dubious research that has attempted to give scientific credence to the presumption that people of color are mentally inferior to the white majority.[14] Invalidation by mental inferiority has also been used to justify sexism: The claim that women are biologically or hormonally predispositioned to be overly emotional (read: irrational or immature) has been invoked by those who feel that women should defer to men, or who feel that women are not capable of dealing with serious or important matters. For example, the suffragists who fought for women's right to vote were regularly dismissed as suffering from "hysteria," which was considered a legitimate mental disturbance at the time.[15]

Given this history, it is no surprise that those who wish to dismiss trans people often do so by claiming that we are delusional, or simply confused about, our genders. For example, back when I decided to transition, the people in my life who voiced the strongest objections invariably stressed that what I was experiencing was simply "all in my head." Some saw my female gender identity as a faulty piece of misinformation that I simply needed to unlearn. Others presumed that what I experienced was akin to an addiction, and they argued that I just needed to be more disciplined in repressing my wayward urge. Their arguments relied on the presumption that my physical anatomy—my male sexed body—was the only relevant, unalterable reality, and that what was going on in my mind—my female gender identity—was unreal and illegitimate by virtue of its invisibility. Of course, this is the opposite of what I actually experienced: The feeling that I had had since childhood that there was something wrong with me being male, and that I should be female, was very real and very unalterable, whereas my physical body has proven to be quite malleable in comparison. But their belief that my external, anatomical sex is most relevant and immutable essentially rendered my inner experience, my mental state, as irrelevant and unstable.

This dualism—that if one's physical sex is "real" and "primary," then the mind must automatically be "secondary" and "faulty"—implies that anything that a trans person says about their own experience, or about gender more generally, is inherently suspect. It effectively ensures that anything that any cisgender person says about gender or trans people automatically trumps what we have to say about ourselves. In effect, it positions cisgender people as de facto experts on gender variance by virtue of the fact that our minds are supposedly faulty while theirs are not. And in my experience, many cisgender people seem to relish in this supposed expert status. I cannot tell you how many times that I have interacted with people who know little to nothing about transgender people and experiences, yet who felt entitled to speak down to me or act intellectually superior to me with regards to the subject; people who repeatedly referred to my "gender confusion" in order to emphasize my presumed mental incompetence; people who have insinuated that I must be delusional because I don't conform to their common sense; people who have dismissed my perspective and experiences on the basis that they are tainted by my supposed mental sickness. To such people, it doesn't matter that I've had unique and enlightening gendered experiences that they have not shared. They don't care that I have a PhD in biology, or that I've written a book and occasionally give keynote talks about gender and transgender people. To them, anything I say is viewed as a mere byproduct of my "mental affliction" and is immediately deemed invalid.

To me, this is the heart of the problem. Words simply cannot convey how intensely frustrating and infuriating it is to be routinely invalidated in this way. Simply talking about it gives me an adrenaline rush. You could call me all sorts of names or profanities, make fun of virtually any other aspect of my body or personality, and it wouldn't even come close to eliciting the anger and outrage that I feel when somebody dismisses my gender identity or insinuates that my gender-related knowledge and experiences are mere figments of my imagination. There is simply no more effective way of hurting me than trans-invalidating me. Trans-invalidations based on mental inferiority are especially triggering to me for three reasons: First, they happen to me repeatedly. Second, they play on the profound shame that I felt back when I was a child when I really did believe the cissexist premise that, since the rest of the world was supposedly "normal," there must be something very wrong with me. Third, those who perpetrate trans-invalidations invariably refuse to acknowledge their own cisgender privilege and how it enables and exacerbates these incidents. After all, while I have had to fight my entire life to have my gender identity be taken seriously, my cisgender detractors simply take theirs for granted. This is the uneven playing field upon which every debate about gender identity and transgender rights plays out. Cisgender people can pretend to have abstract, objective, and purely theoretical conversations about whether gender identity exists, or whether trans people should be allowed to transition, because their identities and life choices are never on the line. But for those of us who are trans, such discussions automatically call into question our identities, our autonomy, and our mental veracity. They literally put our entire personhood up for debate.

Unfortunately, in this culture and at this point in time, dealing with and overcoming trans-invalidations is central to the trans experience. And I would argue that any person who does not understand or acknowledge how injurious these trans-invalidations are to us, simply does not understand transgender people. I'll repeat that: *Any person who does not understand or acknowledge how injurious these trans-invalidations are to us, simply does not understand transgender people.* Period. I further contend that any medical or mental health provider who is sincerely concerned with the health, happiness and well-being of gender-variant people must make challenging and eliminating these trans-invalidations, both within their professional fields and in society at large, a top priority.

Once we understand trans-invalidations, especially those based on mental inferiority or incompetence, it is relatively easy to see why most trans people have a beef with mainstream psychology. First, many mainstream psychologists continue to use what Kelley Winters calls "maligning language."[16] In the psychological literature, trans women are routinely called "male transsexuals" and trans men "female transsexuals." Trans women who partner with men are called "homosexual," while lesbian-identified trans women are called "heterosexual." And the cisgender majority are not called cisgender, or even nontransgender or nontranssexual women and men. Instead, they are generally called "normal" or "biological" women and men. Whenever I hear somebody use the term "biological" as a synonym for cisgender, I always make a point of assuring the person that while I may be trans, I am not inorganic or nonbiological in any way. The purpose of all this terminology is most certainly not clarity. After all, what could be more convoluted and confusing than using the term "heterosexual female transsexual" to describe someone who identifies and lives as a gay man? The only purpose that this terminology serves is to reinforce a hierarchy whereby trans people's assigned sex and anatomies are viewed as primary and relevant, while our gender identities are deemed secondary and irrelevant.

Trans-invalidations are also reinforced by the trans-specific diagnoses in the *DSM*. Two of these—Transvestic Fetishism and GID in Children—were written in such a way that they primarily target people who are not cross-gender-identified, but who simply crossdress or who are gender non-conforming in other ways.[17] This is abominable. Such diagnoses serve no purpose other than to further stigmatize gender variance. The situation is admittedly more complicated for those who wish to socially, physically, and/or legally transition. As I alluded to earlier, a diagnosis is generally required any time one wants to access the healthcare system, and GID has provided that for quite some time. Having said that, having this diagnosis in the *DSM* reinforces the popular assumption that trans people are inherently delusional or confused, and thus, not surprisingly, it is regularly cited by those who wish to invalidate our gender identities. In one chapter of her recent book *Gender Madness in American Psychiatry*, Kelley Winters lists incident after incident in which people who were fighting against the civil rights of trans children and adults cited the GID diagnosis, and the fact that it is listed as a mental illness, in their attempts to invalidate us.[18] This is why so many trans activists favor deleting this diagnosis entirely, or moving it from the psychiatric to the medical realm.

Not only is the conceptualization of trans-as-mental-illness problematic in and of itself (as it plays into the stereotype of mental incompetence), but also the way GID is currently written is especially atrocious. As the name suggests, GID literally states that trans people's gender identities are disordered. Furthermore, it was primarily designed to justify reparative therapy—as a result, trans people who repress their cross-gender identities do not meet the criteria of mental illness, whereas those of us who live happily as members of our identified gender will continue to meet the criteria for GID for perpetuity.[19] Some people have suggested that the diagnosis should be changed to Gender Dysphoria, which would focus solely on the gender dissonance we experience as a result of our bodies and identities not being aligned. Such a change would facilitate access to the means of transitioning while formally ensuring that those of us who are happy post-transition will no longer be deemed mentally disordered. While I agree that such a change would be a vast improvement over the current diagnosis, I do not think that it would be perfect. After all, so long as any form of gender variance is codified in the pages of the *DSM*, it will continue to be cited by trans-invalidators as evidence that we are mentally inferior and incompetent.

Perhaps the greatest example of trans-invalidation within mainstream psychology is the *gatekeeper system*.[20] In order to legally transition in the U.S., one must undergo certain medical procedures, and to obtain those medical procedures, one must first gain approval from one or two mental health professionals. Thus, mental health professionals are viewed as the ultimate "deciders" (as our recent ex-president would say[21]) of who should be allowed to transition and who should not. While some mental health providers are thoughtful, sympathetic, and have lots of experience with trans patients, others are clueless, unsympathetic, and rely primarily on trans-invalidating presumptions about trans folks that exist in the culture. Many also enforce blatant double standards. For example, I can't tell you how many times that I've heard different trans women say that when they first visited some psychiatrist or therapist about transitioning, they were told that they were obviously not a "real" transsexual because they didn't come in wearing a dress and makeup.[22] Because cisgender women always wear dresses and makeup, right?

Now, I acknowledge that there are a small minority of people who do not appear to be trans at all, yet who seek out the means to transition. And there are many people who are gender variant who perhaps hastily rush into the decision to transition, or who have unrealistic expectations about the process, and so forth. So I can understand why many mental health professionals might feel that having this vetting process is important. But, from a trans perspective, this system is unbearably invalidating. It explicitly suggests that many trans-identified people really are confused about our genders and should not transition, and that trans people more generally are not competent enough to make gender-related decisions for ourselves. In other words, it institutionalizes the cultural assumption that what we say about our own lives and our gendered experiences is inherently suspect.

The gatekeeper system deems that any and all mental health professionals have more authority and expertise to speak for and about trans people and issues than trans people do. This is why documentaries and news programs about transsexuality almost invariably include interviews with psychological experts in order to validate (or invalidate) what the trans people in the program say about themselves. So when Paul McHugh describes sex reassignment as "barbaric" and compares it to mutilation, or when Dr. Phil airs a program entitled "Gender-Confused Kids," their supposed expert status necessarily invalidates our experiences, identities, and voices.[23]

On that National Public Radio program about cross-gender-identified children that I mentioned previously, Ken Zucker offered the following quote to justify his reparative therapy: "Suppose you were a clinician and a 4-year-old black kid came into your office and said he wanted to be white. Would you go with that? . . . I don't think we would,"[24] Of course, comparing cross-gender identity—which is a very real pan-cultural and trans-historical phenomenon[25]—to a fictionalized "racial identity disorder" (which does not in actuality exist) is false logic. And I, of course, am free to publicly claim that his argument is utter nonsense. But who's going to believe me? In the marketplace of ideas, my critique will be dismissed as a biased, unobjective perspective from someone who is mentally disordered. Zucker, on the other hand, is a psychologist who has published countless research articles on transgenderism. In the eyes of the world, he is viewed as an expert of me. As long as the *DSM* and gatekeeper system position him as an authority on gender-variant people, what he has to say will always effectively silence me. And that, frankly, makes me very legitimately angry.

Now that I have described what it feels like to be trans-invalidated, and how this phenomenon is reinforced and exacerbated by mainstream psychology, I want to turn our attention to what is perhaps the most insidious form of invalidation: sexualization. A recent American Psychological Association Task Force on the Sexualization of Girls defined sexualization as occurring when any one of the four following criteria are fulfilled: "[A] person's value comes only from his or her sexual appeal or behavior, to the exclusion of other characteristics; a person is held to a standard that equates physical attractiveness (narrowly defined) with being sexy; a person is sexually objectified—that is, made into a thing for others' sexual use, rather than seen as a person with the capacity for independent action and decision making; and/or sexuality is inappropriately imposed upon a person."[26] It is the nonconsensual nature of sexualization that distinguishes it from healthy sexuality.

Trans people are often sexualized in our culture, and this sexualization constitutes a form of invalidation. For example, we live in a culture where it is considered rude, disrespectful, harassing, and even dehumanizing, to ask strangers or even acquaintances graphic questions about their sex lives or their genitals. Yet, those of us who are out as trans, or who are discovered to be trans, are often barraged by these sorts of questions. The very fact that people assume that it's okay to ask a trans person (but not a cis person) such inappropriate questions indicates that we are not seen as fully human or deserving of the same rights and respect that cisgender people receive.

While people may be sexualized in different ways and for different reasons, the fact that our culture is heterosexual-male-centric ensures that the sexualization of those who are female-bodied and feminine in gender expression is the most common and pervasive form of sexualization in our culture. And there is a large body of research demonstrating that sexualization has very serious, negative ramifications on the lives of girls and women. For example, it's been shown that individuals who are sexualized are seen as less than human, are not treated with empathy, are not taken as seriously, and are seen as less competent and intelligent than individuals who are not sexualized.[27] Research also indicates that the media plays an important role in reinforcing the sexualization of women. According to the APA Task Force: "Across several studies, women and men exposed to sexually objectifying images of women from mainstream media . . . were found to be significantly more accepting of rape myths (e.g., the belief that women invite rape by engaging in certain behaviors), sexual harassment, sex role stereotypes, interpersonal violence, and adversarial sexual beliefs about relationships." They conclude that ". . . exposure to sexualized depictions of women may lead to global thoughts that 'women are seductive and frivolous sex objects' . . . and 'foster an overall climate that does not value girls' and women's voices or contributions to society.'"[28]

Like our cisgender counterparts, trans women and others on the trans female/feminine spectrum are routinely sexualized in our culture.[29] In her excellent book *How Sex Changed: A History of Transsexuality in the United States,* Joanne Meyerowitz chronicles the rise of (what she calls) the "eroticization" of trans women."[30] It began in the early 1960s (less than a decade after the mainstream public first became aware of transsexuality), when "tabloid newspapers and pulp publishers produced a stream of articles and cheap paperback books on MTFs who had worked as female impersonators, strippers, or prostitutes," which were often accompanied by "photos that revealed breasts, legs, and buttocks."[31] These stories focused predominantly on the subjects' "unbridled sexual desires," and Meyerowitz comments that they gave the impression that, "the truth of sex change lay in its sexual acts."[32]

By the late 1960s, the sexualization of transsexual women had reached mainstream publishers and movie producers. Perhaps the most notable, early example of this is Gore Vidal's *Myra Breckinridge,*[33] which became a best selling novel in 1968. Myra, who is arguably the first fictional transsexual woman character to garner mainstream attention, embodies several stereotypes projected onto transsexual women that have since recurred over and over again in the media. First, Myra does not identify as a woman, but rather as a homosexual man who has transitioned to female in order to seduce men. In addition to being purposefully sexually deceptive, Myra repeatedly boasts that no man can resist her and she discusses her own female attributes, not in terms of feeling comfortable or right being in her own body (as most transsexuals do), but rather in terms of their capability to entice men. Further, she has an insatiable sexual appetite and engages in sex acts that some would consider deviant or even predatory—for example, there is a thirty-page passage in the book that explicitly chronicles her raping a man with a dildo.[34]

These assumptions—that trans women are inherently sexually promiscuous, sexually deceptive, sexually deviant, and sexually motivated in our transitions—persist in what are perhaps the three most common trans woman archetypes seen in the media over the years: the gay man who transitions to female in order to seduce unsuspecting straight men, the male "pervert" who transitions to female in order to fulfill some kind of bizarre sex fantasy, and the overrepresentation of trans women as sex workers.[35] In sharp contrast, transsexual men are not typically portrayed in a hypersexual manner, nor are they depicted as being sexually motivated in their transitions. Instead, the most common ulterior motive projected onto trans men is that they transition in order to obtain male privilege. Because women are viewed as the "lesser sex" in our culture, people often cannot understand why anyone would give up being a man in order to become a relatively disempowered woman. So they assume that trans women transition in order to obtain the one type of power that women are perceived as having in our society: the ability to be sexualized and to be objects of heterosexual male desire. Thus, the hypersexualization of trans women and our motives for transitioning merely reflects the implicit cultural assumption that women as a whole have no value beyond our ability to be sexualized.[36]

Before moving on, I should make two quick points. First, in her historical analysis of transsexuality, Meyerowitz makes the case that, as the media's (and the public's) interest in trans women became increasingly sexualizing and sexually explicit, their interest in trans men declined reciprocally.[37] Thus, the relative invisibility of trans men in the media is a direct result of media's inability to sexualize them—a difficulty that no doubt stems from the fact that maleness and masculinity are not typically sexualized or objectified in our culture.

Second, the societal sexualization of trans female/feminine identities has a very real negative impact on trans women's lives. Many trans women find that, when others are aware of our trans status, we are often bombarded by objectifying comments and sexually explicit propositions that are typically far more hardcore, debasing, and frequently occurring than what we normally experience when we are presumed to be cis women.[38] Because nonconsensual sexualization is inherently disempowering and dehumanizing, such incidents are quite often linked to transphobic discrimination, harassment, and violence.[39]

The sexualization of trans women, and the reciprocal invisibility of trans men, occurs not only in mainstream culture and in the media, but also in the field of psychology. Historically, psychologists and psychiatrists have regularly sexualized trans people on the trans female/feminine spectrum (while largely ignoring those on the trans male/masculine spectrum) with regards to taxonomy, theories of etiology, descriptions of case histories, and diagnoses.[40] For instance, it is well documented that many gatekeepers have based their recommendations for sex reassignment on whether they considered the trans woman in question to be physically attractive and/or willing to dress and act in a hyperfeminine manner.[41] And while trans people on both the trans female/feminine and trans male/masculine spectrums are currently pathologized under the diagnosis of Gender Identity Disorder (which notably focuses on gender identity and expression rather than sexuality), only trans female/feminine-spectrum individuals can have their gender identities and expressions additionally pathologized as "paraphilias," a category of disorders that are characterized by "recurrent, intense sexual urges, fantasies, or behaviors that involve unusual objects, activities, or situations."[42]

One trans female/feminine-specific paraphilia currently listed in the *DSM-IV-TR* is Transvestic Fetishism. Its main criteria is: "Over a period of at least 6 months, in a heterosexual male, recurrent, intense sexually arousing fantasies, sexual urges, or behaviors involving cross-dressing."[43] As Kelley Winters has pointed out: "The very name equates crossdressing with sexual fetishism and social stereotypes of perversion. It serves to sexualize a diagnosis that does not clearly require a sexual context. Crossdressing by males very often represents a social expression of an inner sense of identity. In fact, the clinical literature cites many cases, considered diagnosable under transvestic fetishism, which present no sexual motivation for cross-dressing and by no means represent fetishism."[44]

So in other words, crossdressing in the trans female/feminine direction is presumed to be of a sexual nature even when it is not. Reciprocally, if a woman was aroused by crossdressing in men's clothing (as some are[45]), she could not be diagnosed with Transvestic Fetishism because the diagnosis is specific for heterosexual males. In fact, psychologist Robert Stoller even argued that women who crossdress must really be transsexuals (read: driven by cross-gender identity) rather than transvestites (read: driven by cross-gender arousal). His reasoning was simple: "Men's clothes have no erotic value whatsoever; these people have no clothing fetish."[46]

While I know plenty of women and gay men who would argue with Stoller's claim, I do believe that he was onto something. Because femaleness and femininity are so routinely sexualized in our culture, female clothing is imbued with a kind of sexual symbolism that male clothing does not have.[47] This naturally leads people to presume that crossdressers on the trans female/feminine spectrum must be doing it for sexual reasons even when they are not. This sexual symbolism also explains why many crossdressers and transsexual women pass through stages where they experience some arousal associated with women's clothing. Indeed, many trans female/feminine-spectrum individuals often refer to their "teenage girl" phase—a period early on when they are particularly interested in sexually revealing or provocative women's clothing. This stage parallels what many young cis women go through as teenagers as they literally try on the sexual symbolism associated with femaleness and femininity in our culture. Many trans female/feminine-spectrum individuals eventually come to realize that there is simply more to their desire to be female than sexuality, just as cis women learn that there is more to being a woman than being sexually appealing to others.

In the late 1980s and early 1990s, psychologist Ray Blanchard took the psychological sexualization of trans femininities to new heights with his theory of "autogynephilia."[48] This theory claims that transsexual women come in two (and only two) subtypes, each with a distinct etiology (or cause). Blanchard refers to the first of these subtypes as "homosexual transsexuals," who are conceptualized as being feminine from a very early age, attracted exclusively to men as adults, and who supposedly never experience cross-gender arousal. Proponents of the theory often depict transsexual women belonging to this group as a type of feminine gay man who ultimately transitions to female in order to attract heterosexual men.[49] The second subtype according to Blanchard's scheme are "autogynephilic transsexuals," who are essentially viewed as a type of heterosexual man who, typically around puberty, begins to experience cross-gender arousal in response to imagining themselves as women. Blanchard argued that this cross-gender arousal is a paraphilia and that it eventually becomes the primary factor that drives these individuals to physically transition to female later in life. Thus, Blanchard's model proposes that all transsexual women are sexually motivated in their transitions, and he forwards two subtypes that suspiciously resemble the sexualizing archetypes of trans women—i.e., the gay man who transitions to female to seduce unsuspecting straight men and the male deviant who transitions to fulfill some kind of bizarre sex fantasy—that appear over and over again in the media. Furthermore, his theory does not even attempt to explain FTM transgenderism, mimicking media depictions that sexualize trans women while ignoring trans men. The fact that this theory so blatantly mimics sexualizing stereotypes of trans women that already exist in the culture explains why proponents of the theory cling to it so desperately despite the many lines of evidence demonstrating that trans women do not fall neatly into two distinct subtypes; that, for most trans women, gender dissonance and/or a desire to be female precedes sexual arousal or attraction by several years; and that fantasies and patterns of arousal that Blanchard labels "autogynephilic" also occur in many cisgender women.[50]

Critics of autogynephilia, including myself, have written extensively about the many methodological and theoretical flaws of this theory. So, rather than rehash that evidence, I want to address what is perhaps an even more salient issue, but which has unfortunately received significantly less attention: Why is it exactly that the overwhelming majority of trans women feel that autogynephilia theory is not merely "wrong," but oppressive and invalidating? First, it is extraordinarily nonconsensually sexualizing. It not only assigns sexual motivations to trans women, but it categorizes us as either "homosexual" or "autogynephilic" based upon those supposed sexual motivations. In other words, it reduces us to sexual motivation. As I alluded to earlier, there is an extensive body of psychological research that shows that when people are sexualized, they are not treated with empathy, are not taken as seriously, and are seen as less competent and less intelligent than those who are not sexualized.[51] This is why historically in rape trials, defense lawyers who wanted to undermine the female victim's testimony would ask her lurid questions about her past (or presumed) sexual history, or mention details about what she was wearing when the incident occurred, especially if her outfit was provocative or revealing.[52] Of course, most reasonable people would agree that, in and of themselves, these matters do not excuse rape. So why do lawyers bring them up? Because sexualizing a person invalidates them! It undermines what they have to say. It enables others to see them as less than fully human and without empathy. This is precisely why feminists have worked so hard to eliminate sexual harassment in the workplace and in the public sphere. And this is exactly why most trans women feel that Blanchard's theory and terminology should be eliminated from psychological discourses.

Here is an analogy that I hope will further elucidate this point. What if Blanchard (or someone like him) claimed that all women fell into two distinct groups: those who have "forced" or "rape" fantasies and those who do not.[53] And suppose he labeled women who have rape fantasies "autoraptophiles" and claimed that their female gender identities were merely a secondary effect of their paraphilic desire to be raped. And suppose he (and other proponents of his theory) argued that this terminology should be widely used in the psychological literature under the presumption that one cannot fully understand autoraptophilic women unless you recognize that they are primarily motivated by their desire to be raped. And what if the psychologist who coined this term was appointed to head the *DSM-5* taskforce that would rewrite the section of adjustment disorders, and he proposed that there should be a modifier to Adjustment Disorder: "with Autoraptophilia." What do you think the outcome of this scenario would be?

First, many women—who are already highly sexualized in our culture—would now have to contend with yet another form of nonconsensual sexualization. This form of sexualization would be potentially more threatening than most though, as it would be legitimized by the psychiatric establishment. Those who sexually intimidate, harass, or assault women could cite autoraptophilia (and the fact that it's in the *DSM)* to argue that the woman in question was literally "asking for it." And, if the woman visited a psychotherapist to work through family or relationship issues, she might instead be barraged by annoying and demeaning questions about her sexual fantasies, as though that were the root cause of all of her problems.

I think that most reasonable people will immediately recognize why this hypothetical scenario is so scary. And if it were real, I am sure that most of you—especially those of you who are female—would do whatever you could to stop it. Well, for trans women, this scenario has pretty much come true with regards to autogynephilia. Ray Blanchard has been named to chair the Paraphilia subworkgroup for the *DSM-5,* and he has proposed changing the Transvestic Fetishism diagnosis to Transvestic Disorder with one of two modifiers: with

Fetishism, or with Autogynephilia.[54] While the diagnosis supposedly targets "heterosexual males" who crossdress, the psychological literature regarding autogynephilia (the bulk of it written by Blanchard) repeatedly claims that lesbian, bisexual, and asexual trans women are really just heterosexual men with a fantasy problem. Therefore, according to Blanchard's proposal, a queer-identified trans woman (such as myself) could theoretically be diagnosed as having "Transvestic Disorder" any time that I have any kind of sexual urge while wearing women's clothing. Since I wear women's clothing pretty much every day of my life these days, my sexuality would presumably be considered perpetually transvestically disordered according to this diagnosis.

I should mention that Blanchard has also proposed significantly expanding the *DSM's* definition of "paraphilia" to include: "any intense and persistent sexual interest other than sexual interest in genital stimulation or preparatory fondling with phenotypically normal, consenting adult human partners."[55] Having read many of Blanchard's writings, I can tell you that he does not consider transsexual bodies to be "phenotypically normal." So, according to this definition, anyone who has an "intense and persistent sexual interest" in me is automatically deemed to have a paraphilia. Thus, Blanchard intends not only to paraphilize[56] all of my present and future sexual partners, but to reduce me to the status of a mere fetish object. To him, my identity, my body, my entire person is nothing more than an expression of aberrant sexuality.

Because autogynephilia sexualizes trans women (thus invalidating us), it has been employed to erase trans women's subjectivity. For example, there are many exceptions to Blanchard's two-type classification scheme: There are lesbian, bisexual, and asexual trans women who have never experienced cross-gender arousal, and there are heterosexual trans women who have. In his writings, Blanchard routinely mischaracterizes the first group as autogynephiles who are lying about not having experienced cross-gender arousal, and the second group as autogynephiles who are lying about their sexual orientation.[57] In addition to being bad science, such accusations essentially portray lesbian, bisexual, and asexual trans women as being both hypersexual and pathological liars. In fact, I would argue that it is Blanchard's hypersexualization of trans women that enables him to portray us as liars (in a manner similar to how defense lawyers portray rape victims as hypersexual or promiscuous in order to invalidate their testimony).

This strategy has been most effectively used by Bailey in his book *The Man Who Would Be Queen*. First, Bailey describes trans women's bodies in sexually graphic terms, he repeatedly comments on how attractive (or not attractive) certain trans women are, he suggests that certain trans women might be "especially well-suited to prostitution," and (of course) he repeatedly stresses that all trans women are sexually motivated in our transitions. While doing that, he also relentlessly accuses those trans women who deny being sexually motivated of lying, misreporting, deceiving, and misrepresenting themselves.[58] The one-two punch of the "hypersexual" and "pathological liar" stereotypes, of course, reinforce the idea that trans women are mentally unstable and unreliable, which (once again) reinforces Bailey's authority as a psychologist to speak on our behalves, as we are presumably too riddled with psychopathology to speak for ourselves. Given the effectiveness of this strategy, it is not surprising that other sexologists have also tried to dismiss trans women's legitimate critiques of autogynephilia theory, or our expressions of outrage over its invalidating terminology, as being mere manifestations of our supposed mental instability and sexual deviancy.[59]

So, in summary, according to mainstream psychology, I am a lying hypersexual deviant whose opinions are unobjective and irreparably tainted by my supposed mental disorder. And this view gives scientific legitimacy to those who wish to invalidate me. This is why I am legitimately angry. And this is why I think that overturning mainstream psychological depictions of trans people is a crucial step if we ever hope to obtain social legitimacy and gender equity. For decades, trans people have raged against the machine, but the machine has not taken us very seriously. But, thankfully, this has slowly started to change, as we have begun to find our collective voice and to speak on our own terms about our experiences, desires, and our perspectives on gender and transgenderism. And there are a growing number of allies and advocates in the medical and mental health fields who have shown a willingness to listen to what we have to say, who recognize how injurious the tropes of sexualization and mental inferiority are to gender-variant people, and who treat gender-variant people, not as mere research subjects or "natural experiments," but as human beings who have autonomy and agency. And together, as activists, allies, and advocates, we can work to displace the current psychological establishment in favor of a system that places trans people's needs first and is free of trans-invalidations.

31

Stop Sexualizing Us!

This is a speech that I gave at the GID Reform Now! protest rally at the Annual Meeting of the American Psychiatric Association in San Francisco on May 18, 2009—the picture of me with the megaphone on the front cover of this book was taken at that protest as I was giving this speech. This chapter is admittedly less nuanced than other things that I have written on this subject, as it was meant to be a crowd-rallying call-and-response chant.

For decades, the general public, and especially the media, have had a lurid fascination with trans people's bodies and sexualities. From talk shows like *Jerry Springer*, to reality shows like *There's Something About Miriam*, novels like *Myra Breckinridge*, and the countless movies that portray trans women almost exclusively as either sex workers, sexual predators, and sexual deviants.[1] This hypersexualization of transgenderism predominantly targets trans women and others on the trans female/feminine spectrum—because in a world where women are routinely objectified, and where a woman's worth is often judged based on her sexual appeal, it is no surprise that many people presume that those of us who were assigned a male sex at birth, but who identify as women and/or dress in a feminine manner, must do so for primarily sexual reasons.

We are here today to say to the APA, stop sexualizing us!

This sexualization of trans female/feminine gender expression also runs rampant in psychiatry. In the current version of the *DSM*, there is a diagnosis called Transvestic Fetishism, which specifically targets "male" expressions of femininity. When nontransgender women wear traditionally feminine clothing, they are viewed as healthy. But when the same behavior occurs in people assigned a male sex at birth, the APA deems it psychopathology. This is hypocrisy!

We say to the APA, stop sexualizing us!

And while crossdressing by men is often an expression of femininity, or of an inner gender identity, Transvestic Fetishism presumes that the act of wearing feminine clothing must (in and of itself) be an expression of aberrant sexuality.

We say to the APA, stop sexualizing us!

Studies have shown that, "Cross-dressers … are virtually indistinguishable from non-cross-dressers."[2] Despite the empirical lack of evidence that cross-dressing is associated with psychopathology, the APA continues to mischaracterize crossdressing as a mental disorder.

We say to the APA, stop sexualizing us!

And if that wasn't bad enough, Transvestic Fetishism has been categorized in the Paraphilias section of the *DSM*—the category that used to be called Sexual Deviations. This section used to be home to diagnoses like Homosexuality and Nymphomania—societal double standards that for decades were reified in the *DSM* as mental disorders. Like its predecessors, crossdressing is a harmless, autonomous, or consensual activity that is unnecessarily stigmatized in both the culture at large and within psychiatry. We are here to call for the removal of all forms of crossdressing and transvesticism from the *DSM*.

We say to the APA, stop sexualizing us!

And while there are many psychologists who understand the distinction between gender and sexuality, who understand that trans people's identities, personalities, and sexual histories are infinitely varied, the APA passed over such people, and instead tapped Ray Blanchard to chair of the subworkgroup for the next *DSM* Paraphilia section.

We say to the APA, stop sexualizing us!

Blanchard is the inventor of the controversial theory of autogynephilia, which claims that all transgender women are sexually motivated in our transitions. Despite the overwhelming scientific and experiential evidence that contradicts his theory, it has gained traction in the psychological literature—including a mention in the current *DSM*—precisely because it reifies hypersexualized stereotypes of trans women.

We say to the APA, stop sexualizing us!

Blanchard views trans female/feminine-spectrum individuals the way most movie producers do. To him, we are all either gay men who become women in order to attract straight men, or we are male "perverts" who become women in order to fulfill some kind of bizarre sex fantasy.

We say to the APA, stop sexualizing us!

Blanchard not only believes that we are sexually deviant, but in the psychological literature, he has forwarded his belief that those people who are attracted to us—our lovers, partners, and spouses—must also suffer from a paraphilic disorder.[3]

We say to the APA, stop sexualizing us!

Blanchard's theories have been challenged by a majority of trans activists, allies, advocates, and countless trans-knowledgeable psychologists and therapists. Yet, the APA selected him to play a lead role in rewriting trans female/feminine gender expression back into the *DSM*.

We say to the APA, stop sexualizing us!

When you sexualize someone, you invalidate them. That's why feminists have worked so hard to put an end to sexual harassment in the workplace, and it's why we as trans activists seek an end to the psychiatric sexualization of trans female/feminine gender expression.

We say to the APA, stop sexualizing us!

Clothing choice does not constitute a psychopathology. We call for the complete removal of crossdressing and transvestism (in any form) from the *DSM*.

We say to the APA, stop sexualizing us!

32

The Beauty in Us

In our culture, there is a correlation between viewing trans people as "abnormal" and "disordered," and assuming that people who find us attractive must also be "abnormal" and "disordered." Sometimes we (as trans people) internalize these messages, and dismiss people who express attraction toward us as "fetishists." In this speech (which I gave at the 2009 San Francisco Trans March), I forwarded a different view of beauty and attraction, one that is more empowering for both trans people and our partners. I expand on some of these ideas in Chapters 42 and 43.

Unfortunately, we live in a society where many people view trans people as unnatural and illegitimate. And one of the most effective ways in which they try to invalidate us is by assuming that we are somehow unlovable, that no one in their right mind would find us desirable. And sadly, many of us end up believing this ourselves.

When I was a teenager and young adult, one of the things that helped keep me in the closet was the fact that I believed that if I did ever come out as wanting to be a girl, or if I were to ever physically transition to female, that others would undoubtedly see me as a freak, and nobody would want me as their partner. I worried that I would become unlovable. And you know something? I was wrong.

Sure, the majority of people in our culture are too insecure about their own gender or sexuality to ever consider dating a trans person. But there are lots of people who aren't that way. When I came out as a crossdresser fifteen years ago, I went onto have relationships with several women who were totally cool with that aspect of my person. And since my transition eight years ago, I have met many people—women, men, and genderqueer—who have expressed sexual or romantic interest in me. For me, the problem hasn't been finding someone who desires me, but rather finding someone whose interests coincide with what I want out of an encounter or relationship. And if you think about it, that is something that everyone, whether trans or not, has to contend with.

This is why I get really frustrated when people automatically presume that any person who is attracted to, or has sex with, a trans person must automatically have some kind of "fetish." This is extremely invalidating, as it insinuates that we cannot be loved or appreciated as whole people, but rather only as a "fetish objects." Sure, there are some people who are specifically attracted to the fact that we are trans, and some of us might find that to be uncomfortable or annoying. But I have also experienced men (who were presumably unaware that I was trans) starring rather obsessively at my chest. But nobody ever seriously accuses such people of having a "breast fetish" or of being "breast chasers," because breasts are seen as a perfectly normal and valid thing to be attracted to. Similarly, there are people out there who specifically date people because of their money or social status, but nobody ever accuses them of having a "fetish." People only use the term "fetish" when they believe that the person in question is inherently undesirable—and I refuse to buy into that mindset!

Instead of buying into the fetish mindset, perhaps we should reconceptualize our transness as though it were any other trait. For example, I happen to be freckly. Some of my lovers are indifferent to my freckles. Others think they are attractive, and they will sometimes tell me how much they like them. These compliments do not bother me in the least, provided that my freckle-admirers are not *only* interested in me for my freckles. In other words, I am fine with people appreciating my freckles provided that they are also interested in other parts of my person.

Truth be told, when it comes to potential lovers, there are only two reactions that I refuse to tolerate. I would never want to date someone who was specifically into the fact that I am trans, but who couldn't care less about the rest of my person—those are the people who truly "fetishize" us, who reduce us to objects. And I would never want to date someone who liked me overall as a person, but who was particularly disturbed by my transness. Anything in between those two extremes is something I can work with. And frankly, I am proud of being trans. So I would much prefer being with someone who appreciates my transness over someone who is uncomfortable about, or unsettled by, that aspect of my person.

We are beautiful people who are legitimately desirable. We are not "fetish" objects! And people who find us attractive are not "chasers," but rather they are simply people who see beauty in us. Because our culture deems us undesirable, our lovers and partners are often expected to explain why they choose to be with us. Others may start to question their sexuality, or they may be ostracized from their straight or gay or lesbian communities. In a sense, they share a bit of our stigma—a stigma that is based on the presumption that we are unlovable. And we shouldn't stand for that!

So, let's purge the phrases "tranny fetish" and "tranny chaser" from our vocabularies. Let's celebrate our lovers, partners, and spouses for seeing the beauty in us. And let's give a big shout out to all of the significant others who are standing by our sides today supporting us. And importantly, let's remember that we are beautiful, and fabulous, and desirable, and deserving of love.

33

Reconceptualizing "Autogynephilia" as Female/Feminine Embodiment Fantasies

This chapter offers a brief summary of my research into, and current understanding of, the phenomenon formerly known as "autogynephilia."

In early conversations that I participated in with other trans activists and advocates in 2008 (in the wake of the new *DSM-5* workgroup appointments), it seemed clear that one of the things working against us in our petitioning for "good" *DSM* revisions (or preventing "bad" revisions from happening) was the lack of peer-reviewed research articles supporting our case, as these are supposedly the only evidence that counts toward reshaping *DSM* diagnoses (although apparently you can avoid this requirement if you chair a *DSM* subworkgroup; see next chapter for details). For instance, while countless thoughtful and thorough critiques of Ray Blanchard's theory of autogynephilia existed on the Internet, in trans-themed publications like *Transgender Tapestry*, and books like *Whipping Girl,* and Kelley Winters's 2008 book *Gender Madness in American Psychiatry,*[1] none of them would officially be taken into consideration. In contrast, the dozen or so (largely redundant) Blanchard articles referencing "autogynephilia" that were published in sexology journals would be considered relevant and may even be referenced in the new *DSM*.

Recognizing this, I began to focus my efforts on writing a critical review about Blanchard's theory of autogynephilia for a peer-reviewed journal. That article was eventually published in 2010 in *The International Journal of Transgenderism* under the title "The Case Against Autogynephilia"—for those interested, a draft of that paper can be downloaded from my website.[2] Unbeknownst to me at the time, Charles Moser was working on a similarly-themed paper, "Blanchard's Autogynephilia Theory: A Critique," which was also published in 2010.[3] Both of our papers presented numerous lines of evidence that disprove the main underpinnings of autogynephilia theory, namely, the assertions that trans female/feminine-spectrum people can be readily divided into two clear-cut categories based upon sexual orientation and the presence or absence of "autogynephilia," and that "autogynephilia" is the primary underlying cause of gender dysphoria and desire to transition in trans women who experience it.

Where our papers differ is that, while Moser continues to use the term "autogynephilia" to refer to sexual fantasies and patterns of arousal in which the "thought or image of oneself as a woman" plays a contributing role, I instead argue that we should no longer use this term for the following reasons:

- There is a several-decades-long history in which "autogynephilia" has been described in the scientific/psychiatric literature as both a sexual orientation and a cause of gender dysphoria and transsexuality. Since neither appears to be the case, it would be misleading to continue using the term in this manner.

- There is a similarly long history of "autogynephilia" being described as a "male"-specific phenomenon and a paraphilia—these notions are interrelated, as (according to psychiatric dogma) paraphilias are extremely rare or nonexistent in women.[4] However, recent studies have shown that many cisgender women (up to 93 percent) have experienced "erotic arousal to the thought or image of oneself as a woman."[5] Therefore, we should no longer use a term that is so closely associated with paraphilias and "erotic anomalies" (as Blanchard calls them) to describe what appears to be a relatively common (and non-pathological) form of sexual thought or fantasy experienced by many female/feminine-identified people.

- "Autogynephilia" (as defined in the scientific/psychiatric literature) conceptualizes trans women as "sexually deviant men," and thus is unnecessarily stigmatizing and invalidating of trans identities. For this very reason, the concept of "autogynephilia" has been increasingly appropriated by lay people who forward anti-transgender ideologies and political agendas.[6]

For these reasons, in my review I argued that we should replace the misleading and stigmatizing label "autogynephilia" with the more comprehensive (and less pathologizing) term *Female/Feminine Embodiment Fantasies (FEFs)*.[7]

Here is the rationale for this nomenclature: I refer to them as "fantasies," because that is what they are: a type of sexual/erotic thought or fantasy. It is widely acknowledged (in both sexology and society) that sexual fantasies vary greatly in the population, and if two people just so happen to have a similar fantasy, it does not necessarily mean that they share the same underlying "condition" or are a similar "type" of person.[8] (In contrast, Blanchard argued that there are two distinct types or categories of trans female/feminine people—"autogynephilic" and "androphilic"—distinguished by the presence or absence of the paraphilic condition "autogynephilia."[9]) The word "embodiment" references the well-accepted notion in philosophy and cognitive studies that our thoughts, perceptions, and desires do not happen in a vacuum—they occur within, and are shaped by, our bodies. As I pointed out in *Whipping Girl,* most of our sexual fantasies involve (at least) two bodies: our own body, and the body of the person we are attracted to (for a more rigorous exploration of this, see Talia Bettcher's excellent article "When Selves Have Sex").[10] In fantasies centered on sexual attraction, most of the attention or emphasis may be placed on our imagined partner's body and behaviors, but our own bodies and behaviors are nevertheless often present (e.g., we may imagine them doing something to our body, or our body doing something to theirs). In "embodiment fantasies," more (or perhaps in some cases, all) of the attention and emphasis is instead shifted toward our own (real or imagined) bodies and behaviors. Finally, the "female/feminine" in FEFs refers to the fact that aspects of our own (real or imagined) female body and/or feminine gender expression play a central erotic role in the fantasy (although other erotic components, such as our imagined partner, may also exist in the fantasy).

For similar reasons, I favor the term Male/Masculine Embodiment Fantasies (MEFs) over the psychopathologizing term "autoandrophilia."[11] While MEFs do exist, they seem to be less common than FEFs. In Chapters 14 and 17 of *Whipping Girl,* and Chapter 30 of this book, I have laid out a compelling case that the relative prevalence of FEFs is foundationally rooted in, and typically viewed through the lens of, our cultural tendency to sexualize and objectify femaleness and femininity. This explains why many people (of diverse sexual orientations and anatomies) who are (or wish to be) female and/or feminine report having experienced such fantasies or erotic thoughts either occasionally or often. It also explains why male- and/or masculine-identified people—whose real or imagined bodies no doubt play some role in their sexual fantasies (e.g., they might imagine other people doing things *to* their penis and/or themselves doing things *with* their penis)—do not typically view their bodies as central to their fantasies, as we all culturally conditioned to view male/masculine bodies as the *subjects* (rather than the objects) of sexual desire.

In the aforementioned *Whipping Girl* chapters and in "The Case Against Autogynephilia," I further argued that a few additional factors are likely to contribute to the observed trends in the prevalence and demographics of FEFs and MEFs. First, while neither of these phenomena is transgender-specific, they do seem to be more common (or commonly reported) in pre- and non-transition transgender-spectrum people. It makes perfect sense that someone who has not yet attained their imagined or identified sexed body, or who are unable to safely share their desired gender expression or presentation with the world, would focus more attention on those elements in their fantasies than people who can take those aspects of themselves for granted. Indeed, this would help to explain the well-documented dramatic decrease in intensity and frequency of FEFs reported by many trans women once they socially and physically transition.[12]

Second, one might expect that the intensity or frequency of FEFs would be more pronounced in individuals who are sexually attracted to femaleness/femininity more generally (e.g., in their partners); an analogous correlation might be expected between MEFs and attraction to maleness/masculinity in others. This would explain the increased levels of FEFs reported in lesbian and bisexual trans women compared to heterosexual trans women (as reported in many previous studies), and numerous lines of anecdotal evidence indicating that MEFs are not uncommon in gay trans men, and in female-assigned people who identify as "girlfags."[13] Similarly, numerous cis femme-identified queer women have told me (in informal conversations) that they regularly experience FEFs. While more formal investigations would be necessary to confirm this anecdotal evidence, the notion that attraction to femaleness/femininity and experiencing FEFs (or attraction to maleness/masculinity and experiencing MEFs) may be correlated to some degree seems reasonable and helps explain previously reported patterns of FEFs in trans female/feminine individuals.

Finally, in addition to our cultural tendency to sexualize femaleness/femininity, I argued that other aspects of traditional sexism (i.e., the assumption that femaleness/femininity is inferior to maleness/masculinity) may help create the correlations in transgender trajectories and sexualities that Blanchard's theory attempted to explain. Throughout *Whipping Girl*, I describe how traditional sexism leads to *effemimania*, where feminine expressions in male-assigned children and adults receive far more scrutiny and derision than masculine expressions in female-assigned people. While the latter group remains relatively free to openly express their masculine inclinations throughout their lives (whether they grow up to be tomboys, butches, or trans male/masculine individuals), the former group faces significant pressure to hide or repress any female/feminine inclinations they may have. Historically, this pressure has resulted in two diverging life paths for people on the trans female/feminine spectrum. Those who were unable to hide or repress their tendencies (e.g., children on the extreme feminine or cross-gender-identified side of the spectrum) came to identify with their femininity, viewing it as simply a natural part of their personality and/or an extension of a female gender identity. In contrast, those children who *were* able to repress such behaviors would come to initially identify as boys, and (as a result of traditional sexism) be embarrassed by any subsequent female/feminine tendencies they experienced. This explains why their initial gender explorations would likely involve a male (public)/female (private) dichotomy that is a hallmark of many crossdressers' identities. And given their initial male identity (and the privileges associated with it), any fascination or eroticization associated with said gender explorations (e.g., FEFs) would likely be fueled by the *mystification/exoticization of the Other*—a phenomenon documented at great length in the humanities and social studies. This repression-mystification hypothesis (which shares some similarities with Veale et al.'s identity-defense model of gender-variant development) provides a nonpathologizing explanation for the two "types" of trans women Blanchard describes, while also being consistent with current trends (e.g., lesbian- and bisexual-identified trans women transitioning significantly earlier in life without a "crossdresser phase") and more recent evidence that FEFs "may be a historically fading phenomenon."[14] In other words, with increasing acceptance of transgender and gender non-conforming children, there is less pressure put on such individuals to repress their female/feminine inclinations, and thus less of a tendency for them to eroticize their own gender explorations later in life.

So that is a brief introduction to my multifactorial model to explain the phenomenon formerly known as "autogynephilia." This model allows for a variety of outcomes, as each of the previously described potential factors simply increases the likelihood of (but does not strictly determine) the presence of FEFs or MEFs within any given individual. Like all sexual fantasies, FEFs and MEFs are not a permanent condition—they may appear, disappear, reappear, intensify, de-intensify, evolve, or vary for unknown/inexplicable reasons. Unlike Blanchard's theory, the existence of FEFs and MEFs does not contradict or deny the known diversity in transgender identities, trajectories, and sexualities.

34

Trans People Are Still "Disordered" in the DSM-5

This chapter is a revised and updated version of two pieces that were originally posted on my blog in December 2012, after the diagnoses in the new DSM-5 had been finalized.[1] An alternative revamping of these blog posts was published in the online journal Social Text *in 2013.[2]*

On the morning of December 3, 2012, I woke up to find my Twitter feed full of article links celebrating the supposed fact that transgender people are no longer considered "disordered" according to the newly finalized *DSM-5*.[3] The *DSM* gets revised every ten to twenty years or so, and diagnoses sometimes get modified, expanded, or completely removed. The change that people on Twitter were celebrating was the fact that the previous diagnosis of Gender Identity Disorder (GID) would be formally changed to Gender Dysphoria in the *DSM-5*.

Admittedly, the new Gender Dysphoria diagnosis is an improvement over GID for a number of reasons—Kelley Winters of *GID Reform* describes some of these improvements, as well as many of the lingering problems with the new diagnosis (for instance, that the biased wording of the diagnosis seems to encourage gender-reparative psychotherapies over transitioning, and renders happy and healthy post-transition trans people as "forever diagnosable" with Gender Dysphoria).[4] Despite some of these drawbacks, many in the trans community seemed excited that the change in name means that transgender people are no longer literally described as "disordered" in the *DSM*.

But the problem is that this is patently untrue.

When the new *DSM-5* workgroup on Sexual and Gender Identity Disorders was chosen back in 2008, virtually all of the focus was on what that committee would do with GID. This was understandable given that this was the diagnosis that trans people were generally required to obtain if they wished to access the means to physical and/or legal transition. In addition, the related diagnosis GID in Children had long been used to justify reparative therapies for gender-non-conforming children.[5] While concern over GID was certainly warranted, the greater trans community gave short shrift to the other *DSM* diagnosis that targeted transgender people, namely, Transvestic Fetishism. And the revised version of that diagnosis remains in the *DSM-5* under the new name Transvestic Disorder.

Unlike GID, Transvestic Fetishism (and now its successor Transvestic Disorder) resides in the Paraphilia section, which contains several sexual crimes (e.g., pedophilia, frotteurism, exhibitionism) and a handful of other generally consensual but unnecessarily stigmatized sexual acts (such as fetishism and BDSM) that are considered to be pathologies by some psychiatrists. While the existence of a trans-specific diagnosis in this particular section of the *DSM* should horrify trans people, many I have spoken with seemed either unaware of, or relatively unconcerned by, the existence of this diagnosis, perhaps because (at the time) it could not be applied to trans male/masculine folks, nor to trans female/feminine-spectrum people who are sexually oriented toward men. While I had been concerned about this diagnosis for quite some time, I became even more alarmed when I learned that Ray Blanchard had been named Chair of the *DSM-5* Paraphilia subworkgroup that would revise it and the other diagnoses in that section.

I sometimes joke that Ray Blanchard is my arch-nemesis (after all, every trans narrative needs an arch-nemesis!). I say this because we so drastically differ in our views on sexuality and trans people. Where I see valid gender identities, Blanchard sees psychopathologies. Where I see autonomous and consensual sexual activities, he sees "erotic target location errors" and "abnormalities." While I have spent a decade challenging trans-misogyny, Blanchard has spent several decades psychiatrically sexualizing trans female/feminine-spectrum people, most notably via his theory of "autogynephilia." So I was extremely concerned about what potential revisions to the Paraphilia section he might concoct.

An early ominous sign came in 2009, during a presentation Blanchard gave in which he proposed significantly broadening the category of "paraphilia" to include: "any intense and persistent sexual interest other than sexual interest in genital stimulation or preparatory fondling with phenotypically normal, physically mature, consenting human partners"—this definition has since been incorporated (almost verbatim) into the *DSM-5*.[6] The term "phenotypically normal" implies that feeling sexual attraction toward anyone who is anatomically or behaviorally atypical—such as people who are differently-sized, disabled, or gender variant, to name a few possibilities—constitutes a paraphilia (and Blanchard's other writings support this interpretation).[7] This language reinforces the cultural belief that able-bodied cisgender women and men are the only legitimate objects of sexual desire.

In addition, Blanchard's proposal asserted that paraphilias include all "erotic interests that are not focused on copulatory or precopulatory behaviors, or the equivalent behaviors in same-sex adult partners."[8] So essentially, all forms of sexual arousal and expression that are not centered on genital penetration sex may now be considered paraphilic. The *DSM-5* specifically lists relatively mundane acts (by today's standards) such as spanking, binding, and phone sex as paraphilias, and one cannot help but wonder whether masturbation in the absence of a partner might also be considered paraphilic according to this definition.[9] And in a subsequent interview, Blanchard insinuated that, if he were to "start from scratch," he would be inclined to reclassify homosexuality as a paraphilia on the basis that it is a non-reproductive sexual activity.[10]

Blanchard and his supporters would likely point out that the new *DSM-5* language states that a paraphilia only becomes a "paraphilic disorder" (i.e., a diagnosable mental illness) when it is associated with "distress, impairment, or harm to others"[11] But as many authors have pointed out, this is basically a distinction without a difference.[12] After all, one can feel distress about being unemployed or being short, but neither "unemployment" nor "small stature" are listed in the *DSM*. Therefore, the new *DSM-5* paraphilia definition implies that atypical and non-reproductive sexualities are disordered *a priori*, otherwise there would be no reason to mention them in the *DSM*. In addition, "distress" and "impairment" will always remain somewhat open to individual mental health professionals' interpretations.[13] For instance, if a male crossdresser is comfortable with that aspect of his person, but is distressed about his relationship (which has been in turmoil since he came out to his partner as a crossdresser), some therapists (particularly those who harbor negative views of crossdressing) might decide that the client's distress is "the immediate or ultimate result of the paraphilia."[14]

Furthermore, outside of mental health settings (and even when not accompanied by distress or impairment), the mere labeling or listing of consensual, noncriminal behaviors as "paraphilias" (e.g., in the *DSM*) can lead to considerable discrimination against individuals who express them (e.g., in the judicial system, healthcare settings, the media).[15] When Blanchard was recently asked about such a possibility for discrimination with regards to Gender Dysphoria or Transvestic Disorder, he flippantly responded, "how many people who make a joke about trannies consult the *DSM* first?"— this ignores the countless examples of people who have cited the *DSM* in their attempts to invalidate trans people.[16]

While the expanded paraphilia definition implies that a plethora of "paraphilic disorders" potentially exist, only eight are explicitly categorized and detailed in the *DSM-5*. One of these is Transvestic Disorder, and it seems to have been personally spearheaded by Blanchard, as he was the author of the original proposed revision that was announced in 2009 (and which I previously critiqued in Chapter 30).[17] That initial revision was rather similar to the Transvestic Fetishism diagnosis in the previous *DSM*, but with the addition of "autogynephilia" (along with "fetishism") as a *specifier* (meaning that one can be diagnosed as having "Transvestic Fetishism *with Autogynephilia*"). While the World Professional Association for Transgender Health (WPATH) repeatedly argued that there is "not enough solid empirical evidence to include these specifiers," they nevertheless remain in the final Transvestic Disorder diagnosis.[18]

But then in 2010, after the formal period for submitting input and comments to the *DSM-5* committees had passed, the diagnosis was quietly revised several more times, and significantly broadened in the process.[19] The first of these changes was the removal of the phrase "heterosexual male" from the diagnosis, which means that it can now potentially be applied to both trans female/feminine- *and* trans male/masculine-spectrum people, and regardless of their sexual orientation.[20] While many trans women and trans men may presume that they are somehow exempt from this diagnosis (on the basis that they do not consider themselves to be "cross-dressed"), as I explained in Chapter 30 this is not necessarily the case. The *DSM-5* does not state whether "cross-dressing" is defined in relation to birth-assigned sex or self-identified gender—presumably this is left up to individual mental health professionals to decide for themselves (and much of the previous psychiatric literature favors the former interpretation). Furthermore, the fact that the *DSM-5* clearly states that an individual can be diagnosed with both Transvestic Disorder and Gender Dysphoria simultaneously (according to both diagnoses), and that Gender Dysphoria does not have an "exit clause" (meaning that post-transition transsexuals are still considered to have the condition), together seem to imply that trans women and trans men can be considered to be in a perpetual state of being "cross-dressed" and therefore diagnosable with Transvestic Disorder if they meet the other criteria (which are discussed below).

Along with this broadening of language, many of us were surprised to find that Blanchard also added "autoandrophilia" (i.e., "sexually aroused by thought or image of self as male") as a new specifier to this proposed diagnosis, even though at the time, no empirical research whatsoever existed on the phenomenon.[21] In a 2013 interview, Blanchard admitted that he did not believe that "autoandrophilia" even existed, and that he only proposed it in order to avoid accusations of sexism—this struck many people as an extremely cavalier way to go about crafting a psychiatric diagnosis.[22] The specifier of "autoandrophilia" was ultimately not included in the final *DSM-5* diagnosis, although its broadening to potentially include "cross-dressed" people of any gender or sexual orientation still remains.

Two other changes were made to Transvestic Disorder during the course of the revision process. The phrase "recurrent and intense sexual fantasies, sexual urges, or sexual behaviors *involving cross-dressing*" was changed to "recurrent and intense sexual arousal *from cross-dressing*, as manifested by fantasies, urges, or behaviors" (emphasis mine). This is a small yet positive change, as it somewhat narrows the scope of the diagnosis, making it less likely that a trans person could be diagnosed with Transvestic Disorder for simply having sexual thoughts or being a sexual person while wearing clothing consistent with their identified gender. However, this potential improvement was completely undermined by the addition of the specifier "in remission."[23] So for instance, a well-adjusted trans woman who does not experience sexual arousal from wearing items of clothing can nevertheless receive a "Transvestic Disorder in remission" diagnosis if she reveals to her therapist that, long ago as a teenager or young adult, she passed through a phase where she was distressed about her desire to crossdress and the associated sexual arousal that she experienced. In other words, there is no "exit clause": Once one experiences "Transvestic Disorder," they are forever diagnosable with the condition.

While one might argue that (despite its many flaws) the Gender Dysphoria diagnosis does at least provide some benefit for trans people (in that it allows those of us who have adequate health insurance or financial means to access trans-related health care), Transvestic Disorder is completely unnecessary and has absolutely no potential benefit to anyone. All it does is stigmatize gender-non-conforming behavior and sexualize transgender-spectrum people. And in a world where anti-trans forces have increasingly turned to using the specter of "sexual deviancy" to undermine our identities and call our motives into question,[24] this newly expanded Transvestic Disorder diagnosis merely reinforces those efforts.

35

An Open Letter to
The New Yorker

After years of working to raise awareness about how Blanchard's autogynephilia theory sexualizes trans female/feminine-spectrum individuals, and thus can be used as a weapon to invalidate our perspectives, it happened to me personally: first, in a book (described in this chapter) released by Routledge, "the world's leading academic publisher in the Humanities and Social Sciences" (according to their website), then subsequently, in the pages of The New Yorker, *a well-respected national magazine. This open letter first appeared in* The Advocate *in August 2014, shortly after the aforementioned* The New Yorker *article was published.*[1]

Dear The New Yorker magazine,

You probably don't remember me—I was the transgender activist who briefly appeared toward the end of that Michelle Goldberg article you ran last week.[2] You know, the one about the "dispute between radical feminism and transgenderism." I know, that topic sounds somewhat bizarre and potentially fascinating—I'm sure you got lots of click-throughs on it! But the thing is, it was a rather awful experience on my end, and I want to share why with you.

For me, the story begins several months ago when Goldberg contacted me about an article she was intending to write about "tensions between trans activists and some radical feminists." She wanted to interview me for her piece, which makes sense for several reasons. I am a trans woman who has written two books about the intersection of feminism and transgender activism. Some of that work critiques strands of feminism that have historically been antagonistic toward transgender people, and trans woman-exclusion policies (i.e., when women's spaces or organizations bar trans women from attending because we were assigned a male sex at birth). As you can imagine, trans-exclusive radical feminists (or TERFs, as they are often called[3])—who believe that transgender activism upholds the patriarchy, and who deny and disrespect trans people's identities—are not especially fond of my work (to put it quite mildly).

To be honest, I was wary when I received the interview request. This is partly because journalists often do a poor job of covering transgender people—sometimes because they do not bother to do background research, or take our perspectives seriously, or else they view us as "fascinating subjects" and present us in a sensationalistic manner. I was also worried because this particular subject is extremely complex and cannot be adequately understood without unpacking the long history of these debates or delving into the nuances of feminist theory. It was hard for me to imagine that a several page piece intended for *The New Yorker's* largely mainstream audience could do this topic justice.

Also, in the past, I have found that mainstream publications seem to enjoy portraying these debates under a false transgender-people-versus-radical-feminists dichotomy ("hey, two groups of gender-freaks just so happen to hate one another—let's publish that!"). In reality, many transgender activists are also feminists, and TERFs tend to be antagonistic toward many other feminists and gender/sexual minorities, including sex-positive feminists, femme/feminine people, bisexuals and other non-lesbian-identified queer people, and sex workers, just to name a few. Really, a more accurate framework for the article would be "the dispute between radical feminists and the vast majority of feminists and LGBTQ activists who disagree with them," but that isn't so sexy and probably wouldn't generate quite as many click-throughs.

I was also a bit hesitant about the fact that the interview request came from Michelle Goldberg. I don't know her personally, although I have read her writings over the years. She mostly writes about mainstream feminism and politics, and on those matters, we probably agree far more than we disagree. However, there is nothing about her previous work to indicate that she has had any previous interest in, or strong familiarity with, transgender issues or LGBTQ communities (i.e., the politics and settings central to these debates).

While I was leery about the situation, I knew that Goldberg was going to write this article anyway. And it was quite likely that (because of my books and activism) I would be a subject in it whether I participated or not. So I agreed to do it. At least that way, I could voice my opinions on the matter (or so I told myself).

Goldberg and I talked on the phone—that first interview was well over an hour long. We discussed many things related to these debates and their history. She asked me about transgender perspectives on these issues, and I shared those with her. She expressed concern about instances where trans people have allegedly personally attacked TERFs, and I shared with her a long list of instances where TERFs have personally attacked me and other trans women without provocation (I mention a few of these instances here, but all you have to do is google "TERF" and you'll find a slew of others).

Goldberg also expressed her concern about TERFs being silenced by trans folks (e.g., their events being protested, boycotted, or venues pulling out after trans people and allies complained). I explained to her that, while I believe that TERFs should be free to assemble and hold their own events if they wish, some of these situations are far more complicated than that. For instance, if an explicitly LGBTQ organization (which sports a "T" for transgender in its acronym) holds an event, wouldn't it be somewhat hypocritical for them to host performers who tacitly support or outright advocate for trans woman-exclusion policies? Or if a college has a policy protecting students and staff from discrimination based on gender identity, and Shelia Jeffreys comes by to give a talk about her new book in which she describes trans men as "women" and trans women as "men," and insists that the latter group are merely sexually deviant men who are trying to take over feminism (we'll get to that in a moment), well then, there is a serious conflict of interest here!

Should the college let Jeffreys speak? If they do, does that mean that they should jettison all of their anti-discrimination policies because they are tantamount to "censorship?" Or should they only remove trans people from those anti-discrimination policies? And if they do that, what are the ramifications? Clearly, there are complex political and ethical issues involved here (none of which, by the way, are given serious consideration in Goldberg's article).

In a follow up email to Goldberg (after our initial interview), I additionally pointed out that the tactics she seemed concerned about when used by trans people are not anything novel:

If an especially homophobic, or sexist, or racist book was being published by a serious academic press, some activists would surely write letters to the publishers to get them to halt that project. If NARTH were to organize a conference, there would surely be gay activists who would try to put pressure on the hotel or conference space to not allow them to use it. Dan Savage no longer uses the controversial word "faggot" in his weekly column because of pressure (exerted mostly by members of his own community) on the papers that publish him. And recently, countless activists were tweeting

#CancelColbert because they found something he did to be racist.[4] *Of course, individual activists may disagree about whether any given campaign is productive or misguided. But the point is that the forms of protests I just described are analogous to protests that trans activists have carried out in the last few years.*

So in general, trans activists' attempts to protest or eliminate things that they feel slander or threaten them is not much different from what other marginalized groups have done. The thing that is new, however, is that for the first time, others are taking trans people's concerns seriously. And this is not because we have become more vocal per se—*trans activists were quite vocal on the Internet a decade ago, I can assure you! Rather, it's because more and more people who are not trans recognize transphobia as a legitimate form of discrimination that should not be tolerated. A decade ago, most people didn't take our identities or what we had to say seriously. Now people are listening to us.*

Anyway, my impression from our initial conversation was that Goldberg was going to write a "she said"/"she said" type of article, sharing perspectives from both trans activists and TERFs about these sorts of incidents. While that is not the article that I would write about the situation, at least it would give a voice to trans people's perspectives on the situation. But unfortunately, that is not how things turned out. Before I explain how it did turn out, I need to tell you about how I became aware that the article might take a hard turn for the worse, because this is also part of the story.

In our email exchanges, I mentioned to Goldberg that I had recently read what Sheila Jeffreys wrote about me in her book *Gender Hurts: A Feminist Analysis of the Politics of Transgenderism* and found it to be vile. Since you don't usually cover radical feminists in *The New Yorker*, you probably don't know much about Jeffreys other than what Goldberg wrote about her (which frankly, made it sound like Jeffreys is the feminist version of Salman Rushdie circa 1990,[5] being shuttled around from secret location to secret location). Well, I am very familiar with Jeffreys's work, as we are diametrically opposed on many feminist issues. For instance, in her book *Beauty and Misogyny*, Jeffreys claims that women who are feminine are that way because they are suffering from a form of Stockholm syndrome,[6] whereas I think feminists should take feminine gender expression seriously. We also differ greatly on our views about sexuality, transgender people, the direction that feminism should take, and other important issues. But you probably don't care so much about those details. You'd probably rather focus on the "catfight" between radical feminists and transgender activists, wouldn't you?

Anyway, I have critiqued Jeffreys's theories on gender in both my books.[7] Her theories. I have never engaged in a personal attack on her, used the wrong pronouns when addressing her, questioned whether or not she is a "real" feminist, or dissected her sexuality or sexual history. However, Jeffreys does all of these things to me in her book.[8] And much of it she does via invoking Ray Blanchard's theory of autogynephilia. Now, I am not going to get into the details of that theory here, because you are probably not interested. Really, all you need to know is that 1) his theory posits that many trans women transition to female in order to fulfill sexually deviant fantasies they have, 2) the theory has been scientifically proven incorrect, and 3) studies by other researchers have found that up to 93 percent of non-transgender women would be characterized as having "autogynephilia" based on Blanchard's definition.[9] Oh, and I almost forgot to mention that Blanchard believes that homosexuality and non-reproductive forms of sex are abnormal.[10]

Honestly, I am not sure how Jeffreys (who is a lesbian and radical feminist) was able to so forcefully promote Blanchard's archaic and male-centric notions about sexuality in her book without her head exploding from cognitive dissonance. But what I do know is why she did it: If Blanchard's theory is true (which it is not), then that means that trans women like me are really sexually deviant men who are infiltrating the feminist movement. This is the thesis she forwards in her book. And instead of seriously addressing my views on gender, feminism, and transgender issues, all she had to do was excerpt portions of my book where I discuss my own sexual history (which I primarily talked about in order to challenge Blanchard's theory and the stigma it has generated). And in doing this, she was then able to caricature me as a sexually deviant man who is trying to "reinvent feminism to fit [my] erotic interests."[11] She seriously says that, almost verbatim, except that she puts the word "feminism" in scare quotes and she misgenders me (because she doesn't consider me to be a "real" feminist or woman).

Goldberg and I discussed all this in a second phone conversation we shared. I described Jeffreys's approach as an ad hominem attack and the transgender equivalent of "slut-shaming" (when people bring up a woman's past or presumed sexual history in order to dismiss her opinions or her as a person). I also shared with her (by email) the "autoraptophilia" analogy that I made in Chapter 30, with the hopes that it would illustrate just how sexualizing and inappropriate it is to define a person based upon sexual fantasies they may have experienced in the past. Goldberg conveyed that she understood my concerns, but she said that she might bring up autogynephilia anyway.

When *The New Yorker* fact checker contacted me to verify the parts of the article that involved me, it became clear that several passages from my book *Whipping Girl* in which I discussed certain aspects of my sexual history were going to be included in Goldberg's article. I got the impression that they were intended to show "my side" of the story in relation to Jeffreys depicting me as an "autogynephile." Being naturally horrified by the possibility of having my sexual history litigated within the pages of a national magazine, I sent another email to Goldberg expressing my concerns about the inclusion of this material (I have since made this and another related email publicly available[12]), and she told me that those passages had subsequently been removed from the final piece.

Last Monday, the article came out. And I was rather dismayed to see its final form. While (thankfully) Goldberg was truthful when she said that the passages of my sexual history would be removed, she hadn't mentioned that the article was going to include Jeffreys's and Blanchard's views about "autogynephilia" without any mention that the theory has been scientifically disproven. And if that weren't bad enough, Goldberg casually mentions that Jeffreys (who is depicted as a sympathetic, if eccentric, character in the article) considers me to be an "autogynephile" without mentioning any of my arguments against the theory and Jeffreys's hypocritical appropriation of it.

I could imagine Goldberg defending herself by saying something like, "I didn't call you an autogynephile, I was merely a journalist reporting on someone else's comments." But as a feminist, she knows that you don't just casually mention that so-and-so thinks the woman in question is a "slut," or that the queer person in question is a "sexual deviant," without that leaving an impression in readers' minds. And as a journalist, she knows that it is unethical to randomly quote some psychologist who believes that some group-in-question is abnormal and sexually deviant without any context or offering of counter arguments from psychologists/scientists who believe that those claims are scientifically invalid. And even if Goldberg was a bad feminist or a bad journalist, she still is not able to claim naiveté here because *I clearly and repeatedly pointed these things out to her.*

Goldberg purposefully played the "autogynephilia" card because her intention in writing the article was to make transgender activists look bad. The numerous biases in the article are discussed at great length in several critical reviews of the piece after its release.[13] For instance, as Mari Brighe (writing for the feminist webzine *Autostraddle)* observes:

Let's start with the numbers. In the piece, Goldberg mentions the names of 14 radical feminist activists (frequently providing physical descriptions), and provides quotes from nine of them—including two from books penned by radfems. In contrast, she mentions and quotes a total of four trans women (zero from books), and two of them are quoted to supporting the radical feminist position. The problem isn't necessarily that Goldberg appears to side with the radical feminist viewpoint; that's perfectly within her rights, and perfectly within The New Yorker's right to print it. The real issue is that Ms Goldberg gives the impression that she's covering the conflict between the trans rights movement and radical feminism—after all, the piece is subtitled "The dispute between radical feminism and transgenderism" —but gives only pass-ing lip service to the transgender community's side of this situation.[14]

And as one of the four trans women in the piece, it is clear to me now that Goldberg merely used me as a prop to give her piece the pretense of balance. I am introduced toward the end of the article, long after readers have likely concluded that transgender activism is out of control. I have a one-line quote that is immediately followed by Jeffreys's description of me (which misgenders me and calls me an "autogynephile"). My views on Jeffreys, Blanchard's theory, feminism, trans activism, my more nuanced opinions about activism more gen-erally, and my experiences being personally attacked by TERFs—none of that is included in the piece (and even if it was, the slut-shaming surely would have undermined what I had to say anyway).

While I am upset about being misrepresented in your magazine, this inci-dent probably won't personally affect me too much within the feminist circles I exist in, where people are already highly skeptical about radical feminists' views—not just of trans people, but of gender, sexuality, and feminism more generally. And given the backlash against Goldberg's "Feminism's Toxic Twit-ter Wars" article from earlier this year (which many felt was biased against feminists of color, and by which some interviewees felt misrepresented),[15] many activists I know will likely view this new article as another "hit piece" against minority groups who engage in forms of activism that Goldberg does not like. (I am not claiming that this was what Goldberg set out to achieve with this article, but it is how the piece is being perceived in some quarters.)

But what really bothers me is that your mainstream readers (most of whom have little-to-no prior knowledge about radical feminism or transgender activism) will most likely not see through the article's journalistic-ish veneer, and will assume that it represents an "objective" and "unbiased" presentation of the situation. And they will assume that transgender activists are mean people and completely out of control, because they have not been offered any evidence to suggest otherwise. And the insinuations that Goldberg makes throughout her article—that trans people act irrationally, are sexually deviant, and potentially dangerous—will seem to have "truthiness" to your readers, because the media has been propagating these very stereotypes of us for almost half a century. And when your readers do eventually meet a real-life trans person, perhaps they will misgender them, or dismiss them as a "pervert," and justify those acts by referencing a *The New Yorker* article they once read.

In the aftermath of your publication of Goldberg's article, I noticed several *The New Yorker* tweets in my Twitter feed. They were there because I follow you on social media. For a brief moment, I considered unfollowing you and making a big public spectacle about it. It would have felt really cathartic, I'd imagine. But I don't really want to unfollow you. I like some of the articles you publish. And I often laugh at your cartoons. And for those reasons, I will not unfollow you, nor will I organize a boycott against you. (I'm sure this may surprise you given Goldberg's mischaracterization of trans activists as death-threat-making vandals who want to censor everything they dislike.)

But to be honest, the next time someone emails me to say, "I am writing an article for *The New Yorker* about fill-in-the-blank transgender issue and I'd really like to interview you," I will definitely be inclined to say no.

Oh, and one last thing: In the last week since you published Goldberg's article, a teenager was stabbed in Washington DC because of the fact that she is transgender, and in the last six weeks, two trans women of color have been found brutally murdered in Baltimore (and some suspect it may be the work of a serial killer who is targeting trans women).[16] So here's an idea: Why don't you publish articles about these more serious matters rather than faux journalism pieces about trans activists purportedly "oppressing" radical feminists? Oh yeah, I almost forgot: You wouldn't get nearly as many click-throughs . . .

Part Four

Communities and Disparities

After spending much of 2008–2010 challenging psychological diagnoses and theories that negatively impact trans people (as detailed in the last section), I finally began to focus in earnest on my second book, which eventually became *Excluded: Making Feminist and Queer Movements More Inclusive*. I see *Excluded* as beginning where the last chapter of *Whipping Girl* ("The Future of Queer/Trans Activism") left off, asking: Why is it that we always seem to create activist movements that erase or exclude many people who have a stake in them?

Sometimes movements become exclusive because they are too focused on one particular marginalized group. This approach (sometimes referred to as *identity politics*) often ignores the needs of those in the community who lie at the intersection of multiple forms of marginalization, and thus, are in most need of advocacy and support. It also invariably leads to attempts to rigorously define or limit who counts as a "bona fide" member of the marginalized group, which can also lead to exclusion. An alternative approach is to focus on shared issues rather than specific identities—this is often called *umbrella activism*. For instance, people who fall under the transgender umbrella might organize around our mutual interest in challenging the gender binary, or we might work together with others who fall under the queer umbrella to challenge all gender and sexual norms. While umbrella activism is more inclusive in theory, typically the most populous or privileged subgroups under the umbrella tend to garner disproportionate influence, and they may champion ideologies or an atmosphere that reflects their own perspectives and values—this may have the effect of disenfranchising or erasing other voices within the movement. In other words, movements centered on identity politics or umbrella activism are both susceptible to homogenization (i.e., the sense that all members should meet certain norms or ideals) and hierarchies (i.e., where certain beliefs, bodies, behaviors, or ways of being are deemed more worthy than others).

In the years just after my transition, when I first began participating in feminism, queer, and trans activism, I came to recognize the existence of homogenization and hierarchies in those settings, and how those forces often conspired to undermine my own identity, perspectives, and issues. So I responded the same way that many activists before me had: Anchored to my own standpoint (e.g., as a transsexual, as a trans woman, as a feminine person), I began to espouse new language, concepts, and calls to action that seemed perfectly logical and righteous from my viewpoint. And what I said (e.g., in *Whipping Girl)* seemed to resonate with many people, so I believe that there was certainly *some* truth in what I was advocating. But I also heard from some people who felt that the way that I phrased or framed certain issues erased their perspectives. And I witnessed other people take what for me was merely a standpoint (i.e., my personal view of gender and society as a transsexual, or as a trans woman), and propose more separatist actions around those identities.

The more that I considered the problem, the more that I came to see activism as a vicious cycle of sorts: one marginalized individual or group forwards well-intentioned ideas and actions to better their standing in society or within the movement, but those undertakings often inadvertently devalue or ignore the concerns of other marginalized people, who then in turn forward their own ideas and actions (which may also be unintentionally exclusive). *Excluded* was my attempt to articulate this problem and to explore how we might circumvent it moving forward. The book begins with a collection of personal essays describing examples of this problem from my own life, then follows with a series of essays that offer holistic strategies to simultaneously challenge *all* forms of marginalization (rather than focus on specific identities or issues) and to move beyond homogenization and hierarchies in activism.

While none of the chapters in this section appear in *Excluded*, they were all written during or immediately after the time period that I was working on the book. In fact, the first four essays in this section were mentioned as potential chapters in the book proposal that I submitted to my publisher, although I eventually decided to cut them from the final manuscript due to concerns about book length. While these chapters differ from one another in topic and tone, they all (in one way or another) touch on various forms of erasure and exclusion that occur within marginalized communities and in activist movements.

36

Bisexual Does Not "Reinforce" Anything

I began publicly identifying as bisexual in 2008.[1] Shortly thereafter, I began routine-ly hearing the meme discussed in this chapter, and this was my initial response to such claims. This piece originally appeared in the webzine TheScavenger.net *in 2010.[2] I later wrote a more extensive follow up essay called "Bisexuality and Binaries Revis-ited," which subsequently appeared in* Excluded.[3]

Increasingly these days, I come across people who are ostensibly bi-sexual—in that they partner with both women and men—but who refuse to identify with that term. Now this, in and of itself, is not necessarily a bad thing, as words (and especially identity labels) evolve over time and invariably go in and out of fashion. What does bother me, however, is the explanation that is often given for this lack of identification: that the word bisexual supposedly "reinforces the gender binary," or "reinforces the notion that there are only two genders." As a bisexual-identified trans woman, I find this argument extremely problematic for a number of reasons.

While a large amount of sex and gender variation exists (as seen in intersex people, gender-non-conforming people, trans folks who physically transition from one sex to the other, trans folks who do not physically transition, or who do not identify within the gender binary, and so on), there are certain aspects of female and male bodies (along with aspects of various gender identities and expressions) that individual people may find particularly desirable (or not).[4] In addition to this, we live in a society in which all people are automatically (and often nonconsensually) read as either female or male, and where different assumptions, expectations, and restrictions are placed on a person based upon which sex they are perceived to be.

The reason why I identify as bisexual is two-fold. First, on a physical level, the attraction that I feel toward male-bodied/identified people feels very different to me on a visceral level than the attraction that I feel toward female-bodied/identified people. And having sex with a female partner feels very different to me than having sex with a male partner. Such feelings are difficult to put into words, and I am not quite sure what the source of this difference is, but presumably it is related to what makes exclusively homosexual or heterosexual people attracted to members of one sex/gender, but not the other. I know that some people describe themselves as pansexual, which may work well for them, but I personally am not a big fan of that label with regards to my own sexuality, as it erases the way in which my attraction toward women is different from the attraction I experience toward men (and vice versa).[5]

The second, and far more important reason (at least for me) why I embrace the word bisexual is that people perceive me and react to me very differently depending upon whether the person I am coupled with is (or appears to be) a woman or a man. In the hetero-mainstream, when I am paired with a man, I am read as straight; when I am paired with a woman, I am read as queer. In queer settings, when I am paired with a woman, I am read as lesbian/dyke/queer and viewed as a legitimate member of the community. But when I am paired with a man (especially when the man in question is cisgender), then I am not merely unaccepted and viewed as an outsider, but I may even be accused of buying into or reinforcing the hetero-patriarchy. So in other words, the "bi" in bisexual does not merely refer to the types of people that I am sexual with, but to the fact that both the straight and queer worlds view me in *two very different ways* depending upon who I happen to be partnered with at any given moment. This aspect of the bisexual experience is not captured by the word "pansexual," nor by the more general word "queer." In fact, I regularly call myself queer, and when I do, people are often surprised when I mention that I date men (as though in their minds, bisexuality does not truly fall under the queer umbrella).

Anyone who is familiar with the history of the bisexual movement can tell you that the reason why some queer people began outwardly identifying as bisexual rather than as gay or lesbian (the two predominant queer identities throughout the '70s and '80s) is precisely because of this insider/outsider issue. So long as a bisexual woman was only sexual with women and called herself a lesbian, she was accepted. But as soon as she admitted to, or acted upon, her attraction to men, she would be ostracized and accused of being a part of the problem rather than the solution. This is why the label bisexual came into prominence—as a way to gain visibility within the queer community and to fight against exclusion.

Back in the '50s and '60s, all LGBTQ people were often simply called "gay" or "homosexual." We were all present during the first queer uprisings and the early days of what was simply called "gay liberation." But as the movement picked up momentum, bisexuals and trans folks were both thrown under the bus, albeit for slightly different reasons. In a world where the straight mainstream assumed that gay men wanted to be women and lesbians wanted to be men, it is not surprising that many lesbians and gay men felt uneasy about the presence of trans people in their movement. And in a world where the straight mainstream insisted homosexuals could become heterosexual if they simply set their minds to it, it is not surprising that many lesbians and gay men felt uneasy about the existence of bisexuals.[6]

While the reasons for bisexual and transgender exclusion from lesbian and gay communities during the '70s and '80s may be somewhat different, the rhetoric used to cast us away was eerily similar: We, in one way or another, were supposedly "buying into," and "reinforcing," heteronormativity. Transsexuals, transvestites, drag artists, butches, and femmes were accused of aping heterosexist gender roles. Bisexuals were accused of purposefully seeking out heterosexual privilege and (literally) sleeping with the enemy. According to many lesbians and gay men (both past and present), bisexuals and trans folks are not merely assimilationist, but we don't even exist! According to this homonormative[7] logic, trans people are really gay men and lesbians who transition in order to pass in the straight world. And bisexuals are really either heterosexuals dabbling in a bit of sexual experimentation, or gay men and lesbians who just haven't fully come out of the closet yet. It is because of this history of erasure and exclusion that bisexual and transgender activists became more outspoken in the late '80s and early '90s, and fought for visibility and inclusion within the lesbian/gay/queer umbrella. While most queer acronyms include B's and T's these days, our communities still remain largely invisible and have little voice in the now relatively mainstream LGBTQ movement. And the rhetoric that has been used against us for decades (i.e., that we are "assimilationist" and "reinforce heterosexism") can still be heard in gay/lesbian/queer communities to this day.

This is precisely what makes my blood boil when I hear people say that the word bisexual "reinforces the notion that there are only two genders." First, it insinuates that self-identified bisexuals somehow oppress trans people. While

I'm sure that there are some bisexuals out there who harbor anti-trans attitudes, in general, I have found that bisexuals are exponentially more accepting of trans folks, and way more likely to consider us to be legitimate romantic and sexual partners, than are the exclusively homosexual majority in our community. So the idea that bisexual-identified people are oppressing trans folks is both wildly inaccurate and ahistorical, as it ignores the decades of marginalization both our communities have faced at the hands of the exclusively homosexual majority.

Second, exclusively homosexual people have been accusing bisexuals of "reinforcing" this or that for decades because of who we sleep with, and now we are supposedly "reinforcing the gender binary" simply by calling ourselves bisexual? Knowing the long history of homosexual attempts to obliterate bisexuality using the "reinforcing" trope, it is difficult for me to view this as anything other than part of the systematic erasure of bisexuality from queer communities. And can somebody please tell me how the term "bisexual" somehow reinforces the binary, yet "gay" and "lesbian" supposedly do not? Most self-identified lesbians use that term to signify that they partner with women, but not men. Most gay men use the term "gay" to signify that they partner with men, but not women. So why are gay men and lesbians not accused of "reinforcing the notion that there are only two genders"? Oh, that's right, because their identities are accepted and seen as legitimate, while bisexual identities are not.

The funny thing about gay/lesbian/queer folks (and this can also be said about many feminists as well) is that often we are just as prejudiced as people in the straight mainstream; we just use different language to express our biases. When somebody is transgender, or transsexual, or bisexual, or engages in BDSM, or sex work, and/or expresses themselves in a feminine manner, we almost reflexively accuse them of "buying into the system" or of "reinforcing" heterosexism/patriarchy/the gender binary/capitalism/insert-evil-hegemonic-ideology-of-choice-here. For me, the word "reinforcing" is a red flag: Whenever somebody utters it, I stop for a moment to ask myself who is being accused of "reinforcing" and who is not. There is almost always some double standard at work behind the scenes. And given the turbulent history of who gets to be considered inside and outside of the gay/lesbian/queer community, it does not surprise me that the only people who are *never* accused of "reinforcing" the hetero-patriarchal-gender-binary are non-feminine, cisgender, exclusively homosexual folks.

The word bisexual may not be perfect, but it does have a rich political history, one that involves fighting for visibility and inclusion both within and outside of the queer community. If the word does not resonate with you personally, then simply do not use it. But if you happen to forgo identifying with the word, don't dare say that it is because you believe that bisexual "reinforces the notion that there are only two genders," as that claim goes beyond personal statement, and enters the realm of accusation, as it insinuates that people who openly call themselves bisexual (e.g., me) are at best, naive about gender politics, and at worst, oppressive of transgender people. If anything, it is the "reinforcing" trope that has historically been used to undermine both bisexuals and trans folks, and we should learn to stop using the very same language that has been used to marginalize us in the past.

37

A "Transsexual Versus Transgender" Intervention

I wrote this piece (which was posted on my blog in September 2011) in response to a largely Internet-driven debate raging within trans circles at the time (and which still persists in various manifestations today).[1] I called this piece an "intervention" as a shout-out to Vivianne Namaste, who often uses that word to describe her own writings and activism.

Over the last year or so, I have read a number of blog entries and Facebook rants about the so-called "transsexual versus transgender" issue. For those who are unaware of this debate, it stems from a subset of transsexuals who feel that the transsexual community is not served well by being included under the transgender umbrella (some even go so far as to insist that there is a mutually exclusive dichotomy between transsexual and transgender people). Along similar lines, these transsexuals also argue that inclusion under the LGBTQ umbrella does a disservice to the transsexual community, as it conflates two very different issues (i.e., sexual orientation and gender identity), and emboldens many cissexual LGB folks to appropriate trans identities and experiences, and to claim to speak on our behalf.

I have purposefully tried to avoid entering into this debate, primarily because many (albeit certainly not all) of the umbrella critiques that I have read invoke horrible stereotypes, and sometimes even hate speech, to help bolster their case. I have seen blatantly homophobic and biphobic remarks made by some anti-umbrella advocates. One post I saw described bisexuals as sexual predators who fetishize and prey upon transsexuals—this comment draws on a long history of monosexist stereotypes of bisexuals as "sex crazed" and desiring "anything that moves," and it deeply offended me as a bisexual trans woman.

Along the same lines, anti-umbrella advocates often self-describe themselves as "real transsexuals" and dismiss those who support the transgender and LGBTQ umbrellas as being poseurs and mere fetishists. Some even cite Ray Blanchard's sexualizing and scientifically incorrect theory of autogynephilia to make their point. It is one thing to disagree with another person's views about whether or not transsexuals should seek inclusion under the transgender and LGBTQ umbrellas. But when people stoop to the level of sexualizing those they disagree with, or dismissing them as "fakes," then they are engaging in name-calling rather than intellectual debate, and I want absolutely no part of it.

So like I said, I have mostly avoided this debate because of the name-calling, disparaging stereotypes, and nonconsensual sexualization that are sometimes associated with it. But recently, I read a post where someone referred to me as being firmly in the "transsexual" (rather than "transgender") camp. This was the second time that I had seen such a claim, and frankly, it surprised me. Granted, in my book *Whipping Girl,* I argued that the transsexual experience is different from other transgender trajectories, and I also decried the manner in which some cissexual gay men and lesbians appropriate transsexual identities. But I never once advocated that transsexuals should completely split off from the transgender or LGBTQ communities. Rather, my intention was constructive criticism—I hoped to make those alliances more aware and respectful of transsexual voices and perspectives.

For the record, I am in the pro-umbrella camp, even though I acknowledge that sometimes umbrella politics are messy and less than equitable. In other words, I believe that the pros of umbrella politics outweigh the cons. But, of course, that is my opinion, and others may disagree. If we are going to have a serious discussion about this issue (i.e., one that does not sink into the abyss of sexualization, stereotypes, and name calling), then it seems to me that there are at least three major issues that need to be addressed, but which have been largely absent from the debate thus far.

Activism Requires Alliances

Anyone who has ever been an activist for any social justice issue can tell you that minority groups, on their own, are never able to fully achieve the positive change they seek in the world without first forming alliances with those who do not share their experience. This becomes even more crucial when the minority group in question is especially small. Even the most liberal of estimates suggest that transsexuals make up about 0.2 percent of the population; more conservative estimates suggest that we are far rarer than that.[2] Therefore, it is simply not possible for us to challenge deeply entrenched and institutionalized societal cissexism without enlisting cissexual allies.

One of the most constructive ways to build alliances is through umbrella groups, where several marginalized groups that share similar concerns band together to work on their shared issues. After all, there is strength in numbers. Transgender activism came about as a way to bring together transsexuals with other gender-variant groups (e.g., crossdressers, intersex people, two-spirit people, genderqueers, butch women, femme men, etc.), not because we are "all the same," but in order to fight together against a mutual problem we share: the way in which our society marginalizes all people who do not conform to gender norms. While not perfect, that coalition has positively impacted most of our lives. One could even make the case that none of us would even be here openly having this debate in a public forum if it were not for the last two de-cades of transgender activism.

Many transsexuals also feel that the LGBTQ umbrella is another useful alliance. After all, it is the common assumption that a person's sex, gender, and sexuality should all nicely and neatly align that lies at the root of the oppression that all of us face. Transsexuals who want to secede from the LGBTQ umbrel-la keep citing the fact that sexual orientation has nothing to do with gender identity. This may be true, but this point has nothing to do with the rationale behind why trans people were initially included in the umbrella—specifically, because LGBTQ individuals are all discriminated against for similar reasons (i.e., because, in one way or another, we challenge the assumption that sex, gender, and sexuality should all be perfectly aligned). This is evident in the way that gay men, lesbians, and bisexuals are often targeted for discrimination for their gender non-conformity, and in the way that transsexuals are often target-ed for discrimination because people fear that sleeping with us might "make them gay." In other words, while sexual orientation and gender identity may be different things, homophobia and transphobia are very much intertwined.

That is the argument for transsexual inclusion under the transgender and LGBTQ umbrellas. Those transsexuals who oppose those umbrellas must an-swer this: If we secede from those alliances, then with whom *should* we ally? What new umbrella groups should we form in order to collectively fight the marginalization we face?

To date, I have only ever seen one opponent of the transgender and LGBTQ umbrellas suggest a viable alternative alliance. That person is Vivianne

Namaste, an amazing Canadian trans activist, writer, and theorist who is sadly underappreciated here in the States. In her book *Sex Change, Social Change: Reflections on Identity, Institutions and Imperialism,* she claims that transsexuals have not been well served by the transgender and LGBTQ alliances, and she argues that transsexuals should instead forge "alliances with advocates for the homeless, activists working for the decriminalization of prostitution, and those who work on prison reform and/or abolition."[3]

While I find her argument to be very reasonable, I have a sneaking suspicion that most anti-umbrella advocates posting on the Internet these days would not embrace such an alliance. Indeed, an underlying sentiment in a lot of their posts seems to be that in order for transsexuals to be considered "normal" or "desirable," we must dissociate ourselves from the undesirable sexual deviants and fetishists who supposedly reside within the transgender and LGBTQ umbrellas. So it is hard for me to envision these same anti-umbrella advocates whose posts I have read suddenly deciding to join forces with sex worker, prison reform, and homeless activists.

It is never in the interest of the powers-that-be to simply give some minority group equal rights or to treat them as fully legitimate individuals. Anyone who has spent any time doing front-line activism can tell you that, in order to create positive change for transsexuals in this world, we need to band together with other disadvantaged groups to fight for our mutual interests. If anti-umbrella advocates want to be taken seriously, then they must move beyond simply decrying the transgender and LGBTQ alliances, and instead propose serious alternative alliances that are both realistic and which will help us achieve our collective goals. Other than Namaste (who, as far as I can tell, has not been involved in the recent Internet umbrella debates), I have yet to see any such alternative offered from anti-umbrella advocates.

Transsexual Is an Umbrella Too

Most of the critiques that I have read arguing that transsexuals should abandon the transgender and LGBTQ umbrellas seem not to take into account the fact that transsexual is an umbrella too! We are a disparate group of individuals who share one thing in common: We all identify and live as members of the sex other than the one we were assigned at birth. Other than that, we differ in almost every way. Some of us are conservative while others of us are liberal. Some of us are middle- or upper-class while others of us are poor or working-class. Some of us are white while others of us are people of color. Some of us are straight while others of us are queer. Some of us are vanilla while others of us are kinky. Some of us are out as transsexual while others of us are stealth. Some of us are able to "pass" or "blend in" as cissexual while others of us are not. Some of us are very feminine, or very masculine, while others of us are less conventional in our gender expression. Like the population as a whole, transsexuals are highly diverse, and we should respect that diversity within our own community.

Some of the anti-umbrella posts that I have read presume that transsexuals are one monolithic group, and that we *all* want out of the transgender and LGBTQ umbrellas, when this is clearly not the case. A lot of us prefer to work toward making these umbrellas function better for transsexuals, rather than abandoning them entirely.

Without a doubt, the most disturbing aspect of this debate is that some anti-umbrella advocates try to erase this diversity in perspectives and experiences in our community by arrogantly claiming that they are "real" transsexuals, and that those who take a pro-umbrella position must be "fake" transsexuals. As I alluded to in the beginning of this post, this "real"/"fake" distinction is often policed via homophobic remarks and blatant sexualization, although it is sometimes policed in other ways.

The most devious way in which this "real"/"fake" distinction is enforced is through a redefining of the word "transgender." Anti-umbrella advocates often use the term transgender, not as an umbrella term that includes transsexuals and other gender-variant people (i.e., the traditional definition of transgender over the last two decades), but rather as a pejorative to describe people who are merely "gender benders," "drag queens," "crossdressed men," "fetishists," and/or "queers." In other words, this use of the word transgender implies that transgender-identified transsexuals are "fakes"—people who pretend to be transsexual, but who are actually something else entirely. This wordplay allows anti-umbrella advocates to outright dismiss any pro-umbrella sentiments on the grounds that the person voicing that opinion is merely "a transgender" rather than a "real transsexual."

About two years ago, on a trans-related email list, I was having an argument with another trans woman about some unrelated issue. And suddenly, out of the blue, she suggested that I was not a "real transsexual" because I still had a "penis" (she mentioned being on my website, so I presume that she figured this out from viewing the video of me performing my spoken word piece "Cocky"). Even though I have pretty thick skin, the accusation that I must not be a "real transsexual" really got to me. It stung badly. Like most of us, I have had to deal with so much shit in my life, first as an isolated trans child, then later as an outspoken transsexual adult. And to have someone, in one swift comment, try to take that all away from me, to invalidate my identity and life experiences, felt like a violation. In writing my response to her, I found myself wanting to mention that, after many years of not being able to afford it, I was finally scheduled to have SRS later that year. But I quickly decided against it for three reasons: 1) it is nobody's fucking business what I do with my body!, 2) it would simply reinforce the fucked up notion that one has to live up to other people's criteria—whether it be surgery, or a diagnosis from a psychiatrist, or "passability," or heterosexuality, or conventional femininity—in order to be deemed a "real transsexual," and 3) it really wouldn't have mattered what I said. She was trying to discredit me, to make the argument we were having about *me*, rather than the subject we were initially arguing about. She would not be satisfied with merely voicing her side of the argument—she also wanted to delegitimize me because I disagreed with her.

People who wish to discredit those they disagree with, rather than engage in honest and serious debate with them, always seem to play the "real" card. This is why right-wing conservatives claim that Obama is not a "real American," or that liberals are not "real patriots." It is why people will claim that hip-hop, or rock-and-roll, or any other music they do not like, is not "real music." And it is why any person who does not conform to conventional assumptions about sex, gender, and sexuality—whether they be transsexual, transgender, LGB or feminist—will inevitably be accused of not being a "real" woman or man.

Transsexuals are people. And like people more generally, we differ with regard to our sexualities, our gender expressions, and our perspectives and opinions. Therefore, we must stop referring to this debate about umbrellas as the "transsexual versus transgender" debate, as that is a misnomer. This is a debate between transsexuals who support transsexual inclusion within the transgender and LGBTQ umbrellas, and those who do not. And anyone who attempts to play the "real transsexual" card should be summarily dismissed, as they are merely engaging in name calling rather than serious debate.

What This Debate Is Really About

When I hear anti-umbrella advocates claim that transsexuals don't want anything to do with the LGB community, it always strikes me as odd given the fact that so many transsexuals are LGB- and/or queer-identified.

Most modern studies examining the prevalence of LGB orientation claim that less that 5 percent of the (predominantly cissexual) population identify as lesbian, gay, or bisexual; the numbers can approach 10 percent of the population when same-sex attraction or experiences (rather than identity) are measured.[4] In contrast, in virtually every survey and research study I have seen (and I've seen quite a few), the percentage of LGB-identified transsexuals falls somewhere between 30 and 60 percent.[5] About ten years ago, I was on a large email list that focused on MTF transitioning, and in a survey there, about one-third of the transsexual women identified as heterosexual, one-third as bisexual, and one-third as lesbian.

There are always problems with measuring the prevalence of sexual orientation, so I would not claim to know exactly how many transsexuals are LGBQ-identified. But I think that it's safe to say that the percentage is way higher among transsexuals than for the greater cissexual population, and that it may even approach or surpass the 50 percent mark.

On top of this, there are many heterosexual-oriented transsexuals who identify as queer, often because they spent their formative pre-transition years within the lesbian/gay/queer communities. For instance, many trans men who are exclusively attracted to women (and therefore heterosexual in orientation) nevertheless identify as queer and continue to participate in queer communities, usually because they were a part of those communities pre-transition and/or because they are partnered to, or have a preference for, queer-identified women. There are also some heterosexual-oriented trans women who spent their pre-transition years in the gay male community, although this admittedly seems to occur far less often than trans men who spend their pre-transition years in lesbian/dyke communities.

This last point may shed some light onto the proverbial "elephant in the room" in this whole umbrella debate: It is almost exclusively a trans woman phenomenon. Now, I am not saying that there aren't *any* trans men out there who want to secede from the LGBTQ umbrella. But frankly, every single anti-umbrella post that I have read has been penned by a trans woman.[6] Now, there may be a number of factors that contribute to this disparity, but I suspect that a major reason is the fact that, in both gay male communities and lesbian/dyke communities, masculinity is celebrated and femininity is dismissed. This generally leads to greater acceptance of transsexual men (who typically express themselves and/or are perceived as masculine), whereas transsexual women (who typically express themselves and/or are perceived as feminine) are often ignored or shunned. To be clear, I am not claiming that all trans women are feminine, or all trans men are masculine. But people do tend to perceive trans women as being feminine, or attempting to be feminine (even when we are not), and vice versa for trans men.

Many transsexual women I have talked to who explored dating in gay male circles during their pre-transition days have told me that they received very little interest from gay men because they were seen as too feminine. In contrast, pre-transition transsexual men do not typically have such a problem dating within lesbian/dyke communities, where butch and trans masculine gender expression are often celebrated.

Here is a thought experiment: Imagine gay men *en masse* warmly welcoming and celebrating heterosexual-oriented post-transition transsexual women into their communities. Sounds quite farcical, doesn't it? And yet, heterosexual-oriented post-transition transsexual men *are* very often welcomed and celebrated in many contemporary queer women's communities.

Given all this, I think that it might be useful to reframe this debate. Arguing that LGBQ folks are inherently anti-transsexual (and therefore, transsexuals should secede from that umbrella) is patently untrue. While some LGBQ individuals may express anti-transsexual sentiments, other LGBQ folks outright embrace certain transsexuals. Instead, a more accurate description is as follows: Negative attitudes toward trans female/feminine individuals runs rampant throughout much of the cissexual queer community. As a result, many heterosexual-oriented trans women never feel welcome in, nor do they ever associate themselves with, the queer community (whereas heterosexually-oriented trans men often do). And queer-identified trans women typically have to work hard to be seen as legitimate members of the queer community (whereas queer-identified trans men are often welcomed within those same queer circles).

This leads to one final point: As a trans woman who has had to fight tooth and nail to try to get the greater cis queer women's community to acknowledge and embrace their trans sisters, the idea of removing transsexuals from the LGBTQ umbrella greatly concerns me. If it were to happen, I believe that it would severely undermine the modest gains that queer-identified trans women have made thus far. So we are left with a dilemma: Heterosexual trans women don't feel like they are a part of the queer community, and so they understandably want to remove transsexuality from the LGBTQ umbrella. Yet, if such a move were to occur, it would have a strong negative impact on queer-identified trans women who still to this day struggle to be acknowledged, accepted, and appreciated within LGBTQ circles.

Reconciling This Debate

Unfortunately, these umbrella debates have created rifts (or exacerbated previously existing rifts) between heterosexual and queer-identified trans women, and between transsexual women and non-transsexual transgender people on the trans female/feminine spectrum. I think that there are a few things that we can do to reconcile these debates and heal the rifts that currently exist within our communities.

First, we should respect the diversity of identities, sexualities, and life histories that exist among those of us on the trans female/feminine spectrums. We should recognize that many transsexual women have been, or currently are, crossdressers, drag performers, androgynous, butch, or genderqueer-identified—such life experiences do not make a person any less transsexual. Furthermore, cissexual women vary in their sexualities and identities, so we should expect transsexual women to vary in these respects too. Heterosexual transsexuals should stop trying to convince the world that all transsexuals are straight and want out of the LGBTQ umbrella. Similarly, queer-identified transsexuals sometimes play up the idea that transsexuality is inherently subversive and super-duper queer in order to gain acceptance within queer circles (I should know, as did quite a bit of that during the first two years after my transition)—this erases the life experiences of our straight-identified trans sisters.

Second, rather than pit trans female/feminine communities against one another, we should all stand together to challenge our shared problem: trans-misogyny within the greater cissexual LGBTQ community.

Finally, we should recognize that umbrellas exist, not because all of their members share the same identity, but rather because their members are marginalized by society in similar or related ways, and thus have formed an alliance to challenge their mutual problems. I believe that transgender and LGBTQ are useful alliances in this regard, but they need not be the only ones. I am a big proponent of creating alliances between cis and trans women to challenge the traditional sexism/misogyny we mutually face. Many people (including me) think that transsexuals should ally ourselves with intersex activists, disability activists, and fat activists to challenge the cultural belief that certain bodies are "better," more "natural," or more valid than others. And Namaste's suggestion that transsexuals should ally with other groups who have been criminalized by society (e.g., sex worker, prison reform, and homeless activists) is another potentially productive one.

If the goal is forwarding transsexual and/or trans women's rights and perspectives, then we should focus our energies on creating more and stronger alliances, rather than tearing down existing ones.

38

Baby Talk

In 2008, Gina de Vries approached me about an idea that she had for a spoken word/performance show that she wanted to create for the following year's National Queer Arts Festival. That show ultimately became Girl Talk—it was billed as "A Trans and Cis Woman Dialogue," and intended to be a show where queer-identified trans women, cis women, and genderqueer folks would read/perform pieces about our shared relationships with one another: "sexual and romantic, chosen and blood family, friendships, support networks, activist alliances."[1] Gina and I co-curated five annual Girl Talk events from 2009–2013, with Elena Rose joining us as a co-curator after the second year. The shows were intense and beautiful—I am honored to have played a role in making them happen.

The pieces that I wrote and performed for the 2009 and 2010 Girl Talk shows ("How to Be an Ally to Trans Women" and "Dating," respectively) were later published in Excluded. *My 2013 Girl Talk piece, "Desirable," appears as Chapter 43 of this book. This chapter and the next are the pieces that I wrote and performed for Girl Talk 2012. An earlier version of this chapter[2] (which appeared on my blog in 2013) generated a few misconceptions and dissenting opinions, which I have tried to address here via edits to the piece and commentary in the Notes section.*

I read blogs. And an unfortunate consequence of reading blogs is that sometimes you stumble upon statements that make you upset. Lately, I've been dwelling over one single sentence from a blog post that I read a few months ago. The author was a femme-identified cis woman who described her identity this way: "I only say I'm queer to steer clear of sex acts with cisgender men whilst simultaneously accommodating my devout lesbianism and propensity towards dating trans men when the butch pool feels too shallow."[3]

I have become preoccupied with this quote, not because it is unusual or extraordinary—on the contrary, these are very commonplace sentiments among queer women these days. Rather, my interest in this quote stems from its subtle and inadvertent messages. Sometimes, the way in which we define ourselves may hint at exclusionary undercurrents that exist within our own community.

First, "queer" seems to be defined here in terms of "devout lesbianism" and "steering clear of cisgender men." Given this framing, a bisexual woman (such as myself) who sometimes *does* have sex with cis men, may be misconstrued as *not* queer—i.e., straight—thus playing into the decades old lesbian tradition of erasing the *B* out of LGBTQ.

Second, the quote seems to imply that trans men are not *really* men, but just another variety of butch woman. Indeed, trans male acceptance and desirability in queer women's spaces often hinges on this assumption, which is partly why so many FTM-spectrum folks who are on "T," prefer the pronoun "he," and move through the world as men, nevertheless disavow any male identification.

But from my perspective, the most poignant aspect of this quote is that there is absolutely no mention of trans women. We are absent, irrelevant, just as we are in most queer women's spaces. I suppose that this isn't surprising. After all, if many cis queer women view trans men as a variant of butch women, then it follows that trans women are merely a variant of cis men. And given this, if they also believe that dating cis men disqualifies them from being queer, then trans women aren't even going to be on their radar.

Lately, I've begun calling this mindset the *FAAB-mentality*. FAAB is an acronym for "female-assigned-at-birth." Both FAAB and its counterpart MAAB (male-assigned-at-birth) were originally coined by trans activists in order to challenge invalidating concepts such as "birth sex," "bio boys," and "genetic girls," and to stress that our gender identities are far more relevant than how the straight world nonconsensually categorized us when we were babies. Yet somehow, over the last few years, FAAB has been appropriated by many cis queer women who wish to convey their affiliation with trans men, and to distance themselves from trans women as well as cis men.

For instance, the musician Bitch recently wrote an open letter explaining why her support of trans woman-excluding women's spaces is not "transphobic."[4] She begins her letter by dismissing cis/trans terminology, and then she reframes the issue in terms of FAABs versus MAABs. Again, this is not an isolated incident—one can see FAAB-mentality rear its ugly head in trans-exclusive radical feminist blogs, and certain butch/femme and trans settings. I've even seen queer folks wearing T-shirts emblazoned with the word *FAABulous*.

So let me state for the record: I am not a fucking MAAB! I am a trans woman. And unlike all the so-called "FAAB FTMs" who move freely in queer women's spaces, I identify and move through the world as a woman. The whole point of trans activism is to get people to respect us for who we are, not for what the straight world expected us to grow up to be when we were mere babies. As far as I'm concerned, anyone who primarily categorizes me based upon how I was coercively assigned at birth is not merely anti-trans, but they are quite literally engaging in baby talk.

But FAAB-mentality isn't only transphobic—it's also biphobic, specifically toward bisexual women who are sexual with cis men, and who are likely to have their "queer credentials" called into question as a result of it. And despite the many cis femmes who now seemingly embrace FAAB terminology (as it allows them to partner with trans men yet still be considered lesbian), FAAB-mentality is highly femmephobic. After all, we live in a queer culture that valorizes sexual and gender non-conformity. So when FAAB-mentality defines womanhood in terms of being labeled "girl" as a baby, then the queerest, coolest thing you can grow up to be is androgynous, or butch, or trans masculine. In other words, FAAB-mentality is inexorably linked to masculine-centrism within queer women's communities. As a result, femmes are viewed as suspect, unless of course they "prove their queerness" by pairing with someone more outwardly gender non-conforming than them.

So I say, let's stop talking in baby talk! Let's acknowledge that, while FAAB and MAAB are sometimes useful clarifying terms, they should not be used as the primary means of defining trans male/masculine and trans female/feminine people, respectively.[5] And most importantly, let's stop viewing the world through the distorted lens of FAAB-mentality, as it inevitably causes femme, bisexual, and trans women to be treated as second-class queer citizens. Instead of obsessing over birth assignments and masculine gender expression, let's create new heterogeneous queer women's communities that celebrate difference—where a woman doesn't have to be born a particular way, or have sex a particular way, or dress or express their genders a particular way, or fulfill some kind of queer stereotype, in order to be appreciated.

39

First Date

This is the second piece that I performed at Girl Talk 2012. Most of my previous Girl Talk pieces delved into some of my more frustrating and disappointing experiences within queer women's communities, so I decided to write this piece about one very positive moment.

I like that we shared smart and silly banter on Twitter long before we stumbled upon one another's OkCupid profiles.

I like that your OkCupid handle had the word "feminist" in it, and that both of our profiles mentioned karaoke.

I like that you described yourself as a switch with top tendencies. Promising, given that I happen to be a switch with bottom tendencies.

I like the fact that, not only are we both femme, but we are both femmes who are primarily attracted to other femmes. There really should be more people like us!

I liked our initial flurry of back-and-forth messages, and how they made me check my email far more frequently than I normally do.

I liked when, on our first date, you told me that you wore heels for me, and that you liked my pink and gray Chuck Taylor's. I like your big pink fuzzy hat and your slight Southern accent.

I liked hearing that you have had numerous past relationships with trans women. Honestly, it's a relief to know that I won't have to be constantly schooling you about trans women's experiences and issues.

I like how it was you, and not me, who complained about the way some trans guys appropriate the label "tranny" without considering the trans-misogyny inherent in that word's history.[1] And I like that you shared my outrage when I ranted about how the acronym FAAB has somehow devolved into a new queer-hipster way of saying "womyn-born-womyn"-only.

I like that you are a long-time disability activist, and I am a long-time trans activist, but we just so happened to meet during a time in our lives when you are questioning your gender identity, and when an auto-immune condition has led me to reevaluate my own relationship with ability.[2]

I like how complex and unique your gender is.

I like the fact that, while assigned-female-at-birth, and non-binary-identified, you don't look or act stereotypically genderqueer. (Seriously, there really should be more than one way to be genderqueer!)

I liked how we flirted in the Shooting Star Cafe, and how, before we even held hands or kissed, we openly discussed our desires and boundaries and triggers with one another.

I like the fact that you find honest communication and consent just as sexy as I do.

I really liked our first kiss, and how we laughed as we managed the logistics of our significant height difference.

I like the fact that we decided that I was cute for being so small and that you were cute for being so tall.

I like how effortlessly we transitioned back and forth between making out, sharing stories, talking theory, and being completely and utterly silly.

I like that you are just as geeky and goofy as me, if not more so. And I like how quickly we seemed to develop an entire repertoire of inside jokes.

I like your long hair, I like your breasts, and I like your hairy calves.

I like that you called me "beautiful." It's so rare for me to hear another queer call me that.

I liked how, toward the end of the night, when we were cuddling, you stroked my face, but in the upward direction, the one that reveals the slight roughness of my stubble. I like that you are attracted to my female body and respect my female identity, but can also appreciate the more gender-discordant parts of me.

I liked how we fell asleep spooning one another, and how at random times throughout the night, we'd wake up and resume kissing and conversation.

I like the how the next morning, when I introduced you to my bird Buddy, she took an immediate liking to you.

I liked walking arm-in-arm with you to breakfast. I like being visibly queer with you.

I liked sitting with you in the corner booth of the Buttercup cafe, holding hands, and sharing more secrets and jokes over coffee, iced tea, and eggs.

I liked our two-minute-long goodbye kiss on the corner of Seventh and Broadway. I like that you are such a great kisser, and that it felt like we could have kept kissing one another forever.

I like how our twenty-hour-long first date inspired me to write this piece—the first love poem that I have written in years.

It suddenly strikes me that the phrase "love poem" has the word "love" in it. We only just met, and we still hardly know each other, so I am not about to drop the L-word yet. But I can say that right now, I am totally crushed out on you. And who knows: Perhaps our current mutual infatuation will grow into something more long term and special. Or maybe this will turn out to be one of those fireworks flings—explosive in the moment, but fizzling out rather quickly.

Even if the latter turns out to be true, I still want to thank you for sharing with me an evening and morning that I will always look back on fondly.

And I want to thank you for giving me hope that two queer femme misfits, who don't fit into today's androdyke, butch/femme, or cis lesbian scenes, can nevertheless find one another and make new and beautiful things happen.

40

Elders

This chapter and the following one were originally written for The Biggest Quake—a series of three spoken word shows curated by Kirk Read for the 2012 National Queer Arts Festival. The subtitle of the series was "New thinking on the San Francisco AIDS epidemic," and Kirk purposefully brought together queer artists of different generations, backgrounds, and identities to create new work related to that epidemic. This is an excerpt from one of the pieces that I performed for the series.

When we think of the AIDS epidemic at its height during the '80s and early '90s, we tend to immediately think of gay men. And for good reason: Gay male communities were decimated by the disease. Yet we tend to completely forget another segment of the LGBTQ community that was also severely impacted by the AIDS epidemic: transgender people, and especially trans women. While gay men in San Francisco had a thriving and visible community with enough activist resources to convey their stories of dying or surviving the epidemic, trans women back then tended to be more isolated, and relegated to more marginalized communities. And for this reason, most of us have never had a chance to hear their stories.

For many years, I was oblivious to this missing generation of trans women. I transitioned to female in 2001, at the age of thirty-three, many years removed from the worst of the AIDS crisis. During the early 2000s, there was a transgender renaissance of sorts here in the Bay Area—a vibrant community full of trans artists and activists. I was really active in the scene, fronting an indie-pop band, performing spoken word, getting involved in Camp Trans, all as a very outspoken trans dyke.

Then around 2005, I saw the documentary *Screaming Queens: The Riot at Compton's Cafeteria,* which tells the tale of transgender women and other queer/trans-spectrum people in the Tenderloin District who stood up to police in an uprising that took place in 1966, three years prior to Stonewall.[1] Upon watching it, I was stunned to discover that this riot took place on the corner of Turk and Taylor, literally half a block away from my band's practice space. For about five years, twice a week, I had been walking right by a piece of queer history without even knowing it. How could this be? How could such an important place and event be virtually lost to history?

While the film never explicitly answers this question, it seems clear that there are only a few first-hand participants and witnesses of that event who are still with us. While there are many reasons why these trans women may not have survived, it's quite likely that many of them were lost to the AIDS epidemic. After this realization, I couldn't help but constantly notice how young my trans community was—almost all of us seemed to be in our twenties and thirties back then. Sure, there were a few prominent older trans activists, but as I listed their names in my head, I noticed that the vast majority of them were either lesbian-identified trans women, or former lesbians who transitioned to become trans men. But the previous generation of trans women who had been sexual with men (such as most of the women involved in the riot at Compton's Cafeteria) remained largely unaccounted for.

It is distressing to contemplate how many trans women may have been lost to the AIDS epidemic. But what is even more tragic is the fact that their deaths are hardly ever remembered, or even acknowledged. While working on this piece, I repeatedly googled various permutations of "HIV/AIDS" and "transgender/transsexual/trans women," hoping to find more information, and perhaps a few of their stories. Many of the results I found discuss HIV/AIDS in the "gay, lesbian, bisexual, and transgender" community, but if you follow the links, the articles almost never actually discuss transgender people. A number of results assessed the current prevalence of HIV in transgender communities. Many of these, unfortunately, lump trans women into the category MSM (men who have sex with men). The few that focus specifically on trans women estimate that somewhere between 25 and 50 percent of trans women today are HIV positive.[2] Some results describe contemporary programs, clinics, and outreach addressing HIV and transgender women, especially those trans women who are at highest risk: those who are poor or homeless, trans women of color, and trans women who engage in sex work.

But in my search, I did not find any names or stories of trans women who lost their lives during the AIDS crisis. It is almost as if they had vanished from contemporary retellings of the AIDS epidemic and transgender history. During the last eleven years that I have spent in queer communities, I've heard countless heartfelt stories of gay men who were lost to AIDS—even though they are no longer with us, it's as if we can still feel their presence in our community. In contrast, the lack of readily accessible stories or information about trans women who died during the epidemic creates a void in our history—they are conspicuous by their absence.

We all know the saying "Silence = Death," intended at the time to encourage people to talk about the AIDS epidemic, to increase media coverage, to raise public awareness. Unfortunately, that equation can go the other way: Some people's deaths are relatively silent, like a branch that falls in the woods when no one seems to be listening, like the previous generation of trans women who were decimated by AIDS, while few people outside of their own personal circles were aware or perhaps even cared.

We tend to pay most attention to the activists who turn out in the largest numbers and who are most vocal. But we also must take it upon ourselves to tune into the silences: to ask ourselves who isn't being accounted for, and whose stories are not being told.

41

Contagious

Like the last chapter, this piece was originally written for The Biggest Quake in 2012. I performed this one on the final night. The second half of it was written directly in response to stories that had been shared by the other writers in the previous shows.

I live with four parrots. Whenever friends come over to visit, I always give them a heads up that my birds can be a bit loud, and that they will likely fly around the room, and such—I can understand how this might be disconcerting for folks who are not used to it. Most of my friends seem to enjoy the experience, or at least they congenially tolerate it. But in a few cases, my friends have been really freaked out by my birds. When I ask why, they almost always tell me that they are afraid of the germs birds carry. I'll empathize with them, tell them that when I was a child, my Mom used to tell me to stay away from birds because they carried germs. But she also told me the same thing about squirrels, and stray dogs and cats. In other words, the germs aren't intrinsic to the animals themselves, but are the result of life in the wild and lack of health monitoring. I'll point out that my birds have been indoor birds their whole lives. They see the vet once a year. They don't have any more germs than indoor dogs or cats do. But even after explaining all that, my friends are not persuaded. They have internalized the idea that birds are disease-ridden. No matter of talk or logic will change their minds.

In other words, dogs and cats are common pets, seen as normal, and not viewed as germ-ridden. But birds are unusual, exotic even, and therefore viewed by some as inherently sick and infectious.

Sometimes, when I come out to straight people as transsexual, I'll notice them slightly distancing themselves from me. When this happens, I wonder whether they consciously or unconsciously see me as sick or infectious. Perhaps they are afraid of catching my transsexual cooties?

Transphobia, homophobia, and biphobia, in their more extreme manifestations, usually evoke this fear of contagiousness. This is evident whenever conservative parents express concern about gay teachers, and fret about how their children might by infected by, and succumb to, some imaginary "homosexual agenda." Or when straight men worry that, if they were to have sex with a trans woman like me, that the experience might somehow "make them gay." I believe that this assumption—that queerness is somehow contagious—is why the "we're just born that way" argument has been so effective in placating straight people and garnering mainstream acceptance. After all, if being queer is a birth defect, not only do we not have a choice in being what we are, but it also implies that straight people can't catch it from us.

Growing up in suburban Philadelphia in the late '70s and early '80s, it seemed as though there were no queer people in the world other than me. Back then, almost all of the out queers lived in cities, far outside of my view. Suburban queers usually remained closeted, even those who were living in plain view. My Great-Uncle Vince never married, and lived with his "best friend" for thirty years, but if you were ever to suggest that they might be a gay couple, everyone in my family would adamantly deny it. During that time and place, words like "gay" and "queer" were to be avoided like the plague.

Ironically, given the utter lack of gay-identified people in our world, kids my age used to throw the word "gay" around all the time. Sometimes it was used as a synonym for "dumb." Other times, when kids said, "that's so gay!" they meant to convey that the object or person was "pathetic" or "gross." Meanings run deep. And so, when I used to dress up as a girl within the privacy of my childhood bedroom, I couldn't help but feel stupid, and pathetic, and gross. I kept quiet about who I was at the time, not only to avoid the stigma of being called "gay" or "queer" by my classmates and peers, but also because I feared that the truth of who I was would implicate my entire family. My parents would be devastated. My younger sisters would be teased for being related to me. It was as if they would all be affected (or perhaps infected) by my queerness. So I tried to keep it all to myself, so that I wouldn't contaminate everyone else around me. You could say that I, and my Great-Uncle Vince, and other suburban queers of the time were "closeted." But sometimes it felt more like a self-imposed quarantine.

I was in high school in the early '80s when AIDS first began garnering national attention. The notion of a so-called "gay disease" really seemed to lit-eralize this metaphor of queerness being contagious (if you'll allow me to wax Susan Sontag-ish).[1] Suddenly, stories of queer people, who had been virtually invisible in my suburban world, started appearing in our newspapers, mag-azines, and TV screens on a daily basis. And correspondingly, homophobia became increasingly blatant and virulent. Urban legends started spreading: tall tales about gay men, bisexuals, prostitutes, and other supposed deviants who set out to intentionally infect innocent straight people. Adults who fancied themselves as open minded when they said, "I don't care what people do in the bedroom, just so long as they don't flaunt it in front of me," suddenly started calling for more invasive measures, such as rounding up and quarantining peo-ple with AIDS, or agreeing with libertarian William F. Buckley Jr.'s suggestion that all HIV-positive people should be tattooed on their forearms and asses in order to protect the uninfected masses.[2]

Of course, these reactions were abominable. But they changed my world in an important way. Within a few short years, suburban folks went from want-ing to believe that nobody they knew was queer, to wanting to know who was queer and who was not. This may have been for the worst possible reason. But for the first time in my isolated, suburban life, people began acknowledging the reality that queer folks lived amongst them. And being queer suddenly seemed like an actual possibility to me—not merely a slur, but something that somebody could actually be.

These days, I am a walking cliché: One of the thousands upon thousands of queer people over the years who have moved to the San Francisco Bay Area with the expressed purpose of more fully exploring our genders and/or sexuali-ties. In the seventeen years that I've been here, I've undergone numerous chang-es in identity. These days, I might describe myself as a bisexual femme-tomboy trans woman who tends to be attracted to other feminine people (independent of gender), and who is currently ethically non-monogamous. Yes, I know, that's a mouthful.

Most people I know who are ethically non-monogamous prefer to call themselves polyamorous or "poly" instead. I have nothing against poly *per se*, but I've met too many people who are super-heavily invested in promoting polyamory as an enlightened, liberating, cutting edge, oppression-shattering way of being, one that challenges the conservative, heteronormative nature of monogamy. As if we need another fucking binary. It seems to me that, regardless of whether a person is mono or poly, some people tend to be good at relationships—respectful of their partners' needs, concerns, boundaries, and desires—while other people are not. Some monogamous relationships work perfectly, while some polyamorous relationships fail miserably. Personally, I have been happy in monogamous relationships, and also in ethically non-monogamous ones. Friends have described me as monogamish or polyflexible. But I've decided to call myself "ambiamorous," because frankly, I like coining new words.

At the end of the previous night's show, Kirk (the curator of The Biggest Quake) gave the audience an assignment: to write about something related to AIDS that no one else is talking about. In mulling it over, it struck me that over the course of these three shows, none of the performers have brought up the subject of monogamy. This is potentially surprising given that some have touted it as a means of reducing one's chances of contracting HIV. Perhaps the subject didn't come up because none of us in The Biggest Quake cast are currently monogamous—although I don't want to be presumptuous about other people's relationship statuses. So allow me to speak in "I" statements:

I didn't have my first HIV test until the age of thirty, when I was on the verge of entering into what turned out to be an almost-ten-year-long monogamous relationship with a queer woman. Back then, we used to joke that we were the only monogamous queer couple in the Bay Area. We knew that it wasn't quite true, but it really did feel that way. Anyway, I digress . . .

I justified not getting an HIV test until the age of thirty on the basis that I consistently used condoms and hadn't engaged in any high-risk behaviors. But frankly, the main reason why I put it off for so long was because I was scared. I moved around a lot in my twenties and did not have a good support network, plus I didn't have adequate health insurance. So I had no idea what I would do if I found out I was HIV-positive. But thankfully, my test came back negative, and so did my partner's, and from that point forward we became "fluid-bonded" (although I'm sure that was before I had even head that term). We separated about five years ago, and since then, I have HIV tests regularly, about once a year. It's become routine, mundane, like having your car's oil changed.

During the last few The Biggest Quake shows, it was interesting for me to hear how HIV status is sometimes navigated in certain gay male communities, as it is very different from what takes place in my own dating circles. My dating pool lies somewhere at the intersection of where queer-identified trans people, trans-friendly queer women, bisexual and pansexual folks, and the poly and

BDSM communities, all overlap. It makes for a very interesting Venn diagram. In my dating circles, sex-positive feminism rules the day, and a lot of value is placed on negotiation, processing, and bodily autonomy; on sane, safe, and consensual sex. Sometimes we talk way more than we actually have sex. But in many cases, all that talk makes the sex way better. Or at least it does for me. I've survived two attempted date rapes in my life, so nowadays it's easier for me to achieve ecstasy when I err on the side of trust and safety.

Queer and kink communities both share the fact that they are fairly small and insular, so everyone ends up knowing one another. It is not unusual to be at a party or event, and to find yourself in a circle of conversation with your ex, her current partner, a mutual friend who also once dated your ex, and one of your current partners' other partners. It reminds me of that famous quote by C. Everett Koop, who was U.S Surgeon General during the onset of the AIDS epidemic. Talking about unprotected sex, he said: "When you have sex with someone, you are having sex with everyone they have had sex with for the last ten years, and everyone they and their partners have had sex with for the last ten years."[3]

When Koop said that, I don't think that he ever imagined us all at a party talking and laughing with one another.

Anyway, in my dating circles, safe-sex practices tend to be a vigorously enforced norm. So it strikes me as odd to hear how much unprotected sex (or conversations about unprotected sex) seem to be going on in certain segments of gay male communities.[4] To be clear, I am not being judgmental here. I believe in bodily autonomy—we each have the right to do whatever the fuck we want with our own bodies. But I am kind of curious. The AIDS epidemic decimated gay male communities, while leaving queer women's communities largely intact. Yet nowadays, it seems as though queer women (and where they intersect with trans, poly, and BDSM communities) may preach and possibly adhere to safe-sex regimes more rigorously than gay male communities do. If this is true, why might this be?

Someone with stereotyped notions of femaleness and maleness might suggest that men are simply far more horny than women. While this might be true on average, I've had a number of female partners who've had insatiable sexual appetites, and who are at least as horny (if not hornier) than most men. But it never caused them to become lax or reckless with regard to safe-sex practices.

As someone who has moved through the world as both a woman and a man, I think that some of this may come down to perceived safety. Women are on the receiving end of all kinds of shit—misogyny, sexual harassment, abuse, and rape—that most men never have to deal with. I think this leads many queer women to seek out safe and self-empowering sexual situations. In contrast, the presumption that men are not vulnerable, and cannot be victims, may lead some queer men to throw all caution to the wind. Like all generalizations, I admit that this is likely overly simplistic. But I offer it to you simply as something to chew over.

42

In Defense of Partners

This essay first appeared on my blog in 2013, where it served as both a reaction to a current event and an introduction to a video performance of my spoken word piece "Desirable" (which is the subsequent chapter). Both pieces expand on Chapter 32, "The Beauty in Us" in empowering trans desirability and critiquing "the fetish concept."

This last weekend, I finally got around to reading Janet Mock's recent essay "How Society Shames Men Dating Trans Women & How This Affects Our Lives," which she wrote in response to the media coverage and public backlash against DJ Mister Cee (a cisgender male hip-hop artist and radio personality) for his attempt to solicit sex from someone who he thought was a trans woman.[1] Mock's piece rightfully points out how the public's shaming of men who are attracted to trans women—e.g., by insulting their manhood, or presuming that they are closeted gay men—undermines our identities too, as the underlying assumption is that we must be "fake women" or "really men."

Mock's essay is very timely, as it shines light onto what I feel has become a huge gaping hole in trans activism. Namely, while we have made some progress in challenging mainstream attitudes toward trans people, we have barely made a dent in the public's attitudes toward, and assumptions about, people who choose to partner with us.

For instance, over the last ten years there has been a noticeable decline in jokes directly targeting transgender people in the media, especially in shows that have more liberal or progressive audiences (e.g., programs like *The Daily Show*, *The Colbert Report*). Yet these same programs continue to regularly make jokes that insinuate that we are undesirable and that there must be something wrong with (and therefore hilarious about) people who are attracted to us.

Why does this discrepancy exist? Well, here is a pragmatic explanation: These days, when shows poke fun at trans people directly, the trans community will strongly protest. Petitions will go up on the Internet, GLAAD and other organizations will start sending out press releases. Suddenly, the show in question will have a big public relations mess on their hands. So while many cisgender comedy writers may still consider us to be laughingstocks, they won't risk making those jokes if they know that there is going to be a big blowback.

However, when they ridicule people who are attracted to us, typically nothing happens. A few people may grumble about the incident on Facebook, Twitter, and other social media outlets, but the community at large does not push back. Why not? Well, the sad truth is that we (the trans community) are often just as suspicious of cisgender people who choose to partner with us as the cis majority is. And while the mainstream regularly belittles people who find us attractive, unfortunately trans people often do the same too.

Admittedly, we do it slightly differently. The cisgender majority will shame Mister Cee and men like him by questioning their manhood and sexual orientation. In my own trans community, people routinely dismiss such men by labeling them as "tranny chasers" and "fetishists."

While there are legitimate critiques to be made of the way in which some (albeit not all) cisgender men who "admire" trans women express their attractions (e.g., by exoticizing us, viewing us as mere sexual objects, not fully respecting our female identities, not treating us as human beings), I believe that the wholesale stereotyping of them and using psychiatric language to pathologize them only worsens the problem—not just for them, but for us as well. Once again, the underlying premise that drives these accusations is that there must be something wrong with them because, after all, they are attracted to us.

This suspicion extends far beyond those men who watch trans porn, solicit trans sex workers, or secretly occasion trans pick-up bars. Cisgender women and men who are in loving committed relationships with their trans partners are also regularly dismissed as being "chasers" and "fetishists." If they want to avoid these accusations, then they have to defend themselves via a convoluted and often contradictory set of claims:

"I am attracted to my trans partner, but not because they are trans, but also not despite the fact that they are trans. Because, after all, I believe that trans people and trans bodies are attractive and deserving of love. But by saying that, I am not trying to imply that I am specifically attracted to my partner's more trans-specific traits, but

at the same time, they do not gross me out either. Honestly, I view my partner's body the exact same way that I view cisgender bodies. Oh God, I hope that last comment doesn't come off as too cisnormative . . ."

Of course, this I-accidentally-fell-in-love-with-a-trans-person-and-I'm-to-tally-okay-with-it-in-a-completely-non-creepy-way spiel only works if you've only ever dated one trans person. If your dating history includes more than one trans partner, then good luck shaking off that "fetish"/"chaser" label.

Way back in the past, I used to assume that people who were attracted to trans people had some kind of a "fetish." But then a trans friend challenged me on this. She asked me why we call men who are attracted to trans women (the vast majority of whom are also attracted to women more generally) "fetish-ists," yet men who limit their dating pool to *just* non-trans women somehow manage to avoid the "fetish" label? Isn't the latter group more restrictive and particular in their desires? Aren't they the ones who really have a "fetish?" Her question stumped me. I thought about it for days, but I couldn't come up with a reasonable rebuttal.

Years later, it became perfectly clear to me what she was getting at. I was doing research to debunk the concept of autogynephilia (see Chapter 33). In the course of that work, I read paper after paper by Ray Blanchard, the psychologist who coined the term. What we lay folks call "fetishes," pathologizing psychologists like Blanchard call "paraphilias." For the latest *DSM* manual, Blanchard was put in charge of defining the term, so unfortunately, here is how "paraphilia" is now described by the most authoritative of psychiatric texts: "any intense and persistent sexual interest other than sexual interest in genital stimulation or preparatory fondling with phenotypically normal, physically mature, consenting human partners."[2] Now I am 100 percent behind the idea that consent is crucial and that adults having sex with children is wrong. But everything else about this definition is horrifying: Basically, if your sexual interests or desires drift in any way outside of what other people perceive as normal, then congratulations, you now have a paraphilia!

By the way, the term "phenotypically normal" means "normal" with regards to observable anatomical or behavioral traits. And as you can probably guess by now, Blanchard does not view trans people as "phenotypically normal." In fact, he coined the paraphilia "gynandromorphophilia" to describe attraction to trans female/feminine people; other researchers have coined the paraphilia "andromimetophilia" to describe attraction to trans male/masculine people.[3]

In lay terminology, gynandromorphophilia is the "fetish" that Mister Cee, my girlfriend, everyone I've dated post-transition, and all of my trans woman friends' partners, supposedly have in common.

Attraction is a messy and complicated matter. I have researched it extensively, and I can tell you that absolutely nobody knows why people turn out to be heterosexual, homosexual, bisexual/pansexual, or asexual. Nobody understands why some people prefer certain body or personality types or traits over others, while other people have different (sometimes extremely different) predilections.

I have no idea why some people are attracted to trans people. And let me be clear: When I say "attracted to trans people," I am not talking about that extraordinarily rare person (who I'm not sure even exists) who is *only* attracted to trans people, but not at all to cis people. Rather, I am talking about a heterogeneous population of people who are attracted to many cisnormative and non-gender-related human traits, but who also (additionally!) happen to be attracted to some human traits that are considered to be gender non-conforming or non-cisnormative. Sure, some of these traits may be bodily traits (these being the ones that garner the most attention and consternation in discussions about so-called "fetishes"). But such gender-non-conforming or non-cisnormative traits may also be behavioral traits (e.g., related to gender expression) or personality traits. Indeed, I have had partners tell me that they find trans women attractive because, in their experience, we tend to be especially self-assured, interesting, and/or critical of societal norms. The point is that being attracted to trans people can take on many forms and can vary significantly from person to person.

So to restate: I have no idea why some people are attracted to certain gender-non-conforming/non-cisnormative human traits (and who therefore find trans folks particularly attractive). But I do know why most people *are not* attracted to such traits: because trans people and bodies are highly stigmatized throughout society. This stigmatization inflicts shame on those of us who are trans—a shame that many of us work hard to overcome.

But this shame also affects people who find us attractive—not in the same way, nor to the same extent, but it does affect them. Rather than seeing their attraction toward us as "normal" and "healthy," society teaches them to view it as a "fetish." This shame encourages them to keep their attraction secret—this applies to both cis people who self-identify as "admirers," "fetishists," or "chasers" and purposefully seek out trans partners, as well as to those cis people who are surprised to find out that the person they are attracted to, or dating, or have fallen in love with, is trans and who subsequently hide that info (and sometimes even their partner's existence) from friends and family.

If we want to move past all this shame, then we need to embrace the fact that trans people are worthy of desire, and that some cis people (as well as some trans people) will find us attractive. To accomplish this, we need to destroy the psychopathologizing myth that so-called "fetishists" and "chasers" exist.[4] And we need to create space for cis partners of trans people to respectfully discuss their desires and to articulate (in concert with trans people) how the fetish concept demeans both them and us. I am not suggesting that we should bend over backwards to include cis people who invalidate our gender identities or view us only as sexual objects. But we should amplify the voices of cis partners who are willing to challenge cissexism and who truly appreciate us as living breathing people.

43

Desirable

This piece was written for Girl Talk in 2013. It is my most thorough critique of "the fetish concept" to date, and I additionally discuss the more specific negative ramifications this mindset has had for trans women within queer women's communities.

In the early 2000s, I hosted a trans, intersex, and genderqueer-focused performance series called GenderEnders. One of my most successful shows, and the one for which I received the most positive feedback, took place nine years ago, in May 2004. It featured readings by cis partners of trans people, and I billed it as "The Tranny Lovers Show."

I often think back to that show, in part because it was such an amazing night. But also because it's hard for me to reconcile that amazingness with the fact that, if I proposed the exact same show today, I would probably get run out of town.

For starters, many would complain about my use of the word "tranny," which many of us regularly used in a reclaimed way back then, but which has since become extremely controversial, taboo even (as I discuss in Chapter 45). Admittedly, if I were putting on a similar show nowadays, I wouldn't include the "T-word" in the title, not because I personally hate it (frankly, I'm rather ambivalent toward it), but because I wouldn't want to alienate potential audience members. But even with that change, there remain two other reasons why my "Tranny Lovers Show" would likely be critically panned today. Let's call them the "A-word" and the "F-word."

The A-word is *appropriation*. The argument goes something like this: Trans people are an oppressed minority, whereas cis people are the privileged majority. So when cis people define or describe themselves in relation to their couplings with trans people, they are appropriating our circumstances and the oppression we face. Therefore, the only non-appropriative way for cis partners to view themselves is as trans allies. And as allies, they shouldn't put the focus on themselves (for instance, by talking about their experiences being partnered to us), but rather they should simply work to have the voices of actual trans people be heard.

Now personally, I have a lot of reservations about how the word "appropriation" is sometimes used, because it can mean very different things to different people (as I discuss in detail in Chapter 44). For instance, I could claim that drag queens, cis women who undergo hormone replacement therapy, and crossdressed trick-or-treaters all "appropriate" trans women's experiences. Conversely, trans-exclusive radical feminists often insist that trans women "appropriate" cis women's bodies and circumstances. Appropriation is a fancy way of saying that some people should be allowed to do certain things while others should not, and thus lends itself rather easily to policing other people's gender expressions and perspectives. Rather than fixate on appropriation, I believe that we should instead critique acts that exploit, erase, or denigrate trans people. And I don't see how cis partners do any of these things when they talk about their relationships with us.

Furthermore, reducing our cis partners to the status of being "merely allies," or silencing them because they have cis privilege, ignores the fact that they too are marginalized—they are often shunned by family and friends, and may even become targeted for violence (if you don't believe me, look up the name Barry Winchell).[1] And this marginalization isn't merely the result of what is sometimes called "courtesy stigma" (where people are viewed negatively if they associate or partner with a member of a stigmatized group).[2] Rather, our partners are singled out because of their own sexualities. In a world where trans bodies and genders are viewed as gross and illegitimate, respectively, other people will question our partners' sexual orientations, sexual proclivities, and sometimes even their gender identities. And because we are seen as freaks, our partners are often accused of being indiscriminate, promiscuous, desperate, or deviants.

Rather than challenge this marginalization that our cis partners face, sometimes we as a trans community participate in and perpetuate it. For instance, many of us automatically view people who find us attractive with suspicion or derision. Indeed, this leads us directly to the third reason why a "Tranny Lovers Show" would probably go over like a lead balloon today: Some trans folks would inevitably dismiss the cis participants as "creepy" and discredit their desires by invoking the dreaded "F-word": *fetishist*.

The word "fetish" is derived from the Portuguese word for artificial. Fetishes are literally viewed as fake forms of attraction. When applied to partner choice, the fetish concept is used to delegitimize attraction to any and all bodies that are not considered normative. This is why people are accused of having "transgender fetishes," "fat fetishes," or "disability fetishes," but not "cisgender fetishes," "thin fetishes," or "able-bodied fetishes" (even in cases where the person in question exclusively partners with these latter groups). In talking about a woman I find attractive, I'm allowed to praise any of her cisnormative features and no one will flinch. But if I said that I was attracted to her beard stubble, her tall stature, or her pre-op or non-op genitals, then suddenly most people—cis and trans alike—would argue that I must be suffering from some kind of fetish.

The fetish concept is an unusual form of marginalization in that it targets two different groups simultaneously. One group (in this case, trans folks) is deemed to be an illegitimate object of desire that cannot be loved for the entirety of their person, but rather only as "fetish objects." The second group consists of people who find us attractive, and who therefore are presumed to suffer from an abnormal and abominable form of desire. Laypeople call it a fetish. Psychiatrists call it a paraphilia, and they describe people who are attracted to trans women as suffering from gynandromorphophilia. (Apparently, they have a thing for words with way too many syllables.) In other words, our culture pathologizes our cis partners. And the fetish concept sexualizes both of us: Our partners are reduced to the status of "sexual deviants," while we are reduced to the status of "fetish objects."

Admittedly, some people dislike their trans bodies and thus experience discomfort when others express attraction or appreciation toward their transness. While this is an understandable reaction, it does not by any means make that attraction a "fetish." As someone who believes that being trans is just as legitimate as being cis, I believe that it is perfectly natural for people to be attracted to my transness, and I don't protest it provided that they 1) fully respect my self-identified gender, 2) appreciate me as a whole person, and 3) refrain from sexually harassing me. And even if they fail to meet these three criteria, that doesn't make them a "fetishist," it just makes them an asshole.

There is a popular assumption (among pathologizing psychiatrists and laypeople alike) that so-called "fetishists" are singularly focused and relentless in pursuit of their "fetish objects." This explains why many trans people use the pejorative "tranny chaser" (with its connotations of stalking and obsession) interchangeably with "tranny fetishist." And can I take a second to point out what should be blatantly obvious: If the word "tranny" is truly a beyond-the-pale insult (as some trans folks insist), then isn't it hypocritical for us to use it in a slur against people who are attracted to us? And if we really believe that the *DSM* maligns and invalidates us, then why the fuck do we use psychiatric language and concepts to pathologize cis people?

For the life of me, I can't fathom why we need the term "tranny chaser." Sure, when men know that I'm trans, sometimes they'll hit on me aggressively. But men also aggressively hit on cis women, but nobody ever calls them "cissy chasers." Can't we just call all sexually harassing and objectifying behavior "sexualization" rather than perpetuating the psychiatric myth that so-called "fetishes" exist?

A failure to distinguish between everyday sexualization and the fetish concept lies at the heart of trans dykes' dilemma in contemporary queer women's communities. Basically, trans men constantly complain about how they are "fetishized" by cis queer women who find them attractive and purposefully seek them out. First off, smallest violin in the world—most trans dykes would kill for that kind of appreciation from other queer women.[3] Second, it's a total misnomer to call this "fetishization" because trans guys are generally seen as *legitimate objects of desire* in contemporary dyke communities, unlike trans women. If you're a cis queer woman who is partnered to a trans guy, nobody blinks an eye. But if you start dating a trans woman, some queer women will view you as aberrant, question your motives, and may even ostracize you.

It is important to note that trans guys weren't always considered legitimate partners for cis dykes. Back in the '80s and '90s, being partnered to a trans man typically led one to be shut out of lesbian communities. So what changed? How did dating trans men go from being anathema to being acceptable or even admirable?

It's quite simple really. Back then, most trans men didn't protest when their cis dyke partners openly discussed their relationships and the difficulties inherent in being a queer woman partnered to a trans man within a community founded on separatism and rallying against the patriarchy. Those discussions proliferated, and as they did, the stigma associated with dating trans men slowly lifted. Eventually, many cis queer women began proudly referring to themselves as "trans-sensual" and "trans-amorous." And say all the negative things you want about those labels and their doppelgänger "trans admirer," but at least they challenge the societal assumption that trans people are inherently undesirable.

Anyway, that was the atmosphere that existed nine years ago when I first curated the "Tranny Lovers Show," which is why cis and trans folks both appreciated it so. But in the years that followed there was a pushback, primarily from trans men who felt "fetishized" by cis dykes, and who made it impossible for cis queer women to talk about their desires without being threatened by the specter of "tranny chaser." Conveniently for trans guys, this trend occurred after they had already been deemed to be legitimate partners in queer women's communities. It was as if they pulled up the ladder behind them.

And now, as a result, trans dykes are left stranded on the outside, along with our cis partners, who feel like they can neither publicly discuss the lack of support they get in their own dyke communities, nor express the attraction they experience toward trans women, without being accused of "appropriation" or being dismissed as "chasers."

As queer trans women, it is in our best interest for us to work to put an end to these trends. Discussions like the one we are having tonight are an important start. But honestly, in the five years that we have put on Girl Talk shows, I'm not sure that I've once heard anyone explicitly say, "trans women are hot." All of us here tonight are dancing around the fetish concept—we are allowed to express romantic love and affection, but we're all deathly afraid to say that "trans women are fucking sexy" or (god forbid) "I prefer dating trans women to cis women." Until cis queer women can openly express such thoughts without fear of being dismissed as appropriators and fetishists, we will never see any progress.

In order to foster this change, we trans women need to do two things. First, we must support our partners if they wish to speak out about their experiences being in relationships with us: both the wonderful and the difficult parts, the internalized trans-misogyny they may have had to overcome, as well as the derision they face from other queer women or society more generally. Their stories will help legitimize cis-and-trans dyke relationships and make clear that trans women are desirable and worthy of love.

Second, we must learn to embrace the fact that, while we may personally feel sadness or a sense of loss regarding our trans bodies and histories, others may nevertheless view us as attractive, powerful, courageous, interesting, and sexy *because* of the fact that we are trans, not in spite of it. My body, personality, and perspectives may not be perfect (nobody's are), but they are special because they transcend our culture's cisnormative ideals. To appropriate a phrase from

Fight Club: I am a beautiful and unique snowflake.[4] And I expect that some people—especially those who are more discerning and open-minded—will be able to appreciate that.

Male admirers often praise trans women for being "versatile," "the best of both worlds," or "girls with something extra." I've always hated the way such language seemingly ranks trans women according to how well we adhere to traditional she-male-porn standards. But having said that, I must say that I have come to appreciate the way that these clichés portray trans women as being special for the ways in which we are different from cis women. Perhaps we can create similar, albeit less phallocentric, language to express why trans women are special and worthy of queer women's desire. Maybe we should praise trans women for being secret double agents who spent our childhoods embedded in the enemy camp, and as a result, we now have insights into gender and sexism that cis women are not privy to. Trans women are sexy because we have bucked the patriarchy in the most flagrant way possible. Trans women are hot because, unlike our cis counterparts, we have chosen to be women and we have gone to incredible lengths, and overcome incommensurable obstacles, in order to make that reality possible. Trans women are attractive because we are tenacious, impervious, relentless, and badass. We don't take shit lying down—we are survivors and we are fucking desirable.

Part Five

Differences of Opinion in Trans Activism

As activists, we will often point to something out in the world—a word, assumption, action, media depiction, and/or some person—and we will sincerely and passionately argue that it contributes to our marginalization. And although we forward such claims with the best of intentions (e.g., making the world safer or more just for gender-variant people), stating them in an adamant or matter of fact manner essentially creates a binary opposition: Other people can only ever side "with us" or "against us." If the person who disagrees with our claim is a member of the dominant majority, it is easy enough to dismiss their stance as being the result of them being "the oppressor." But when disagreement comes from within our own community, we may feel threatened because the opposing party's stance seems to undermine our position, and we may be tempted to accuse them of being naive, dupes, assimilationists, or traitors who are "reinforcing" our oppression and/or holding back the movement. These sorts of claims are being made constantly in all spheres of activism. They not only create rifts in our movements, but they are a major cause of erasure and exclusion: People who disagree with the majority of their own marginalized group (or its most vociferous faction) may feel compelled to remain silent about their opinion, or may be personally smeared if they voice their dissent.

Most people associate activism with taking steadfast and strident positions. Despite this stereotype, in *Excluded* I argue that being a thoughtful and productive activist often requires us to learn to accept differences of opinion within our movements. After all, activists of different (or even similar) backgrounds will inevitably face different issues, have different concerns, view the world from different vantage points, draw from different experiences, and advocate for different courses of action. Therefore, if we want our movements to move beyond homogenization and hierarchies, then we must abandon fixed one-size-fits-all views of activism, and instead learn to accept a multiplicity of perspectives—each with potential benefits and drawbacks, and each being potentially useful or misguided depending on the context.

Since I finished writing *Excluded* in March 2013, I have tried to apply this idea to a variety of contentious contemporary issues within transgender activism. This work has led to a series of essays that have appeared on my blog over the last two years;[1] a handful of the pieces that I am most proud of are reproduced as chapters in this section.

44

Considering Trans
and Queer Appropriation

This essay first appeared on my blog in October 2013. It grew out of a year-long thought process during which I grappled with three big questions: When an activist claims that some action or undertaking constitutes "appropriation," what exactly do they mean? When two activists disagree with one another regarding whether something is "appropriative" or not, what is the underlying logic that leads them to their differing conclusions? Are there instances when claims of "appropriation" potentially do more harm than good? What follows is the result of said ruminations.

Within the activist circles I run in, I routinely hear people accuse others of *appropriation*, or claim that certain behaviors or endeavors are *appropriative*. I myself have written about how certain people (e.g., cisgender academics and media producers) sometimes appropriate transgender identities and experiences (discussed more below). So I am certainly sympathetic to the concept.

At the same time, however, I have seen the concept of appropriation used (or misused) in order to undermine marginalized groups. For instance, cisgender feminists have long accused trans women of "appropriating female dress" or "appropriating women's identities"—this was part of the justification for why Sylvia Rivera was kicked off the stage at a 1973 Pride rally in New York City.[1] On the TERF website "Pretendbians," the byline at the top of the webpage says: "We don't hate you, we hate appropriation"—the implication being that trans women cannot ever be actual lesbians, but rather we can only appropriate lesbian identities and culture.[2]

Recently, on several occasions, I have heard trans people claim that cisgender people who perform drag, or who crossdress as part of a Halloween costume, appropriate trans people's identities and culture. Such statements surprised me, in part because they are so eerily similar to the aforementioned accusations of appropriation that trans-exclusive radical feminists have levied against us. But what struck me even more was how such claims represent a complete about-face from the direction that transgender activism took during the '90s and early '00s. During that era, we tended to celebrate binary-shattering activities. Trans activists didn't merely discuss our own gender non-conformity, but we emphasized the fact that most of us (whether trans or not) transgress gender norms at some points in our lives. Indeed, trans activists often encouraged forms of gender transgression in the cisgender majority, as we generally believed that such expressions would help undermine binary gender norms throughout society.

And suddenly now in 2013, some trans people are essentially taking the exact opposite approach by discouraging cisgender people from transgressing gender norms (via accusations that such actions represent an appropriation of transgender identities and culture).

In the wake of all these claims, I have done a lot of thinking about appropriation over the last year. And I have come to the conclusion that the issue is way more complicated than the cut-and-dried "appropriation-is-always-bad" perspective that seems to predominate in activist settings. While we should be concerned about appropriation (especially certain manifestations of it), we should also be cognizant of some of the negative ramifications that can arise from the indiscriminate or overzealous use of the concept. In this essay, I will share some of my thoughts on this matter.

For the record, my main focus here will be accusations of appropriation with regards to gender and sexuality, and what they mean for transgender and queer (e.g., LGBTQIA+) communities and activism. Some of what I say may have relevance to other instances of cultural appropriation (e.g., with regards to ethnicity, class, religion, nationality, etc.). However, LGBTQIA+ identities and cultures are unique in a number of ways (which I will address toward the end of the piece), and this may limit the usefulness of applying what I say here to other such instances of appropriation.

What Is "Appropriation" and Why (or Perhaps When) Is It Bad?

In the most general sense, appropriation occurs when we take something that somebody else has created and use it for our own purposes. For example, I can appropriate a certain chord progression others have previously used in order to create a new song. Or I could appropriate another person's theory and apply it to a new problem. If I like your fashion sense, I may appropriate your style. Human beings are highly social animals: We are imitators, and we learn language, fashion, traditions, expressions, and ideas from one another. As the saying goes, there is nothing new under the sun. Almost everything we create has its origins elsewhere—we are constantly adopting, adapting, and repurposing other people's past creations and reconstructing them in novel ways. So appropriation—in the most general sense—is an everyday part of human life.

Within social justice movements, we typically use the word "appropriation" in a more specific sense: to describe instances where a dominant and/or majority group takes up some tangible or intangible aspect of a marginalized and/or minority community. Sometimes it is the marginalized/minority group's identity that gets appropriated—for instance, members of the dominant/majority group may claim that identity for themselves, or create their own depictions of members of that group (which typically resemble the dominant/majority group's assumptions and stereotypes rather than the marginalized/minority group's lived realities). Other times, it is the minority group's culture (e.g., their language, art, beliefs, religions, traditions, rituals, and fashions) that gets appropriated. Often cited examples include when Western countries appropriate art and artifacts from nations they have colonized, or appropriate their spiritual practices and traditions (as seen with the popularity of Yoga and Buddhism here in the U.S.). Or in how white America has historically appropriated musical styles that had their origins in African-American communities (e.g., jazz, rock-and-roll, hip-hop). And so on.

So if appropriation (in the most general sense) is a basic human tendency, why is it considered to be bad when dominant/majority groups appropriate from marginalized/minority groups? I would argue that there are at least three non-mutually-exclusive reasons why this is so:

- *Erasure:* Marginalized/minority groups have little power or voice in society. Therefore, when the dominant/majority group takes up their identities, ideas, and other cultural creations, it tends to undermine or erase the context in which they were created, and the original meanings and symbolism that underlie them. In other words, the dominant/majority typically takes up the marginalized/minority group's creations while disregarding their perspective. Sometimes the fact that the appropriated items had their origins within the marginalized/minority group (rather than the dominant/majority) gets overlooked or forgotten.

- *Exploitation:* Sometimes members of the dominant/majority group will materially profit from aspects or acts that they have appropriated from a marginalized/minority group without ever giving anything back to that community. This tends to further exacerbate economic disparities that may already exist between the two groups.

- *Denigration:* This can refer to a couple different things. Denigration can mean "to treat or represent as lacking in value or importance; belittle," which applies to instances where important or sacred aspects of the marginalized/minority group's identity or culture are appropriated by the dominant/majority group in an irreverent or disrespectful manner. Denigration can also mean "to speak damagingly of; criticize in a derogatory manner; sully; defame: to denigrate someone's character," which applies to instances where the dominant/majority group appropriates some aspect of the marginalized/minority group's identity or culture in order to purposefully ridicule, parody, or insult members of that group.[3]

As I mentioned earlier, in my past writings (specifically in *Whipping Girl*), I have critiqued the way in which cisgender media producers and academic researchers have appropriated trans people in their art and theories, for instance, when they hold us up as examples of gender ambiguity or liminality.[4] Such instances are problematic because:

- They erase the marginalized group's voice and perspective (as trans people are depicted as merely symbols or metaphors, while our real-life circumstances and issues as a marginalized population are completely ignored).

- They exploit the marginalized group (as certain cisgender media producers have made lots of money capitalizing on the exoticness of gender-variant lives, and some cisgender gender theorists have garnered success and built their careers upon interpreting trans people's bodies and identities, without giving anything back to the trans community).

- They denigrate the marginalized group (in that cisgender media producers and academic researchers often outright dismiss or discount trans people's self-accounts, fail to take trans people's struggles seriously, and sometimes even blatantly ridicule or demean trans people in the process).

I believe that these three phenomena—erasure, exploitation, and denigration (or "EED" for short)—encapsulate most, if not all, of what typically concerns activists when they critique instances of appropriation.

Once we recognize EED, it becomes clear why dominant/majority groups' appropriation of marginalized/minority identities and cultures can be a bad thing, but not vice versa. After all, marginalized/minority groups have relatively little power or voice in society, and thus are not in a position to erase or exploit the identity and culture of the dominant/majority group. And while marginalized/minority groups may choose to denigrate the dominant/majority group, it will only have a limited effect, as the dominant/majority group is already taken for granted, respected, and viewed as the norm throughout society.

Non-EED Appropriation

Thus far, I have argued that appropriation is a bad thing when it leads to erasure, exploitation, and/or denigration of the marginalized/minority group. And most activists (including myself) would agree that instances of EED appropriation should be challenged and critiqued. However, there are other occurrences where appropriation (in the most general sense) occurs, but it does not necessarily erase, exploit, or denigrate the marginalized/minority group—I will refer to these instances as *non-EED appropriation*.

Here are a few examples of non-EED appropriation of trans people:

- A cisgender academic could carry out a research project that focuses on issues and obstacles that trans people are most concerned about. This project could be done in a way that respects trans people's perspectives and opinions, and portrays us in a realistic manner (rather than relying on stereotypes or reducing us to metaphors). The final product (e.g., an article or book) could be described as appropriative in that it uses trans people's realities, ideas, perspectives, and experiences, despite the fact that it amplifies trans voices and has the potential to create positive change for trans communities.

- There have been several instances in which cisgender students have attended school crossdressed in order to show support for a transgender classmate.[5] Such acts could be described as appropriative, yet they are done out of respect and in support of trans people. Much like students who shave their heads in support of a student who is going through chemotherapy, such acts can help destigmatize and lend legitimacy toward the marginalized/minority group in question.

- Over the years, I have met a number of cisgender people who appreciate transgender perspectives and culture. For instance, they might have learned a lot from trans authors, and they may recommend those books to others. They might enjoy performances by transgender spectrum artists or patronize transgender film festivals. They do this out of genuine respect, and their actions do help to promote trans voices and to put money into the hands of trans performers and writers. Yet the person in question could be described as appropriating trans culture in a non-EED sense.

- Cisgender people who are partners of trans people sometimes start their own support or discussion groups. While such groups may focus a lot on partner-specific issues, they will also discuss how to be supportive of the trans people in their lives and how to challenge societal cissexism. Such groups may have a net-positive effect on trans communities, by directly supporting relationships in which trans people are involved, and by demystifying and destigmatizing trans sexualities and relationships. Despite these benefits, some trans people may claim that the group members appropriate trans identities (by positioning themselves as "trans partners") and/or appropriate the oppression trans people face by discussing how it impacts their own lives.

Now it is quite likely that these four examples have evoked a range of feelings among trans people who read this. Some may have positive feelings about the cisgender people in question—they may be described as allies or advocates, and their actions (while arguably appropriative in the most general sense) may be welcomed with open arms. Other trans activists might have a negative view of said people, dismissing them as "tourists" who are privileged in ways that trans people are not, and who are reaping the benefits of a marginalized/minority population while not having to endure the harsh realities of actually being trans themselves. (Indeed, I have heard these latter critiques made with increasing frequency lately.)

In other words, while most activists would agree that EED appropriation is a bad thing, there is significant disagreement about whether non-EED appropriation is bad, neutral, or good. In thinking through these differences of opinion, it seems to me that whether a marginalized/minority group member has a positive or negative view of non-EED appropriation hinges on two interrelated axes: *stigma versus acceptance* and *integration versus separatism*.

Stigma Versus Acceptance

The more highly stigmatized a group is, the less likely it is that the dominant/majority group will even attempt to appropriate aspects of their identity or culture, as doing so will only lead to them becoming tainted by said stigma. However, if the marginalized/minority group becomes more accepted over time, there will be less of a social price to pay for associating oneself with that group. Thus, as acceptance of the group increases, so do the chances that others will engage in non-EED appropriation.

From the marginalized/minority group's perspective, non-EED appropriation is often welcomed when the group is highly stigmatized, as the group appreciates any genuine outsider interest and support they can get. But as the group becomes more established and accepted in society, such appropriation starts to feel more like an invasion, as more and more dominant/majority members seemingly want to associate with their identity and take part in their culture.

When I was a young adult (e.g., in the '80s and '90s), there was a ton of stigma associated with being trans—way more than there is today. Because of that stigma, very few cis people would have dared to go to a transgender event or taken part in a trans-related demonstration, as the cisgender majority would likely have viewed them as suspect as a result. The rare cis people who were willing to associate with trans people back then were often viewed in a positive light and welcomed into the community. For instance, the first transgender-spectrum support/social group that I belonged to had the phrase "and friends" tacked onto the end of the title, and partners, family, and friends were regularly welcome to attend meetings.[6] Even in the early '00s, when I was active in the San Francisco Bay Area's trans community, there was a sense that cis partners and close friends of trans folks were a part of our community too, and they would often take the stage at trans events (as described in Chapter 19). I'm sure that some people today would dismiss this as "cis people using their privilege in order to take up space at trans events," but that would overlook the very different reality of that time. Back then, very few people supported trans people, and those that genuinely did were embraced as part of our community.

Things are very different now. There is still quite a lot of cissexism out there, but in certain segments in our culture (e.g., especially in queer, feminist, and social justice circles) there is an acknowledgement that trans people are legitimate, and that cisgender people should be good allies to gender-variant folks. In such settings, being aware of transgender politics and culture may be seen as a sign that a person is a good progressive or activist. Indeed, this may lead to an increase in what might be called "faux allies"—people who are not especially concerned with trans people and issues, nor personally invested in trans communities, yet who nevertheless regard themselves as allies of trans people because to do otherwise would potentially garner disdain from other progressives or activists.

Furthermore, the fact that we currently exist in an era where there is a mix of both societal cissexism and trans acceptance—and where the former is viewed as conservative and close-minded, and the latter viewed as progressive and open-minded—means that an awareness of trans culture and politics can allow a person to be seen by others as worldly, cutting edge, or "hip." Thus, just as hipster straight folks began to appropriate aspects of gay and lesbian identity and culture during the '90s and '00s, more and more cisgender people are now appropriating aspects of trans identities and culture.

It would be relatively easy for someone like myself, who lives in a very progressive part of the country, to pan the influx of cisgender people who suddenly seem interested in trans people and culture. While it may potentially be annoying, it is also a sign of our increasing legitimacy in the eyes of society. And frankly, having lived through the past, I would much rather be in our current situation than where we were several decades ago (or where other trans folks in more conservative parts of the country remain today) where trans people are viewed as pariahs, and nobody wants anything to do with us, appropriation or otherwise.

Integration Versus Separatism

Activists who have a positive or neutral view of non-EED appropriation often imagine the ultimate goal of their activism as being the complete integration of their group within mainstream society. By integration, I mean that the group's identity, perspectives, and culture are viewed as unique, but also as a legitimate part of the culture at large.

One can see examples of integration in how certain groups that have immigrated to the U.S. from other countries are now seen as both distinct yet legitimately part of the culture. For example, I am of Italian (father's side) and Irish (mother's side) heritage. A century ago, when my grandparents and great-grandparents lived in the U.S., they were highly marginalized. The dominant/majority (primarily Protestants of Northern European ancestry) blatantly discriminated against them with regards to employment and housing, and used derogatory slang terms to refer to them. They were routinely ridiculed for their religion (Catholicism), and stereotyped as criminals, drunkards, lazy, etc. Some of my older relatives have told me about how, when they were young, neighborhood parents wouldn't let their children play with them because of their ethnicity. Even during my parent's generation (in the '50s), many in the dominant/majority group wouldn't have approved of their children marrying someone of Irish or Italian descent.

Nowadays, Irish- and Italian-Americans are generally seen as part of U.S. culture, and this integration is due to both U.S. culture rubbing off on Irish- and Italian-Americans, as well as Irish- and Italian-Americans influencing U.S. culture.[7] Americans of various persuasions eat at pizza parlors and drink at Irish pubs; we all watch Martin Scorsese films and celebrate St. Patrick's Day. While such activities are clearly examples of non-EED appropriation, they are not viewed by most people (both within and outside of Irish- and Italian-American communities) as "appropriation" in the negative sense. Rather, they are viewed more as "cultural appreciation" than "cultural appropriation."[8]

One can also see this integration and growing cultural appreciation in mainstream attitudes toward gay and lesbian people, at least in some sectors of the country. The first Gay Pride events in the '70s were far more like protests or demonstrations rather than celebrations, and the average straight person wouldn't dare set a foot anywhere near them. Nowadays, Queer Pride parades are (for better or for worse) endorsed by mainstream corporations, covered by the mainstream media, and many (if not most) of the audience members are straight (not unlike the countless people of non-Irish heritage who show up to New York City's annual St. Patrick's Day parade). This non-EED appropriation/cultural appreciation can also be seen in the rise in popularity of gay-themed TV shows and movies, the embrace of gay artists and celebrities, and so on.

As these examples illustrate, when marginalized/minority groups are highly stigmatized (as Irish- and Italian-Americans were in the early 1900s, and as gay people were in the '60s and '70s), they tend to be relegated to their own communities, and there is not much *culture permeability* between them and the dominant/majority group. But as stigma lessens and integration begins to occur, the boundary between the marginalized/minority group and the dominant/majority group inevitably becomes somewhat culturally permeable. And non-EED appropriation plays a major role in this process, as both a contributing factor to, and the net result of, that permeability.

Of course, not all members within a particular marginalized/minority group will strive for integration, or welcome the cultural permeability that comes with it. Some individuals may feel that their unique identities, language, and traditions are being watered down or made impure by mainstream non-EED appropriation. Such people may want to keep their culture pure via taking a more separatist stance, such as discouraging or limiting the dominant/majority group's access to their culture. Such people are way more likely to critique non-EED appropriation as "oppressive appropriation" rather than "cultural appreciation," and to view it as just as bad as (or as merely an extension of) EED appropriation.

It should be noted that people who take on more separatist stances typically look down upon members of their own group who strive for integration, often dismissing them as being "assimilationists." For example, separatist-oriented queers who complain about straight mainstream folks who appropriate Queer Pride and queer culture more generally are also likely to dismiss LGBTQIA+ people who dress gender-normatively, or same-sex couples who seek out legal recognition of their marriages, as being assimilationist. This usage of the word "assimilationist" is usually intended to be pejorative, and synonymous with the words "sell out" or "traitor."

This conflating of integration with assimilation is rather off the mark. After all, true assimilation would be to completely blend in with straight culture—to be "closeted" or "stealth." In contrast, someone who moves through the world as an out queer person (regardless of how they dress), and who is part of a visibly same-sex marriage, isn't engaging in assimilation by any means. Rather, they are part of an integration process.

So one might ask: What purpose do these accusations of "assimilation" serve? It seems to me that they are meant to undermine members of one's own community who strive for integration, by insinuating that such individuals are traitors, and thus illegitimate or inauthentic members of the group. This sort of identity policing helps to maintain a level of cultural impermeability between the marginalized/minority group and the dominant/majority group. Indeed, understanding this allows one to recognize that accusations of "assimilation" and non-EED "appropriation" are essentially flip sides of the same coin: the latter maintains cultural impermeability by delegitimizing members of the dominant/majority group who cross identity or community boundaries, while the former delegitimizes members of the marginalized/minority group who are perceived as doing the same.

Now, I could make some grandiose claim like, "Integration is the righteous path, whereas separatism will ultimately lead to our doom" (or vice versa), but I am not about to do that. In my book *Excluded: Making Feminist and Queer Movements More Inclusive*, I decry such one-size-fits-all approaches to activism. The truth is that both approaches have some negative drawbacks. Separatism generally favors sameness over difference, and in doing so, it leaves behind many members of the marginalized/minority group in question. For instance, separatist-oriented queers who decry assimilationists and instances of straight people engaging in non-EED appropriation seem to want to preserve some kind of idealistic notion of queer culture that they have experienced, enjoyed, and/or felt empowered by in the past. That version of queer culture probably resonated with them because they were accepted within that culture. In contrast, while I am politically queer, I have never felt fully welcome in queer communities and spaces, mostly because I am a transsexual woman, but also because I am bisexual and femme—three identities that often lead me to be dismissed as an inauthentic or illegitimate queer in those spaces.

Of course, I could turn around and create (or participate in) femme, or bisexual, or trans woman separatist movements. But even if I did feel welcome and empowered in such communities, there would inevitably be many other members of my marginalized/minority group who would feel excluded from them.[9]

While I tend to fall on the integrationist side of the spectrum, I do understand why separatist tendencies exist. Some marginalized/minority group members may feel irrevocably injured or violated by the dominant/majority group, and as a result, they may not want to have anything to do with them. As a result, they might view people (like myself) who seem to blur strict distinctions between queer and straight (on the basis that I am bisexual, femme, and/or trans), and who strive for integration rather than separatism, as potentially threatening because we "undermine the movement." (And of course, whenever people refer to "the movement," what they really mean is "their movement.")

Furthermore, while I will never feel welcome or relevant in certain queer spaces—such as the Michigan Womyn's Music Festival, which explicitly excludes trans women from attending—I nevertheless recognize that such separatist communities do develop their own unique culture, and that the cultural permeability that comes with integration and non-EED appropriation would inevitably change that culture. While I might view such an evolution in a positive light, I understand that others would view it negatively, and perceive any such changes as a loss of the original culture that they very much cherished.

So rather than frame integration and separatism in terms of a good-versus-bad binary, I believe that it is more useful to recognize them as two general tendencies that always seem to arise within marginalized/minority groups. And while we (i.e., integrationists and separatists) might agree that EED appropriation is a bad thing that should be challenged, we will invariably view instances of non-EED appropriation very differently.

The Case for Cultural Permeability with Regards to Gender and Sexuality

While disagreements about integration versus separatism exist within most marginalized/minority groups, there are a few additional reasons why those of us who are marginalized because of our genders and/or sexualities should think twice before enforcing cultural impermeability via accusations of non-EED appropriation.

The first has to do with what I refer to in *Excluded* as the *insider/outsider myth*.[10] The myth assumes that some of us (for instance, members of a particular LGBTQIA+ subgroup) are legitimate members of the group—that is, "insiders"—who are allowed to freely participate in queer cultures, whereas other people (e.g., the straight majority) are "outsiders" who can only appropriate our identities and culture.

This sort of insider/outsider mentality may make some sense in thinking about cultural appropriation based on nationality, ethnicity, religion, etc., where some people are born into and socialized within that culture, whereas others are not. Of course, even in such cases, there will always be people who are of mixed nationality, ethnicity, religion, etc.—people who Gloria Anzaldúa famously described as living in the borderlands between two identities or cultures.[11]

However, this insider/outsider framing completely falls apart when considering the identities and cultures of gender and sexual minorities. After all, almost all of us grow up in straight families and communities. While we may have experienced ourselves as different from the straight majority in some way as young children, we did not initially have LGBTQIA+ identities or culture to help us make sense of our lives. Rather, we tend to discover these identities over time: We hear someone mention the identity, we seek out books and websites to learn more about them, we try these identities on for size ourselves, we connect with other people who we believe are "like us" in that way, and so on.

The first time we enter a particular LGBTQIA+ space (whether it be a gay bar, a trans support group, or an asexual online discussion group) we often feel like outsiders, and we experience a steep learning curve in trying to understand the language and customs associated with the group.

In other words, we *discover* LGBTQIA+ identities and cultures. And one could say that virtually all gender and sexual minorities are appropriators, as virtually all of us have adopted identities and participate in cultures that others created before us, and which we were not initially socialized into. Indeed, the only people who are immersed in queer cultures from the start of their lives are children of queer parents, and the majority of them turn out to be straight!

Permeability between straight and queer identities and culture is essential for LGBTQIA+ self-actualization and empowerment. Furthermore, when a straight person engages in a stereotypically queer activity, it may be an act of appropriation, but it could also be experimenting or questioning on their part. I have heard queer people accuse straight people who make out with one another of "queer appropriation"—when I do, I often reply, "Well how do you know that neither of them will come to identify as gay/lesbian or bisexual/pansexual someday?[12] And even if the people in question do end up being straight, isn't the fact that nowadays people can engage in same-sex kissing without being ostracized a sign that that heterosexist norm is eroding?

Along similar lines, don't instances where cisgender people crossdress or engage in other forms of non-EED gender non-conformity help to deteriorate binary gender norms? Shouldn't we be celebrating such instances of permeability between genders and sexualities rather than condemning them as appropriation?

And if we do decide to call out certain people's genders and sexualities as appropriative, then where exactly do we draw the line? And who gets screwed as a result? Doesn't the claim that "heterosexuals shouldn't appropriate queer culture" pretty much leave bisexual/pansexual folks especially vulnerable to accusations of appropriation? And doesn't the claim that "men shouldn't appropriate women's oppression" leave trans women especially susceptible to similar criticism?

This leads us to another crucial point: Accusations of appropriation are essentially claims about authenticity.[13] Specifically, they create a binary wherein certain people (i.e., the marginalized/minority group) are considered to be authentic when they engage in a particular activity, whereas others (i.e., the dominant/majority group) cannot authentically engage in that same act. Rather they can only appropriate it.

This specter of "inauthenticity" isn't nearly so troubling when it comes to other forms of cultural appropriation. For instance, the implication that white folks/Westerners are "inauthentic" when they perform reggae or practice yoga is not meant to be an indictment of their natural abilities. After all, nobody is born performing reggae or practicing yoga—these are leaned skills and traditions. Rather, the "authenticity" that is invoked simply refers to whether one was socialized within the culture that originally created these practices versus whether one was raised in an outsider culture and only discovered and took up such practices later in life.

In sharp contrast, there is ample evidence that sex, gender, and sexuality naturally vary in the population, not only because of culture and environment, but also because of biological variation.[14] And all of us are socialized into cultures where there are a multitude of different expressions of gender and sexuality. Some of these expressions may be considered feminine, masculine, or androgynous. They may be described as queer or straight, or as unusual or normal. But regardless of what labels and meanings others might project onto these different gender and sexual expressions, all of these variations exist within the society in which we are raised. They are arguably all a part of our culture.

While sex, gender, and sexuality naturally vary within the population, we live in a world where such expressions and identities are highly policed. And they are primarily policed via the tropes of "authenticity" and "naturalness."

In the culture at large, feminine gender expressions and attraction toward men are viewed as authentic and natural when expressed by women, but not by men. Masculine gender expressions and attraction toward women are viewed as authentic and natural when expressed by men, but not by women. Penile-vaginal penetration sex between monogamous partners is viewed as the only authentic and natural form of sex, whereas most other sexual interests and acts are dismissed as inauthentic and unnatural.

The concepts of "authentic," "natural," and "real" lie at the heart of almost all manifestations of societal cissexism. The notion that transsexuals are not "authentic" women or men, or that two-spirit or genderqueer people have not chosen an "authentic" gender, enable the cisgender majority to dismiss our identities as "inauthentic," and thus misgender us as they see fit. The "trans panic" phenomenon is steeped in assumption that trans people are deceivers who pose as an "inauthentic" gender while hiding our supposed "real" gender. It is commonly presumed that people who partner with trans people do not experience "authentic" attraction to us, but rather that they are driven by some kind of "fetish"—derived from the Portuguese word for "artificial."

The point is that, while gender and sexuality naturally vary, sexual and gender non-conformity is rigorously punished in our society via accusations of inauthenticity, whether it be claims that trans people's gender identities are "inauthentic," that asexual/bisexual/lesbian/gay people's sexual attractions (or lack thereof) are "unnatural," or that straight cisgender people are not "real women" or "real men" because of some relatively minor gender transgression they may have committed (e.g., not shaving their legs, expressing too much emotion, or having a gender atypical occupation). And calling someone's non-EED expressions of gender or sexuality "appropriative" is really just another way of dismissing them as "inauthentic" (which is precisely why trans-exclusive radical feminists so frequently accuse trans women of appropriation, as it depicts us as merely fakes, pretenders, impersonators, and imposters).

There are no "authentic" expressions of gender and sexuality. There are merely those that are deemed legitimate in society and those that are dismissed as inauthentic. While I understand why some LGBTQIA+ people might be inclined to describe non-EED acts of sexual and gender non-conformity as "appropriation" (especially when the person engaging in them appears straight, cisgender, etc.), I fear that such accusations may only perpetuate the real/fake, natural/unnatural, and authentic/inauthentic binaries that are so often used to undermine our own genders and sexualities.

Conclusion

This essay was intended to illustrate that the concept of appropriation is way more complicated than many people seem to realize, and that non-EED appropriation is not necessarily a bad thing, depending on your politics and perspective. Furthermore, I hope that people will recognize that cultural permeability is an absolute necessity for LGBTQIA+ communities to exist and flourish, and that claims that certain non-EED expressions of gender or sexuality are "appropriative" will only lend support to existing binary gender norms and to the false notion that certain genders and sexualities are more "natural," "real," or "authentic" than others.

Moving forward, I believe that we should continue to critique instances of EED appropriation, but it would help if we were more explicit about why such instances are bad. Specifically, rather than simply crying "appropriation" (which often conflates EED and non-EED appropriation, and can also implicate acts that merely resemble those that occur in marginalized/minority groups), we should explicitly discuss how such acts either erase, exploit, and/or denigrate the marginalized/minority group in question.

45

A Personal History of the "T-Word"
(and some more general reflections on language and activism)

This piece first appeared on my blog in April 2014. It is intended to be but one trans woman's take on what has become a highly controversial term, written in the (perhaps implausible) hope of fostering more nuanced and historically situated dialogue about the word moving forward. The second half of the piece (i.e., the section entitled "Words don't kill people, people kill words . . .") moves beyond debates about whether specific words should be reclaimed or denounced, and instead considers the (typically undiscussed) potential long-term ramifications of (what I refer to here as) the Activist Language Merry-Go-Round.[1]

Language evolves. Words that were once commonplace now come off as anachronistic. And words that once had good or neutral connotations are now seen as problematic or politically incorrect, and vice versa. It happens all the time. But within my own lifetime, I cannot think of a single word that has undergone such a quick and dramatic shift as the word "tranny" has, particularly with regards to how it is used within transgender-spectrum communities.

A decade ago, "tranny" was a word that most trans folks I knew used self-referentially, and occasionally to refer to other trans people. Nowadays, it is viewed as highly controversial. The Internet is chock full of articles and blog posts making the case that the term is an irredeemable slur that no one should utter, or which argue that the word can only be used by certain trans people in certain specific contexts.

For the record, I do not have a horse in this race. I used to use the word all the time, but now I very rarely use it. I have not penned this piece to make the case for re-reclaiming the word "tranny," nor to argue that we should do away with it. Rather, I feel that amidst all of the current debates about the term, some important history is being lost. So in this piece, I want to revisit that history, to provide some context for why the term initially gained popularity as a reclaimed word and how feelings about it have evolved over time. Toward the end of this essay, I will attempt to situate contemporary debates about the word within the context of activist responses to language more generally.

This is a highly personal account of the word from my standpoint as a trans woman who first began participating in urban, predominantly white, queer-centric trans communities in the U.S. in the 1990s and early 2000s. Gender-variant folks of different backgrounds, geographies, and communities might have very different yet equally valid stories to tell about the word.

Thirteen Years Ago

So I transitioned in 2001, and shortly thereafter became involved in the San Francisco Bay Area's rapidly growing gender-variant community, both as an out trans performer and an event coordinator (as discussed in Chapter 19): I organized and emceed a performance series called GenderEnders, put together numerous benefit shows for Camp Trans, and helped organize an annual Trans/Intersex/Genderqueer & Buddies Community Picnic. During that time and in those settings, just about everybody seemed to use the term "tranny." It was generally viewed as a reclaimed word—that is, a word that has been used in a disparaging way by the dominant majority, but which the marginalized minority reclaims for itself to use in a self-empowering way.[2] The idea is simple: If people are going to try to insult me for being a "tranny," then why not take the word and turn it into a source of pride—"yes I'm a tranny, and there's nothing fucking wrong with that!"

Some words are successfully reclaimed, a few examples being "queer," "gay" and "dyke," which are all now regularly used in non-disparaging ways by people who share those identities as well as by people who do not. Other reclamation projects do not fare quite so well. Some feminists have tried to reclaim the words "bitch" and "slut," yet these words are still far more often used as insults than as self-empowered identities. Back in the early 2000s, "tranny" seemed (at least to me) to be well on its way to being positively reclaimed. There were community-based events like the Tranny Fest film festival; performance troupes like the Tranny Roadshow; people often referred to the aforementioned Trans/Intersex/Genderqueer & Buddies Community Picnic as simply the "Tranny

Picnic" and the annual Trans March as the "Tranny March"; and so on.

During this time period, I regularly used the word "tranny" in a reclaimed way. It appears in my 2003 slam poem "Cocky" as well as in many of my other early spoken word pieces.[3] When I first pitched *Whipping Girl* to my publisher in 2005, the working title was actually *Hot Tranny Action*—it referenced a trans woman-focused activist website that I was in the process of creating at the time. The phrase was meant to be a play on words, as "hot" can mean intense or angry, and "action" can refer to protests and activism. We decided not to use it as the book title though, as we felt it would create too many misconceptions about what the book was actually about.

In my 2005 spoken word piece "On the Outside Looking In," I not only refer to myself as a "tranny," but I also used the plural term "trannies" to refer to trans people more generally. Today, such a move would offend many trans folks (and for that reason, I have removed the word from the version of that piece that appears in my recent book, *Excluded*).[4] However, when I performed the piece back in 2005 (a mere nine years ago) nobody even flinched. It was viewed (at least in my local trans community) as just as legitimate a turn of phrase as using the plural term "queers" is in many LGBTQIA+ spaces today.

There are several important aspects about being a trans person in the 1990s and early 2000s that I believe help explain the popularity of the word as a reclaimed identity label during that time period.

First, trans folks had almost no visibility back then. I know that trans invisibility is still an issue today, but believe me when I tell you that it was exponentially worse back then. There was virtually zero media coverage of trans people and issues outside of a handful of sensationalistic movies and the occasional *The Jerry Springer Show*. When I was first coming out to people in 2001, most told me that they had never (to their knowledge) seen or met a real-life transsexual before. So the simple act of being out as trans was often read by the cis majority as a shocking in-your-face sort of move.

Given that people already viewed us as surprising and shameless for simply existing and being out, many of us played up this shock value ourselves in order to challenge societal cis assumption (i.e., when people assume that every person they meet will be cisgender/cissexual). I believe that this tendency to flaunt our trans identities in the face of a cis majority who didn't want to believe that we were part of their reality contributed to the popularity of reclaiming the provocative word "tranny" as a self-identity label, and it can also be seen in activist groups of the time who sported unapologetic in-your-face names such as Transexual Menace or the intersex group Hermaphrodites with Attitude.[5]

A second and related point: Back then, most cis people had not yet heard of any of the self-identity labels that trans folks have created for ourselves. In the early 2000s, when I would come out to people as "trans" or as "transgender," most acted completely oblivious or confused until I clarified things by calling myself transsexual or a "tranny." People seemed to be familiar with the words "transvestite" and "tranny," and to a lesser extent "transsexual," although admittedly most did not have any kind of nuanced understanding of the differences in meaning between these terms.

In other words, at the time, there were no "respectable" labels for trans people. All trans-related labels were either unknown to the public or highly stigmatized. Back then, cis people used the word "transsexual" with just as much disdain as they used the term "tranny." I think this helps to explain why many of us (at least in my community) didn't tend to get quite so upset about the use of the term "tranny"—it wasn't viewed as significantly more soiled in society's eyes than other well known trans-related labels.

Today we have a few labels ("transgender," "gender non-conforming," "gender variant," "trans," and even "transsexual") that have garnered a modicum of recognition and respect in our culture. I feel that it is this respectability (as limited as it may be) that has led many trans folks to want to purge less respectful-sounding labels—such as "tranny" and "transvestite"—from the lexicon. Not coincidentally, these latter words also happen to be more closely associated with sex (and specifically with sex work, pornography, and fetishism) in the public's mind, which surely contributes to some trans people's desire to distance themselves from such labels.

Another observation: I've heard trans people today say that they hate the word "tranny" because it seems to make light of, or trivializes, trans identities and experiences. I respect that sentiment. But in retrospect, I think that might actually be part of the reason why many of us back then (in that very different era) gravitated toward it. Flippantly referring to oneself as a "tranny" made it seem like it was no big deal, which provided a useful way to defuse the oh-my-god-you're-a-transsexual-monster-serial-killer attitude that some cisgender people would express upon trans disclosure moments.

To put it a different way, back when trans people were more often viewed as abominations and as downright dangerous or shocking, there were advantages to playing down or making light of our predicament. But nowadays, when many cis people think that trans is "no big deal" because they personally know trans people, or they regularly see trans individuals on talk shows and reality television, perhaps it is more useful to remind people of the seriousness of trans issues and experiences rather than making them seem mundane and not especially noteworthy.

Anyway, these are a few of my thoughts on why "tranny" was such a popular word among trans activists during the '90s and '00s, and why its apparent usefulness back then may not translate well during this very different time—a time in which public backlash against trans people and activism is arguably a more pressing concern than trans-invisibility.

In doing research for this essay, I discovered yet another possible explanation for why the word was once popular, one that pre-dates my participation in trans communities. In Kate Bornstein's piece "Who You Calling A Tranny?" she points out that the word "tranny" was initially coined by trans female/feminine-spectrum folks in Sydney, Australia during the '60s and '70s as a way to unite drag queens and transsexual women.[6] She describes the term as "our first own language word for ourselves that has no medical-legacy" and says that only later was it "picked up and used as a denigrating term by mean people in the world."

Thus, much like the word "transgender," the initial popularity of "tranny" may have stemmed from the fact that it was a community-created, non-pathologizing identity label. And while I have framed the matter here in terms of trans people reclaiming a derogatory slur, the history of the word appears a bit more complicated than that. In fact, the word "tranny" has a number of parallels with the word "gay": both began as in-community self-referential labels, which then garnered negative meanings when the mainstream public discovered them and began using them in derogatory ways, thus forcing members of these communities to have to reclaim the very words that they themselves originally forwarded.[7]

Why I Stopped Using the Word

Eight years ago (i.e., 2006), I pretty much stopped using the word "tranny." My reasoning had nothing to do with contemporary debates regarding the word (which are discussed below). Rather, I stopped because I was in the process of noticing and critiquing disparities that existed within trans communities, especially with regards to how we were accepted within feminist and queer circles. Some of these disparities were driven by trans-misogyny, masculine-centrism, subversivism,[8] and forms of cissexism that specifically target transsexuals—all of which became topics that I addressed in my book *Whipping Girl.*

As a result of my growing awareness of these disparities, I pulled back from referring to myself with more general trans terms (e.g., "transgender," "tranny"), and began using more specific identity labels such as "transsexual" and "trans woman," as I felt that these identities and standpoints were in more need of being articulated. (This is why I purposefully chose to describe myself as a "transsexual woman" in the subtitle of *Whipping Girl.*) In other words, I stopped routinely using the word "tranny," not because I found it inappropriate or offensive, but rather because I found it to be too generic for the activism that I was engaging in at the time. (For the record, I do believe that broader umbrella terms such as "transgender" or "trans" serve important purposes—see Chapter 37.)

Six Years Ago

During the early '00s, I would sometimes come across trans people who expressed that they personally did not like the word "tranny," but such occasions were relatively sporadic. It wasn't until 2008 that I first remember hearing arguments denouncing the word on a more regular basis. Much of this appears to have been part of a backlash against Project Runway's Christian Siriano's popular catch phrase "hot tranny mess."[9] While I never saw that show personally, I do remember cis folks at the time suddenly using the word "tranny" and "tranny mess" quite a lot, almost as if they now owned the word. It was admittedly quite annoying.

One common response to this was for trans folks to argue that "tranny" was a derogatory word that nobody should ever use. Such arguments seemed to discount the fact that many trans folks at the time were regularly using it to refer to themselves in a positive, self-empowered way.

Other trans folks made what I call the *ingroup argument*: Because of its history as a slur, it is inappropriate for any cis person to use the word "tranny" under any circumstances. However, trans people are free to use it amongst ourselves as a special in-community word. While I understand the reasoning behind this argument, I believe that it overlooks the original intention behind why many trans activists set out to reclaim the word "tranny" in the first place. A common goal of reclaiming words is to turn a disparaging term into a legitimate one, as part of a strategy to assert that the referents of the label (in this case, trans people) are a legitimate thing to be.[10] Many of us believed that we were working toward a future where "tranny" no longer carries bad connotations, and where anyone is free to use it in a non-derogatory manner, much like how both queer and straight folks use words like "gay" or "queer" today.

In any case, over the last five years, all of these arguments stressing that "tranny" is an inherently bad word have (for better or worse) created an environment where it is potentially controversial for anyone to use the word in any setting. For instance, I've been in trans woman-only settings where individual trans women have been interrogated by others for self-labeling themselves in that way.

Who Is Allowed to Call Themselves "Tranny"?

Around the same time that trans folks were pushing back on the use of "tranny" in the mainstream public, two other debates surfaced regarding which gender-variant subpopulations have the right to try to reclaim the word, or to use it self-referentially.

The first of these is the argument that people on the trans female/feminine spectrum have the right to reclaim "tranny," while those on the trans male/masculine spectrum do not. My introduction to this idea came from Hazel/Cedar Troost's excellent two-part blog post series entitled "Re-Reclaiming Tranny (or not)."[11] Hazel/Cedar's posts made the following points:

- When the word "tranny" is used as a slur, it is specifically meant to target trans female/feminine-spectrum folks. For instance, it evokes the hypersexualization of trans femaleness/femininity in our culture (as seen in the phrases "tranny porn" and "hot tranny action"), which does not directly implicate or affect trans male/masculine folks.

- In addition to sexualization, in our culture, "tranny" is used as a slur that implies "doing femininity or womanhood badly," and thus is used to insult trans women and occasionally cis women, but not trans men. In other words, tranny is never used to call maleness or masculinity into question.

- Many of the people who are most insistent on reclaiming the word "tranny" are folks on the trans male/masculine spectrum who are not only not personally targeted by the word, but who also sometimes dismiss trans women who are offended by the word via subversivism (e.g., claiming that trans women who distance themselves from the word "tranny" do so because they are too conservative, assimilationist, or binarist).

Hazel/Cedar's posts won me over when I first read them, and for the last several years, I have tended to lean toward the trans-guys-reclaiming-the-word-tranny-is-problematic camp.[12] And this perspective has since gained significant support within various segments of the trans community.

But in thinking through this issue more recently, I feel that there is a counter argument to this that is often overlooked. Historically, people on the trans female/feminine spectrum have garnered virtually all of the public's attention and backlash, whereas (until recently) trans male/masculine folks have been almost entirely invisible.[13] So perhaps people associate the word "tranny" with trans female/feminine-spectrum folks because they are more aware of our existence? And therefore, as the public becomes more aware of trans male/masculine identities, perhaps they will begin to use word "tranny" as a slur against them as well?

There is some evidence to suggest that this may be the case. For instance, I have heard some trans male/masculine individuals say that they have been targeted by the word. Sure, this may not occur very frequently, but that could simply be because the public is less likely to read trans male/masculine individuals as trans (as a result of said invisibility). Here is more convincing evidence: If you google the word "tranny" along with either Chaz Bono or Thomas Beatie/"pregnant man" (the two trans men who have garnered the most mainstream attention) you will find plenty of instances where people unflattering or dismissively refer to them as being a "tranny."

By no means am I suggesting that trans men are just as targeted by the word "tranny" as trans women. That is clearly not the case, at least not at this point in time. But as I said, words evolve. And I wouldn't be surprised if the word "tranny" eventually becomes a word that is used to target all trans people independent of the direction of their gender non-conformity and/or transition. And it could potentially become a slur that is used to dismiss anyone (whether cis or trans) who is perceived as falling short of being a "real woman" or "real man."

A second argument that has arisen asserts that drag queens should not use the word "tranny," or that when they do, they are appropriating trans women's experiences. People who make this case often point to RuPaul, who has been a vocal supporter of the word.[14] Because RuPaul does not identify as transgender, it is relatively easy for trans activists to portray him as a cis gay man who has no right to reclaim a word that primarily targets trans women. In addition, on his show *RuPaul's Drag Race*, he has routinely done other things that trans women find highly offensive or insensitive (e.g., using the even more controversial term "she-male," and running skits that seem to encourage the audience to clock trans women).[15] So it is fairly easy (and arguably justified) for trans activists to make the case that he is a cissexist gay man who has no right to reclaim the word.[16]

In other cases, the claim that drag queens are "cisgender gay men" and thus have no right to reclaim the term is more specious. After all, some drag queens present as female/feminine in their day-to-day lives, and as such, they are often targeted by the word "tranny." Still others eventually transition to female. There isn't a sharp boundary that one can draw between drag queens and trans women any more than there is a sharp boundary that one can draw between butch women and trans men: While many people clearly fall into one camp or the other, there are others who blur those lines, or have inhabited both identities at different times in their lives.[17]

In an excellent essay called "Let's Talk About 'Tranny'," Tobi Hill-Meyer makes this very relevant point:

While breaking down who can and can't use the term based on identity is an easy shorthand for some very complicated issues, it has downsides. One of the big downside[s] is that it can cause an increase in policing the boundaries of trans and trans female/feminine identity. Can a drag queen use the term? A trans man? A genderqueer trans man? An uber feminine fag? Not to mention that it creates a situation that encourages judgment of how trans someone is or how valid a female identity is, which can leave transfeminine genderqueers in a difficult situation. The same goes for any trans woman who is misread as either not trans or not a woman. And such people who also happen to fit aspects of the stereotypically tranny image are left in an even more tenuous position. The downside of black and white rules is that you spend a lot of time parsing the gray areas and trying figure out how to put people in their place rather than evaluating the value of the rule in such situations.[18]

The "T-Word" in 2014

It seems that within the last year or so, the tide seems to have shifted even farther away from skirmishes over who has the right to reclaim the word "tranny," and more toward the realm of nobody-should-use-the-word-period. An argument that is increasingly made to justify this latter position is that trans women often experience the word in association with abuse or violence. According to this argument, even if I (as a trans woman) were to use the word in a reclaimed and self-empowering way, I may inadvertently trigger others who have had the same word hurled at them during an assault, or in a harassing or threatening situation.[19]

Now, I am sensitive to this as someone who has had slurs hurled at me during harassing or abusive altercations, and who has subsequently experienced intense reactions to those words after the fact. Part of the reason why I no longer use the word "tranny" today (with the exception of reading my older writings, or pieces such as this where I am looking back on how the word has been used in the past) is that I have no desire to needlessly or flippantly toss around a word that is likely to trigger or upset other people. Having said that, I do think that it is important for us to interrogate this argument, as it has some unforeseen implications and drawbacks.

First, I believe that the reason why many trans people (and especially trans women) experience "tranny" in association with harassment and abuse is that 1) many cis people have extremely negative views of trans folks, and 2) "tranny" is the only word (or most familiar word) they have to refer to us. Hence, the word is often used in a derogatory fashion. So what happens when people become familiar with more "respectable" words such as trans or transgender?

Well, they may end up using these words in a similarly negative way. In fact, this is already starting to happen: I have heard of numerous instances (whether it be on the streets, or on TERF websites and Internet comment threads) where cissexist individuals use the words "trans" or "transgender" in a similarly disparaging or degrading manner. In other words, the problem is not these words *per se*, but the negative meanings that people try to convey with such words. Given this, it doesn't make much sense for us to simply purge every trans-related label once others begin using them in a derogatory fashion. Rather, it makes more sense for us to challenge the underlying negative meanings themselves (a point that I will return to in the final section).

Second, there is diversity among trans people in what words they find upsetting and/or what words they have experienced in association with abuse. For instance, while I have on multiple occasions been called a "tranny" in association with harassment, I don't find the word to be triggering, perhaps because I came out into a trans community where the word was regularly used in a reclaimed way. But as I allude to in the last chapter of *Excluded*, I am often triggered by the word "trap," even when it is used in a non-cissexist manner.[20] My life would be a lot easier to manage if people simply stopped saying that word, but I don't expect the trans community to collectively work to purge that word from the lexicon. Indeed, I have heard other trans women say that they are not really bothered by the word "trap," even when it is used to refer to us.

Along similar lines, I have had harassers call me a "she-male," and I have found it distressing—I experience it as an affront to my identity. And yet, I have met non-op trans women who use the term self-referentially. From their standpoint, they feel that they need the term because so many transsexuals actively try to invisibilize and invalidate trans women who do not seek out bottom surgery. In their eyes, "she-male" is the most easily recognized term in our culture for a woman with a "penis," so they have sought to reclaim it. While this honestly squicks me (as the word has been used in disparaging ways toward me), who am I (as a post-op trans woman) to say that they should not be able to reclaim that word?

Those who have read my writings may know that I personally abhor the term "transwoman" (i.e., spelled as one word).[21] While I wouldn't say that I find it triggering, I have had numerous instances where others have non-consensually described me as a "transwoman," or where editors of articles that I have written have removed the spaces between "trans" and "woman"—I have found those experiences to be highly invalidating. And yet, at the same time, I know there are other trans folks who regularly use the one-word variation and they can have legitimate rationales for doing so.[22]

The point is that there is diversity among trans women, and trans people more generally. We will never all agree on language, as we necessarily have different experiences and come from different perspectives. So I am concerned about how assertions that the word "tranny" is offensive or unacceptable in all cases, regardless of context or intent, presumes that there is some kind of universal trans perspective. Any time an activist movement starts asserting that their constituents are all uniform in their views on a particular matter, it leads to the erasure of certain voices within the movement. And this is not a trivial problem—I spend most of *Excluded* explaining precisely why such one-size-fits-all approaches inevitably lead to far smaller movements with far more narrow and distorted agendas. Typically, those individuals who fail to adhere to the consensus view will be dismissed as not being "real" or "legitimate" members of the marginalized group, or accused of "reinforcing" the oppression the marginalized group faces—indeed, I have already witnessed numerous accusations along these lines being made in contemporary debates about the word "tranny."

Finally, as I alluded to at the beginning of this section, it is relatively easy for me to give up the word "tranny" in order to accommodate other people, as I stopped using it as an identity label years ago. It would surely be more difficult for trans folks who continue to find it to be a self-empowering identity label.[23] But what if the next word we seek to do away with *is* a label that I find to be important and self-empowering?

For instance, lots of trans folks seem to dislike the word transsexual—a word that I use in a reclaimed way and which has become an important part of my identity and activism. What if the community moves to purge that word over the course of the next five or ten years? Do I become a pariah if I continue to use it? What if it's some other identity label that I (or you) use nowadays? What are the ramifications of that?

Some may find this suggestion to be far-fetched or alarmist. But honestly, I could not have imagined this large of a community pushback on the word "tranny" as recently as seven years ago. So it seems to me that this scenario is entirely plausible.[24]

Those who oppose the purging of the word "tranny" will often trot out the trope of "word policing." It is an easy way to demonize those who detest the word as being "too authoritarian," just as accusations of "political correctness" dismiss the same people as being "too sensitive." Such accusations deny the reality that words have meanings and can be used to wield power over people. But at the same time, power can also be wielded via attempts to eradicate words that others have long used as part of their identity, activism, and/or culture. I believe that it is incumbent upon us as activists to consider the negative effects that eliminating such words can have on those marginalized individuals—an issue that I have discussed in greater depth regarding attempts by some to eradicate the word "bisexual."[25]

Words Don't Kill People, People Kill Words . . .

I wrote most of this essay in 2013 (all of it except for the previous "2014" section and this revamped "conclusion"). I didn't post it back then because frankly I was worried about misinterpretation and blowback. I worried that people who abhor the word "tranny" would disparage me for not taking a hardline stance against the word and/or for giving "potential ammunition" to the other side of the debate. And I worried that people who like to carelessly drop the word without regard for how others feel about it would either cite this essay in order to bolster their claims, or else accuse me of kowtowing too much to those who wish to "censor language." I suppose this all may still occur: A negative drawback of holding complicated or ambivalent views on a contentious matter is that one runs the risk of being misunderstood and denounced by people on all sides of the debate.

I started writing this essay simply because I thought that it would be interesting to chronicle how dramatically community reactions toward this word have shifted over the last decade. As the title suggests, I initially viewed this piece as a personal historical project. And I decided to shelve a previously completed version of this piece last summer, again, because I feared that it would be misinterpreted and misunderstood. But a couple of months ago, I found myself wanting to revisit this piece. As I did, it became increasingly clear to me that I was not *really* writing about the word "tranny" *per se*. After all, I do not have a personal stake in the word, so if it dies a slow death, I won't personally mind. And even if I did harbor strong opinions about the word, I highly doubt that anything I could say would really make much of a difference: There is so much critical mass against the word within trans communities these days that I have a hard time imagining it ever making a comeback.

So why did I bother spending countless hours over the course of a year to write a eight-thousand-ish word essay about a term that I have no personal investment in? Well, because I realized over time that what this essay is *really* about is language. And more specifically, about how we, as trans activists, constantly and continually attempt to transform any and all language that relates to us.

As activists, we often stress how crucial words and language are. You don't need to convince me of this—I literally (pun intended!) named myself after a character in a George Orwell book.[26] The problem that we often make, however, is that we mistakenly assume that words have fixed meanings: that they are inherently good or bad, righteous or oppressive, revolutionary or conservative. The truth is that the meanings that we assign to words (or presume they have) are often extraordinarily arbitrary. One subpopulation of trans folks will celebrate a particular word as a self-empowering label, while another will claim that the same combination of letters and syllables is problematic for some reason, or does the community more harm than good. We denounce people for their attempts to reclaim words that we detest despite the fact that we ourselves routinely use reclaimed words (e.g., gay, queer, dyke) that others detested and protested in the past. And we complain about how neologisms look "too foreign" or are "too confusing" despite the fact that many words we regularly use nowadays started out as neologisms. In some cases, we point to a word's troubled history to make the case that we should completely do away with it (e.g., when people who dislike the word "transsexual" point to its origins as a pathologizing term), and in other cases, we completely ignore any positive history a word may have had (e.g., how people who dislike the word "tranny" ignore its origins as a community-created, non-pathologizing identity label, or how it was used in a positive way by activists in the '90s and early '00s). Frankly, there is no rhyme or reason to any of this.

Once again, this goes well beyond consternations regarding the word "tranny." I can't tell you how many conversations I have participated in over the past two decades about trans terminology. Should we refer to our community as transgender, gender variant, gender non-conforming, trans, trans*, or other?[27] Are we MTFs, transwomen, trans women, women of transsexual experience, girls like us, survivors of Harry Benjamin Syndrome, or other?[28] Should we call it a "sex change," sex reassignment surgery, gender reassignment surgery, gender confirmation surgery, bottom surgery, or other? Is it transsexuality or transsexualism?[29] Should we spell "transsexual" with one or two *S's*?[30] Are we "transgendered" or "transgender"?[31] Can transgender and transsexual be used as nouns and/or as plural words?[32]

It used to be okay to refer to someone as a "transvestite" (still is in the U.K., from what I gather), but then the preferred term in the U.S. became "crossdresser." However, some activists pointed out that "crossdresser" and "crossdressing" make too many assumptions about a person's life history and current gender identity. So to avoid such assumptions, many of us began simply describing people as "presenting as female (or male)," but some have objected to that on the grounds that such phrasing is pathologizing (with analogies being made to patients "presenting" symptoms of an illness), even though this phrasing had activist (rather than medical/psychiatric) origins.

I have informally started referring to this phenomenon as the *Activist Language Merry-Go-Round*, as these continual shifts in terminology never seem to end. In some cases, a particular word replacement may seem to be a vast improvement over the previous term (I don't hear too many people lamenting the loss of "sex change," for instance). But most of these word swaps seem to be fairly arbitrary and/or provide incremental (if any) improvement over previously existing terms. A few terms blatantly espouse a particular ideology (e.g., the usage of "Harry Benjamin Syndrome" implies a belief that transsexuality is an intersex condition), but most seem to be more about aesthetics (e.g., in many of the terminology debates I have alluded to above, there are linguistic precedents to support both sides of the argument).[33]

It is true that words and language are important. This importance stems not from the actual words themselves, but rather the meanings that we attach to them and ways in which we use them. Case in point: The words "gay" and "lesbian" are generally considered to be inoffensive, and even respectable, words to use to refer to people of those particular sexual orientations these days. And yet, those labels have very different histories. The word "gay" has a long (as in several-hundred-year-long) history as a pejorative lay people used to refer to people who were considered to be promiscuous, prostitutes, and/or sexually deviant, before it became an in-community term for gay men.[34] As the straight majority learned of this latter usage, they began using it in a derogatory fashion toward gay men, as well as other people and things they did not like. "Lesbian" is a historical reference to the Greek Island of Lesbos, which was home the poet Sappho (circa sixth century B.C.). The term was used by sexologists for years before it was reclaimed by lesbian activists.[35] As the straight majority learned of this usage, they began using it in a derogatory fashion toward lesbians, any woman who is not conventionally feminine, and/or primarily associating it with a particular genre of pornography that had virtually nothing to do with actual lesbians.

The words "gay" and "lesbian" have been used as both slurs and as self-empowering identities at different times by different people. One is used primarily as an adjective, while the other can be used as an adjective or a noun. Nobody takes these words literally (e.g., assuming that all gay men are happy, or that all lesbians are of Greek descent), nor does the historical usage of these terms take precedence over their contemporary usage (e.g., nobody assumes that "gay" implies promiscuity or prostitution, or that "lesbian" implies pathology or geographic origin). Their prominence today is not due to the fact these were the magical "perfect words" that allowed these groups to finally challenge the oppression they face and garner mainstream acceptance. Rather, these words are merely accidents of history—one can rather easily imagine that, under slightly different circumstances, other neologisms or reclaimed terminologies (e.g., homosexual, homophile, sapphist, queer, dyke, fairy, woman-identified woman, to name but a few possibilities) could have become the accepted terms for these populations.

In other words, the Activist Language Merry-Go-Round does not stop when the marginalized group finally finds "all the perfect words" to convey their identity and circumstances. It stops when people (or at least, a big chunk of society) cease projecting stigmatizing meanings, assumptions, and stereotypes onto those identities and circumstances. And for trans people, this obviously has not happened yet.

Stigma is the engine that keeps the Activist Language Merry-Go-Round in perpetual motion. We grow up in a culture where everything related to being trans is deemed illegitimate, suspect, fake, immoral, ridiculous, gross, etc. These meanings seep into the words that people use to describe our bodies and lives, our identities and partners, the things that we do, and virtually anything associated with us. These negative meanings and the systemic social structures that propagate them run deep and remain largely out of our reach. One of the few areas in our lives in which we can exert a modicum of control is through language: the words that we personally choose to embrace (or discard), and the words that we will tolerate (or not tolerate) from the mouths of others.

There is an understandable tendency for us to be suspicious toward (and perhaps even despise) trans-related language that was popularized before our time, as such words may seem to symbolize or embody the very stereotypes and negative meanings that we are trying to disentangle and dissociate ourselves from. This desire to destroy previously existing terminologies, and to replace them with novel alternatives, or freshly minted reclaimed words, seems to occur in every activist movement to some degree.

Historically, this process has been fairly slow moving—a gradual evolution in word usage over time. But in the Internet age, an idea or argument regarding language can catch on like wildfire (as I discuss in Notes 24 and 31 for this chapter). This is perhaps even more true with regards to trans communities, where the people who tend to be most active on Internet community forums and social media are younger trans folks, those who are in the process of coming out or transitioning, and/or who are not too far removed from those life events. Furthermore, many trans people ultimately become far less active in, or completely dissociate themselves from, the community after a few years of vigorous involvement (I am admittedly an anomaly in this regard). Together, these trends can create a wave-like phenomenon: Newly engaged activists are constantly forwarding their own word preferences designed to replace the previously existing terminology (which they find problematic for understandable reasons), just as the activists who initially championed that previous terminology (and who also did so for understandable reasons) are pulling back and thus remain largely unavailable to defend that language or explain why those language preferences resonated with them in the first place. Hence, the Activist Language Merry-Go-Round keeps on spinning.

At this juncture, a few points need to be made before people start hating on me. First, I am not in anyway implying that newer activists are "naive" whereas their predecessors "have historical perspective." I believe that ahistoricity runs rampant among all generations, and especially within LGBTQIA+ circles, where (with a few exceptions) we suddenly "come out" into communities that we were neither raised nor socialized into, and for which we have little previous historical knowledge about (unless we go out of our way to purposefully seek it out). Second, while the Activist Language Merry-Go-Round often results in a mere "re-branding" of previously existing identities, objects, expressions, and ideas, it is also true that each new wave of trans activists contributes new and important concepts that further our understanding of trans people and our experiences. And many of these concepts will be responses to present circumstances that could not have been envisioned by activists of the previous wave. So while some shifts in language may be somewhat arbitrary, others may be vitally important.

Some people may assume that my discussion here is self-serving: "Well, now that Julia has written her books and articles forwarding the language that she wants, she is trying to prevent future generations from replacing her preferred trans-related words with their own." Nothing could be further from the truth. For one thing, I do not have the power to stop any one person, let alone an entire trans community, from forwarding or protesting whatever language they wish. The phenomenon that I am describing here is bigger than any of us.

Furthermore, I have accepted the fact that the Activist Language Merry-Go-Round will not stop until trans identities, expressions, bodies, etc., are viewed as legitimate in our culture. When that time comes, trans-related words and labels will no longer be saturated with stigma, and only then will trans folks not feel compelled to eradicate such language or replace every term with novel (or reclaimed) alternatives.

Returning to the initial topic of this essay: The word "tranny" is, on one level, merely an ensemble of letters and syllables. But on another level—one in which many of us viscerally experience—the word is often (albeit not always) used to unleash an onslaught of negative sentiments. My fear is that we, as trans activists, are focusing all of our ire and wrath on the word itself, while not challenging the negative sentiments it seems to embody (and which are our true foe). And I am worried that the message that we are inadvertently conveying to the cis majority is "don't ever use the T-word," rather than encouraging them to interrogate and challenge the numerous negative meanings, assumptions, and stereotypes that people sometimes try to convey via that word.

In this essay, both directly and indirectly (via articles I've described or referenced) I have discussed a plethora of different meanings that different people have associated with the word "tranny" over time:

- "Our first own language word for ourselves that has no medical-legacy" and which was coined in order to unite drag queens and transsexual women in Sydney during the '60s and '70s (as pointed out by Kate Bornstein).

- A word co-opted by pornographers and the sex industry in order to market trans women and others on the trans female/feminine spectrum as sexual objects.

- A word that people who are attracted to trans people have subsequently adopted to describe their attractions to us (e.g., "tranny chaser," "tranny fetish"), and which some trans people also use to dismiss those very people (e.g., "He's just a fucking tranny chaser").

- A word that the mainstream public employs to ridicule trans women, and sometimes cis women, for "doing womanhood/femininity badly" (as discussed by Hazel/Cedar Troost).

- A word that trans people reclaimed during the '90s and early '00s in order to challenge trans invisibility and cis assumption (as I discussed earlier).

- A word that some transgender-spectrum people use in a subversivist manner in order to imply that their gender identities, expressions, or politics are more radical and subversive than other people's (as discussed by Hazel/Cedar Troost).

- A word that cisgender hipsters bandy about in order to give the impression that they are politically progressive or cutting edge because they supposedly have some familiarity (usually a highly superficial familiarity) with trans communities and culture (e.g., Christian Siriano and his slogan "hot tranny mess").

- A word that trans-unaware cisgender people use, not as a slur, but rather because they have heard other trans people (e.g., Julia Serano, circa 2001–2005) use the term self-referentially, and thus presumed that it was a neutral term that transgender-spectrum people use to describe themselves.

My purpose in listing these various meanings is not to imply that "tranny" is a special magical fairy-dust word that can mean anything to any person, and therefore all people are entitled to freely use it however they wish. The word does have a history as a slur (albeit only over the last few decades), and some trans people have experienced the word in association with sexual harassment and/or transphobic violence. People should be aware of this history, and if they choose to use the word, they should be responsible for their decision to do so. At the same time, we should all be cognizant of the complex history of the word, and (I would argue) we should judge people primarily according to their intent and the context in which they use it.

Earlier in this essay, I cited "queer," "gay," and "dyke" as examples of words that have been positively reclaimed. Despite being successfully reclaimed, these words are still sometimes (by certain people, in certain contexts) used as slurs. Most of us can rather easily distinguish between positive or neutral uses of these words—e.g., "Zachary Quinto came out as gay a few years ago" or "The Dyke March is this Saturday"—and negative ones—e.g., "That show is so gay, I can't believe you like it" or "Fucking dykes!" (as angrily shouted from a passing car at me and my girlfriend).

I would love to see conversations about the word "tranny" reach this level of nuance. Rather than calling out the mere utterance of "tranny," let's call out instances in which the word is used to exploit, erase, or denigrate trans people. And rather than simply calling out the fact that someone has used the word, let's call out the negative meanings behind the usage (e.g., "When you called her a 'tranny' just then, you were trying to sexualize/objectify her," or ". . . you were implying that she's not a 'real' woman").

I would argue that it's the negative meanings behind word "tranny" that invalidate us, not the word itself. If we only strive to eradicate words (whether it be "tranny" or others), those negative meanings will continue to persist, and they will inevitably latch themselves onto other words. And it is only when we have convinced much of the cis majority to abandon those negative meanings that the Activist Language Merry-Go-Round will finally stop spinning.

I, for one, am looking forward to a time when trans activism and trans-related language is not so dizzying all the time.

46

On People, Polarization, Panopticons, and #ComplexFeelingsAboutActivism

This chapter first appeared on my blog in April 2014. It was written in response to an escalating online debate (or in Internet parlance, a "kerfuffle") amongst trans women activists who differed in their opinions on several topical issues—most pertinently, RuPaul and drag, the word "tranny," and Jared Leto's portrayal of a trans woman in the film Dallas Buyers Club. *In this piece, I largely ignore the specifics of this particular melee (although those details can be found in sources cited in the Notes section), and instead focus on the tendency within activism for people with differing views to become entrenched into opposing camps, and to depict their opponents (or perceived opponents) as "oppressive" and a threat to the movement. And in the process, I invent a largely disregarded hashtag.[1]*

Over the last month or two, I have had numerous conversations amongst trans woman friends, and quite a few inquiries from other trans-identified and trans-aware folks, about the rather high profile "kerfuffle" that has taken place within trans female/feminine-spectrum circles recently. I rather vaguely alluded to the situation in my recent blog post, "a few thoughts on drag, trans women, and subversivism."[2] Other folks have written about it, but my personal favorite synopsis thus far is Jen Richards's recent piece.[3] I wouldn't be surprised if the principal actors at the center of this story disagree with certain aspects of this particular review. But Richards explores many of the issues regarding community, difference, and consensus (or the lack thereof) that have been on my mind lately. The thing that I appreciate most about the piece is that Richards puts herself into the shoes of others, not to be presumptive or to replace their viewpoints with her own, but rather to try to understand where they are coming from. It was a refreshing change of pace from the this-camp-is-evil/

oppressive/censoring/humorless/hurtful versus this-camp-is-righteous/op-pressed/human/less-pretentious/more-like-you-dear-readers dichotomy that has formed the backbone of most descriptions of this kerfuffle thus far.

The strategy of putting oneself into other people's shoes (in a hopefully understanding rather than presumptive way) is one of my personal foremost tenets of writing and activism. I may not always do it successfully. But I try really hard to understand what people on the "other side" of a debate or dispute believe, why they believe it, and what life circumstances led them to gravitate toward that perspective rather than others. Even if you strongly disagree with their views, it may help you find new and more productive ways to challenge their reasoning, or to re-frame your argument in ways that resonate with them a bit more. Even if you remain in disagreement, at the very least, it allows you to see your opponent as a living breathing person rather than as an abomina-tion or an evil oppressor.

But the thing is, seeing things from other people's perspectives can often make being an activist rather dicey and difficult to navigate.

For instance, with regards to this recent kerfuffle: I understand why RuPaul (who has been using the "T-word," as drag performers historically have, long before many of us became involved in trans and queer communities) would be reluctant to give up that self-identity label, even if I find several aspects of his TV show to be problematic and consider his response to recent controversies to be rather flippant.[4] I understand why trans folks who were never a part of the historical period that gave rise to RuPaul would be appalled by his continu-ing use of the "T-word." I understand why trans women (whether it be Parker Molloy, Calpernia Addams, or others) might have differing opinions about RuPaul, or drag, or Jared Leto, even if I don't necessarily agree with them on that particular issue(s). I understand why both Molloy and Addams probably felt misunderstood and invalidated by what the other was saying about them, even if I disagree with some of the things each of them said.[5] I understand why Andrea James would want to support her friend Addams (who she probably felt was being unfairly characterized), even if I disagree with much of what she said in her "take down" piece of Molloy.[6] I understand why people started hashtagging #IStandWithParker, and why Zinnia Jones started the petition,[7] and why many trans women signed it, even though I felt that some of the ar-guments being made by folks in that camp were virtually identical to the ones Addams and James were making: both sides were supposedly "conservative" and "assimilationist" and "homophobic/heteronormative" and "abusing their public platforms" and "on the wrong side of history."

The whole thing reminded me of that scene from the movie *V for Vendetta* with the dominoes: one thing causing another to happen, each person unknowingly playing a small role in what was becoming a far bigger story. The end result, of course, was entrenched polarization within the community. And as it was all unfolding, I felt like all I could do was watch. Because I knew that if I tried to intervene or add my voice in any way, I would simply get sucked up into the story.

Molloy and I follow each other on Twitter (as activists sometimes do). A couple weeks ago, I was tweeting about baseball (as I sometimes do), and she and a few other folks chimed in, and we had a harmless conversation about how bad our favorite teams have historically been. As this was happening, it suddenly struck me that others might perceive the exchange as being a tacit endorsement: that I must be on "her side" of the debate, even though we were merely discussing baseball. It made me extremely self-conscious. A few days later, in an online piece about the kerfuffle, it was mentioned that Molloy liked sports, and I wondered if the writer knew this because they had seen our Twitter exchange. After all, social media (especially in activist circles) is one giant panopticon[8]: We are all watching one another all of the time.

Last week, on my Twitter notifications, I saw that James tweeted something about buying my book *Excluded*. Often, when people tweet something about liking my books, or buying my books, I will re-tweet them (as you do), but I knew that if I did that in this case, I would become part of the story: I would be perceived as "siding" with James. And since that is the unpopular side of the debate (at least within younger trans women's circles), the ramifications could be dire. Perhaps my name might even be added to the petition against James and Addams: I would become one of the older elite white trans women with a platform who are oppressing the younger generation of elite white trans women with a platform.

People who are unfamiliar with this situation might expect that I am wildly exaggerating here, but I don't believe that I am. A few weeks back, on the Internets, I saw one trans activist seemingly calling out another trans activist for the fact that they follow musician Amanda Palmer on Twitter. Why, pray tell? Well, from what I could gather, it seems that Palmer positively mentioned James's article somewhere on social media. I would imagine that Palmer has no idea who James is, nor understands any of the details of this kerfuffle. I would imagine that Palmer simply liked the fact that James critiqued (to put it politely) "hashtag actvism."[9] I would imagine that someone with as high of a public profile as Palmer has probably felt unfairly attacked on social media before, and perhaps this is why she liked James's piece. I don't know—this is admittedly all just speculation on my part. The main point is that Palmer (probably unknowingly) "took a side" in the kerfuffle. And now, every trans activist who owns a Dresden Dolls album or enjoys Neil Gaiman novels is potentially suspect.[10]

I abhor this "picking a side" mentality, where if you have ever enjoyed a RuPaul performance, or think Jared Leto is a good actor, or if you want to nominate Jayne County for this year's Godwin's Law award,[11] then others will automatically assume that you belong to a particular camp, and that you must hold certain views that are commonly associated with that camp. I don't like being constantly placed into situations where I have to be either for or against Molloy, Addams, or James, and if I choose the "wrong side," then I will be ostracized. I think that all three women have done some positive things for our community, while at the same time, all three have said or done things at times that I disagree with. Frankly, there are *no* trans women who I agree with 100 percent of the time on all matters, so I resent feeling forced into "taking sides" with some trans women against other trans women, as that denies the complexity of people and situations.

I have complicated thoughts and feelings about many people and many things. So I resent how kerfuffles amongst activists (and there have been too many to count) always seem to result in polarization and over-simplified, cut-and-dried positions.

I believe that putting myself into other people's shoes in order to try to understand where they are coming from is a crucial part of my activism. So I resent how polarized activist positions attempt to coerce me into *not* identifying with, nor relating to, nor trying to better understand, certain people.

I resent how polarized activist positions try to compel me to see people as monsters and demons rather than as complex and fallible human beings.

As I alluded to above, this kerfuffle has touched on what has become a hot topic of late in activist circles (not to mention the media at large), namely, "hashtag activism." Many people have critiqued the phenomenon (including James), and I think many of those arguments are quite silly. Basically, it's just another way of getting one's opinions out there, no different really than starting a petition, or writing a blog or Facebook post that you hope others will share. While I am not against the phenomenon, I almost never participate in hashtag campaigns when they do occur. I hadn't really thought much about why that is until the recent #IStandWithParker campaign. In that case, it became clear to me that I felt like I was being compelled to "take a side" in a debate that I felt ambivalently about. Not every hashtag campaign falls into the category of being for or against people, but a lot of them do. Even when campaigns don't explicitly mention people, they are still often *about* people: If you're involved in that particular activist circle, then you know who wrote the blog post or article or tweet that made another activist you know upset, and which led them to start the hashtag campaign. Like I said, social media-based activism is a panopticon—we are all watching one another. We see who is tweeting with the hashtag and who is not, and sometimes (albeit not always) these tweets express allegiances to people and/or condemnations of other people. We watch our Twitter feeds—or in other cases, we notice who signed which petition, or who commented on which blog post—and we start imagining people as being on one side or another.

I can get behind hashtags like #TransphobiaSucks and #StopSexism and so forth. But if I know that a particular hashtag is intended to imply that I am "with this person" and "against that person," then I generally don't want any part of it. This is especially true when I know that both parties are activists, or members of the same marginalized group, who simply have differing opinions about some matter.

That is why I put the hashtag #ComplexFeelingsAboutActivism in the title of this post. I don't necessarily expect people to use it, and I certainly do not expect it to "trend."[12] But I do think that it is potentially productive to get the word out that it is okay for us to have complicated or ambivalent feelings about an issue, or about our fellow activists, sometimes. It is okay for us to agree with another activist about some matters but not others. It is okay for us to see both sides of an issue. It is okay for us to be critical of an individual's actions without tearing them down as people.

As I say in the last chapter of *Excluded*, we should stop constantly framing activist kerfuffles in terms of "righteous activist"/"evil oppressor" or "infallible activist"/"ignorant oppressor" dichotomies.[13] We are all trying to change the world for the better. We all make mistakes. We all hurt people. We are all still learning. All of us are right some of the time and wrong other times. And in many cases (as much as we may hate to admit it), there simply isn't a clear right or wrong stance, just differences in opinion. #ComplexFeelingsAboutActivism

47

Cissexism and Cis Privilege Revisited
(Part One: Who Exactly Does "Cis" Refer To?)

Originally published on my blog in October 2014, this is the first piece in a two-part series that revisits "cis terminology," exploring the varying usages of this language, and proposing an alternative (but not necessarily mutually exclusive) framework for considering gender non-conformity, marginalization, and privilege.

My first book *Whipping Girl* helped to popularize cis terminology—that is, language that uses the prefix "cis" to name the unmarked dominant majority (i.e., people who are not trans) in order to better articulate the ways in which trans people are marginalized in society. In 2009, I wrote *"Whipping Girl* FAQ on cissexual, cisgender, and cis privilege" (Chapter 25 of this book), which explained my reasoning in forwarding cis terminology and addressed some of the more common arguments made against such language. That blog post ended with a section discussing some of the limitations of cis terminology and the concept of cis privilege—a topic that I will revisit in this two-part series.

Over the years, I have observed that many people now use cis terminology in a manner that is somewhat different from how I attempted to use it in *Whipping Girl*, thus leading to potential ambiguity—I will address such matters in this first essay. In the last section of this essay, I will suggest another possible model for describing how people are differentially viewed and treated with regards to gender non-conformity, and which may (in some cases) provide a more effective framework than a cisgender/transgender dichotomy.

In the second essay, I will describe two differing approaches to activism, each of which leads to very different understandings of cissexism and the cis/trans distinction. Rather than simplistically arguing that one approach is "good" and the other "bad," I will instead forward a more contextual approach, one that acknowledges both the advantages and limitations of different ways of employing cis terminology, and that encourages us to strategically use whichever approach might be most effective within a given situation.

Cisgender, Cissexual, and Cissexism in Whipping Girl

Whipping Girl was written from an explicitly transsexual perspective and addressed issues that I felt were overlooked by the open-ended approach taken by the transgender movement in the 1990s (as that perspective continued to dominate in trans communities in 2005–2006 when I was writing the book). Here is what I mean by "open-ended": Transgender was a broadly defined umbrella term intended to be inclusive of all people who defy societal gender norms. This includes many of us who nowadays identify as "trans" for one reason or another, but it was also meant to potentially include other people who are unconventionally gendered in some way.[1] This open-ended definition allowed a wide variety of individuals to claim a spot under the transgender umbrella if they chose to do so.

This open-ended approach may seem counterintuitive to trans activists today, but there was an intentional logic to it. Trans folks had been largely left behind during the feminist and gay liberation movements of the 1970s and 1980s, primarily because these were identity-based movements centered on women and gay people, respectively. When movements are rooted in identity, there will inevitably be turf wars over who counts as a "real" woman or an "authentic" gay person. So despite the fact that trans people often face traditional sexism and heterosexism—the forms of sexism that feminism and gay liberation, respectively, were designed to challenge—we were nevertheless excluded from these movements.

In order to circumvent such problems, transgender activists during the 1990s purposefully created an anti-identity movement, where one was not required to meet any specific criteria for being transgender in order to participate. Anyone could take part in trans liberation so long as they opposed binary gender norms. Transgender activists of that time often highlighted the countless ways in which *all* people (whether trans or non-trans, queer or straight, female or male or both or neither), to varying degrees, are negatively impacted by the same gender binary system. This strategy was extremely productive in creating alliances between trans activists and other queer activists and feminists.

I still believe that this open-ended approach has its merits—especially with regards to creating a larger and more diverse movement, and enabling the non-trans majority to see the benefits (for both themselves, as well as for us) in challenging binary gender norms. However, in practice, it can lead to the false impression that all gender norms are similarly policed, or that all gender-variant people face the same set of obstacles. As I argue in *Whipping Girl*, while we all may have a stake in challenging rigid binary gender norms, we are not necessarily viewed and treated in the same ways by society at large.

Throughout *Whipping Girl*, I primarily focused on two such differences that are relevant to my own life. One was articulating how folks on the trans female/feminine spectrum face trans-misogyny (as discussed throughout Part 2 of this book). The second was highlighting the obstacles that are more specifically faced by transsexuals (i.e., those of us who identify and live as members of the sex other than the one we were assigned at birth). I focused on transsexuality because, at the time, it felt like most of the discussion about transgender issues (especially within feminist and queer circles) placed more interest and concern for those who challenge societal norms with regard to gender expression, while often ignoring or outright dismissing issues faced by transsexuals (who primarily defy norms with regard to gender identity and sex embodiment). Nowhere is this more evident than in the writings of many gender and queer theorists of the time, who often celebrated drag, androgyny, and female masculinity, while simultaneously dismissing transsexuals for supposedly being too conservative, assimilationist, or for "reinforcing" the gender system.[2]

I felt that this prioritization of gender expression over gender identity invisibilized some of the most pertinent obstacles faced by transsexuals. After all, while a non-transsexual drag performer, or feminine man, or masculine woman, may experience ridicule or harassment in their day-to-day lives for being visibly gender non-conforming, their gender identities and sex embodiments are not typically called into question. They do not have any problems obtaining legal documentation (e.g., driver's licenses, passports) that recognize their lived and identified genders; they do not run the risk of being locked up in the wrong jail cell or forced into some other inappropriate gender-segregated space; they do not have to deal with being mischaracterized as "deceiving" other people or being accused of "impersonation" when they move through the world as members of their self-identified gender.[3]

I wanted to address these issues in *Whipping Girl*. And as I was writing the book, I stumbled onto cis terminology (as I describe in Chapter 25) and found it to be invaluable for articulating such differences in how transsexuals are viewed versus how cissexuals (i.e., people who are not transsexual) are viewed by society. Throughout *Whipping Girl*, I used the word "cissexism" to describe this particular double standard, and I most thoroughly critique it in Chapter 8, "Dismantling Cissexual Privilege."[4] I make it clear in that chapter (and elsewhere in the book) that the purpose of using this language is not to reinforce the assumption that transsexuals are inherently different from cissexuals (as I do not believe that we are), but rather to examine the differences in how people are viewed and treated by others depending upon whether they are perceived or known to be transsexual or cissexual—I will return to this particular point in the following chapter.

While the word "cissexual" is used throughout *Whipping Girl* (according to Google Books, it appears on a whopping seventy-six pages, and often multiple times per page), the word "cisgender" only appears six times in the entire text. I used the word cisgender in the same way that activists today typically do, namely, as a synonym for non-transgender. I also make a distinction between cissexism (i.e., the assumption that transsexual gender identities and sex embodiments are less legitimate than cissexual ones) and cisgenderism (i.e., the assumption that people who defy gender norms are less legitimate than people who conform to them). (Note: I use "cissexism" somewhat differently today, as I explain in the next section.) Cisgenderism only appears once in the book, and my usage of the term to describe the delegitimization of people who defy binary gender norms is consistent with how others have used the word.[5]

So why did I focus almost entirely on cissexual privilege and cissexism while largely ignoring cisgender privilege and cisgenderism? As I've already discussed, the main reason is that I felt that transsexual-specific issues had not been adequately addressed by the transgender movement. But in addition to that, it occurred to me as I was working on the book that there was an obvious tension or inconsistency between the broad open-ended approach of the transgender movement and the specificity that is necessary in order to discuss how some people may be privileged in ways that others are not. While transsexuals are a heterogeneous group, there are specific things that we share in common (i.e., we identify and live as members of the sex other than the one we were assigned at birth) that lead us to be viewed and treated in very particular ways by society, and this treatment (particularly with regards to our gender identities and sex embodiments) differs significantly from that typically experienced by cissexuals.[6] In stark contrast, the label transgender is used in an open-ended, all-encompassing way—it could refer to "full-time" transsexuals as well as people who occasionally crossdress; people who strongly identify within the binary as well as people who do not; people who come off as explicitly androgynous, butch, or effeminate, as well as people who superficially seem to be gender conforming (that is, until others discover that they are transsexual, or genderqueer, or intersex, or two-spirit, etc.).

It was relatively straightforward for me to describe cissexual privilege—the assumptions that drive it and how it (or the lack of it) plays out in transsexuals' lives. But cisgender privilege seemed more like a nebulous blob to me. There are numerous different cisgender privileges out there, many of which are experienced by certain transgender subgroups but not by others.

For instance, while I may not have cissexual privilege, I do have what might be called *binary privilege*, in that I identify within the male/female binary. And while my female identity may be viewed as "lesser than" or "not as real as" that of a cissexual woman, the fact that I identify as a woman makes my identity far more legible and understandable to most people than that of a genderqueer person who does not identify within the binary.

Similarly, while I am not especially gender conforming as a woman (as I am somewhat tomboyish), I am femme enough that my appearance does not stand out as being particularly gender transgressive. As a result, I do not regularly face the specific forms of ridicule or harassment that visibly androgynous and butch women do[7]—this is another way in which one could say that I am privileged with respect to them, despite the fact that they have cissexual privilege whereas I do not.

Given that there are countless gender norms out there, and that many of us defy some of these norms while conforming to others, it did not seem clear to me that we can easily divide up the world up into people who have cisgender privilege and those who do not. The reality is that many of us experience both cisgender privileges and the lack thereof simultaneously in our lives. Furthermore, transgender activists of the 1990s purposefully intended for "transgender" to be an open-ended label that anyone who defies gender norms could potentially embrace. For one to begin to discuss "cisgender people" as a class unto themselves, it seemed to me that we would necessarily have to precisely define who "transgender people" are. I felt uncomfortable doing this, as it would have defied the explicit intentions of the transgender activists who forwarded the term in the '90s.

Anyway, for all of the aforementioned reasons, I decided not to delve too much into cisgender, cisgenderism, and cisgender privilege(s) in *Whipping Girl*.

Cis Terminology circa 2014

Language evolves. Some words catch on and others do not. And some of the differences in how cis terminology is used today seem to stem from aesthetic and/or political preferences for certain words over others.

One example of this is the failure of "cisgenderism" to really catch on. Perhaps this is because it is a somewhat clunky word. In any case, trans activists these days tend to use the word "cissexism" in its place. In other words, while I used cissexism in a transsexual-specific manner in *Whipping Girl*, nowadays trans folks generally use the word in a broad way to describe societal double standards wherein transgender bodies, identities, and expressions are deemed less legitimate than their cisgender counterparts. I have since gone with the flow on this, using this latter definition of cissexism in my second book *Excluded* and in other post-*Whipping Girl* writings.

Here is another language trend: People of transsexual experience often prefer labels like "trans" and/or "transgender" over "transsexual." The most commonly heard justification for this preference is that transsexual contains the word "sex" within it, which plays into misconceptions that we transition for sexual reasons rather than to live as members of our identified genders (although I would counter that "sex" in this context is clearly meant to refer to femaleness and maleness, not sexual activity). Now this trend began well before I began working on *Whipping Girl*—in fact, I was purposefully trying to reclaim the word transsexual by using it in the subtitle and throughout the book. While I still proudly use it, many folks have moved away from it, which is totally fine. But this trend does have a significant unintended consequence: It means that few people these days (other than me) regularly refer to "cissexuals" or "cissexual privilege." Instead, it is far more common to come across references to "cis" or "cisgender" people, and "cis" or "cisgender" privilege.

As stand alone words, "trans" and "cis" can sometimes refer to transsexuals and cissexuals, respectively—specifically when they precede the words "woman" and "man" (e.g., trans woman, cis man). But many other times, "trans" is used as a broad, open-ended umbrella term that is synonymous with transgender. Indeed, many folks these days put an asterisk on the end of trans (i.e., trans*) in order to emphasize its broad umbrella nature.

Thus, in practice, when someone says "cis people," it is often unclear whether they are talking about cissexual or cisgender people. And this can lead to significant discrepancies, as there are far more cissexual people than cisgender people, and many cissexual people are in fact transgender!

This slippage in meanings between cis, cisgender, and cissexual is often acutely felt by people who are cissexual but who nevertheless fall under the transgender umbrella. Several friends of mine who identify as crossdressers, genderqueer, and/or intersex have told me that they feel uncomfortable with cis terminology because, on the one hand, they don't want to deny the "cis privilege" they experience (by which they seem to mean cissexual privilege), but at the same time, they feel erased by the assumption that they are "cis people" (as they fall under the transgender umbrella). Still others who are cissexual and identify within the binary (and acknowledge those privileges), but have a history of being gender variant and participating in gender-variant communities, have expressed unease with how the labels "cis" and "cisgender" seem to oversimplify their gendered histories.[8]

Admittedly, there are some people who clearly do not fall under the transgender umbrella (nor do they wish to) yet who reject the labels cis/cisgender and deny having cis/cisgender privileges. Such individuals will often cite definitions in which "cisgender" is described as being synonymous with being "gender conforming" or "gender normative," and they will then point to various ways in which they are not especially conforming or normatively gendered. Thus, in their minds, they cannot be cis/cisgender, nor can they possibly possess cis/cisgender privilege. Because such claims seem to purposefully ignore how cis privileges play out in everyday life,[9] it is easy to dismiss these arguments as examples of the knee-jerk denial that often accompanies discussions about privilege. However, while these claims may be misguided, it is worth recognizing that they are enabled by the same vagueness in the terms cis/cisgender that has also caused confusion and disillusion within transgender spectrum communities.

So to summarize: The terms "cis" and "cisgender" are often used ambiguously, and this is partly due to the fact they are defined in relation to the broad, open-ended, umbrella terms "trans" and "transgender," which lack precise definitions or boundaries. This ambiguity has caused some concern within trans communities (regarding potential erasure of non-transsexual transgender identities) and confusion outside of trans communities (specifically, ostensibly cisgender people who misunderstand the purpose of this language and therefore reject it).

Rethinking Gender Non-Conformity and Social Legitimacy

There are a few things that we can do to help alleviate some of the aforementioned problems. For one thing, if we are specifically talking about privileges experienced by non-transsexuals, then perhaps it might be best to explicitly say "cissexual privilege" rather than "cis privilege." And if we are talking more generally about privileges experienced by cisgender people, then maybe we should refer to them as "cisgender privileges" (plural), and make clear that these privileges can vary somewhat from person to person, both within the transgender umbrella and outside of it. Also, given that we (i.e., trans activists) often tout the diversity that exists within the transgender/trans/trans* umbrella, we should also keep in mind that diversity exists among cisgender/cis/cis* people as well, and that there is no clear-cut line that one can draw in the sand between these two groups.

Most importantly, we need to stress (both within trans communities and to the general public) that the primary purpose of the cis/trans distinction is not to simply describe differences in identity. Rather, its main purpose is to articulate differences in *societal legitimacy*. By this reasoning, what is significant about me being "trans" is not the fact that I have rejected my birth-assigned gender (as in a perfect world, that might not be particularly noteworthy), but the fact that my gender is deemed to be less socially legitimate than other people's genders because of that fact. And cis people experience cis privileges, not because they are one hundred percent happy with their gender status or completely free from gender-based oppression, but because they do not face the same obstacles that I do as a trans person (as a result of their genders being deemed socially legitimate in ways that mine is not; see Note 9 for this chapter).

I would argue that the terms transgender/trans/trans* are not especially suited for this task of discussing discrepancies in social legitimacy, as they are meant to be catch-all categories for people who in various ways "defy gender norms" or are "gender non-conforming." And most people who are ostensibly cisgender can probably point to instances in their lives when they have defied certain gender norms and were criticized for it. I believe that it is in our best interest to encourage the cisgender majority to consider and express outrage over how gender norms negatively impact them, as such discussions are necessary if we want them to join us in a campaign to eliminate binary gender norms. But at the same time, not all gender norms are created equal. A man might wear a pink shirt, or a woman might choose not to shave her legs, and they may both receive negative comments from others. But they probably won't get fired from their jobs, be accosted in public restrooms, have doctors refuse to treat them, or face transphobic violence on account of those acts. In other words, acts of gender non-conformity may differ greatly in their social legitimacy (or lack thereof).

Given all this, perhaps a more advantageous way of discussing gender norms with regards to social legitimacy is to consider a three-tiered system rather than a cisgender/transgender dichotomy. These three groupings are not meant to define discrete classes of people, but rather three general tiers of social legitimacy.

Some people in our society are perceived as being *gender conventional*, in that they generally adhere to the accepted societal norms and expectations that are projected onto boys/men and girls/women in our culture. Because these individuals seemingly fall within those accepted parameters, their gender identities, expressions, and bodies are generally viewed as "normal" and legitimate. To be clear, this is not to say that such individuals are fully "gender privileged." After all, while they experience certain privileges for being seen as conventionally gendered, they may simultaneously be delegitimized because they are a woman, or feminine, or because of the way their gender intersects with other forms of marginalization.

Other people might be perceived as being somewhat *gender unconventional* because they defy some of these norms. This group might include people whose body or build is somewhat atypical for their gender, as well as tomboyish women, flamboyant or effeminate men, or people who prefer unisex or androgynous fashions. It might also include people who espouse feminism, or who have interests or professions that are atypical for their gender. Maybe they engage in more extreme acts of gender non-conformity, but only within certain socially sanctioned settings (e.g., while on a stage as part of an act or performance, or at costume or role-play-themed events). Others may view such individuals as "odd" or "weird," and they will certainly catch some flak for this. However, at the same time, these particular traits are also generally seen as being either a part of human variation (i.e., it is commonly accepted that some people will simply be that way) or as having more to do with politics, style, or social roles (which many people recognize as flexible and evolving over time). For this reason, gender unconventional people are generally seen as "outliers," but are not viewed as constituting a pernicious threat to male and female gender categories or categorization. In other words, while they are not seen as entirely socially legitimate, they are usually considered to be socially acceptable or tolerable.

Still other traits are seen as belonging exclusively to one sex or another, or are considered to be determinative for gender categorization—examples may include primary and certain secondary sex characteristics,[10] one's gender identity, and the gender that one lives and presents as. When a person defies these norms, they are often viewed as downright *gender transgressive.*[11] So for instance, a man who wears a single item of feminine clothing may be seen as gender unconventional, whereas if they fully present as a woman with the intention of being read as female, then they will likely be deemed gender transgressive. A woman who wants to be on top during sex may be seen as gender unconventional, but if they always imagine themselves as having a penis during the act, they will likely be viewed as gender transgressive. Unlike gender unconventional traits (which are commonly viewed as "bending" gender norms), gender transgressive traits are often perceived as downright "breaking" the laws of gender. This explains why our society has historically condoned the punishment of gender transgressive people (e.g., via violence and dehumanizing acts, denying of legal rights, or ruining their lives in other ways), and why such individuals are often misconstrued as "deceivers" and "impersonators" (i.e., "criminals" guilty of the gender equivalent of "fraud"). Thus, gender transgressive traits are viewed as completely unacceptable and socially illegitimate.

At this point, a few crucial points about this model need to be made. First, to reiterate, these three tiers are not intended to represent identities (as I can assure you, I do not identify as "gender transgressive"—frankly, my gender feels rather mundane to me personally, having to live with it every day). Rather, these tiers simply represent different ways in which gendered traits (and the people who possess them) may be perceived and treated by others. Second, these tiers are not intended to represent fixed and discrete classes. For instance, in certain times or places, people might view the fact that I am transsexual as highly gender transgressive and punish me accordingly, whereas for people in other times or places (e.g., communities that are largely trans aware, positive, or welcoming) that facet of my person may be seen as merely gender unconventional. Similarly, in more liberal or progressive settings, traits such as being a feminist or being in a same-sex relationship may be seen as ordinary and legitimate, whereas in more conservative settings (where especially rigid or fundamentalist ideas about gender predominate), these same traits might be considered to be transgressive and illegitimate.[12]

This model highlights numerous aspects of marginalization based on gender non-conformity (and activism designed to challenge it) that are obscured by other models (e.g., a cisgender/transgender dichotomy). First, it accounts for the concerns of people who are viewed as gender unconventional—that is, it acknowledges that people who are ostensibly cis (yet gender unconventional) often face disapproval and penalties for their gender non-conformity—without trivializing the more extreme ramifications and punishments faced by many trans people (on the basis that we are perceived as gender transgressive).

It also helps to explain the slow arc of progression that activism often takes. Specifically, groups that are deemed transgressive (and dehumanized as a result) are not in a logistical position to claim that they are just as legitimate as the dominant majority, as such claims will not be taken seriously. Instead, such groups often have to make the case that they are merely unconventional, rather than a violation of the laws of society, morality, or nature. Upon reaching the status of being seen as merely unconventional (rather than transgressive), they can then more effectively work to completely eliminate the "convention" (in this case, the gender norm) that undermines them. This process involves convincing people that, while certain ways of being (e.g., with regard to gender) may be atypical or uncommon, they are nevertheless just as socially legitimate as more typical or common ways of being. Recognizing this progression may lead to an understanding that trans activism needs to be occurring on both of these "fronts" simultaneously, since individuals within a given population will likely differ in whether they view gender atypical people as transgressive, unconventional, or socially legitimate.[13]

Because gender unconventional people may be perceived as gender transgressive in certain contexts, and because trans people are slowly but increasingly being perceived as gender unconventional rather than gender transgressive, it is in all of our best interests to work together to challenge all binary gender norms, and to argue that all gender atypical traits should be considered socially legitimate. This is a cause that could unite numerous groups in addition to trans people, including many feminists, other LGBTQIA+ activists, other people who consider themselves to be gender unconventional in some way, and even gender conventional people who find gender norms to be restrictive or unfair. Indeed, this coalition is similar to the one that 1990s era transgender activists attempted to build, although we seem to have gotten away from this strategy a bit in recent years.

To be clear, I am not suggesting that we completely replace the cisgender/transgender dichotomy with the three-tiered system I have just described. Both are simply models that explain certain aspects of marginalization based on gender non-conformity. Each model is limited in its explanatory powers, and may be more useful in certain situations or contexts but not others. While the three-tiered model may be more likely to win over other activists—especially those who are gender unconventional but not transgender-identified—it is perhaps a bit too complicated to resonate with people who do not have an especially nuanced view of gender. And while I personally prefer activist approaches that focus on how individuals are differentially perceived and treated by society, history has repeatedly shown us that identity-based approaches (e.g., I am transgender, and transgender people are oppressed, whereas cisgender people do not face this oppression) invariably seem to garner the most momentum, both within marginalized communities and in persuading the dominant majority.

It should also be pointed out that many of the problems associated with the cisgender/transgender distinction that I detailed earlier stem not from the fact that this model is dichotomous (rather than three-tiered, or some other variation), but rather because of how it is employed. In the second essay in this series, I will discuss two common albeit different ways in which people tend to conceptualize and utilize the cisgender/transgender distinction, each of which arises from differing activist philosophies, and may lead to considerably different potential outcomes.

48

Cissexism and Cis Privilege Revisited
(Part Two: Reconciling Disparate Uses of the Cis/Trans Distinction)

Members of the same marginalized population may take rather different approaches toward articulating the obstacles they face. Two especially common activist approaches are "decentering the binary" and "reverse discourse" strategies. In this essay (originally published on my blog in November 2014), I discuss the logic behind these differing approaches to activism, and explain why they tend to result in very different understandings of cissexism and the cis/trans distinction. In fact, some of the most common complaints about cis terminology are actually critiques of "reverse discourse" approaches to activism. Rather than outright championing one approach over the other, I encourage activists to familiarize themselves with the pros and cons of each strategy in order to use them in the most judicious and effective way possible.

In the previous chapter, I discussed how the way in which cis terminology is often used today can sometimes invisibilize certain forms of gender-based oppression, and potentially exclude people who exist at the margins of the transgender umbrella (i.e., people who don't fit quite so neatly into a cis/trans binary). In this essay, I want to talk about the different ways in which a cis/trans distinction may be employed, as this can greatly shape the nature and ultimate goals of trans activism.

"Decentering the Binary" versus "Reverse Discourse" Approaches

One of the more commonly heard complaints about cis terminology is that it supposedly "creates a new binary" (i.e., trans versus cis). I strongly disagree with this argument. After all, people already make a distinction between non-transsexuals and transsexuals, and between gender-conforming and gender-non-conforming individuals. So the cissexual/transsexual and cisgender/transgender binaries already exist in people's minds. It's just that now we (trans activists) have explicitly named the unmarked majority as "cis."

This naming of the unmarked majority can be undertaken toward one of two potential ends. First, it can be used to undermine the binary in question by *decentering the dominant group perspective*. So, rather than the standard perspective that trans people's genders are illegitimate and suspect (which presupposes that cis people's genders are legitimate and "normal"), we can instead argue that there are really two groups at play here: trans and cis people. Both are legitimate things to be. And trans people are not inherently different or distinct from cis people, but rather we are merely perceived, interpreted, and treated differently. Here, the cis/trans distinction and cis privilege serve as conceptual tools in order to make this under-discussed and often invisible set of cissexist double standards appear visible to people. The end goal here is to get people to recognize and relinquish these cissexist double standards, thus reducing the social significance of the cis/trans distinction. Presumably, in a post-cissexist world, there would still be people who are gender variant, or who socially and/or physically transition,[1] but their gender identities, expressions, and embodiments would not receive undue scrutiny, nor be viewed as less legitimate than their cis counterparts. This is the approach that I strove to articulate in *Whipping Girl*.

A second and rather different way in which the naming of the unmarked majority can be employed is as part of a *reverse discourse*.[2] A reverse discourse occurs when a group takes a designation or distinction that has historically been used to marginalize them (in this case, being "trans") and uses it as a standpoint from which to prioritize their own beliefs, desires, and perspectives. So instead of the cis majority defining, discussing, and critiquing trans people, trans folks now define ourselves and describe our own identities, lives, issues, communities, and culture. What cis people say about us, our predicament, and perhaps even gender more generally, is rendered irrelevant—we are the only authority on issues that impact our lives. Indeed, in a reverse discourse, cis people and perspectives may even be deemed as inherently suspect, illegitimate, or oppressive.[3]

While the first approach that I described merely decenters the dominant group (thus creating two legitimate groups: cis and trans people), reverse discourses re-center the binary on the marginalized group. Rather than reducing the social significance of the cis/trans binary, a reverse discourse emphasizes it—after all, one only gains the authority to speak about trans people and related matters of gender if one can indisputably claim a trans identity. And in this reverse discourse, discussions of cis privilege are not merely a tool to make unconsciously-held cissexist double standards appear visible, but rather they are used to make cis people accountable for their relative power and the long history of anti-trans oppression. This approach compels cis people to explicitly acknowledge their position of power and privilege as members of the oppressor class—for example, by stepping aside to allow trans people's voices to be heard, or qualifying anything they say about trans issues or even gender more generally with the admissions like "Well, as a cis person . . ."

Of course, trans people did not invent this reverse discourse approach. Michel Foucault initially coined the phrase "reverse discourse" to describe the approach taken by gay liberationists who re-appropriated the heterosexual/homosexual distinction in order to forward the narrative of a homosexual class that was oppressed at the hands of the heterosexual majority.[4] Within feminist theory, the phrase "reverse discourse" has been used to describe certain strands of feminism that conceptualize sexism solely in terms of "men are the oppressors, women the oppressed, end of story." (Note: in some of my previous writings, I have used the term "unilateral feminism" to describe this particular approach to feminism.) Reverse discourses have also arisen in other activist movements, where they are often described under the rubric of "identity politics."[5] So it is unsurprising that trans activists would adopt a similar approach.

Having come into activism during the heyday of third-wave feminism and queer theory, I was taught to be highly suspicious of reverse discourses for several reasons. First, they divvy up all people into two mutually exclusive groups: the oppressors and the oppressed. This move excludes countless "liminal" people who do not fall neatly into one group or another. This is why feminists who forward reverse discourses have such a horrendous track record in dealing with people who fall under the transgender umbrella, and why gay men and lesbians who forward reverse discourses have such a horrendous track record in dealing with people who fall under the asexual and bisexual umbrellas.

Reverse discourses also tend to be highly unilateral, focusing primarily on that one particular axis of oppression, while ignoring other forms of marginalization that intersect with that "primary axis" (as well as with one another).[6] As a result, reverse discourses tend to depict the marginalized group in a homogeneous manner—e.g., by making claims that all members share the same perspectives, beliefs, needs, and desires—when this is typically far from the truth. Reverse discourses also tend to portray the "oppressor class" (who in reality are a heterogeneous mix of people who vary greatly in their experiences, privileges, and forms of marginalization they may face) in a monolithic and stereotyped manner. As Judith Butler once said: "The effort to identify the enemy as singular in form is a reverse-discourse that uncritically mimics the strategy of the oppressor instead of offering a different set of terms."[7]

A disdain for reverse discourses and the way they exclude people who do not neatly fit into binary categories is what compelled transgender activists of the 1990s to try to create an open-ended anti-identity movement for anyone who saw themselves as a "gender outlaw" of one stripe or another (as I discussed in the previous chapter). So when writing *Whipping Girl,* I tried not to fall into the reverse discourse trap, and instead I tried to adhere to the decentering the binary approach that I described earlier. And while I think that I did a pretty decent job to that effect, in retrospect, I have to admit that there were a few passages where I got a bit reverse discourse-y.[8] Frankly, it's hard not to. When you are a delegitimized minority, members of the dominant majority will often not take you seriously unless you can somehow prove that you have superior knowledge (due to your unique standpoint) and deserve to be listened to (because you have been unfairly oppressed by the dominant group). Reverse discourses provide this. In contrast, the both-identities-are-just-as-legitimate sentiment of the decentering the binary approach often fails to gain much traction at first, especially if the marginalized group is highly stigmatized.

In addition to creating a narrative that gives the marginalized group the authority to speak on its own behalf and compels the dominant group to listen, reverse discourses can also be very cathartic for members of the marginalized group. It provides a justification for them to rightfully vent the anger and hurt that they have been made to feel as a result of the marginalization they have faced. And because reverse discourses "flip" the original hierarchy, members of the marginalized group may suddenly feel a sense of superiority over members of the dominant group, and this can understandably feel empowering. In contrast, the nobody-is-superior-to-anyone sentiment of the decentering the binary approach does not offer this possibility for self-satisfaction.

Finally, while reverse discourses are primarily concerned with identities (in this case, whether people are cis or trans), the decentering approach is primarily concerned with a mindset (in this case, cissexist double standards that influence how we see and interpret the world) that affects both the dominant and marginalized groups. Therefore, according to the decentering approach, members of the dominant group are just as capable of overcoming cissexist beliefs as members of the marginalized group are. As a result, members of the dominant group have the potential of becoming righteous allies who can help us challenge the marginalization we face. In stark contrast, reverse discourses tend to portray members of the dominant group as inherently oppressive and suspect, and thus the very notion that such individuals can become "allies" or "advocates" seems somewhat self-contradictory. Indeed, in reverse discourses, people who position themselves as allies are often accused of asserting their privilege and/or erasing the voices of the marginalized group by attempting to speak on their behalf.[9]

Given all this, it seems obvious why reverse discourses tend to galvanize marginalized groups far more so than decentering the binary approaches. But the problem is that reverse discourses have no endgame: the distinction forever remains important, even if discrimination decreases over time. And as I already discussed, reverse discourses have a host of other problems (e.g., they unilaterally focus on one or a few axes of oppression; they erase and exclude people who do not fit neatly into one of the two mutually exclusive groups; they view members of the two groups in a uniform, and sometimes essentialist, manner) that are not shared by the decentering the binary approach.

Who Faces Cissexism?

We can see the profoundly different implications of these two approaches if we ask the simple question: "What is cissexism and who faces it?"

A decentering-the-binary approach would encourage us to view cissexism as a set of assumptions that people (whether individuals or institutions) hold (either consciously or unconsciously) that lead them to perceive, interpret, and treat gender-variant/gender-non-conforming bodies, identities, and expressions as illegitimate or inferior to their gender-normative/gender-conforming counterparts. Thus, any given person (whether cis or trans) can behave in a cissexist manner. And any given person (whether cis or trans) could potentially experience cissexism (although for obvious reasons, this form of marginalization will be experienced most frequently and intensely by trans people). In *Whipping Girl*, I described cissexism (along with heterosexism) as but one form of *oppositional sexism*—the belief that female and male are rigid categories, each possessing a mutually exclusive set of traits, abilities, and desires. And oppositional sexism works hand in hand with *traditional sexism* (the belief that femaleness and femininity are inferior to, and less legitimate than, maleness and masculinity) to ensure that only straight men who were assigned a male sex at birth and are sufficiently masculine can ever be viewed as fully legitimate.[10] In other words, cissexism is part of an overarching system that (along with other forms of sexism) works to *keep all people in their place*. Thus, any person can face cissexism.

Take, for instance, an otherwise cisgender man who never had a gender-variant thought in his life. If he were to suddenly, on a whim, decide to wear a dress to work, he would very likely face cissexist ridicule and harassment on his way to his job, and possibly even get fired from his job as a result. If an otherwise cisgender woman who never had a gender-variant thought in her life decided that she was tired of plucking all the hairs on her chin and upper lip (which a considerable number of women experience), she would surely face cissexist reactions and comments once her facial hair grows out. In fact, cissexism (or at least the threat of it) is the force behind both the low level gender anxiety faced by cisgender people who worry that they will be perceived as insufficiently feminine or masculine if they do "the wrong thing," as well as the more severe forms of gender policing and punishment experienced by those of us who more regularly or blatantly transgress gender norms.

By no means does this decentering the binary perspective suggest that all people are equally hurt by societal cissexism. Clearly, some of us grapple with cissexism on a routine basis, while other people experience it infrequently and/or far less severely. But the decentering approach does encourage us to challenge all expressions of cissexism, regardless of who the perpetrator or target is.

Those who adhere to a more strict reverse discourse approach will likely see things very differently. They may be inclined to see cissexism as a form of marginalization that specifically oppresses trans people, because after all, cis people materially benefit from the systematic oppression of trans folks. Because they are privileged by this system, instances where cis people face cissexism in some form may be dismissed as unimportant or illegitimate.

This latter tendency is most certainly not specific to trans activist reverse discourses. Feminists who are entrenched in a reverse discourse approach often claim that only cis women can face traditional sexism—such claims ignore how traditional sexism sometimes impacts certain men's lives and how it wreaks havoc on many trans people, especially those of us on the trans female/feminine spectrum.[11] Similarly, gay men and lesbians who are steeped in reverse discourse-thinking often insist that they alone are targets of heterosexism—this ignores how heterosexist ideology is often used as a weapon to police straight individuals' behaviors, and how it greatly impacts the lives of those of us who fall under the bisexual/pansexual umbrella.

Indeed, there are a series of tropes that people who are inclined toward reverse discourse approaches often trot out in order to dismiss both the dominant group's, as well as liminal people's (i.e., those of us who do not neatly fall into the reverse discourse's binary) experiences with the form of marginalization in question. Here are a few examples of how these tropes (which arise in reverse discourses more generally) are sometimes applied to cisgender people and/or those who exist at the borderlands between cis and trans:

- *The not-the-true-target trope:* When cis people are subjected to acts of cissexism (e.g., if they are called a "sissy" or ridiculed for "looking like a tranny"), some trans people will discount that person's experience by claiming that they were not the true target of cissexism. After all, since such comments insinuate that there is something wrong with, or funny about, being transgender, trans people are the primary intended target of such remarks, whereas the cis person is only indirectly affected.

- *The lack-of-history trope:* Trans people have long personal histories grappling with societal cissexism. And over time this can have an accumulative effect, whereby we become highly sensitive to and possibly even triggered by cissexist acts, since they exacerbate the oppression we have already faced. In contrast, a cis person who is subjected to a cissexist act will not nearly be as negatively impacted by the incident, as it represents more of an aberration for them rather than part of a continual systemic experience.[12]

- *The dabbling trope:* Unlike trans people (whose gender variance/gender non-conformity is real and authentic), other individuals who behave in a gender-non-conforming manner are merely pretending or "playing" with gender. Because their acts of gender non-conformity are occasional and frivolous in nature, the oppression they face as a result should not be taken too seriously.

- *The tourist trope:* People who are not authentically trans may experience instances of cissexism, for instance, related to being partnered to a trans person, or for occasionally dabbling in acts of gender non-conformity. However, because they are merely "tourists," they can always stop engaging in such acts (e.g., by leaving their partners, ceasing their "gender play"), thereby escaping cissexism—something that authentic trans people are unable to do.

- *The slumming trope:* Because trans people are sometimes viewed as fascinating, exciting, or radical in certain circles, some people who are not authentically trans themselves may associate with trans people or engage in acts of gender non-conformity in order to appear "edgy" or to obtain "hipster cred." Because such individuals are merely "appropriators" (rather than authentic trans people) the cissexism they face should not be taken seriously.[13]

- *The parodying trope:* Trans individuals may presume that people who they view as outsiders, or "not trans" in the way that they are, must be purposefully mocking or parodying authentic trans people when they engage in acts of gender non-conformity. Because they are merely parodying trans people, such individuals are pretty much asking for any cissexism they face.

- *The infiltrator trope:* Trans individuals may presume that people who they view as outsiders, or "not trans" in the way that they are, must be purposefully infiltrating their community, most likely for nefarious reasons.[14] Because they are up to no good, such individuals are pretty much asking for any cissexism they may face.

Now of course, there may be some instances or contexts in which some of the above claims may be relevant or bear some truth. But many times they are flat out wrong. The more important point is that, taken together, these claims serve the purpose of dismissing or denying the reality that some cisgender people, and many folks who inhabit the borderlands between cis and trans, sometimes face cissexism. As a trans and bisexual woman who has been subjected to analogous claims within reverse-discourse-inclined feminist and gay/lesbian circles, I can tell you that these tropes are pervasive and can be highly damaging to people who do not neatly fit the canonical image of a "woman" or a "gay" or "lesbian" person. So I find it distressing when I hear similar claims being made about people who do not fit the canonical image of a "trans person."

Additionally, the aforementioned claims highlight an important inconsistency in our activism that I touched upon in the previous chapter. Namely, trans activists use the term "trans" as an umbrella for all people who are gender non-conforming, or gender variant, or who transgress gender norms. And yet, some people who do these very things may be dismissed as not experiencing cissexism because they are not considered to be "bona fide" trans people, but rather merely dabblers, tourists, appropriators, parodists, infiltrators, and so on. This raises the question: What is it that supposedly makes someone a "bona fide" trans person, one who is capable of experiencing "authentic" cissexism?

Well, many reverse-discourse-inclined folks will resort to blatant essentialism to make their case, as evidenced by those trans-exclusive feminists who insist that I can never be a "real woman" (and therefore, can never experience "real sexism") because I am not "biologically female." Or Harry Benjamin Syndrome-identified "real transsexual" women who insist that they were born with a specific brain anomaly that drag queens, crossdressers, genderqueers, and queer/transgender-identified trans women are missing, and which supposedly makes the cissexism they experience real and authentic, whereas the rest of us are merely "poseurs" and "appropriators" in their eyes.[15]

Admittedly, most of us who are trans activists are highly cognizant of the problems associated with essentialist thinking, so we tend to avoid invoking it in our arguments. However, rather than resorting to blatant essentialism, we instead tend to define "bona fide" trans people in a manner reminiscent of U.S. Supreme Court Justice Potter Stewart's famous definition of obscenity (which he offered during a 1964 court case regarding pornography): "I know it when I see it . . ."[16]

Many of us are painfully aware of how this "I know it when I see it" mentality tends to play out within transgender communities:

If you are a post-transition transsexual, you are clearly a "bona fide" trans person. However if you are pre-transition, or not "out" as trans, then we will presume that you are cis, and all the cissexism you face doesn't count. Until, of course, you *do* transition or come out as trans, then those experiences will become retroactively authentic.

Drag queens do not count as "bona fide" trans people—after all, they are merely cis gay men who have *all the cis privilege*. Unless they eventually transition to female (as some do), then they were really trans people all along, and drag was merely something that they had to do in order to survive in a cis-centric world.

Genderqueer folks are "bona fide" trans people. Although we will likely doubt that they are *really* genderqueer unless they offer us some kind of visible sign of their genderqueerness. So if you are a FAAB genderqueer who happens to be femme, or a

MAAB genderqueer who isn't femme, then screw you—you are merely poseurs! On the other hand, if you *look* genderqueer (you know, FAAB dressed masculinely or androgynously), then totally, you're a legitimate genderqueer. Unless you call yourself a "butch," in which case we'll have to assume that you're merely a cis lesbian with *all the cis privilege*.

Oh, and regarding potential MAAB genderqueers: 1) is that even a thing? I thought only FAAB people could be genderqueer? 2) if you *are* genderqueer, then the least you could do is wear a dress, or put on some makeup, so that we don't assume that you're a cis dude poser, 3) but don't dress *too femininely*, or else we'll assume that you're a drag queen (a.k.a., a cis gay dude) with *all the cis privilege*, 4) also, be sure to dress that way *all the time*, otherwise we'll assume that you're merely a crossdresser.

And speaking of crossdressers: Sorry, but you cannot be "bona fide" trans people. After all, you live most of your life moving through the world with *all of the cis privilege*. Get back to us if/when you eventually decide to transition, and then we may retroactively authenticate your prior experiences with cissexism.

If you are intersex, then you are definitely a "bona fide" member of our community (if you choose to be, as many intersex folks do not identify as trans). But be sure to explicitly and frequently mention that you are intersex, otherwise we will have no choice but to assume that you are a cis person infiltrating our space. But so you know, if you *do* explicitly and frequently mention that you are intersex, then we will likely take that as a sign that you are totally cool with talking about it, and we will probably ask you all sorts of inappropriate questions about your anatomy or medical history as a result.

<!-- end satire ---\>

For many of us, being trans is a deeply personal and largely internal experience. I spent years contemplating, struggling with, and privately exploring my inner sense of gender before I ever dared to engage in any kind of public act as a trans person (e.g., presenting as female in public, interacting with trans communities, coming out to people as trans). And as trans activists, we often vociferously challenge the mainstream public's tendency to constantly invade our privacy (e.g., when they insist that we must always reveal our trans status to them, or answer their inappropriate questions about our anatomy or childhoods). So it seems odd—if not downright contradictory—that we often forward a reverse discourse strategy that compels people to constantly show and/or explicitly state where they fall on the cis/trans continuum, and which may even dismiss their experiences with cissexism if they have not yet come to fully identify as trans, or if they choose not to be out as trans, or if they do not live up to other people's criteria of what counts as trans.

Embracing a More Contextual Approach to Trans Activism

Here is an excellent bell hooks quote:

Feminism is the struggle to end sexist oppression. Its aim is not to benefit solely any specific group of women, any particular race or class of women. It does not privilege women over men. It has the power to transform in a meaningful way all our lives.[17]

Analogously, I would argue that trans activism should be the struggle to end cissexist oppression.[18] Its aim should not be to benefit any specific group of trans people, any particular race or class of trans people. It should not privilege trans people over cis people. It has the power to transform in a meaningful way all our lives.

A decentering the binary approach that challenges all expressions of cis-sexism (regardless of where the perpetrator and intended targets fall along the cis/trans continuum), and works to lessen the negative impact that gender norms have on *all* of our lives, most closely approaches this lofty goal. In contrast, reverse discourse strategies fail us for numerous reasons that I have detailed over the course of this essay.

It would be fairly easy for me to simply reiterate the same arguments that were made by third-wave feminists and queer activists well over twenty years ago: that reverse discourses (or "identity politics," as such approaches are some-times called[19]) tend to deny diversity and intersectionality, are horribly exclu-sionary, and for these reasons, we should abandon them. But I believe that such a flat-out condemnation would ignore the underlying forces and human tendencies that ultimately compel activists to turn to reverse discourses again and again. Here are a few of these forces and tendencies (some of which I've already alluded to during this two-part series):

- *Activist movements tend to get co-opted.* Upon learning about a partic-ular form of marginalization, members of the dominant majority of-ten reflexively focus on how that form of marginalization potentially impacts themselves, while largely ignoring how it impacts those most severely targeted. Reverse discourses refute this tendency.

- *We all want to believe that we are right.* For members of the dominant majority, this often means that they assume that their opinions about marginalized minorities (and the oppression they face) are informed, objective, and righteous, when often they are anything but. Reverse discourses refute this tendency, while simultaneously enabling members of the marginalized minority (who also want to believe that they are right) to assume the status of "expert" on the situation (even though their opinions may differ significantly from other members of their own group).

- *The existence of "faux allies."* When groups are highly stigmatized, very few people are willing to stand by the group, and the few who do are usually genuine in their sentiments. But as the group becomes more accepted by society, members of the dominant majority will increasingly feel pressure to be on the "right side" of the argument, and may declare themselves "allies" of the group in order to avoid accusations that they are prejudiced. Upon doing so, they may then make highly uninformed or problematic claims on behalf of the marginalized group in question. Reverse discourses directly undermine such efforts.[20]

- *Guilt by association.* One of the easiest ways to delegitimize a minority/marginalized group is to conflate them with some other marginalized group, or to highlight a subpopulation within the group who are viewed as especially illegitimate. This is why people who wish to undermine trans women tend to compare us to male crossdressers, female impersonators, and drag queens, and/or emphasize the existence of trans female/feminine folks who engage in sex work, have been incarcerated, have a history of fetishism or practicing BDSM, who are pre- or non-op, who have since de-transitioned, and so on. The insinuation, of course, is that these supposedly inferior or stigmatized qualities are intrinsic to the group as a whole. Reverse discourses—which typically imagine some sort of "ideal" or "canonical" group member—provide a convenient logic for those activists who wish to dissociate themselves from these "less desirable" individuals. However, such an approach inevitably results in other marginalized individuals (especially members of the group who are liminal or multiply marginalized) being thrown under the proverbial bus.

- *Members of the marginalized minority may differ in their ultimate goal.* Some members may carry out activism with the hopes of fully integrating into, and being seen as respectable members of, society at large. In contrast, others may no longer trust members of the dominant group, nor want anything to do with them. Individuals in this latter category may prefer to reside primarily within their own marginalized communities with as little interaction with the dominant majority as possible. Reverse discourses offer those in this latter, more separatist, camp the justification to create and uphold such insular communities.[21]

While I generally distrust reverse discourse approaches to activism (having been personally undermined by them as both a bisexual and trans woman), I completely understand why they arise and why many activists embrace them. And I honestly don't expect them to go away any time soon, given the human tendencies I just outlined. So rather than outright condemning them, I instead encourage trans activists (and activists more generally) to learn to recognize reverse discourses and to understand their limitations and flaws. Perhaps we can learn to use them more judiciously or effectively—for instance, employing them when challenging a member of the dominant majority who arrogantly presumes they have "authority" or "superior knowledge" over us, while refraining from using them simply as a tool to invalidate other people's expressions or perspectives, or as a method for discounting or excluding other marginalized individuals.

For me, the hardest part about being an activist has not been speaking truth to power. I have become fairly comfortable and adept at expressing my views about gender and trans issues to members of the cis majority. But what I have found to be most difficult, especially early on, was learning to accept the fact that there will always be some trans people who will disagree with me on such matters. Initially, their disparate or dissenting views seemed to somehow undermine the veracity of my opinion, and my knee-jerk reaction to such incidents was to presume that such people were politically naive, cis apologists who were selling out the movement, or reckless activists whose extreme views would likely set the movement back. These sorts of sentiments abound in all activist movements. But over time, I realized that my reactions were steeped in a cissexist double standard. After all, I certainly do not expect the cis majority to ever all agree about some particular issue. So why is it then that I (or anyone else for that matter) would expect the trans community to all line up and agree with one another all the time?

It is true that some people are politically naive (e.g., someone who is first coming into the community, and is unfamiliar with our movement's history or activism more generally). But more often than not, when I come across a trans activist who I disagree with about some particular issue, it is usually because we differ in our vantage points and/or our understanding or beliefs about trans people and activism.

This two-part series has been part of an even larger endeavor that I have embarked upon over the last few years. In my recent book *Excluded*, I argued that our movements become exclusionary when we embrace fixed models of how gender and sexuality, and sexism and marginalization, work. These fixed models typically lead us to propose one-size-fits-all solutions to challenge the oppression we face, and as a result, we tend to accuse activists who propose alternate opinions or courses of action of "reinforcing" that oppression. In the second half of *Excluded*, I offered strategies that enable us to challenge all forms of sexism and marginalization without becoming entrenched in any one particular fixed perspective.

Since completing that book, I have given considerable thought to recent debates within trans activism regarding language, appropriation, generational divides, the tendency of activists to coalesce into opposing factions, and of course, cis terminology.[22] Rather than (or sometimes in addition to) simply taking a side in the debate in question, I have tried to understand why people who disagree with me, or disagree with other trans activists, came to their differing views. I attempted to understand their vantage points (inasmuch as possible), and the underlying logic or beliefs that led them to that conclusion. And I gave serious consideration to the possibility that their differing approach might possibly make sense or be the correct course of action in certain times or circumstances, but perhaps not in others. I have carried out this work, not to seem like a "nice person," nor to find some kind of "compromise" that will make all sides happy. Rather, I have done this because I believe that activism needs to be flexible and contextual if it is going to accommodate a diversity of people.

If we are going to accept heterogeneity and differences of opinion within our community, then it starts with us trying to understand where other trans activists are coming from. I hope that my articulating the "decentering the binary" and "reverse discourse" approaches in this essay, if nothing else, at least helps other activists better understand why they may have come to differing conclusions than their peers.

There Is No Perfect Word
(A Transgender Glossary of Sorts)

As I mentioned in the Introduction, I have created an online glossary of transgender (and related) terminology that I use throughout this book and in my other writings—it can be accessed at **http://juliaserano.com/terminology.html**. *What follows here is a brief essay that accompanies that online glossary, in which I summarize some of my current thinking regarding trans-related language.*

Glossaries can be quite useful, especially for books on specialized topics (e.g., transgender activism) that rely on subject-specific terminology. However, a drawback of glossaries is that they tend to give the impression that the words listed have cut-and-dried meanings that remain largely undisputed. While this might generally be true for glossaries of terms related to geology, grammar, or guitars, it most certainly is *not* the case for trans-related terminology. Many of the words and phrases listed here are only several decades old (if that), so they are by no means set in stone. And nearly every single word that refers to some aspect of transgender identities, bodies, or life experiences exists in a perpetual state of debate or dispute, with individual trans people espousing differing word preferences and alternative definitions. In Chapter 45, I describe this lightning-speed language evolution as the Activist Language Merry-Go-Round: In response to the societal stigma that permeates everything associated with trans people (including the words used to describe us), we are constantly inventing new untainted terms and/or reclaiming, redefining, or eliminating older ones.

Here is an analogy to help illustrate this dilemma: I have been a guitarist for about thirty years, and during that time, guitar-related language has barely changed at all. And the reason why it hasn't changed is that guitarists are not marginalized in our culture—thus everything associated with guitar playing (including terminology) is generally free of negative connotations. However, if guitarists did face severe stigma and undue scrutiny in our culture, then I can assure you that there would be debates over language and calls to eliminate or replace certain words. Some guitar activists would likely argue that the phrase "minor chord" trivializes our existence; that the word "fret" gives the false impression that people should be afraid of us; that "power chord" and "hammer on" play into media stereotypes of guitarists as violent; that "pickup" and "G string" perpetuate the sexualization of guitarists. There would also likely be claims that "guitar-playing person" is a more appropriate and respectful term than "guitarist," arguments over whether people who additionally play other (less stigmatized) instruments count as "real guitarists," and calls for more inclusive labels because "guitarist" does not seem to include people who play other stigmatized stringed instruments like the banjo, ukulele, and others.

I am by no means mocking activist responses to language here. To the contrary, I think that it is perfectly understandable why marginalized individuals (whether fictional stigmatized guitarists, or real-life transgender people) would want to change the language that is often used to undermine or injure them. But I also worry about the (typically under-discussed) negative ramifications of these constant shifts in language. What happens to trans folks who have long used a particular term as part of their activism when other trans activists deem that word to be anachronistic or problematic for some reason? Will the former group now be painted as "out of step" with the community, or accused of "reinforcing the oppression" the group faces? (I have seen both happen.) Insisting that everyone use the "correct" language and avoid "inappropriate" language is a surefire way to exclude community members from differing generations, geographies, and cultures, or even activists who simply have different opinions or impressions about those words.

All of us have word preferences (including me), and I think that it is fine for us to advocate on behalf of our preferred terminologies. But nowadays, I strive to avoid *word sabotage*—when our belief that our favored word is inherently appropriate, righteous, liberating, and/or inclusive, leads us to automatically presume that people who use alternative language must be behaving in an offensive, incorrect, repressive, and/or exclusionary manner.[1] I have also become suspicious of *word elimination* strategies—when we point to some aspect of a word's origin, history, aesthetic quality (or lack thereof), literal meaning, alternate definitions, potential misinterpretations or connotations, or occasional exclusionary or defamatory usage, and use that as an excuse to claim that the term is oppressive and should be eliminated from the lexicon. While in an individual instance, word elimination may seem perfectly justified (especially in cases where the term has a long history of being used predominantly as a slur), the reality is that any and all words can be readily subjected to this sort of defamation—even our personal favorites! Over the years, I have witnessed word elimination campaigns against virtually every trans-related word that I can think of (many specific examples are given in Chapter 45). This approach ignores the fact that most words are highly contextual, exhibiting multiple meanings or differing connotations depending upon the context. Many words and phrases can be used in both positive and negative ways, or in productive and disparaging ways. Yet, word elimination strategies insist that *any* negative usage (whether present or past, commonplace or occasional, real or perceived) automatically trumps all potentially neutral, positive, or productive uses of the term.

Instead of condemning the words themselves, we should instead focus our attention on the ways in which people are using, misusing, or abusing them. And we will be best served if we challenge the negative connotations and false assumptions associated with those misuses and abuses, rather than trying to eliminate the words themselves.

Notes

Introduction

1. Julia Serano, *Whipping Girl: A Transsexual Woman on Sexism and the Scapegoating of Femininity* (Emeryville, CA: Seal Press, 2007); Julia Serano, *Excluded: Making Feminist and Queer Movements More Inclusive* (Berkeley, CA: Seal Press, 2013). A second edition of *Whipping Girl* was released in 2016; with the exception of a newly added Preface (see Part 2, note 7), the page numbers listed here should correspond equally to both editions.

2. Many of my additional writings on trans woman-exclusion can be found at Julia Serano, "Frustration" (http://juliaserano.com/frustration.html), and a thorough collection of my writings on psychiatric depictions of trans people can be found at Julia Serano, "Debunking Psychological Diagnoses and Theories about Transsexual and Transgender People" (http://juliaserano.com/TSetiology.html).

3. My blog can be found at: http://juliaserano.blogspot.com. An archive of many of my writings can be found on my website at: http://juliaserano.com/writings.html.

4. Phyllis Burke, *Gender Shock: Exploding the Myths of Male and Female* (New York: Anchor Books, 1996), 3–136.

5. *What Sex Am I?*, directed by Lee Grant (New York: Joseph Feury Productions, 1984); Jan Morris, *Conundrum* (New York: Harcourt Brace Jovanovich, 1974).

6. Kate Bornstein, *Gender Outlaw: On Men, Women and the Rest of Us* (New York: Vintage Books, 1994).

7. Within trans communities, the word "stealth" is sometimes used to refer to not being "out" as trans to most people in one's life. As with most trans language related to "passing," the term is considered to be problematic by some. See Serano, *Whipping Girl,* 176–180.

8. Transexual Menace and Hermaphrodites with Attitude are discussed throughout Riki Anne Wilchins, *Read My Lips: Sexual Subversion and the End of Gender* (Ithaca, NY: Firebrand Books, 1997), and Transgender Nation is discussed in Susan Stryker, *Transgender History* (Berkeley: Seal Press, 2008), 91–111.

9. Leslie Feinberg, *Transgender Warriors: Making History from Joan of Arc to Dennis Rodman* (Boston: Beacon Press, 1996); Leslie Feinberg, *Trans Liberation: Beyond Pink or Blue* (Boston:

Beacon Press, 1998); Wilchins, *Read My Lips;* Pat Califia, *Sex Changes: The Politics of Transgenderism* (San Francisco: Cleis Press, 1997).

10. I discuss this personal evolution in Chapters 10 and 17 of Serano, *Whipping Girl.*

11. Jaime M. Grant, Lisa A. Mottet, Justin Tanis, Jack Harrison, Jody L. Herman, and Mara Keisling, *Injustice at Every Turn: A Report of the National Transgender Discrimination Survey* (Washington: National Center for Transgender Equality and National Gay and Lesbian Task Force, 2011).

12. Sam Brodey and Julia Lurie, "Get Ready for the Conservative Assault on Where Transgender Americans Pee," *Mother Jones*, March 9, 2015 (http://motherjones.com/politics/2015/03/transgender-bathroom-discrimination-bills).

Part 1: Performance and Poetry

1. The Bitesize website hosts my "coming out as trans" open letter (http://bitesize.net/julia.html) and an interview with the band that discusses my then recent transition (Mike Henry, "Bitesize: Big Evil," *West Coast Performer*, November 2002, http://bitesize.net/press.html#WCPcover).

2. A poetry slam is a competitive spoken word event in which the writer/performer's work is judged (on a scale from zero to ten) by randomly selected audience members. This competitive element tends to encourage more performative and accessible poems relative to those primarily written for the page.

3. Serano, *Whipping Girl*, 315–317.

4. Julia Serano, *Either/Or* (Oakland, CA: Switch Hitter Press, 2002); Julia Serano, *Draw Blood* (Oakland, CA: Hot Tranny Action, 2004).

5. Serano, *Excluded*, 22–36.

6. The spoken word pieces "Deconstructive Surgery," "Self-Deception," "Submissive Streak," and "Barrette Manifesto" appeared in Serano, *Whipping Girl*, and "On the Outside Looking In" and "On Being a Woman" were later included in Serano, *Excluded.*

7. For instance, throughout both my chapbooks, I repeatedly used the word "transgendered" (with an "-ed"), which was consistent with how trans activists spoke at the time. Here, I replace that word with "transgender," which is considered to be more appropriate in this day and age (see Chapter 45, Note 31). I also used the word "tranny" and its plural form "trannies" quite a lot in my early spoken word pieces. While this reclaimed usage was commonplace back then, the word "tranny" is increasingly viewed as controversial, as discussed in Chapter 45. While I have edited out most of the more superfluous instances of "tranny," a few remain intact, especially when I refer to organizations or events that used the word in their title. Finally, for some inexplicable reason, I hyphenated the term "trans-woman" throughout *Draw Blood*—perhaps I intended this to be a compromise between my preferred spelling "trans woman" and the one-word variation "transwoman" used by others. In any case, here, I have replaced those hyphens with a space.

1 – Vice Versa

1. *Big Ugly Review*, Issue 1, Fall 2004.

2. In the original version of this piece, I referred to them as "transvestites" rather than "cross-dressers," as at the time, both were considered to be acceptable synonyms to describe men who sometimes dress or present themselves as women. Indeed, the acronym "TV/TS" (for transvestite/transsexual) was a common label for trans organizations and events before the term "transgender" fully caught on. While "transvestite" has since garnered negative connotations here in the U.S., it is still regularly used (sans negative connotations) in the U.K. (as I allude to in Chapter 45).

3. Some trans people today might be disturbed by my referring to these individuals as being "equal parts aunt and uncle," as this might seem to invalidate the female persona they were publicly presenting as at these meetings. However, during that time (the early 1990s), many of us who identified as crossdressers did view ourselves as possessing both male/masculine and female/feminine qualities simultaneously, and my description here was intended to capture the beauty in that state of being, rather than to undermine anybody's gender.

4. At the time that I wrote this, it was still quite common in trans communities to refer to people's (presumed) genetic status. I explain why such designations are now considered to be problematic in Serano, *Whipping Girl*, 172–174. Also, for the record, Joan went by she/her pronouns during the time that we knew one another.

5. I have mixed feelings about including my birth-assigned name (or "deadname," as many contemporary trans folks call it) here, as well as in Chapter 12. At the time that I wrote this piece, I was genderqueer-identified and recently transitioned, so this inclusion seemed natural to me. But nowadays, that name feels almost foreign to me. While many trans folks (including myself) object to such gratuitous references to our birth assigned names (as such citations are often intended to invalidate our gender identities), I have decided to leave this passage intact in order to be true to the original piece, plus also my previous name is already floating around out there in the universe (due to my pre-transition exploits in biology and music).

6. In the *Star Trek* universe, the Trill are a humanoid species that often contain another sentient symbiotic species inside them—in such cases, the individual's personality represents a merging of the two entities. In this particular episode ("The Host"), Beverly Crusher falls in love with a male Trill whose humanoid body dies, and the symbiont is then transferred to the body of a female Trill. Predictably, the change of sex is too much for Crusher to accept and she ends the relationship.

2 – Ophelia Revisited

1. Mary Pipher, *Reviving Ophelia: Saving the Selves of Adolescent Girls* (New York: Putnam, 1994).

2. Stacey May Fowles and Megan Griffith-Greene (eds.), *She's Shameless: Women Write About Growing Up, Rocking Out and Fighting Back* (Toronto: Tightrope Books, 2009).

3 – Either Or

1. *Transgender Tapestry*, Issue 105, Spring 2004.

2. While the phrase "pass as a woman" was quite commonplace at the time, many transsexuals (including myself) have since made the case that we do not "pass" as women or men, but rather we "pass" as cisgender/cissexual—see Serano, *Whipping Girl*, 126, 176–180.

4 - Scared to Death

1. I no longer remember where this specific statistic is from. But a recent study reported that 41 percent of transgender adults have attempted suicide—see Jody L. Herman, Ann P. Haas, and Philip L. Rodgers, "Suicide Attempts Among Transgender and Gender Non-Conforming Adults," The Williams Institute, UCLA School of Law, January, 2014 (https://escholarship.org/uc/item/8xg8061f).

2. "Once every two weeks" is not intended to be a factually accurate statistic. Rather, it is the roughest of estimates based on the fact that the *Remembering Our Dead* website had documented that at least twenty-seven gender-variant people had been murdered that year (https://web.archive.org/web/20021211213037/http://www.rememberingourdead.org/day/who.html). Also, while I wasn't fully cognizant of it at the time (being relatively new to trans activism), in retrospect I regret my saying that these individuals were "murdered for being transgender," as this ignores the multiple, intersectional forces that (far more often than not) also contribute to these murders. As numerous subsequent analyses have made clear, the overwhelming majority of instances of transphobic violence target trans people of color, poor and working class trans folks, individuals on the trans female/feminine spectrum, and/or trans sex workers—see Chapter 27, especially Notes 20 and 21.

3. I was most certainly not suggesting that gender-variant people comprise a "species" unto ourselves here. This was merely a metaphor meant to express the fact that we are endangered.

5 - Small Blue Thing

1. Tristan Taormino (ed.), *Take Me There: Trans and Genderqueer Erotica* (Berkeley: Cleis Press, 2011).

2. Viagra is a drug for erectile dysfunction that comes in the form of a blue pill. The title "Small Blue Thing" was borrowed from a Suzanne Vega song of the same name, which would often pop into my head when I would take those pills.

6 - Class Dismissed

1. *The Crying Game* was a 1992 film that featured a famous "trans reveal" scene. I discuss this film in the context of other media depictions of trans people in Serano, *Whipping Girl*, 36–41.

2. Actually, this turns out not to be true. While young children learn to make gender distinctions as they begin to pick up language, their understanding of gender is way more vague and fluid than that of adults. It is not until a developmental stage known as "gender constancy" (which usually occurs around ages four through seven) that children start to believe that gender is fixed and unchanging—a prerequisite for viewing girls and boys as "mutually exclusive" or "opposites."

3. I made this claim because, at the time, it was believed that there were about 25,000 human genes, and that the Y chromosome (the only sex-specific chromosome in humans) contained about a hundred genes, which works out to less than one percent of total genes. While these numbers still roughly hold true today, they admittedly ignore other biological processes that seem to contribute to sex differences (e.g., X-inactivation, sexually dimorphic gene expression). Having said that, I stand by the basic point that I am making here: that women and men are way more similar than different, and that we are primed to see differences between the sexes even when they do not exist (or barely exist). For a more recent and thorough take on how I view the intersection of biology and sex/gender, see Serano, *Excluded*, 138–168.

4. When I wrote this piece, I was a die-hard social constructionist with regards to gender. My position has evolved quite a bit and become more nuanced since then. Recently, I have forwarded a "Holistic View of Gender and Sexuality" that acknowledges the multitude of influences that shared biology, biological variation, shared culture, and individual experience may play in the development of gender and sexual traits—see Serano, *Excluded*, 138–168.

5. *The Bell Curve: Intelligence and Class Structure in American Life* was a 1994 book that controversially claimed that disparities in intelligence (e.g., as measured by IQ tests) observed between people of different races/ethnicities are largely due to inherited genetic/biological differences. For a powerful critique of its claims, see Stephen Jay Gould, "Curveball," *The New Yorker*, November 28, 1994, 139–149.

7 – Super Hero

1. Barbie is a popular fashion-themed doll marketed to girls, whereas G.I. Joe is a military soldier-themed "action figure" (which is what they call dolls when they are marketed to boys). Most of the super hero references in this piece pertain to the DC Comics character Superman, who has super-human powers because he was born on another planet. Superman loses his powers when exposed to Kryptonite, a piece of his now-destroyed home world. Like many super heroes, Superman spends much of his life pretending to be a normal "mild-mannered" person (in his case, his alter ego Clark Kent). Lois Lane is our protagonist's primary love interest, and she is typically portrayed as being enamored with Superman, but disinterested in Clark—this dilemma results in his love for her to remain unrequited in most reiterations of the story. Phone booths are antiquated enclosed spaces where people could use a public phone in relative privacy or, if you are Clark Kent, change into his Superman outfit. The Hall of Justice is from the cartoon *Super Friends* (one of my favorite shows as a young child), where it served as headquarters for many of the DC Comics super heroes.

8 – Book Worm

1. Lee Brewster and/or Lee's Mardis Gras stores are briefly discussed in the following pieces: Mariette Pathy Allen, "Momentum: A Photo Essay of the Transgender Community in the United States Over 30 Years, 1978–2007," *Sexuality Research & Social Policy*, 4, no. 4 (2007), 92; Helen Boyd, *She's Not the Man I Married: My Life with a Transgender Husband* (Emeryville, CA: Seal Press, 2007), 296, Note 6; Douglas Martin, "Lee Brewster, 57, Style Guru For World's Cross-Dressers," *The New York Times*, May 24, 2000 (http://nytimes.com/2000/05/24/nyregion/lee-brewster-57-style-guru-for-world-s-cross-dressers.html); Deborah Rudacille, *The Riddle of Gender: Science, Activism, and Transgender Rights* (New York: Pantheon Books, 2005), 237; Stryker, *Transgender History*, 87; Zagria, "Lee Brewster (1943–2000) retailer, activist," *A Gender Variance Who's Who*, October 3, 2009 (http://zagria.blogspot.com/2009/10/lee-brewster-1943-2000-retailer.html).

2. Some of these potential issues are likely to arise from the fact that I tried to write this piece from the trans-naive perspective that I personally possessed during 1990–92, the time period when I routinely visited the store. Other issues may stem from the highly sexual and sexualized nature of the publications discussed herein. While I empathize with this concern (I discuss the sexualization of trans bodies and identities at great length in Parts 2 and 3 of this book), as a sex-positive feminist (how I identify both now and back when I wrote this) I believe that there is value in speaking openly and honestly about aspects of our bodies and sexualities that others typically view as shameful and stigmatized. Finally, there is likely a generational divide here: Younger trans folks these days often first access trans people and culture through transgen-

der-run/populated online communities centered upon direct conversation and the exchange of information. In contrast, due to the extreme trans invisibility/isolation that I describe in the Introduction, for many trans people of my generation, our first exposure and access to trans people and culture was often indirect through trans-themed pornography and erotica.

3. I discuss the phenomenon of "forced feminization" fantasies (both my personal experiences and my trans feminist analysis) in Serano, *Whipping Girl*, 273–276.

4. To be clear, I am *not* insinuating that non- and pre-op trans women are "in between" or "not quite women" here (although having grown up in a cissexist culture, that is admittedly how I naively viewed these women at the time). My views on pre- and non-op trans women have dramatically evolved since then (e.g., see Chapters 10 and 26).

5. I worry that this statement may disturb some trans women who view themselves as being nothing like cisgender men who are attracted to trans women. For starters, I am sure that many of these "men" I saw in the store were (like me) crossdressers or other trans female/feminine-spectrum people, and it seems reasonable that some of them (like me) have since transitioned to female. Second, at the time that I visited that store, I viewed male admirers as struggling with similar issues of shame and stigma that I was dealing with (e.g., having to hide our desires). While I would never equate the two (neither then nor now), I do believe that our issues are interconnected (as I discuss in Chapters 42 and 43).

9 – Introduction to Draw Blood
1. See Chapter 15.

2. See Chapter 10.

3. *Oprah* was a talk show hosted by Oprah Winfrey that is singled out here because of a groundbreaking show they aired in 2003, which introduced mainstream audiences to Jennifer Finney Boylan and her memoir *She's Not There: A Life in Two Genders*. Discovery Channel is a cable TV channel that (at the time) seemed to routinely air sensationalistic documentaries about transgender people. I mentioned it by name here because, shortly before writing this piece, I was "shopping" for a new therapist, and one of the questions I would always ask potential candidates was "Have you worked with any transgender clients before?" And one therapist actually responded: "No, but I did see this documentary on the Discovery Channel once . . ."

4. See Chapter 17.

10 – Cocky
1. I discuss the media's coverage of Araujo's murder in Serano, *Whipping Girl*, 247–251.

2. Excerpts of "Cocky" have previously appeared in Michelle Tea, "Transmissions from Camp Trans," *The Believer*, November 2003; Rona Marech, "Throw out your pronouns: 'he' and 'she' are meaningless terms in the Bay Area's flourishing transgender performance scene," *The San Francisco Chronicle*, December 29, 2003; Serano, *Excluded*, 34. A fictionalized version of my 2003 performance of "Cocky" at Camp Trans also appears in Ariel Schrag's 2014 book *Adam*.

11 – Sleeping Sickness
1. *Clamor Magazine*, Issue 23, November/December 2003. I discuss my personal experiences

with, and current views on, religion in greater depth in Serano, *Excluded*, 240–242.

2. *CCD* is Catholic religious education administered to children (such as myself) who attend public (rather than Catholic) schools. It is similar to Sunday School, except that it usually takes place on weekdays after school.

12 – Mix and Match
1. *Holy Titclamps*, Issue 19, Summer 2003.

2. Back when this piece was written, "radical feminist" was sometimes used in a generic way by feminists who wished to distinguish themselves from straight mainstream feminists. My partner (who I am describing in the piece) was "radical" in a queer-minded, sex-positive way, rather than adhering to the specific brand feminism espoused by the self-identified "radical feminists" who I discuss in Chapter 35 and elsewhere.

14 – Period Piece
1. When I used to perform this poem, I would express over-the-top outrage and exasperation that alternated between comical and dead serious. The emotional back-and-forth was itself an inside joke (i.e., a reference to "mood swings") which the audience seemed to appreciate, as it is my only slam poem (in three years of performing) to garner a perfect score.

2. Serano, *Whipping Girl*, 65–76.

3. Midol is an over-the-counter drug marketed to relieve premenstrual syndrome. For the record, nobody ever literally shoved bottles of Midol in my face (this is what we in the literary business call hyperbole). Although on multiple occasions, people who were unaware that I was trans did attribute my behaviors to my presumed menstrual cycle, which is what led me to write this piece.

4. This was something that a few trans women on one of my MTF-transition-themed email lists recommended. I tried it for a while, but did not notice any discernable effects on my body nor my mood, so I eventually stopped trying to cycle my hormones.

5. The three sentences immediately preceding the endnote were later re-used (with slight alterations in language) in Serano, *Whipping Girl*, 67. In that chapter of *Whipping Girl*, I go onto say that while hormones do exert real effects, they do not do so in the overly simplistic and essentialist manner that people often claim (Serano, *Whipping Girl*, 71–76; Serano, *Excluded*, 166–167).

6. This statement is not literally true: In trying to verify this claim for this book, I found sources that suggest that women's androgen levels are slightly higher during ovulation, and other sources that say that androgen levels are relatively stable over the course of the menstrual cycle. However, what is true (and what I was likely referencing with this line of the piece) is that the relative ratio of testosterone to estrogen tends to be highest in women during menstruation (as a result of the decline in estrogen after ovulation).

16 – Open Letter to Lisa Vogel
1. See also Serano, *Whipping Girl*, 233–245, and Serano, *Excluded*, 22–36.

2. Trudy Ring, "This Year's Michigan Womyn's Music Festival Will Be the Last," *The Advocate*, April 21, 2015 (http://advocate.com/michfest/2015/04/21/years-michigan-womyns-music-

festival-will-be-last).

3. Feminist perspectives can also sometimes be reductionist, e.g., when they reduce gender to mere socialization or social constructs—I explain this further in Serano, *Excluded*, 138–168.

4. "Birth privilege" was a concept I began forwarding during 2003–05 to describe double standards regarding legitimacy that nowadays fall under the umbrella of cis/cisgender/cissexual privilege (see Serano, *Whipping Girl*, 161–193, and Chapters 25, 47, and 48 of this book). The term also appears in my 2005 essay "Hot Tranny Action Manifesto," in Julia Serano, *On the Outside Looking In* (Oakland, CA: Hot Tranny Action, 2005; http://juliaserano.com/outside.html).

17 – Fighting Words
1. Carolyn Connelly, "Fuck You (A Poem for Monty)," *a brooklyn diary* (self-published, 2003); Serano, *Excluded*, 34.

2. All of the people mentioned in this passage were popular television or radio hosts at the time.

3. While I came out to other queer/trans people in my early twenties (e.g., see next chapter), it wasn't until I was twenty-seven that I came out to (some) straight friends as trans.

4. This line is not intended to be a denial of what some call "passing privilege," or what I have described as "conditional cissexual privilege" (see Serano, *Whipping Girl*, 176–180)—I most certainly recognize that I often benefit from such privileges. Rather, I am simply calling out the cissexist presumption that it is inherently better to look like a cissexual than it is to look like a transsexual.

18 – Cherry Picking
1. Morty Diamond (ed.), *Trans/Love: Radical Sex, Love & Relationships Beyond the Gender Binary* (San Francisco: Manic D Press, 2011); Rachel Kramer Bussel (ed.), *Best Sex Writing 2013: The State of Today's Sexual Culture* (Berkeley, CA: Cleis Press, 2013).

2. From what I recall, I did this on a couple of occasions, then stopped out of fear. Not so much the fear of being caught (although that certainly concerned me), but rather the fear of what it all possibly meant. While I stopped briefly, I eventually sublimated this subconscious desire into play—specifically, stories I'd create wherein the protagonist was turned into a girl as part of the narrative (as described in Chapter 13, "Endgame").

3. This eventually became the premise for the Bitesize song "Switch Hitter"; audio and lyrics for the song can be found at http://bitesize.net.

4. The Billy Squier song "The Stroke" was a hit song in the early '80s, and perhaps the least subtle song about a hand job ever known to humankind (although some of the Internet search results I encountered suggest that the song is actually about the music industry, in which case the hand-job imagery is merely a metaphor). The main line of the chorus of the song is, "Stoke me, stroke me," immediately followed by (what sounds like) children shouting in unison "Stroke!"

5. Depeche Mode is a band who became popular in the '80s and whose songs sometimes evoked BDSM imagery. This is perhaps most evident in their song "Master and Servant," which (for better or worse) was not the song playing on his stereo when I walked into his apartment.

19 – San Francisco Bay Area Trans Performance and Activism

1. My "Events" webpage can be found at http://juliaserano.com/events.html, and the GenderEnders website is preserved at http://juliaserano.com/genderenders/index.html. Artists' and organizers' names reflect their public personas at the time—that is, the names they performed under and/or used in promotional materials (such as fliers, posters, websites, online announcements, etc.). My apologies to any artists and organizers from the scene whose names have since changed unbeknownst to me, and to those whose contributions I may have inadvertently omitted.

2. Notably, some of the artists who performed at the Picnic were not transgender themselves. While this might seem strange today, back then (when few people wanted to be associated with trans people) there was a general sentiment in the community that our partners, close friends, and staunchest supporters were also a part of our community, and we were happy to include them in our events. I discuss the logic behind this in the "Stigma versus acceptance" section of Chapter 44, "Considering Trans and Queer Appropriation."

3. As with Note 2, some contemporary trans people might contest this assertion, and instead frame such participation as "cis people appropriating or taking up space in trans communities." In Chapters 44, 47, and 48, I analyze the activist logic behind both the open-ended all-inclusive approaches that many trans activists of the '90s and early '00s (including myself at the time) forwarded, and more recent "reverse discourse" approaches (which rely on drawing sharper distinctions between cis and trans people) that prevail in trans activist settings today. In those chapters, I make the case that neither perspective is "right": they both have potential benefits and drawbacks, and may differentially appeal (or not appeal) to activists in different situations or settings.

4. Needless to say, the idea of having TIG Week being the last week of May ushering in Pride month never caught on. But (conspicuous by its absence in this piece), the first Trans March—which came together in an impromptu manner (apparently via an anonymous email) on the Friday before Pride weekend in 2004—did eventually grow into an annual event in the Bay Area, and is also now celebrated in many other cities as well (http://transmarch.org/about). To the best of my knowledge, the annual Picnic petered out sometime after 2006.

5. Marech, "Throw out your pronouns" (see Chapter 10, Note 2, for full citation).

6. I revisit the "Tranny Lovers Show" in Chapters 43 and 45, wherein I address both the show's name and theme, which many contemporary trans people are likely to take issue with.

7. Julia Serano, "Skirt Chasers: Why the Media Depicts the Trans Revolution in Lipstick and Heels," *Bitch Magazine*, Issue 26, Fall 2004 (later revised to become Chapter 2 of *Whipping Girl*).

8. As I discuss in the introduction to the next section, this book collection eventually evolved into *Whipping Girl*. The original *Hot Tranny Action* website is now preserved for prosperity's sake at http://juliaserano.com/hottrannyaction/index.html. The reasoning behind this purposefully provocative name is explained in Chapter 45.

Part 2: Articulating Trans-misogyny

1. Serano, "Skirt Chasers."

2. Serano, *On the Outside Looking In.*

3. I would describe the two other major contributing factors to this phenomenon as straightforward transphobia/cissexism (which leads some queer women to view trans men as "really female" because of their birth-assigned sex, genital status, etc.) and history (as many trans men identify as lesbians prior to their transition, and thus have the opportunity to become close with, and gain the trust of, many queer women within the community before ever identifying/presenting as male). For clarifying points about such disparities in acceptance between trans men and trans women within queer women's communities and beyond, see Chapter 27, Note 17.

4. According to *Wikipedia* (https://en.wikipedia.org/wiki/Cisgender), the term cisgender did appear in print on at least one occasion prior to the publication of *Whipping Girl*, namely, in Eli R. Green, "Debating Trans Inclusion in the Feminist Movement: A Trans-Positive Analysis," *Journal of Lesbian Studies*, 10 no. 1–2 (2006), 231–248. Cristan Williams recently reported that a variant of "cis" (cisvestitismus) was used to describe non-trans people in the German medical literature back in 1914 (Cristan Williams, "So, I hear trans people recently invented this whole cis/trans thing . . . ," *The TransAdvocate*, August 12, 2013, http://transadvocate.com/so-i-hear-trans-people-recently-invented-this-whole-cistrans-thing_n_9982.htm), although there is no indication that the trans activists who first began using cisgender/cissexual were aware of that literature. It seems unsurprising that such terms may have been independently invented numerous times given the long history of the prefix "cis" being used as the complementary pair of "trans."

5. Jacob Anderson-Minshall, "Bring in the Noise," *SF Bay Times*, August 31, 2006.

6. Julie Foster, "Transsexual finds sexism in feminism," *San Francisco Chronicle*, June 17, 2007.

7. Julia Serano, *Whipping Girl: A Transsexual Woman on Sexism and the Scapegoating of Femininity* (Berkeley, CA: Seal Press, 2016), ix–xxvi.

8. Julia Serano, "Whipping Girl FAQ: on the words, transsexual, transgender and queer" (http://juliaserano.blogspot.com/2011/08/whipping-girl-faq-on-words-transsexual.html); Julia Serano, "Whipping Girl FAQ: the necklace issue" (http://juliaserano.blogspot.com/2011/08/whipping-girl-faq-necklace-issue.html); Julia Serano, "Whipping Girl FAQ: Submissive Streak" (http://juliaserano.blogspot.com/2011/08/whipping-girl-faq-submissive-streak.html).

9. Julia Serano, "Expanding Trans Media Representation: Why Transgender Actors Should Be Cast in Cisgender Roles" (https://medium.com/gender-2-0/expanding-trans-media-representation-why-transgender-actors-should-be-cast-in-cisgender-roles-f880cb7bb36e).

20 – Her Own Femme
1. Serano, *Excluded*, 48–69.

21 – Frustration
1. Jacob Anderson-Minshall, "Michigan Or Bust: CampTrans Flourishes for Another Year," *San Francisco Bay Times*, August 3, 2006.

2. Indeed, this reasoning was forwarded by the two trans male/masculine-spectrum individuals interviewed in the article cited in Note 1.

3. It was certain attendees who made these accusations of "divisiveness," not the conference or-

ganizers (who were very supportive of us). My concerns with the film and keynote are described in more detail in Serano, *Excluded*, 48–69.

4. Osento was a women-only bathhouse in San Francisco that allowed entrance based on genital status. Trans women who had not had bottom surgery were not allowed in, whereas trans male/ masculine folks who had not had bottom surgery were often free to enter. Osento had a "no bathing suit" policy, and refused to accept pre- and non-op trans women even if they promised to remain clothed or wear bathing suits. Locally, this policy was just as controversial and hotly debated in queer and trans circles as the Michfest policy was.

22 – Questionable

1. While my intentions in writing this paragraph should be clear, (just in case) let me state for the record that I am in no way attempting to disrespect breast cancer survivors in this passage. As a cancer survivor myself, I acknowledge that if you do have cancer, there may be some occasions when people ask you intrusive or unwanted questions. But the majority of people (in my experience, at least) recognize that cancer is a serious and sensitive matter, and they will usually refrain from engaging in potentially uncomfortable lines of questioning. In contrast, while some people are respectful of my transsexuality and transition, many others (especially back in the early-to-mid '00s when I wrote this) subjected me to a seemingly relentless interrogation, which is what inspired this piece.

2. These are all celebrities of the time who hosted eponymous daytime talk shows that would occasionally air episodes featuring transsexuals. And these episodes always followed the same formula: The transsexual(s) would first share their trans narrative, then the host and audience would ask them all the same predictable questions (i.e., the very ones that I was routinely asked, and which I recite in the first part of this piece).

23 – Finally

1. A thorough list of examples of this anti-trans sentiment, and descriptions of this purging of trans women from feminism, can be found in Note 2 for "On the Outside Looking In," in Serano, *Excluded*, 302.

2. Rudacille, *The Riddle of Gender*, 149, 158; Stryker, *Transgender History*, 102; "O'Leary, Jean (1948–2005)," *GLBTQ* (http://glbtq.com/social-sciences/oleary_j.html).

3. Alice Echols, *Daring to Be Bad: Radical Feminism in America, 1967–75* (Minneapolis: University of Minnesota Press, 1989), 255–256; Joanne Meyerowitz, *How Sex Changed: A History of Transsexuality in the United States* (Cambridge: Harvard University Press, 2002), 259–260; Robin Morgan, *Going Too Far* (New York: Random House, 1977), 170–188; Stryker, *Transgender History*, 102–105.

4. Califia, *Sex Changes*, 106–107; Meyerowitz, *How Sex Changed*, 260; Stryker, *Transgender History*, 105; Cristan Williams, "TERF hate and Sandy Stone," *The TransAdvocate*, August 16, 2014 (http://transadvocate.com/terf-violence-and-sandy-stone_n_14360.htm).

5. Kay Brown, "20th Century Transgender History and Experience" (http://web.archive.org/web/20100329081244/http://jenellerose.com/htmlpostings/20th_century_transgender.htm); Califia, *Sex Changes*, 98–99; Janice Raymond, *The Transsexual Empire: The Making of the She-Male* (Boston: Beacon Press, 1979), 117.

6. Stryker, *Transgender History*, 110, 112–113, 171; Cristan Williams, "TERFs & Trans Healthcare," *The TransAdvocate*, October 12, 2013 (http://transadvocate.com/terfs-trans-healthcare_n_10275.htm); Cristan Williams, "Fact Checking Janice Raymond: The NCHCT Report," *The TransAdvocate*, September 18, 2014 (http://transadvocate.com/fact-checking-janice-raymond-the-nchct-report_n_14554.htm).

7. Califia, *Sex Changes*, 86.

8. Califia, *Sex Changes*, 86.

9. Mary Daly, *Gyn/Ecology: The Metaethics of Radical Feminism* (Boston: Beacon Press, 1990), 70–71.

10. Gloria Steinem, "If the Shoe Doesn't Fit, Change the Foot," *Ms.*, February 1977, 76–86 (this article later re-appeared as the chapter "Transsexualism" in Steinem's book *Outrageous Acts and Everyday Rebellions*, which became a national bestseller). Steinem has since stated her support of transgender people and claimed that her previous words had been taken out of context (see Gloria Steinem, "Op-ed: On Working Together Over Time," *The Advocate*, October 2, 2013). Robin Morgan made these particular claims during her speech at the West Coast Lesbian Conference, where she (according to Alice Echols) united lesbian and heterosexual feminists, in part, by turning them both against trans women—see Echols, *Daring to Be Bad*, 255–256; Morgan, *Going Too Far*, 170–188 (specific quotes are on 181). My highlighting *Ms.* here is not intended to single them out (for the record, they have published my writings, including Chapter 29, in recent years), but rather to demonstrate that during this period, anti-trans sentiment was just as prevalent in mainstream feminist circles as it was within radical feminist circles.

11. While trans women were effectively forced out of the women's movement in the 1970s, by no means did that stop trans women from being feminists—see Stryker, *Transgender History*, 123–153; Jessica Xavier, "A Look Back at *TransSisters: The Journal of Transsexual Feminism*" (https://learningtrans.files.wordpress.com/2010/11/a-look-back-at-transsisters.pdf). During the 1990s, newer strands of feminism that were more inclusive of gender-variant people—such as sex-positive feminism, poststructuralist feminism, queer theory, and intersectionality—gained more prominence, and helped to eventually pave the way for trans women to be taken seriously within feminism (as I discuss in more depth in Chapter 27).

24 – Trans-misogyny primer

1. Fuller descriptions and sources for all these claims can be found in Serano, *Whipping Girl*. This primer can be downloaded and freely distributed (provided I am properly cited) at http://juliaserano.com/av/TransmisogynyPrimer-Serano.pdf.

2. As I explain in Serano, *Whipping Girl*, 261–262, while the latter two stereotypes are mere concoctions of the cisgender imagination, there is a reality to trans women who engage in sex work. I have no problems with media attempts to seriously and respectfully consider the lives and issues of trans sex workers. However, the vast majority of such media depictions are superficial and purposefully sensationalistic, and in *Whipping Girl*, I argue that this superfluous overrepresentation of trans female/feminine sex workers stems from the more general assumption that trans women must transition for sexual reasons. Another manifestation of this same assumption is the phenomenon of "walking while trans"—where police profile trans women (especially trans women of color) as sex workers (often without any justification or probable cause) simply because they are or appear trans—see Darby Hickey, "Policing Gender and Sexuality: Trans-

gender sex workers, HIV, and justice," *Positively Aware,* July/August 2008, 40–42; Amnesty International, *Stonewalled: Police abuse and misconduct against lesbian, gay, bisexual and transgender people in the U.S.,* September 2005, 20–25; Make the Road New York, *Transgressive Policing: Police Abuse of LGBTQ Communities of Color in Jackson Heights,* October 2012, 12–13. As but one of many examples of this profiling, in the aforementioned Amnesty International report, one LAPD Captain claimed that he believed that 80 percent of the transgender community is involved in sex work, and that this is largely due to their supposed "sexual addiction" (p. 21).

25 – Whipping Girl FAQ on cissexual, cisgender, and cis privilege

1. Serano, *Whipping Girl,* 364; Emi Koyama, "Cissexual/Cisgender: decentralizing the dominant group," June 7, 2002 (eminism.org/interchange/2002/20020607-wmstl.html). See also "Part 2 – Articulating Trans-misogyny," Note 4 for further discussion of early uses of cis terminology.

2. Koyama, "Cissexual/Cisgender."

3. In the original piece, I referenced posts from two bloggers (Queen Emily and cannonball) who had recently written about the cis-is-too-academic trope. Unfortunately, like many things on the Internet, they have seemingly disappeared, so I am unable to cite them properly here.

4. I further expound upon this unmarked/marked distinction in Serano, *Excluded,* 169–199. See also Wayne Brekhus, "A Sociology of the Unmarked," *Sociological Theory* 16, no. 1 (1998), 34–51; Linda R. Waugh, "Marked and unmarked: A choice between unequals in semiotic structure," *Semiotica* 38 (1982), 299–318.

5. I discuss this in more depth in Serano, *Whipping Girl,* 307–313.

26 – 96 Percent

1. That promotional material can be found at http://juliaserano.com/Pissue.html.

2. Such poems often included "Small Blue Thing" (Chapter 5), "Cocky" (Chapter 10), and "Deconstructive Surgery" (which later became Chapter 11 of *Whipping Girl).*

3. Suzanne J. Kessler and Wendy McKenna, *Gender: An Ethnomethodological Approach* (Chicago: University of Chicago Press, 1978), 142–155.

4. "Mentally disordered" is a reference to the (then current) psychiatric diagnosis Gender Identity Disorder, which is discussed in more detail in Chapter 30.

5. Fiona Giles (ed.), *Dick for a Day: What Would You Do If You Had One?* (New York: Villard, 1997).

6. The other performers that evening were Charlie Jane Anders, Ryka Aoki, Sherilyn Connelly, solidad decosta, and Shawna Virago.

27 – Talking Past One Another

1. For a list of sources discussing Michfest's trans woman-exclusion policy, how it has evolved over the years, and debates and protests challenging it, see Serano, *Excluded,* 301–302 (specifically, Chapter 2, Note 1). This issue is also discussed in Chapters 16, 19, and 21 of this book.

2. Originally published as Julia Serano, "Rethinking Sexism: How Trans Women Challenge Feminism," *AlterNet*, August 4, 2008 (http://alternet.org/story/93826/rethinking_sexism%3A_ how_trans_women_challenge_feminism).

3. Radicalesbians, "The Woman Identified Woman," in Anne Koedt, Ellen Levine, and Anita Rapone (eds.), *Radical Feminism* (New York: Quadrangle/The New York Times Book Co., 1980), 241.

4. I unpack the logic behind such unilateral approaches to activism (often called "reverse discourses") in Chapter 48.

5. I debunk these feminist presumptions about femininity in Chapter 29, and more thoroughly in Serano, *Whipping Girl,* 319–343.

6. Morgan, *Going Too Far,* 180; Mary Daly, *Gyn/Ecology,* 67.

7. Morgan, *Going Too Far,* 181; Raymond, *The Transsexual Empire* (in particular, Chapter 4, "Sappho by Surgery").

8. For an accessible introduction to queer theory, see Riki Wilchins, *Queer Theory/Gender Theory: An Instant Primer* (Los Angeles: Alyson, 2004).

9. For examples, see Bornstein, *Gender Outlaw;* Feinberg, *Trans Liberation;* Feinberg, *Transgender Warriors;* Wilchins, *Read My Lips.*

10. Emi Koyama, *A Handbook on Discussing the Michigan Womyn's Music Festival for Trans Activists and Allies* (Portland, OR: Confluere Publications, 2003), 8; Tristan Taormino, "Trouble in Utopia," *The Village Voice,* September 12th, 2000. This shift in focus from specifically challenging trans woman-exclusion to more generally challenging the festival's binary views on gender is also evident in the interview cited in Note 12.

11. I critically examine this debate over whether transsexuals (or any other gender or sexual minority, for that matter) "reinforce" or "subvert" the gender binary in Serano, *Excluded,* 117-137.

12. Interview with Riki Anne Wilchins, along with Gunner and Kate from the Lesbian Avengers of Boston, on *GenderTalk,* program 277, on September 25, 2000 (http://gendertalk.com/ radio/programs/251/gt277.shtml). The interview begins at 65:11 into the program, and the quote in question occurs around 71:52.

13. Jacob Anderson-Minshall, "Michigan Or Bust"; Emi Koyama, *A Handbook on Discussing the Michigan Womyn's Music Festival for Trans Activists and Allies,* 12; Serano, *Whipping Girl,* 233–245; Serano, *Excluded,* 22-36.

14. That experienced is described in Serano, *Excluded,* 22-36.

15. Patricia Hill Collins, *Black Feminist Thought: Knowledge, Consciousness and the Politics of Empowerment* (New York, Routledge, 2000); Emi Koyama, "Whose Feminism is it Anyway? The Unspoken Racism of the Trans Inclusion Debate," in Susan Stryker and Stephen Whittle (eds.), *The Transgender Studies Reader* (New York: Routledge, 2006), 698–705. The term intersectionality first appeared in Kimberlé Crenshaw, "Demarginalizing the Intersection of Race and Sex:

A Black Feminist Critique of Antidiscrimination Doctrine, Feminist Theory and Antiracist Politics," *The University of Chicago Legal Forum*, Volume 139, (1989), 139–167, although the general concept had been forwarded in classic texts such as Cherríe Moraga and Gloria E. Anzaldúa (eds.), *This Bridge Called My Back: Writings by Radical Women of Color* (Berkeley, CA: Third Woman Press, 2002); bell hooks, *Ain't I a Woman?: Black Women and Feminism* (Boston: South End Press, 1981); Audre Lorde, *Sister Outsider: Essays and Speeches* (Freedom, CA: The Crossing Press Feminist Series, 1984).

16. Michigan Womyn's Music Festival, "Michigan Womyn's Music Festival Sets the Record 'Straight'," August 22, 2006 (http://eminism.org/michigan/20060822-mwmf.txt).

17. As I explicitly addressed earlier during "Part 2: Articulating Trans-misogyny," this passage (and others like it) are not intended to imply that "trans men are privileged, and trans women are not, end of story." Back in 2008, when I was writing this essay, there were relatively few discussions about how various forms of privilege (such as male/masculine privileges, or white and middle-class privileges discussed later in this chapter) impact individuals within trans communities differently, and how a failure to recognize this intersectionality can result in certain voices and issues being overlooked or erased within trans activism.

18. My introduction of the "wave" metaphor here was not intended to draw sharp lines between eras, but rather to suggest that this increasing articulation of differences in experiences (especially due to intersectionality) in "second-wave" transgender activism is analogous to what had occurred during the rise of "third-wave" feminism. I refer to 1990s–era transgender activism as the "first wave" here because it was the first to organize around the label "transgender," not because it marked the beginning of trans activism. Earlier eras of trans activism are described in Meyerowitz, *How Sex Changed*, and Stryker, *Transgender History*, plus Chapter 23 of this book.

19. Sylvia Rivera Law Project (http://srlp.org); TransJustice (http://alp.org/TransJustice); TGI Justice Project (http://tgijp.org).

20. GenderPAC, "50 Under 30: Masculinity and the War on America's Youth," (2006). Similar findings have since been reported in Grant et al., *Injustice at Every Turn;* National Coalition of Anti-Violence Programs, "Lesbian, Gay, Bisexual, Transgender, Queer, and HIV-Affected Hate Violence in 2013 (2014 Release Edition)" (http://equalitymi.org/files/2013-ncavp-hv.pdf).

21. Viviane Namaste, *Sex Change, Social Change: Reflections on Identity, Institutions, and Imperialism* (Toronto: Women's Press, 2005), 90–93.

22. Monica Roberts's blog can be found at http://transgriot.blogspot.com. To the best of my knowledge, the Transsistahs and Transbrothas Conference is not currently ongoing.

23. Michigan Womyn's Music Festival, "Michigan Womyn's Music Festival Sets the Record 'Straight'."

29 – Empowering Femininity
1. Julia Serano, "Empowering Femininity," *Ms. Magazine* Blog, July 28, 2014 (http://msmagazine.com/blog/2014/07/28/empowering-femininity). Many of the ideas contained herein were previously expressed in Serano, *Whipping Girl*, 17–20 and 319–343.

2. Serano, *Whipping Girl*, 18.

Part 3: Pathological Science Revisited
1. Serano, *Whipping Girl*, 115–160.

2. Serano, *Whipping Girl*, 253–271 and 283–306.

3. Julia Serano, "A Matter of Perspective: A Transsexual Woman-Centric Critique of Dreger's 'Scholarly History' of the Bailey Controversy," *Archives of Sexual Behavior* 37, no. 3 (2008), 491–494. Dreger's article and numerous peer commentaries are cited in Chapter 30, Notes 1, 4, and 6.

4. These critiques are compiled in Julia Serano, "Alice Dreger's disingenuous campaign against transgender activism" (http://juliaserano.blogspot.com/2015/04/alice-dreger-and-making-evidence-fit.html).

5. Julia Serano, "Debunking Psychological Diagnoses and Theories about Transsexual and Transgender People" (http://juliaserano.com/TSetiology.html).

6. Sheryl Ubelacker, "CAMH to 'wind down' controversial gender identity clinic services," *The Globe and Mail*, December 15, 2015 (http://www.theglobeandmail.com/news/toronto/camh-to-wind-down-controversial-gender-identity-clinic-services/article27766580/); "Support Affirmative Care for Trans and Gender Diverse Kids!," (http://www.ipetitions.com/petition/support-affirmative-care-for-trans-kids). The backlash is described (and critiqued) in Casey Plett, "Zucker's 'Therapy' Mourned Almost Exclusively By Cis People," *Harlot*, April 11, 2016 (http://harlot.media/articles/2582/zuckers-therapy-mourned-almost-exclusively-by-cis-people).

7. Julia Serano, "Placing Ken Zucker's clinic in historical context," February 9, 2016 (http://juliaserano.blogspot.com/2016/02/placing-ken-zuckers-clinic-in.html).

30 – Psychology, Sexualization and Trans-Invalidations
1. For instance, Ray Blanchard—who has carried out research on trans people at Centre for Addiction and Mental Health (formerly the Clarke Institute of Psychiatry) for decades—when asked "Do you think that classifying transgender people as having a disorder does contribute to stigma against the trans community?" callously replied "No. I mean how many people who make a joke about trannies consult the *DSM* first?"; see Laura Cameron, "How the Psychiatrist Who Co-Wrote the Manual on Sex Talks About Sex," *Motherboard*, April 11, 2013 (http://motherboard.vice.com/blog/heres-how-the-guy-who-wrote-the-manual-on-sex-talks-about-sex). In J. Michael Bailey. *The Man Who Would Be Queen: The Science of Gender-Bending and Transsexualism* (Washington D.C.: Joseph Henry Press, 2003), 158, Bailey seemingly admires his colleague's contemptuous attitude when he says, "Blanchard is irreverent, cynical, and politically incorrect … He has little patience for arguments about whether research is good for people (such as 'Are homosexual people hurt or harmed by research on the genetics of sexual orientation?')." But the example that was fresh in my mind when writing this speech was Alice Dreger, "The Controversy Surrounding *The Man Who Would Be Queen*: A Case History of the Politics of Science, Identity, and Sex in the Internet Age," *Archives of Sexual Behavior*, 37, no. 3 (2008), 366–421, in which she repeatedly played down and dismissed trans people's legitimate concerns about Bailey's book and its potential ramifications (as noted in most of the peer commentaries cited in Note 4).

2. The word "transgenderism" has a long history of being used as a neutral term to describe the phenomenon of transgender people and experiences, much like "transsexuality" or "transsexualism" is the phenomenon of transsexual people and experiences. However, some contemporary

trans activists have tried to claim that the term is derogatory, mostly due to how it has been misappropriated in recent years by trans-exclusive radical feminists (e.g., Sheila Jeffreys in her book *Gender Hurts*; see Chapter 35) to give the impression that it refers to an aberrant political ideology rather than the phenomenon of gender variance. This is but one of many examples of the Activist Language Merry-Go-Round phenomenon that I describe in the second half of Chapter 45. I discuss the history of the word "transgenderism," and why I feel that we should not abandon it, in Julia Serano, "Regarding Trans* and Transgenderism" (http://juliaserano.blogspot. com/2015/08/regarding-trans-and-transgenderism.html).

3. Throughout this piece, I use the term "mainstream psychology" as an umbrella term to refer to those psychological, psychiatric, and sexological discourses on gender variance, transgenderism, and transsexuality that have dominated the medical/mental health literature or have been institutionalized in our society (e.g., via the gatekeeper system and the *DSM*) over the last half century. I chose the word "psychology" (rather than "psychiatry") primarily because most of the theories and diagnoses that I critique here have been invented and/or forwarded by psychologists.

4. A few examples include: Walter O. Bockting, "Biological reductionism meets gender diversity in human sexuality," *The Journal of Sex Research*, 42 (2005), 267–270; Madeline H. Wyndzen, "The world according to J. Michael Bailey inside 'The Man who would be Queen: The Science of Gender Bending and Transsexualism'," *All mixed up: A transgendered psychology professor's perspective on life, the psychology of gender, & "gender identity disorder"* (http://GenderPsychology. org/autogynpehilia/j_michael_bailey); and peer commentaries from John Bancroft (426–428), Ben A. Barres (429), Talia Mae Bettcher (430–433), John H. Gagnon (444–447), Riki Lane (453–456), Charles Moser (472–475), Margaret Nichols (476–480), Julia Serano (491–494), and Elroi J. Windsor (495–497) in *Archives of Sexual Behavior* 37, no. 3 (2008).

5. Zak Szymanski, "DSM controversy could overshadow opportunities," *Bay Area Reporter*, May 29, 2008 (http://ebar.com/news/article.php?sec=news&article=3018).

6. The quote is a reference to Anne Lawrence, "Shame and Narcissistic Rage in Autogynephilic Transsexualism," *Archives of Sexual Behavior* 37, no. 3 (2008), 457–461, which is her peer commentary on Dreger's article (cited in Note 1). Both Lawrence and Dreger depict trans people as engaging in an irrational, mass overreaction to mainstream psychology, although Lawrence's article is admittedly significantly more psychopathologizing than Dreger's.

7. The World Professional Association for Transgender Health (WPATH) Standards of Care (SOC) is a set of guidelines for trans health providers. While early versions of the SOC were rather horrific (see Serano, *Whipping Girl*, 116–126), recent revisions have incorporated changes suggested by the trans community—see Eli Coleman et al., "Standards of Care for the Health of Transsexual, Transgender, and Gender-Nonconforming People, Version 7," *International Journal of Transgenderism* 13 (2011), 165–232.

8. American Psychiatric Association, *Diagnostic and Statistical Manual of Mental Disorders, Fourth Edition, Text Revision (DSM-IV-TR)* (Washington D.C.: American Psychiatric Association, 2000).

9. Alix Spiegel, "Two Families Grapple with Sons' Gender Identity," *National Public Radio (NPR)*, May 7, 2008 (http://npr.org/2008/05/07/90247842/two-families-grapple-with-sons-gender-preferences). Throughout this chapter, I will use the phrase "cross-gender-identified" in reference to people who identify as the gender other than the one they were assigned at birth.

10. Definition according to *Dictionary.com* (http://dictionary.reference.com/browse/invalidate).

11. Reviewed in Viviane K. Namaste, *Invisible lives: The erasure of transsexual and transgendered people* (Chicago: University of Chicago Press, 2000); Currah, P., Juang, R. M. and Minter, S. P. (eds.) *Transgender Rights* (Minneapolis: University of Minnesota Press, 2006); Serano, *Whipping Girl.*

12. Talia May Bettcher, "Appearance, Reality, and Gender Deception: Reflections on Transphobic Violence and the Politics of Pretence," in Felix Ó. Murchadha (ed.), *Violence, Victims, and Justifications* (Oxford: Peter Lang Press, 2006); Talia May Bettcher, "Understanding Transphobia: Authenticity and Sexual Abuse," in Krista Scott-Dixon (ed.), *Trans/Forming Feminisms: Transfeminist Voices Speak Out* (Toronto, Canada: Sumach Press, 2006); Talia May Bettcher, "Trans Identities and First Person Authority," in Laurie J. Shrage (ed.), *You've Changed: Sex Reassignment and Personal Identity* (Oxford: Oxford University Press, 2009).

13. Further discussion of the depiction of trans people as mentally incompetent can be found in Kelley Winters, *Gender Madness in American Psychiatry: Essays from the Struggle for Dignity* (Dillon, CO: GID Reform Advocates, 2008). Bettcher, "Trans Identities and First Person Authority" (see previous Note) offers an in depth philosophical analysis to explain why trans people are not typically viewed as having legitimate "first person authority" regarding gender identity. Serano, *Whipping Girl,* 161–193, provides a framework to challenge many of the foundational assumptions that enable such trans-invalidations.

14. Elizabeth Ewen and Stuart Ewen, *Typecasting: On the Arts and Sciences of Human Inequality* (New York: Seven Stories Press, 2006); Stephan Jay Gould, *The Mismeasure of Man* (New York: W.W. Norton and Company, 1996).

15. Mara Mayor, "Fears and Fantasies of Anti-Suffragists," *The Connecticut Review* 7 (1974), 64–74.

16. Winters, *Gender Madness in American Psychiatry,* 45–49. See also Madeline H. Wyndzen, "The banality of insensitivity: portrayals of transgenderism in psychopathology," *All mixed up: A transgendered psychology professor's perspective on life, the psychology of gender, & "gender identity disorder"* (http://GenderPsychology.org/psychology/mental_illness_model.html).

17. Winters, *Gender Madness in American Psychiatry,* 19–43.

18. Winters, *Gender Madness in American Psychiatry,* 71–78.

19. Winters, *Gender Madness in American Psychiatry,* 161–167.

20. Critiques of the gatekeeper system can be found in Anne Bolin, *In Search of Eve: Transsexual Rites of Passage* (South Hadley, MA: Bergin and Harvey, 1988), 48–68; Namaste, *Invisible Lives,* 157–234; Arlene Istar Lev, *Transgender Emergence: Therapeutic Guidelines for Working With Gender-Variant People and Their Families* (Binghamton: The Haworth Clinical Practice Press, 2004), 25–54; Jacob C. Hale, "Ethical Problems with the Mental Health Evaluation Standards of Care for Adult Gender Variant Prospective Patients," *Perspectives in Biology and Medicine* 50 (2007), 491–505; Serano, *Whipping Girl,* 115–160.

21. This is a reference to George W. Bush, who while president, once said: "But I'm the decider,

and I decide what is best."

22. For other examples of trans women not being taken seriously by gatekeepers because they did not dress especially feminine, see Bolin, *In Search of Eve*, 107–108; Namaste, *Invisible Lives*, 163–164.

23. Paul McHugh is a psychiatrist who does not believe in sex-reassignment and who has become the "go to" authority and interviewee for those wishing to invalidate trans people—the specific quotes cited here are from Bailey, *The Man Who Would Be Queen*, 206; FoxNews.com, "Critics Slam Boston Doctor Who Offers Sex Change Treatment to Kids," May 19, 2008 (http://fox-news.com/story/0,2933,356592,00.html). Dr. Phil is a psychologist and television host whose eponymous show ran an episode called "Gender-Confused Kids" on October 29, 2008 (http://drphil.com/shows/show/1138).

24. Spiegel, "Two Families Grapple with Sons' Gender Identity."

25. For a comprehensive list of references supporting this fact, see Serano, *Excluded*, 308, Note 4.

26. American Psychological Association Task Force on the Sexualization of Girls, *Report of the APA Task Force on the Sexualization of Girls* (Washington, DC: American Psychological Association, 2007), 2 (www.apa.org/pi/wpo/sexualization.html). Note: the American Psychological Association is different from the American Psychiatric Association (who publishes the *DSM*).

27. American Psychological Association Task Force on the Sexualization of Girls, *Report of the APA Task Force on the Sexualization of Girls*, 27–35.

28. American Psychological Association Task Force on the Sexualization of Girls, *Report of the APA Task Force on the Sexualization of Girls*, 31–32.

29. Serano, *Whipping Girl*, 134–138 and 253–271.

30. Meyerowitz, *How Sex Changed*, 168–170 and 196–207.

31. Meyerowitz, *How Sex Changed*, 197–198.

32. Meyerowitz, *How Sex Changed*, 168, 202.

33. Gore Vidal, *Myra Breckinridge* (Boston: Little, Brown & Company, 1968). For a description of the impact that *Myra Breckinridge* had on popular culture (and thus, popular assumptions about trans female/feminine people) see Meyerowitz, *How Sex Changed*, 203–206.

34. Vidal, *Myra Breckinridge*, 166–197.

35. Serano, *Whipping Girl*, 16, 134, 261–262.

36. This case is made in more detail in Serano, *Whipping Girl*, 35–52 and 253–271.

37. Meyerowitz, *How Sex Changed*, 206.

38. I describe my own personal experiences of this in Serano, *Whipping Girl*, 255–259. While

such experiences (which many other trans women have shared with me) are admittedly anecdotal, they are indirectly documented in the sexual harassment and abuse statistics cited in Note 39.

39. Recent reports have chronicled that up to 64 percent of transgender people have been the victims of sexual assault, and that 76 percent of transgender students had experienced sexual harassment, including unwanted sexual remarks or being touched inappropriately—see Grant et al., *Injustice at Every Turn;* Emily A. Greytak, Joseph G. Kosciw, and Elizabeth M. Diaz, *Harsh Realities: The Experiences of Transgender Youth in Our Nation's Schools* (New York: GLSEN, 2009). The phenomenon of "walking while transgender" (discussed in Chapter 24, Note 2) is also an example of the sexualization of trans women being linked with discrimination and harassment. The interconnectedness of sexualization, discrimination, and violence is further explored in Bettcher, "Understanding Transphobia: Authenticity and Sexual Abuse"; Talia Mae Bettcher, "Evil Deceivers and Make-Believers: On Transphobic Violence and the Politics of Illusion," *Hypatia: A Journal of Feminist Philosophy* 22, no.3 (2007), 43–65.

40. Serano, *Whipping Girl,* 126–139 and 253–271; Lev, *Transgender Emergence,* 132–143.

41. Reviewed in Serano, *Whipping Girl,* 126–139. See also Bolin, *In Search of Eve,* 106–120; Namaste, *Invisible Lives,* 163–164 and 202–205.

42. American Psychiatric Association, *DSM-IV-TR,* 535. As I describe in the more recently written Chapter 34, this statement is no longer accurate for the *DSM-5.* For critiques of the *DSM's* Paraphilia section, see Charles Moser, "Paraphilia: A Critique of a Confused Concept," in Peggy J. Kleinplatz (ed.), *New Directions in Sex Therapy: Innovations and Alternatives* (Philadelphia: Brunner-Routledge, 2001), 91–108; Charles Moser and Peggy J. Kleinplatz, "*DSM-IV-TR* and the Paraphilias: An argument for removal," *Journal of Psychology and Human Sexuality* 17, no. 3/4 (2005), 91–109.

43. American Psychiatric Association, *DSM-IV-TR,* 574–575. For critiques of the Transvestic Fetishism diagnosis, see Charles Moser and Peggy J. Kleinplatz, "Transvestic fetishism: Psychopathology or iatrogenic artifact?" *New Jersey Psychologist* 52, no. 2 (2002), 16–17; Serano, *Whipping Girl,* 127–129 and 263–265; Winters, *Gender Madness in American Psychiatry,* 33–43.

44. Kelley Winters, "Issues of Psychiatric Diagnosis of Cross-Dressers," *GID Reform Advocates* (http://web.archive.org/web/20090510090634/http://www.gidreform.org/tf3023.html).

45. Gordene Olga MacKenzie, Transgender Nation (Bowling Green: Bowling Green State University Popular Press, 1994), 52–53, 88–89; Lev, *Transgender Emergence,* 141; Niklas Långström and Kenneth J. Zucker, "Transvestic fetishism in the general population: prevalence and correlates," *Journal of Sex and Marital Therapy* 31 (2005), 87–95. See also Chapter 33, Note 11.

46. Robert J. Stoller, *Sex and Gender: On the Development of Masculinity and Femininity* (New York: Science House, 1968), 195. On the numerous occasions that I have shared this Stoller quote while giving talks on trans, queer, and/or feminist issues, it consistently evokes uproarious audience laughter. I point this out to show the huge disparity between what is taken for granted within mainstream psychology (e.g., that men's clothing has no erotic value, or that female-assigned people cannot possibly experience any bona fide arousal via crossdressing) and what real people outside of the psychological establishment actually experience in real life.

47. Serano, *Whipping Girl,* 283–306.

48. Ray Blanchard, "The Classification and Labeling of Nonhomosexual Gender Dysphorias," *Archives of Sexual Behavior* 18, no. 4 (1989), 315–334; Ray Blanchard, "The Concept of Auto-gynephilia and the Typology of Male Gender Dysphoria," *The Journal of Nervous and Mental Disease* 177, no. 10 (1989), 616–623;

49. For example, Bailey, *The Man Who Would Be Queen,* 146.

50. These and many other facts and findings that together disprove Blanchard's autogynephilia theory are reviewed in Julia Serano, "The Case Against Autogynephilia," *International Journal of Transgenderism* 12, no. 3 (2010), 176–187; Charles Moser, "Blanchard's Autogynephilia Theory: A Critique," *Journal of Homosexuality* 57, no. 6 (2010), 790–809; Julia Serano, "The real 'autogynephilia deniers'," July 13, 2015 (http://juliaserano.blogspot.com/2015/07/the-real-autogynephilia-deniers.html).

51. American Psychological Association Task Force on the Sexualization of Girls, *Report of the APA Task Force on the Sexualization of Girls,* 27–35.

52. Lynda Lytle Holmstrom and Ann Wolbert Burgess, *The Victim of Rape: Institutional Reactions* (New Brunswick: Transaction Books, 1983), 171–188. While somewhat tangential, it is worth noting that Bettcher (in "Trans Identities and First Person Authority") points out that the denial of first person authority plays a central role in both rape and in trans-invalidations. In the first case, a rapist will dismiss the fact that the woman explicitly said "no" to his sexual advances, and instead privilege his own interpretation of her (e.g., arguing that she must have really meant "yes" because of what she was wearing, or supposedly communicating with her body language). Similarly, a trans-invalidator will ignore what a trans woman (or man) says about her own gender identity and experiences in favor of their own interpretation of her gender.

53. "Forced" or "rape" fantasies are fairly common in women. Anywhere between 31 to 57 percent of women report having them—reviewed in Joseph W. Critelli and Jenny M. Bivona, "Women's erotic rape fantasies: an evaluation of theory and research," *The Journal of Sex Research* 45 (2008), 57–70. The term "autoraptophilia" does not exist in the psychological or sexological literature—I invented it for the sole purpose of demonstrating how invalidating and potentially damaging it can be to define people based upon their sexual fantasies, especially if the population in question is already routinely sexualized in the culture at large.

54. Ray Blanchard, "*DSM-V* Paraphilia Options: General Diagnostic Issues, Pedohebephilic Disorder, and Transvestic Disorder," a paper presented at the Annual Meeting of the Society for Sex Therapy and Research on April 3, 2009, at Arlington, Virginia (http://individual.utoronto.ca/ray_blanchard/index_files/SSTAR_2009_Talk_on_DSM.html). Unbeknownst to me at the time, this proposed diagnosis would undergo numerous subsequent revisions—see Chapter 34 for specifics.

55. Blanchard, "*DSM-V* Paraphilia Options." I discuss this definition (and the many problems with it) in more depth in Chapter 34.

56. Paraphilize (transitive verb): to deem a person's autonomous or consensual sexual desires, urges, and/or orientations to be abnormal, unhealthy, or psychopathological.

57. For example, see Ray Blanchard, "Typology of male-to-female transsexualism," *Archives of Sexual Behavior* 14 (1985), 247–261.

58. Bailey, *The Man Who Would Be Queen*. Bailey's hypersexualization of trans women is mostly found on pp. 141–212. The "especially well-suited to prostitution" quote can be found on p. 185. Most of the trans-women-as-pathological-liars depictions can be found on pp. 157–176.

59. Discussed more in depth in Winters, *Gender Madness in American Psychiatry*, 107–116.

31 – Stop Sexualizing Us!

1. *Jerry Springer* and *There's Something About Miriam* were television series that portrayed trans women in a sensationalistic and sexualizing manner (described in Serano, *Whipping Girl*, 37–38), and *Myra Breckinridge* was discussed in the previous chapter.

2. This quote is found in Moser and Kleinplatz, "Transvestic fetishism: Psychopathology or iatrogenic artifact?"

3. He does this in Ray Blanchard and Peter I. Collins, "Men with sexual interest in transvestites, transsexuals, and she-males," *Journal of Nervous and Mental Disease* 181 (1993), 570–575, wherein he coined the term "gynandromorphophilia" to describe the supposed paraphilia of being sexual attracted to trans female/feminine-spectrum people. It is also implied in Blanchard's broadening of definition for "paraphilia" for the *DSM-5* (mentioned in the last chapter and discussed in more depth in Chapter 34), as it is clear that he does not consider trans people as "phenotypically normal."

33 – Reconceptualizing "Autogynephilia" as Female/Feminine Embodiment Fantasies

1. Serano, *Whipping Girl*, 126–139 and 253–271; Winters, *Gender Madness in American Psychiatry*, 117–140.

2. Serano, "The Case Against Autogynephilia"—full citation in Chapter 30, Note 50; available for download at http://juliaserano.com/av/Serano-CaseAgainstAutogynephilia.pdf.

3. Moser, "Blanchard's Autogynephilia Theory: A Critique"—full citation in Chapter 30, Note 50 (available for download at www.tandfonline.com/doi/pdf/10.1080/00918369.2010.486241).

4. American Psychiatric Association, *DSM-IV-TR*, 568. While the accuracy of this claim is debatable, the crucial point here is that this notion (that paraphilias are male-specific) is what allowed Blanchard to portray "autogynephilia" as a paraphilia in the first place: In his 1989 paper in which he first introduces the concept (Blanchard, "The Classification and Labeling of Nonhomosexual Gender Dysphorias"), Blanchard considers the presence of "autogynephilia" in many trans women, and the supposed lack of its counterpart in trans men, to be evidence that it must be a paraphilic impulse (under his presumption that trans women are "men" and trans men are "women"). In stark contrast, recent findings (see Note 5) indicate that what Blanchard calls "autogynephilia" is likely to be a more general sexual phenomenon associated with female/feminine-identified people (both cis and trans), rather than being a trans-specific paraphilia.

5. Charles Moser, "Autogynephilia in Women," *Journal of Homosexuality* 56, no. 5 (2009), 539–547. See also Jaimie F. Veale, Dave E. Clarke, and Terri C. Lomax, "Sexuality of male-to-female transsexuals," *Archives of Sexual Behavior* 37 (2008), 586–597; Noah Berlatsky, "Why Are Trans Women Penalized For Body Fantasies Everyone Has?," *The Establishment*, May 16, 2016 (http://www.theestablishment.co/2016/05/16/why-are-trans-women-penalized-for-body-fantasies-

we-all-have).

6. Numerous examples of this are compiled in Julia Serano, "The real 'autogynephilia deniers'."

7. Serano, "The Case Against Autogynephilia."

8. Harold Leitenberg and Kris Henning, "Sexual fantasy," *Psychological Bulletin* 117 (1995), 469–496; Emily Dubberley, *Garden of Desires: The Evolution of Women's Sexual Fantasies* (London, UK: Black Lace, 2013). See also Berlatsky, "Why Are Trans Women Penalized For Body Fantasies Everyone Has?"

9. Blanchard's taxonomic view of trans female/feminine people (centered on the presence or absence of "autogynephilia") is reviewed and debunked in Serano, "The Case Against Autogynephilia"; Moser, "Blanchard's Autogynephilia Theory: A Critique"; Jaimie F. Veale, "Evidence Against a Typology: A Taxometric Analysis of the Sexuality of Male-to-Female Transsexuals," *Archives of Sexual Behavior* 43, no. 6 (2014), 1177–1186.

10. Serano, *Whipping Girl,* 268–269; Talia Bettcher, "When Selves Have Sex: What the Phenomenology of Trans Sexuality Can Teach About Sexual Orientation," *Journal of Homosexuality* 61, no. 5 (2014), 605–620 (https://learningtrans.files.wordpress.com/2013/12/whenselves.pdf).

11. "Autoandrophilia" seems to have first appeared in the sexological literature in a singular case study of a cisgender gay man; see Anne A. Lawrence, "Anatomic autoandrophilia in an adult male," *Archives of Sexual Behavior* 38, no. 6 (2009), 1050–1056. For less pathologizing examples, see Tracie O'Keefe, "Autogynephilia and Autoandrophilia in Non-Sex and Gender Dysphoric Persons," Paper presented at the World Association for Sexual Health conference, Sydney, April, 2007 (http://tracieokeefe.com/autogynephilia-and-autoandrophilia-in-non-sex-and-gender-dysphoric-persons); Jack Molay, "Autoandrophilia, on women who fantasise about having a man's body," *Crossdreamers,* February 13, 2010 (http://crossdreamers.com/2010/02/autoandrophilia-on-women-who-fantasise.html).

12. See Serano, "The Case Against Autogynephilia," and references therein.

13. For evidence of MEFs in gay trans men, see the Discussion section of Matthias K. Auer, Johannes Fuss, Nina Höhne, Günter K. Stalla, Caroline Sievers, "Transgender Transitioning and Change of Self-Reported Sexual Orientation," *PLOS ONE* 9, no. 10 (2014), e110016. "Girlfag" is a term (mostly used in online communities) to describe androphilic (i.e., attracted to men) female-assigned individuals who identify with gay men, gay male culture, and/or fantasize about being gay men having sex with other men—e.g., see Ili, "'I am something that does not exist!' (On queer schwulwomen, girlfags and guydykes)," *Crossdreamers,* September 1, 2014 (http://crossdreamers.com/2014/09/i-am-something-that-does-not-exist-on.html), and other posts listed in Jack Molay, "A Reader's Guide to the Crossdreaming and Autogynephilia Blog," January 1, 2008 (http://crossdreamers.com/2008/01/readers-guide-to-confessions-of.html).

14. The "repression-mystification" hypothesis I describe here was first forwarded (in much greater detail) in Serano, *Whipping Girl,* 283-306. The "identity-defense" model is described in Jaimie F. Veale, Terri C. Lomax, and Dave E. Clarke, "Identity-defense model of gender-variant development," *International Journal of Transgenderism* 12, no. 3 (2010), 125-138. While these models vary in certain respects, they both posit that the two "types" or "classes" of trans female/feminine-spectrum people frequently cited in the psychiatric/sexological literature represent dif-

ferent reactions or defense mechanisms in response to societal transphobia/trans-misogyny. The "current trend" I mention here is a personal observation based on informal conversations that I've shared with numerous young (typically college-aged) queer-identified trans women. The claim (and supporting data) that FEFs (more specifically, in the form of transvestic fetishism) "may be a historically fading phenomenon" is from Larry Nuttbrock, Walter Bockting, Mona Mason, Sel Hwahng, Andrew Rosenblum, Monica Macri, and Jeffrey Becker, "A further assessment of Blanchard's typology of homosexual versus non-homosexual or autogynephilic gender dysphoria," *Archives of Sexual Behavior* 40, no. 2 (2011), 247-257.

34 – Trans People Are Still "Disordered" in the DSM-5

1. The original 2012 blog posts are Julia Serano, "Trans people still 'disordered' according to latest *DSM*" (http://juliaserano.blogspot.com/2012/12/trans-people-still-disordered-according.html) and Julia Serano, "Follow up on *DSM*-still-considers-trans-folks-'disordered' post" (http://juliaserano.blogspot.com/2012/12/follow-up-on-dsm-still-considers-trans.html). This piece also draws from my 2009 piece: Julia Serano, "Why feminists should be concerned with the impending revision of the *DSM*," (http://juliaserano.com/TSetiology.html#FeministingParaphilias).

2. Julia Serano, "Trans People Still Disordered in *DSM*," *Social Text,* DSM-CRIP issue (http://socialtextjournal.org/periscope_article/trans-people-still-disordered-in-dsm).

3. Twitter is a social media platform that allows people to share short messages (which are referred to as "tweets"). As I searched the Internet for such articles, I found that most of them were quite short, used similar language, offered no critical analysis, nor included comments from any trans activists or advocates who had been critical of the *DSM-5* revision process. It seems to me that the most likely scenario is that the American Psychiatric Association (who publishes the *DSM*) probably sent out some kind of press release touting their supposed "trans-friendliness," and that several news outlets simply passed the misinformation along as "news" to their readers.

4. Kelley Winters, "Third Swing: My Comments to the APA for a Less Harmful Gender Dysphoria Category in the DSM-5" (http://gidreform.wordpress.com/2012/06/19/third-swing-my-comments-to-the-apa-for-a-less-harmful-gender-dysphoria-category-in-the-dsm-5). The diagnosis itself can be found in the "Gender Dysphoria" section of American Psychiatric Association, *Diagnostic and Statistical Manual of Mental Disorders, Fifth Edition (DSM-5)* (Washington D.C.: American Psychiatric Association, 2013).

5. Serano, "Placing Ken Zucker's clinic in historical context" (and references therein); Winters, *Gender Madness in American Psychiatry.*

6. The definition that appears in the text is from the "Paraphilic Disorders" section of American Psychiatric Association, *DSM-5*. It is identical to the one Blanchard proposed in 2009 (see Blanchard, "*DSM-V* Paraphilia Options"; full citation in Chapter 30, Note 54) with the exception that the phrase "physically mature" has replaced the word "adult." The vast array of problems with this definition are dissected in Andrew C. Hinderliter, "Defining Paraphilia in *DSM-5:* Do Not Disregard Grammar," *Journal of Sex and Marital Therapy* 37, no. 1 (2011), 17–31; see also Charles Moser, "Yet another paraphilia definition fails," *Archives of Sexual Behavior* 40 (2011), 483–485.

7. In Blanchard, "*DSM-V* Paraphilia Options," he explicitly describes sexual attraction to "amputees, paralyzed persons, physical deformities" as paraphilic, and in Blanchard and Collins, "Men with sexual interest in transvestites, transsexuals, and she-males," he described attraction to trans

female/feminine individuals as a paraphilia that he named "gynandromorphophilia." Blanchard is also a co-author on a paper that argues that people who have a sexual interest in individuals outside of the age range of seventeen to forty-five are paraphilic (see Hinderliter, "Defining paraphilia in *DSM-5:* do not disregard grammar"). See Chapters 42 and 43 for my argument against conceptualizing such forms of attraction as "paraphilias."

8. Blanchard, "*DSM-V* Paraphilia Options." While this specific language does not appear in the final *DSM-5*, the sentiment clearly remains—see Note 9.

9. The *DSM-5* explicitly lists "interests in spanking, whipping, cutting, binding," and "telephone scatologia (obscene phone calls)" as examples of paraphilias, and the Fetishistic Disorder diagnosis additionally includes "recurrent and intense sexual arousal" in response to various articles of clothing or footwear, or "a highly specific focus on nongenital body part(s) (see "Paraphilic Disorders" section of American Psychiatric Association, *DSM-5)*. Hinderliter, "Defining paraphilia in *DSM-5:* do not disregard grammar," discusses how the *DSM-5* paraphilia definition could be interpreted to deem masturbation, orgasming without genital stimulation, watching pornography, reading erotica, and sexual role play as paraphilic as well.

10. Cameron, "How the Psychiatrist Who Co-Wrote the Manual on Sex Talks About Sex" (full citation in Chapter 30, Note 1).

11. "Paraphilic Disorders" section of American Psychiatric Association, *DSM-5*.

12. Charles Moser, "Problems with Ascertainment," *Archives of Sexual Behavior* 39 (2010), 1225–1227; Patrick Singy, "What's Wrong With Sex?" *Archives of Sexual Behavior* 40 (2011), 483–485. Both these authors point out that this sort of false distinction is precisely why the diagnosis "Ego-dystonic Homosexuality" was removed from previous *DSM* revisions. Hinderliter, "Defining paraphilia in *DSM-5:* do not disregard grammar," additionally points out that the term "paraphilia" has a several-decade-long history in the psychiatric literature (including previous *DSM* revisions) to refer to a set of diagnosable mental disorders, and thus is entirely unsuitable as a label to describe nonpathological behaviors.

13. Charles Moser and Peggy J. Kleinplatz, "*DSM-IV-TR* and the Paraphilias: An argument for removal," *Journal of Psychology and Human Sexuality* 17, no. 3/4 (2005), 91–109.

14. Charles Moser and Peggy J. Kleinplatz, "Transvestic fetishism: Psychopathology or iatrogenic artifact?" *New Jersey Psychologist* 52, no. 2 (2002). "The immediate or ultimate result of the paraphilia" is language that appears in the "Paraphilic Disorders" section of American Psychiatric Association, *DSM-5*.

15. Marty Klein and Charles Moser, "SM (Sadomasochistic) Interests as an Issue in a Child Custody Proceeding," *Journal of Homosexuality* 50 (2006), 233–242; Peggy J. Kleinplatz and Charles Moser, "Towards clinical guidelines for working with BDSM clients," *Contemporary Sexuality* 38, no. 6 (2004), 1, 4; Keely Kolmes Wendy Stock, and Charles Moser, "Investigating Bias in Psychotherapy with BDSM Clients," *Journal of Homosexuality* 50 (2006), 301–324; Charles Moser, "A Different Perspective," *Archives of Sexual Behavior* 37 (2008), 366–421; Serano, "The real 'autogynephilia deniers'."

16. The Blanchard quote is from Cameron, "How the Psychiatrist Who Co-Wrote the Manual on Sex Talks About Sex," and numerous examples of people citing *DSM* diagnoses (e.g., GID)

as justification for discriminating against trans people can be found in Winters, *Gender Madness in American Psychiatry*, 71–78.

17. Ray Blanchard, "The DSM Diagnostic Criteria for Transvestic Fetishism," *Archives of Sexual Behavior* 39 (2010), 363–372.

18. Luk Gijs and Richard A. Carroll, "Should Transvestic Fetishism be classified in *DSM 5*? Recommendations from the WPATH Consensus Process for Revision of the Diagnosis of Transvestic Fetishism," *International Journal of Transgenderism* 12 (2010), 189–195.

19. Between April 2010 and June 2011, there were at least three different proposed versions of "Transvestic Disorder"—these are all listed in Gail Knudson, Griet De Cuypere, and Walter Bockting, "Second Response of the World Professional Association for Transgender Health to the Proposed Revision of the Diagnosis of Transvestic Disorder for *DSM 5*," *International Journal of Transgenderism* 13, no. 1 (2011), 9–12. The final diagnosis differs somewhat from all of these, and can be found in the "Paraphilic Disorders" section of American Psychiatric Association, *DSM-5*.

20. Many trans activists and advocates working to eliminate this diagnosis from the *DSM* (including myself—see Serano, *Whipping Girl*, 127–128) often pointed out that the diagnosis was sexist in that it singled out "heterosexual men" (whereas people of other genders and sexual orientations were presumably free to crossdress without the stigma of pathology). Our purpose in doing so was to point out the ludicrousness inherent in the diagnosis, in the hopes that it would ultimately be removed. Frankly, it never occurred to me (although perhaps it should have) that Blanchard might use these accusations of sexism as an excuse to expand it to include even more people (he essentially admits to this in the article cited in Note 22).

21. For more on "autoandrophilia," see Chapter 33, Note 11.

22. Cameron, "How the Psychiatrist Who Co-Wrote the Manual on Sex Talks About Sex."

23. WPATH also opposed both the specifiers "in remission" and "in a controlled environment" (not discussed here) on the grounds that they "exclude the possibility of an 'exit clause.'"—see Knudson, De Cuypere, and Bockting, "Second Response of the World Professional Association for Transgender Health to the Proposed Revision of the Diagnosis of Transvestic Disorder for *DSM 5*." In the final *DSM-5*, the specifier is listed as "In full remission" and requires one to experience "no distress or impairment in social, occupational, or other areas of functioning for at least 5 years," which seems to imply that someone who has not experienced those issues for four years still qualifies for the full diagnosis sans specifier.

24. See for example Luke Brinker and Carlos Maza, "15 Experts Debunk Right-Wing Transgender Bathroom Myth," *Media Matters for America*, March 20, 2014 (http://mediamatters.org/research/2014/03/20/15-experts-debunk-right-wing-transgender-bathro/198533); Serano, "The real 'autogynephilia deniers'."

35 – An Open Letter to The New Yorker
1. Julia Serano, "Op-ed: An Open Letter to The New Yorker," *Advocate.com*, August 5, 2014 (http://advocate.com/commentary/2014/08/05/op-ed-open-letter-new-yorker).

2. Michelle Goldberg, "What Is a Woman? The dispute between radical feminism and trans-

genderism," *The New Yorker,* August 4, 2014 (http://newyorker.com/magazine/2014/08/04/woman-2).

3. Some TERFs claim that "TERF" is a slur (Goldberg highlights this without explanation in her article), but this ignores the history of the term: It was popularized by a cisgender feminist who felt the need for "a deliberately technically neutral description" to distinguish between trans-exclusive radical feminists (i.e., TERFs) and "trans*-positive/neutral" radical feminists—see Cristan Williams, "TERF: what it means and where it came from," *The TransAdvocate,* March 15, 2014 (http://transadvocate.com/terf-what-it-means-and-where-it-came-from_n_13066.htm).

4. NARTH (National Association for Research and Therapy of Homosexuality) is an organization that promotes the use of "conversion therapy" to "cure" same-sex attraction. Dan Savage writes a sex advice column called *Savage Love,* which early on sported the catchphrase "Hey Faggot!"—Savage (a gay man himself) meant the phrase to be used/interpreted in a reclaimed, rather than derogatory, way. #CancelColbert was a social media campaign that was directed at *The Colbert Report* (a television show that parodied right-wing news outlets) because of a sketch they aired that was intended to satirize an incidence of racism, but which many people subsequently interpreted as racist.

5. Salman Rushdie is an author whose book *The Satanic Verses* was interpreted by some as blasphemous—it was banned in many Muslim countries, and Rushdie spent most of the 1990s in hiding because Iran's Ayatollah Khomeini had called for his assassination. With this reference, I am obviously poking fun at Goldberg's attempts to portray Jeffreys as though she lives under a similar sort of threat. No one has called for Jeffreys's death, and her books have not been banned or censored—in fact you can purchase them right now online. Rather, much like authors who write racist, sexist, or homophobic books, Jeffreys is simply having problems finding venues that want anything to do with her.

6. Sheila Jeffreys, *Beauty and Misogyny: Harmful Cultural Practices in the West* (New York: Routledge, 2005), 24–27.

7. Serano, *Whipping Girl,* 334; Serano, *Excluded,* 120–123.

8. Sheila Jeffreys, *Gender Hurts: A Feminist Analysis of the Politics of Transgenderism* (New York: Routledge, 2014), 49–51.

9. Moser, "Autogynephilia in Women" (full citation in Chapter 33, Note 5). Unsurprisingly, Jeffreys does not mention this, nor any other of the numerous lines of evidence that challenge Blanchard's theory (see Chapter 33, and references therein).

10. Cameron, "How the Psychiatrist Who Co-Wrote the Manual on Sex Talks About Sex." See also Chapter 34.

11. Jeffreys, *Gender Hurts,* 50.

12. Julia Serano, "Two articles (plus thoughts on autogynephilia as the transgender equivalent of slut-shaming)," July 28, 2014 (http://juliaserano.blogspot.com/2014/07/two-articles-related-to-femininity-and.html).

13. A few examples include: Jos Truitt, "Why The New Yorker's radical feminism and trans-

genderism piece was one-sided," *Columbia Journalism Review,* August 6, 2014 (http://cjr.org/minority_reports/new_yorker_feminism_transgenderism_jos_truitt.php?page=all); Leela Ginelle, "TERF War: The New Yorker's One-Sided Article Undermines Transgender Identity," *Bitch Media,* August 1, 2014 (http://bitchmagazine.org/post/terf-war-the-new-yorkers-one-sided-article-undermines-transgender-identity); A.V. Flox, "A Pity Party for Trans-Exclusionary Radical Feminists," *Slantist,* July 28, 2014 (http://slantist.com/terfs-new-yorker/).

14. Mari Brighe, "The New Yorker's Skewed History of Trans-Exclusionary Radical Feminism Ignores Actual Trans Women," *Autostraddle,* July 29, 2014 (http://autostraddle.com/the-new-yorkers-skewed-history-of-trans-exclusionary-radical-feminism-ignores-actual-trans-women-247642/).

15. Michelle Goldberg, "Feminism's Toxic Twitter Wars," *The Nation,* February 17, 2014 edition (it appeared online January 29, 2014). The aftermath of that Goldberg article is described in Katherine Cross, "The Chapel Perilous: On the Quiet Narratives in the Shadows," *Nuclear Unicorn,* February 6, 2014 (http://quinnae.com/2014/02/06/the-chapel-perilous-on-the-quiet-narratives-in-the-shadows/).

16. Parker Marie Molloy, "Man Arrested for Allegedly Stabbing 15-Year-Old Trans Girl," *Advocate.com,* July 31 2014 (http://advocate.com/politics/transgender/2014/07/31/watch-man-arrested-allegedly-stabbing-15-year-old-trans-girl); Parker Marie Molloy, "Second Baltimore Trans Woman Found Murdered Since June," *Advocate.com,* July 16 2014 (http://advocate.com/politics/transgender/2014/07/16/second-baltimore-trans-woman-found-murdered-june).

36 – Bisexual Does Not "Reinforce" Anything

1. My 2008 coming-out-as-bisexual spoken word piece ("Three Strikes and I'm Out") appears in Serano, *Excluded,* 70–74.

2. Julia Serano, "Bisexuality does not reinforce the gender binary," *The Scavenger,* October 9, 2010 (http://thescavenger.net/glb/bisexuality-does-not-reinforce-the-gender-binary-39675-467.html).

3. Serano, *Excluded,* 81-98.

4. When this essay was originally published, a few people mistakenly assumed that, in this passage, I was claiming that a person's physical sex (or the sex that others perceive them to be) somehow trumps a person's gender identity. I most certainly do not believe that, and I have reworded this passage here to better reflect what I was trying to convey—namely, that aspects of physical sex (such as bodily changes that result from sex hormones) are a salient or significant part of many people's experiences of sexual attraction.

5. In retrospect, I now find this particular claim to be somewhat superfluous, as all bisexual/pansexual-spectrum people will no doubt differ from one another in our experiences of sexual attraction. In my follow up essay, "Bisexuality and Binaries Revisited" (Serano, *Excluded,* 81–98), I instead argue that, from an activist perspective, it is potentially more productive to organize around some kind of umbrella term that enables us to challenge our shared issues (i.e., monosexism/biphobia and bi-invisibility) rather than dwell on the many differences that exist in how we experience, practice, and/or categorize our sexualities.

6. This is admittedly an oversimplification of why trans- and bisexual-exclusion occurred within

gay and lesbian communities and movements. Nevertheless, I believe that the main point that I make here—namely, that both our existences challenged lesbian and gay ideologies and ortho-doxies—most certainly contributed to our exclusion.

7. I am using the term "homonormative" here in accordance with Susan Stryker, "Transgender History, Homonormativity, and Disciplinarity," *Radical History Review* 100 (2008), 145–157, to describe how "gay" and "lesbian" are viewed as the unspoken norm within queer communities, thus erasing or excluding other gender and sexual minorities such as transgender people and (as I argue here) bisexuals. An alternative usage of "homonormative" (attributed to Lisa Duggan) refers to when queer communities embrace heteronormative ideals (e.g., marriage, monogamy, gender conformity).

37 – A "Transsexual Versus Transgender" Intervention

1. Julia Serano, "A 'Transsexual Versus Transgender' Intervention," September 8, 2011 (http://juliaserano.blogspot.com/2011/09/transsexual-versus-transgender.html).

2. Femke Olyslager and Lynn Conway, "On the Calculation of the Prevalence of Transsexualism," paper presented at the WPATH Twentieth International Symposium, September 2007 (http://ai.eecs.umich.edu/people/conway/TS/Prevalence/Reports/Prevalence%20of%20Transsexualism.pdf).

3. Namaste, *Sex Change, Social Change*, 29.

4. Gary J. Gates, "How many people are lesbian, gay, bisexual, and transgender?" The Williams Institute, UCLA School of Law, April 2011 (http://williamsinstitute.law.ucla.edu/wp-content/uploads/Gates-How-Many-People-LGBT-Apr-2011.pdf).

5. For instance, the many articles I reference in Serano, "The Case Against Autogynephilia" that categorized transsexual women according to their sexual orientations typically reported numbers within this range. A more recent survey of 6,450 trans people (Grant et al., *Injustice at Every Turn)* found that only 23 percent of MTF respondents and 25 percent of FTM respondents identified as heterosexual, whereas 67 and 72 percent, respectively, listed their sexual orientation as either gay, lesbian, same-gender, bisexual, or queer (with the remainder identifying their orientation as either asexual or other).

6. While this seemed true in 2011 when I wrote this essay, an analogous separatist movement among trans men has arisen in recent years; see Jack Molay, "Truscum and the Transgender War of Words," *Crossdreamers,* December 16, 2013 (http://crossdreamers.com/2013/12/truscum-and-transgender-war-of-words.html) for parallels and differences between these two movements.

38 – Baby Talk

1. Quote from promotional material for the 2009 Girl Talk show (http://queerculturalcenter.org/Pages/QFest09/GirlTalk.html). Most of the Girl Talk shows were recorded—links to these audio and video archives are compiled on my website at http://juliaserano.com/girltalk.html.

2. Julia Serano, "FAAB-mentality," March 7, 2013 (http://juliaserano.blogspot.com/2013/03/faab-mentality.html).

3. The quote is from Katie Liederman, "Not That into Sex," *PrettyQueer.com,* September 17,

2011 (http://prettyqueer.com/2011/09/17/not-that-into-sex). For the record, Liederman subsequently clarified to me that the quote was not intended to erase trans women or invalidate anybody's identity, and I accept this, especially given how many other cis queer female friends and acquaintances I have who are respectful of my identity as a bisexual trans woman, yet would likely describe their own sexual orientation and identity in language similar to this quote. This piece is not intended to be a "call out" of the quote, or of any queer woman's sexual preferences or self-description. Rather, I cited the quote simply because I felt that it provided a particularly useful jumping-off point to discuss more general trends I've noticed with regards to how "queer," "lesbian," and "woman" are often conceptualized within queer women's communities, and how this framing undermines trans women, bisexuals, and femmes within these same settings.

4. Bitch, "An open letter from Bitch: Dispelling The Rumor of my supposed Transphobia," March 24, 2011 (https://facebook.com/notes/bitch/an-open-letter-from-bitch-dispelling-the-rumor-of-my-supposed-transphobia/10150162614373255).

5. In the years prior to writing this piece, I had countless conversations with other trans activists regarding inclusive language for trans-spectrum trajectories. I eventually settled on *trans female/feminine* and *trans male/masculine* because they accommodate both gender identity and/or expression, and they place the focus on our self-identities and self-understandings, rather than non-consensual birth assignments. After posting this piece on my blog, I had a few people who identify as agender or genderqueer tell me that they prefer MAAB over trans female/feminine because they feel that they are neither female nor feminine. This appears to be an example of irreconcilable differences in trans language and activism that sometimes arise, and which I dedicate the final section of this book toward discussing.

39 – First Date

1. My numerous and complicated thoughts regarding the word "tranny," and about arguments over who can and cannot legitimately use the word, are discussed at great length in Chapter 45. For the record, I was happy that she (the love interest in this piece) raised this point, not because I personally believe that trans men should never be able use the term, but rather because it demonstrated that she was familiar with arguments that many trans women during that time were making.

2. I discuss this in Julia Serano, "Skin," December 19, 2010 (http://juliaserano.blogspot.com/2011/08/skin.html).

40 – Elders

1. Susan Stryker (who co-directed the film) also discusses this event and the circumstances surrounding it in Stryker, *Transgender History*, 63–75.

2. Some of these studies are reviewed in Kimberly Keller, "Transgender health and HIV," *BETA* 21, no. 4 (2009), 40–50. A recent report examining fifteen countries estimates that HIV prevalence in transgender women is 48.8 percent, which is fifty times higher than in the general population—see Frits van Griensven, Prempreeda Pramoj Na Ayutthaya, and Erin Wilson, "HIV surveillance and prevention in transgender women," *The Lancet Infectious Diseases* 13, No. 3 (2013), 185–186.

41 – Contagious

1. This is a reference to the Susan Sontag book *AIDS and Its Metaphors*.

2. William F. Buckley Jr., "Crucial Steps in Combating the AIDS Epidemic; Identify All the Carriers," *The New York Times,* March 18, 1986.

3. This is how the quote is attributed to Koop on numerous Internet pages, although I could not find a definitive source for it. If this is not what Koop said verbatim, it is at least similar in spirit.

4. This was anecdotally described in some of the other The Biggest Quake cast members' pieces, and is also observed in recent research studies—see Donald G. McNeil Jr., "Rise in Unprotected Sex by Gay Men Spurs H.I.V. Fears," *The New York Times,* November 27, 2013.

42 - In Defense of Partners
1. Janet Mock, "How Society Shames Men Dating Trans Women & How This Affects Our Lives," September 12, 2013 (http://janetmock.com/2013/09/12/men-who-date-attracted-to-trans-women-stigma).

2. American Psychiatric Association, *DSM-5.* For further critique of this definition, see Chapter 34 and references therein.

3. Blanchard and Collins, "Men with sexual interest in transvestites, transsexuals, and she-males"; John Money and Margaret Lamacza, "Gynemimesis and gynemimetophilia: Individual and cross-cultural manifestations of a gender-coping strategy hitherto unnamed," *Comprehensive Psychiatry* 25, no. 4 (1984), 392–403.

4. I have had subsequent conversations with several trans activists who feel that the term "chaser" serves a purpose as an in-community pejorative to describe cis people who sexually objectify or harass trans people. If the word were *only* used in this manner, I would not be so concerned. But the fact is that the term *is* routinely applied (by both trans and cis people) to denigrate the sexual desires, identities, and experiences of potential and actual partners of trans folks, even when they do not engage in objectifying or harassing behavior; see also Avery Brooks Tompkins, "'There's No Chasing Involved': Cis/Trans Relationships, 'Tranny Chasers,' and the Future of a Sex-Positive Trans Politics," *Journal of Homosexuality* 61, no. 5 (2014), 766–780.

43 - Desirable
1. Barry Winchell was an army soldier who was murdered in 1999 by another soldier because he was dating a trans woman.

2. Courtesy stigma is described in Erving Goffman, *Stigma: Notes on the Management of Spoiled Identity* (Englewood Cliffs, NJ: Prentice-Hall Inc., 1963), 30–31.

3. "World's smallest violin" is a visual joke (which I did when I performed this piece) intended to express sarcastic sympathy toward somebody who you believe is unjustly or excessively complaining about something. As I state earlier in the piece, I completely understand why any given trans man might object to people who invalidate his male identity and/or sexually objectify or harass him, and I have no issues with complaints to this effect. My critique here is specifically directed at those trans men who primarily partner with cis queer women, yet who simultaneously complain when such women (in a general sense) express their interest in, or attraction toward, trans men.

4. In the 1999 film *Fight Club,* the character Tyler Durden tells his followers, "You are not a beautiful or unique snowflake." I have obviously turned this quote around.

Part 5: Differences of Opinion in Trans Activism

1. Links to these posts and other similarly themed pieces are compiled in Julia Serano, "Activism, Language, and Differences of Opinion (a compilation of essays)," (http://juliaserano.blogspot.com/2016/07/activism-language-and-differences-of.html).

44 – Considering Trans and Queer Appropriation

1. See Chapter 23, Note 2.

2. Unlike some TERF websites that express cissexism through the medium of feminist theory and rhetoric, *Pretendbians* is pure unadulterated ad hominem attacks and slander targeting trans women. I refuse to share the web domain here.

3. Definitions from *Dictionary.com* (http://dictionary.reference.com/browse/denigration).

4. Serano, *Whipping Girl,* 195–212.

5. For example: The Associated Press, "High school students crossdress to support transsexual sophomore," May 7, 2008 (http://nydailynews.com/news/high-school-students-crossdress-support-transsexual-sophomore-article-1.328652).

6. This is the same group that I describe in the Introduction to this book. For the record, the group did occasionally have closed meetings where only trans folks could attend. But many, if not most, of the meetings were open to partners and friends as well.

7. It must also be said that these groups were more readily able to integrate because they are both white and Christian, and thus they did not have to overcome the entrenched racism and Christian-centrism that continue to predominate in the U.S.

8. I have appropriated the phrase "cultural appreciation" from Susan Scafidi, *Who Owns Culture?: Appropriation and Authenticity in American Law* (New Brunswick, NJ: Rutgers University Press, 2005), 6–11. Admittedly, some Irish-Americans may view St. Patrick's Day parades as exploitative, and some might view Scorsese-esque depictions of Italian-Americans as denigrating. In other words, members of the same marginalized/minority group may disagree about what constitutes EED versus non-EED appropriation, much like they may disagree over whether non-EED appropriation is bad, neutral, or potentially good.

9. For example: fakecisgirl, "The New Trans Separatism is the same old White Supremacy," July 25, 2013 (http://fakecisgirl.wordpress.com/2013/07/25/the-new-trans-separatism-is-the-same-old-white-supremacy).

10. Serano, *Excluded,* 99–104.

11. Gloria Anzaldúa, *Borderlands/La Frontera: The New Mestiza* (San Francisco: Aunt Lute Books, 1999).

12. Here is a real life example of this: My band Bitesize was actively playing for several years before my transition. And back then, on a few occasions, a male friend from another band and I would kiss on stage during our set. We did it primarily for the same reason that Kurt Cobain and Krist Novoselic of Nirvana famously kissed on national TV—to make homophobes uncomfortable, to challenge heterosexism. I suppose that some people in the audience could have viewed

us as two "straight dudes" who were trying to garner "indie-cred" by appropriating queerness, but in reality, both of us had been sexual with men previously and we both eventually wound up identifying as bisexual.

13. This is discussed in great length in Scafidi, *Who Owns Culture?*, 52–66.

14. Serano, *Excluded*, 138–168 (and references therein).

45 – A Personal History of the "T-word" (and some more general reflections on language and activism)

1. I flesh out this concept further in Julia Serano, "On the 'activist language merry-go-round,' Stephen Pinker's 'euphemism treadmill,' and 'political correctness' more generally," June 2, 2014 (http://juliaserano.blogspot.com/2014/06/on-activist-language-merry-go-round.html); Julia Serano, "Regarding Trans* and Transgenderism" (http://juliaserano.blogspot.com/2015/08/regarding-trans-and-transgenderism.html). See also "There is No Perfect Word: a Transgender Glossary of Sorts" (pp. 283–285 of this book).

2. An excellent review of reclaiming words (centering on "queer," but discussing other reclaimed labels as well) can be found in Robin Brontsema, "A Queer Revolution: Reconceptualizing the Debate Over Linguistic Reclamation," *Colorado Research in Linguistics* 17, no. 1 (2004), 1–17.

3. As found in their original form in Serano, *Either/Or* and Serano, *Draw Blood*. Over the years, I have subsequently swapped out many instances of "tranny" in these pieces, in part, due to the word's increasingly polarizing nature.

4. Compare Serano, *On the Outside Looking In*, 19–29 (http://juliaserano.com/outside.html#outside) to Serano, *Excluded*, 22–36.

5. See Introduction, Note 8.

6. Kate Bornstein, "Who You Calling A Tranny?" July 12, 2009 (http://katebornstein.typepad.com/kate_bornsteins_blog/2009/07/who-you-calling-a-tranny.html). Zagria, "Some observations on the tranny word," *A Gender Variance Who's Who*, May 1, 2014 (http://zagria.blogspot.it/2014/05/some-observations-on-tranny-word.html) also describes community usage of the words "tranny" and "transy" during the 1970s.

7. This evolution of the word "gay" is described in Brontsema, "A Queer Revolution." The corresponding evolution of the word "tranny" is inferred from its apparent in-community usage in the 1970s (sources cited in Note 6), the way it subsequently became picked up by the media and sex industry starting in the 1980s and 1990s (see Cristan Williams, "Tranny: An Evidence-Based Review," *The TransAdvocate*, April 28, 2014, http://transadvocate.com/tranny-an-evidence-based-review-2_n_13593.htm), and my experiences in trans settings in the early 2000s where many of us felt like we were reclaiming the word. Admittedly, much of the early usage of the word "tranny" has been lost to history, so others may arrive at different interpretations (e.g., Williams, "Tranny: An Evidence-Based Review").

8. *Subversivism* is a term that I introduced in *Whipping Girl* (pp. 346–349) to describe the belief (held by some feminists and queer people) that certain expressions of gender or sexuality subvert the gender binary/heteronormativity/patriarchy/insert-oppressive-gender-system-of-your-choice-here, which implies that other expressions of gender and sexuality must "reinforce"

that oppressive system. The many problems inherent in this worldview are dissected throughout Serano, *Excluded*.

9. Margaret Price, "Is Christian Siriano making a hot mess of the term 'tranny'?," *Bitch Media*, March 14, 2008 (http://bitchmagazine.org/post/is-christian-siriano-making-a-hot-mess-of-the-term-quottrannyquot).

10. Admittedly, this is an oversimplification, as people can have alternative goals for reclaiming words—see Brontsema, "A Queer Revolution." Personally, I think the "ingroup argument" often gains momentum (at least initially) because it functions as a compromise of sorts between those who view the word as inherently bad (and who thus remain able to push for the eradication of the term within mainstream society) and those who embrace it as a reclaimed word (who thus remain able to use the term self-referentially). However, a negative side effect of this compromise is that it often leads to "border wars" over who is a legitimate member of the group or target of the word (and thus are allowed to reclaim it) and who is not; I discuss such border wars later in the essay.

11. Hazel/Cedar Troost, "'Tranny' and Subversivism: Re-reclaiming 'Tranny' (or not) part 1," November 10, 2008 (https://takesupspace.wordpress.com/2008/11/10/tranny-and-subversivism-re-reclaiming-tranny-or-not-part-1); Hazel/Cedar Troost, "'Tranny' & Cis Women: Re-Reclaiming Tranny (or not) part 2," January 8, 2009 (https://takesupspace.wordpress.com/2009/01/08/tranny-cis-women-re-reclaiming-tranny-or-not-part-2).

12. I say that I "leaned toward" the trans-guys-reclaiming-the-word-tranny-is-problematic camp because I agreed with the logic behind the argument. However, I did not personally feel comfortable with the idea of telling trans male/masculine folks that they have no right to use the word. This is especially true for those who were out in the '90s and early '00s, and who embraced the word in order to challenge the rampant cis assumption and trans male/masculine invisibility that existed back then. However, I would insist that trans male/masculine folks who choose to use the word "tranny" are responsible for educating themselves about trans female/feminine perspectives on the word.

13. In *Whipping Girl*, I argued that this difference in visibility is due to trans-misogyny, plus the fact that, in our culture, male/masculine physical cues trump female/feminine ones when it comes to how we gender people (leading trans women to be read as trans more frequently than trans men). In Chapter 30, I also discuss how trans male/masculine invisibility is closely linked to the public's tendency to sexualize trans female/feminine folks.

14. Daniel Reynolds, "RuPaul: 'I Love the Word Tranny'," *Advocate.com*, May 22, 2014 (http://advocate.com/arts-entertainment/television/2014/05/22/rupaul-i-love-word-tranny).

15. Parker Marie Malloy, "RuPaul Stokes Anger With Use of Transphobic Slur," *Advocate.com*, March 18, 2014 (http://advocate.com/politics/transgender/2014/03/18/rupaul-stokes-anger-use-transphobic-slur). "Clock" (verb) is a slang term for recognizing that a person is transgender.

16. I say "arguably justified" because it depends on one's interpretation of the word. If you view "tranny" as a slur that specifically targets people who are transgender-identified, then this argument is indeed justified. However, if you view the word (à la Kate Bornstein) as a word created by trans women and drag queens to unite both camps, then RuPaul does seem to have a stake in the term (even if he is not doing a very good job on the "uniting" front). I am not arguing for or

against either of these interpretations, just acknowledging that both viewpoints exist and seem to be contributing to this ongoing debate.

17. For instance, two drag queen contestants on RuPaul's show have since transitioned to female (Monica Beverly Hillz and Carmen Carrera, see Note 14). Sylvia Rivera, Candis Cayne, and many other trans women spent periods of their lives when they self-identified as drag queens.

18. Tobi Hill-Meyer, "Let's Talk About 'Tranny'," *Handbasket Productions* (http://blog. handbasketproductions.com/?p=187). This essay originally appeared as a three-part series on *Bilerico.com* in December 2010. In correspondence with the author, Hill-Meyer added the following clarification: "While I was talking about how policing the identity of the speaker can create problems, my ultimate point was that *context* matters so much more than who is speaking. And by that I don't mean the 'I meant it positively' defense, but the context of a private conversation with your friends as opposed to using it in the title of a public event and flyering the town with it. Or the context of using it as a reference to the transphobic way people see you as opposed to shouting it from stage or putting it on a poster in a community center. The rules people set up often feel more like morality judgments, but what I care about is who is impacted, who is kept from accessing a space, who is made to feel unsafe in their own space."

19. Another historical note: In the trans communities that I participated in in the early '00s, there was a lot of talk about people taking responsibility for their own triggers, rather than citing them as a justification for removing potentially distressing words, opinions, people, etc. Much of this seemed to be a direct response to the then commonplace claims that the presence of trans women in women-only spaces would trigger survivors of sexual abuse (I discuss such claims in Chapter 16 and also in Serano, *Whipping Girl*, 242; Serano, *Excluded*, 30–31). This was also in the wake of 9/11, when many Americans felt that they were entitled to "be free of" (i.e., to remove or censor) any language, political or religious views, people, songs, etc., that made them feel "unsafe"—this atmosphere also likely fueled discussions about people taking responsibilities for their own triggers in my community. I'd like to think that there is some sort of middle-ground for us to both be respectful of people's triggers while at the same time acknowledging that people will differ in what they may find triggering, and that attempts to make "safe spaces" often result in "same spaces" that favor homogeneity over diversity.

20. "Trap" is a derogatory slang term for trans women, popularized by cis men who believe that we supposedly "deceive" them into being attracted to someone who is "not really a woman." A number of years ago (while self-googling), I stumbled upon a message board where someone lifted a photo of me from my website, and others started gawking at it, with some of the commenters referring to me as a "trap." I found it highly violating, and I believe that it is why I continue to have such an intense negative reaction toward the word.

21. I discuss my reasoning for this in Serano, *Whipping Girl*, 29–30; Serano, *Excluded*, 303.

22. For example: Cristan Williams, "Transwomans vs Trans Woman," July 17, 2013 (http:// cristanwilliams.com/b/2013/07/17/transwomans-vs-trans-woman).

23. See for example, Kate Bornstein, "To T, or Not to T. That's The Frakking Question," November 18, 2010 (http://katebornstein.typepad.com/kate_bornsteins_blog/2010/11/to-t-or-not-to-t-thats-the-frakking-question.html); James Nivhols, "Jayne County, Transgender Icon, Allegedly Banned From Facebook For 'Transphobic Slurs'," *The Huffington Post*, April 17, 2014 (http://huffingtonpost.com/2014/04/17/jayne-county-transgender_n_5169324.

html). Both women were out as trans decades before me, and were trans pioneers during a time that was far more fraught than anything that I experienced during my coming out in the early '00s. Even if we do not agree with their views on this word (or other issues), I personally believe that both have earned the right to call themselves whatever they want, as many of us wouldn't even be here without their trailblazing lives. Admittedly, other trans folks may strongly disagree with me about this.

24. As I allude to in the following paragraph in the text (and the following Note), attempts to purge the word "bisexual" in recent years (stemming from forces both within and external to bisexual/pansexual-umbrella communities) is another example of how previously taken-for-granted identity labels and activist terminologies can rather suddenly find themselves to be subjected to undue scrutiny and potential eradication.

25. See Chapter 36 and Serano, *Excluded*, 81–98.

26. One of the most formative books in my life was George Orwell's *1984*. I read it several times in the years before my transition. And during those years, I very much related to the circumstance of having to navigate my way through a dangerous and repressed world without letting anyone find out who I really was or what I was thinking. While not a perfect character, Julia despises the society she lives in, but is adept at keeping secrets and not being found out. Julia is a survivor. She takes risks, but calculated ones. She is a passionate person, but only indulges in that side of herself when she knows that it's safe to let her guard down. That is how I saw myself pre-transition and why I chose Julia as my name. That, plus the fact that I had always aesthetically liked the name Julie for reasons that remain unclear to me.

27. All of these terms—including trans*, which in 2014 (when I originally wrote this essay) was touted by some as the "most inclusive" variant, but which has subsequently come under some scrutiny and criticism—are discussed in Serano, "Regarding Trans* and Transgenderism."

28. "Girls like us" is a term popularized by Janet Mock and that many younger trans women have embraced and/or prefer. "Harry Benjamin Syndrome" is a term favored by some people who (instead of identifying as "transsexual") view themselves as having an "intersex brain condition."

29. This debate (which I remember occurring during the mid-'00s) was often centered on perceived negative connotations associated with the suffix "-ism." Such concerns are similar to more recent consternation regarding the term "transgenderism," which is dissected and discussed in Serano, "Regarding Trans* and Transgenderism."

30. For a period in the '90s, trans activists began spelling it "transexual" with one *S* (as seen in the name of the activist group Transexual Menace). Presumably, this purposeful misspelling was done to free the word from its pathologizing past. A problem with alternate spellings is that, while they may feel reclaiming and radical when written, or when reading them off the page, they typically sound identical to the non-reclaimed variations when spoken.

31. In the '90s and early '00s, the word "transgendered" was commonplace—one can find it in classic books like Kate Bornstein's *Gender Outlaw* and Leslie Feinberg's *Trans Liberation*, and I routinely used it in my early writings (e.g., my chapbooks *Either/Or* and *Draw Blood*). We routinely talk about people being "gendered," so it makes sense that one might describe someone as being "transgendered." But at some point in the mid-'00s, there were increasing complaints about "transgendered." Many of these centered on the assumption that, because the word is an

adjective, it is grammatically incorrect to add an "-ed" to it, or that the "-ed" implied "past tense"; others have pointed out that these claims (from a purely grammatical sense) are specious—e.g., see Semanticide, "Transgender vs Transgendered," November 4, 2012 (http://semanticide. tumblr.com/post/35039846184/transgender-vs-transgendered); Helen Boyd and Jennifer Finney Boylan, "About 'Transgendered': Some History & Grammar," *en/Gender*, July 13, 2015 (http://myhusbandbetty.com/2015/07/13/about-transgendered-some-history-grammar).   In any case, such complaints started to garner critical mass around the time that I was writing *Whipping Girl*. I remember using the "Replace" function to change all instances of "transgendered" to "transgender" in my manuscript. It initially felt so strange to say that someone was "transgender" rather than "transgendered"; nowadays, the exact opposite is true: "transgendered" feels horribly wrong to me. While trans folks these days often say that they find the phrasing "transgendered person" to be offensive, other trans folks have argued that they find "transgender person" to be offensive—e.g., see Matt Kailey, "Transgender v. Transgendered: Changing My Policy, Not My Mind," July 27, 2009 (https://mattkailey.wordpress.com/2009/07/27/ transgender-v-transgendered-changing-my-policy-not-my-mind). As I have argued throughout this piece thus far, there is no pleasing everybody when it comes to activist language.

32. The current GLAAD Media Reference Guide (http://glaad.org/reference/transgender) claims that both words should be used as adjectives only. However, it is still quite common within the community for people to describe themselves as "a transsexual," or to use "transsexuals" plural—indeed, I have done this throughout my own writings, and this usage has a very long history. In contrast, there is a growing consensus that "transgender" should not be used as a noun, and the plural term "transgenders" will usually generate complaints. However, much like the move away from "transgendered," this is a relatively recent development, as "transgenders" appears in 1990s trans activist books such as Kate Bornstein's *Gender Outlaw* and Leslie Feinberg's *Transgender Warriors*.

33. While I prefer "trans woman," those who prefer "transwoman" can point to words like "congresswoman" as precedents. People who like the term "transsexuality" can point to "bisexuality," whereas those who prefer "transsexualism" can point to "lesbianism." Those who hate the usage of transgender or transsexual as a noun can point to the word "gay" (i.e., we don't talk about people being "a gay"), whereas those who do not mind will cite the fact that it's okay to talk about someone being "a lesbian" or "a bisexual." Those who hate the plural versions "transgenders" and "transsexuals" can stress how inappropriate it is to refer to "gays," whereas others can point to the frequently used plural words "lesbians" and "queers." The arbitrary nature of the "transgender" versus "transgendered" debate is discussed in Note 31.

34. "Gay," *Online Etymology Dictionary* (http://etymonline.com/index.php?term=gay); Daven Hiskey, "How 'Gay' Came to Mean 'Homosexual'," *Today I Found Out*, February 25, 2010 (http://todayifoundout.com/index.php/2010/02/how-gay-came-to-mean-homosexual); Cara Giaimo, "More Than Words: Gay Pt. 1—We're Going Gay," *Autostraddle*, January 13, 2014 (http://autostraddle.com/more-than-words-gay-pt-1-were-going-gay-215984).

35. "Lesbian," *Online Etymology Dictionary* (http://etymonline.com/index.php?term=lesbian); "Lesbian," *Wikipedia* (http://en.wikipedia.org/wiki/Lesbian).

46 – On People, Polarization, Panopticons, and #ComplexFeelingsAboutActivism

1. On social media sites (particularly Twitter), a hashtag is a word or phrase preceded by the symbol #, which denotes it as a keyword or search term for potential topics of interest.

2. Julia Serano, "a few thoughts on drag, trans women, and subversivism," April 27, 2014 (http://juliaserano.blogspot.com/2014/04/a-few-thoughts-on-drag-trans-women-and.html).

3. Jen Richards, "Moving beyond hurt: On Calpernia Addams, Andrea James, and Parker Molloy," *The Daily Dot*, April 28, 2014 (http://dailydot.com/opinion/trans-community-debates-middle-ground).

4. Reynolds, "RuPaul: 'I Love the Word Tranny'."

5. The specific articles in question include: Parker Marie Molloy, "Op-ed: What People Don't Get About Dismay Over Jared Leto," *Advocate.com*, March 10, 2014 (http://advocate.com/commentary/2014/03/10/op-ed-what-people-dont-get-about-dismay-over-jared-leto); Calpernia Addams, "Transphobic and Homophobic Slurs Don't Matter, but Our Response Does," *Huffington Post*, April 2, 2014 (http://huffingtonpost.com/calpernia-addams/parker-marie-molloy_b_5077322.html).

6. Andrea James, "I F*cking Hate @RuPaul," *Boing Boing*, April 4, 2014 (http://boingboing.net/2014/04/04/rupaul.html).

7. Zinnia Jones, "Open Letter: 350+ Trans Women and Transfeminine People Stand Against Calpernia Addams and Andrea James" (http://freethoughtblogs.com/zinniajones/2014/04/open-letter-100-trans-women-stand-against-calpernia-addams-and-andrea-james).

8. A panopticon is a circular institutional building (such as a prison) where one guard is capable of watching all of the inhabitants simultaneously. The philosopher Michel Foucault theorized about how people respond (e.g., by self-policing their own behaviors) upon living under such a constant state of surveillance. Admittedly, my claim that "social media . . . is one giant panopticon" is an imperfect metaphor, as instead of a single guard watching us, we are all constantly observing and reacting to one another. But I do believe that the knowledge that our peers are constantly observing our every move online coerces us into publicly "performing" our allegiances and condemnations in such settings.

9. "Hashtag activism" is a loose term for any attempt to use a specific hashtag to generate awareness and/or coordinate conversations about a particular activist cause. While it can be extremely effective in this regard, it can also be used to target individuals who (whether justly or unjustly) are perceived to have said or done something immoral or oppressive.

10. Amanda Palmer first garnered attention for her band The Dresden Dolls. Palmer is currently married to novelist Neil Gaiman.

11. Godwin's Law states that, "As an online discussion grows longer, the probability of a comparison involving Nazis or Hitler approaches 1" (i.e., becomes inevitable; https://en.wikipedia.org/wiki/Godwin%27s_Law). Jayne County is a trans musician who was briefly banned from the social media platform Facebook for using the word "tranny," and she later compared the incident to Nazi Germany—see James Nichols, "Jayne County, Transgender Icon, Allegedly Banned From Facebook For 'Transphobic Slurs'," *The Huffington Post*, April 17, 2014 (http://huffingtonpost.com/2014/04/17/jayne-county-transgender_n_5169324.html).

12. In Internet parlance, when a hashtag "trends," that means that a lot of people are actively using it.

13. Serano, *Excluded*, 288–299.

47 – Cissexism and Cis Privilege Revisited – Part 1: Who Exactly Does "Cis" Refer To?

1. For instance, Leslie Feinberg asked 1990s–era transgender activists to list who they felt should be included under the transgender umbrella; the list included: "transsexuals, transgenders, transvestites, transgenderists, bigenders, drag queens, drag kings, cross-dressers, masculine women, feminine men, intersexuals . . . androgynes, cross-genders, shape-shifters, passing women, passing men, gender-benders, gender-blenders, bearded women, and women body builders . . ." (Feinberg, *Transgender Warriors*, x). In *Gender Outlaw*, Kate Bornstein suggested that gay men and lesbians are excluded by society more for their breaking of gender codes than for their sexual practices, and for that reason, one could make the case that they are "transgendered" (although she quickly acknowledges that "this will offend everyone")—Bornstein, *Gender Outlaw*, 135.

2. I provide numerous examples of such claims, and thoroughly eviscerated this notion that transsexuals are inherently "conservative," "assimilationist," or "reinforce the gender system," in Serano, *Whipping Girl*, 115–160, and Serano, *Excluded*, 110–137.

3. Here is why this discrepancy in experiences exists: The very notion that people either "defy" or "conform" to gender norms is anchored in the assumption that they belong to one sex (i.e., their assigned sex) while expressing themselves in ways that are more stereotypical of the other sex. Indeed, this is how many (albeit certainly not all) non-transsexual transgender-spectrum people understand themselves. In contrast, transsexuals are typically misread as "misrepresenting" ourselves as members of the other sex. While I may understand myself to be a woman, others may interpret me as an "extremely effeminate man" or a "female impersonator." This is why coming out as transsexual is often more fraught than coming out in other ways. After all, if someone comes out as a gay man, or a crossdresser, or a drag performer, other people will likely see them as they see themselves (i.e., as gay man, a crossdresser, a drag performer, respectively). In contrast, when I come out to people as transsexual, other people may misinterpret that as me confessing that I am "really a man" rather than recognizing that I have simply shared the truth that I am a woman of transsexual experience.

4. Serano, *Whipping Girl*, 161–193. I also discuss how cissexism functions in Serano, *Excluded*, 113–132.

5. Serano, *Whipping Girl*, 20. A similar use of the term "cisgenderism" can be found in Y. Gavriel Ansara and Peter Hegarty, "Cisgenderism in psychology: pathologising and misgendering children from 1999 to 2008," *Psychology & Sexuality* 3, no. 2 (2012), 137–160. The terms "genderism" and "binarism" are also sometimes used in a similar manner.

6. Some might suggest that the cissexual/transsexual distinction is blurred by transsexuals who "pass" as cissexual. But as I argue in *Whipping Girl*, this is not actually the case: What these transsexuals experience is more accurately described as *conditional cissexual privilege*. It is conditional because they lose it as soon as they come out as, or are discovered to be, transsexual. Admittedly, the cissexual/transsexual distinction can become muddied when one retroactively views transsexual lives. For example, if someone consciously identifies as a man for many years before eventually coming to identify as a transsexual woman, did they experience cissexual privilege as a man in the past (since that's how they identified at the time)? Similar complications arise with regards to people who identify as transsexual for a period of their lives, but who later

de-transition. The distinction can also get murky in those rare instances when people who are ostensibly cissexual live as members of the other sex, not because they identify as members of that sex, but for some other reason—for instance, to gain access to a gender-specific occupation or to write a book (in the case of Norah Vincent's 2006 book *Self-Made Man: One Woman's Journey into Manhood and Back Again*). In such cases, these individuals may face many of the same allegations that transsexuals do (e.g., of being "deceivers" or "impersonators"), although it comes without having their underlying gender identities invalidated in the process. Anyway, these exceptions aside, I believe that the cissexual/transsexual distinction is relatively sharp compared to the vague open-ended nature of transgender (which makes it impossible to precisely define cisgender) and the fact that different transgender subgroups are often perceived, interpreted, and treated quite differently from one another (which results in a multiplicity of cisgender privileges that are differentially experienced within transgender populations).

7. Of course, this can drastically change if people discover that I am transsexual, at which point they are likely to misperceive me as an especially gender transgressive "man" rather than as a relatively gender-conforming woman.

8. This is discussed in Helen Boyd, "Jeez Louise This Whole Cisgender Thing," *en/Gender*, September 17, 2009 (http://myhusbandbetty.com/2009/09/17/jeez-louise-this-whole-cisgender-thing); A. Finn Enke, "The Education of Little Cis: Binary Gender and the Discipline of Opposing Bodies," in Anne Enke (ed.), *Transfeminist Perspectives in and beyond Transgender and Gender Studies* (Temple University Press: Philadelphia, 2012), 60–77.

9. I discuss some of these privileges in Serano, *Whipping Girl*, 161–193; Serano *Excluded*, 113–132. I also recommend Hazel/Cedar Troost, "Cis Privilege Checklist," *Taking Up Too Much Space* (http://takesupspace.wordpress.com/cis-privilege-checklist) for a thorough elucidation of such privileges as they play out in everyday life.

10. So-called "primary sex characteristics" are ones we are born with (e.g., genitals and other reproductive organs), and "secondary sex characteristics" are those that develop in response to sex hormones during puberty (or hormonal transition), e.g., breasts in women, facial hair in men.

11. I appropriated this nomenclature from Kate Bornstein's notion that some people are "transgressively gendered" (Bornstein, *Gender Outlaw*, 135), although I am using it in a somewhat different manner. To be clear, I am not insinuating that gender-transgressive people are inherently transgressive or purposefully engaging in transgressions. Frankly, most of us just wake up every day and are being ourselves, just like everyone else. Rather, it is other people who view our genders as transgressive (because they believe that there are "gender laws" and they perceive us as "breaking" those laws).

12. To be clear, I am not conflating gender and sexual orientation here. While members of a particular gender may vary in their sexual orientations (e.g., heterosexual, bisexual, homosexual, asexual), it is also true that there are societal gender norms regarding sexual attraction. According to these gender norms, a woman who partners with a man will be seen as gender conventional, whereas if she partners with a woman she may be viewed as gender unconventional or gender transgressive.

13. This helps explain certain disagreements that regularly occur within activist movements over what strategies will best serve the cause. For instance, the "we can't help it, we're just born this way" argument that many LGBTQIA+ people have forwarded can be quite effective in convincing people that our queerness or transness is merely unconventional rather than transgressive.

Yet this same argument (which some may take as an admission that we represent biological "mistakes" or "anomalies") can be a hindrance for those activists who are trying to make the case (often to a different audience) that we should be considered wholly socially legitimate rather than merely socially tolerable or accepted.

Here is another example: Back when I was first getting involved in trans activism in the early '00s, one of the most common formats for raising awareness about trans people and issues was to conduct "Transgender 101" workshops, wherein we discussed our lives, identities, and experiences. In other words, the implicit purpose of these workshops was to humanize trans people, and to convince others that while we may be "gender unconventional," we are not "transgressive" (i.e., immoral, unnatural, deceptive). In the years since, I have heard many trans activists argue that we should be doing "Cissexism 101" workshops rather than "Transgender 101" workshops. While I agree in a general sense, I think that it is important to recognize that such campaigns have very different audiences and goals in mind. A "Cissexism 101" workshop would encourage people to see trans people as just as socially legitimate as cis people, and while such work is vital, this particular approach might not be so effective on people who view us as downright "transgressive" and therefore unworthy of consideration in the first place.

48 – Cissexism and Cis Privilege Revisited – Part 2: Reconciling Disparate Uses of the Cis/Trans Distinction

1. Sometimes those who forward strict social constructionist stances on gender have argued the opposite—that if people's genders had less social significance than they currently do, there would be no need for transsexuals to transition, and that transsexuality as a phenomenon would cease to exist. I explain why such claims are misguided in Serano, *Whipping Girl*, 139–160, and Serano, *Excluded*, 117–168.

2. To the best of my knowledge, this idea of a "reverse discourse" originated in Michel Foucault, *The History of Sexuality, Volume I: An Introduction* (New York: Vintage Books, 1990), 101–102.

3. As I discuss in great detail in Serano, *Excluded*, 169–199, double standards are generally characterized by the *unmarked/marked distinction*, wherein members of one group (typically the dominant majority) are deemed unmarked—their existence and perspective are taken for granted, and they are viewed as unquestionable, normal, and legitimate. In contrast, the other group (typically a marginalized minority) is marked—they are viewed as inherently remarkable, questionable, abnormal, suspect, and illegitimate. In reverse discourses, this hierarchy becomes flipped: The marginalized minority's views are suddenly deemed unquestionable and legitimate, whereas the dominant majority perspective is deemed inherently questionable, suspect, and illegitimate (at least within the context of the reverse discourse). It should be noted that marginalized minorities may have very understandable reasons for viewing the dominant majority with suspicion, especially in cases where they are invalidated and injured by members of that group on a regular basis. Such instances will no doubt be cited by the marginalized group to justify their suspicion and delegitimization of the dominant group. My purpose here is *not* to dismiss such understandable reactions to oppression, but rather to point out how reverse discourse hierarchy-flips often impede more intersectional and inclusive approaches to challenging marginalization (as I discuss over the course of this essay and throughout my book *Excluded*).

4. Foucault, *The History of Sexuality, Volume I*, 101–102.

5. The *Wikipedia* entry for "identity politics" (http://en.wikipedia.org/wiki/Identity_politics) cites Barbara Smith and the Combahee River Collective as the originators of the term, stating that they used the phrase to refer to "a politics that grew out of our objective material experiences

as Black women." Identity politics may be carried out in different ways. For instance, people who share a particular marginalized identity (or identities) may describe the world and the obstacles they face from their particular vantage point, while simultaneously acknowledging that other identities and perspectives are also possible and legitimate (this contextual and intersectional approach is what I advocate for in Serano, *Excluded*). Other times, identity politics takes the form of a reverse discourse wherein a person's perspective and concerns only gain legitimacy if they are indisputably viewed as belonging to that particular identity. When activists talk pejoratively about "identity politics" (as third-wave feminists, and queer and transgender activists of the 1990s often did), they are usually referring to the negative ramifications of reverse discourses (which I describe throughout the course of this chapter) rather than the more general phenomenon of marginalized groups voicing their own unique perspectives (which seems to be an essential element of any activist movement).

6. Sometimes reverse discourses recognize more than one axis of marginalization, yet still manage to dichotomously divide the world into "oppressors" and "oppressed" based on identity. For instance, some activists regularly decry "straight men," thus designating them as "oppressors" of both women and queer folks. In the activist circles that I run in, I often see complaints about "cis white feminists," which depicts such individuals as "oppressors" of both trans people and people of color within the movement. There are countless other variations (e.g., understandable complaints about "middle-class able-bodied femmes," or "white middle-class trans activists," and so on). On the one hand, these conversations can provide important avenues to discuss relative privilege within movements, and how people who are privileged in certain ways may be viewed as ideal members of the group and/or advocate strategies that do not take into account the additional obstacles faced by multiply marginalized members of the group. Personally, I want to see more of these conversations. But at the same time, the tendency toward identity-based condemnations (e.g., blanket statements about "straight men" or "cis white people") seems to erase the fact that members of each of these particular dominant groupings, as well their marginalized counterparts (in this case, "queer folks plus women" or "trans folks plus people of color," respectively) are all heterogeneous, differing with regards to the privileges and marginalization that each individual member faces.

7. Judith Butler, *Gender Trouble: Feminism and the Subversion of Identity* (New York: Routledge, 1999), 19. And yes, it is true: I really did just cite both Butler and Foucault in the same essay.

8. This is especially true for Chapter 7 ("Pathological Science: Debunking Sexological and Sociological Models of Transgenderism") and Chapter 9 ("Ungendering in Art and Academia") of *Whipping Girl*. Notably, both of these chapters focus on challenging the assumptions and theories about trans people that have been forwarded by certain cissexual doctors, scientists, psychologists, sociologists, and gender and queer studies scholars—that is, those who are deemed by society to be "authorities" on trans people and lives. Their "expert status" ensured that anything that they claim about me will be viewed as having more legitimacy or validity than anything that I say about myself. The only way to effectively disrupt this power dynamic was for me to engage in a reverse discourse—i.e., by forcibly arguing that trans people are the only true authorities on trans identities, experiences, and lives. Toward the end of this essay, I will make the case that this is precisely the type of situation in which reverse discourses can be most effectively employed. However, when taken to the extreme, even this tactic can have negative and/or spurious consequences (e.g., see Note 9).

9. The potential problems associated with this became especially evident to me during 2009–2013, when revisions to the *DSM* (and specifically, the trans-specific diagnoses therein) were

being contested. Among those who were most directly active in that process—which included a mix of psychiatrists, psychologists, therapists, trans health providers, trans advocates and activists, some of whom were trans and others who were cis—the debate tended to break down along the lines of whether one believes that gender minorities arise as a result of pathology or natural variation. There were both trans and cis people on either side of this debate. Many of the folks on the natural variation side of the debate who I interacted with were cis professionals who had worked with trans clients for many years, and who were very knowledgeable and respectful of trans people's experiences and circumstances. And yet, during the *DSM* debates, I would often read or hear trans people outright dismiss these advocates solely on the basis that they were cis—the presumption being that because they were cis, they could not possibly understand trans people's circumstances and needs, and therefore, they must be attempting to silence or delegitimize us in some way. Notably, a couple of the trans folks I observed making these claims had only recently come out into trans communities, and based on their comments, they did not seem nearly as aware of the diversity of gender-variant people and experiences as some of the cis professionals whom they were condemning.

I offer this as an example of how simply being a member of a marginalized group does not automatically make one's perspective more righteous, nor does it automatically enable one to better empathize with or understand other members of their own group.

If we are honest with ourselves, we can all admit to having occasionally met a particular queer-positive straight person who happens to be more knowledgeable about LGBTQIA+ issues than certain queer folks, or a particular male feminist who happens to be more aware and critical of sexism and gender inequities than certain women, and so on. As activists, we may find such instances troubling. After all, if we openly admit that some cis people may be more knowledgeable about trans issues than certain trans people, it seems to open the door for any cis person (e.g., a cissexist bigot) to claim that they have superior knowledge over us. Alternatively, a more positive interpretation of such instances is that we (the minority/marginalized group) are sometimes successful in convincing and evangelizing members of the dominant group to relinquish that form of marginalization and fight on our behalf. In other words, such instances may offer us hope that a post-cissexist world might someday be achievable (a possibility that appears unobtainable in perpetuity from a strict reverse discourse perspective).

10. Serano, *Whipping Girl*, 13–14.

11. I discuss this throughout *Whipping Girl*.

12. While this can be true, sometimes the opposite holds true. I often find that comments directed toward cisgender people that imply that they are insufficiently feminine or masculine, or that they do not live up to female or male ideals or standards, seem to upset them far more than how similar comments affect me. I'd like to believe that this is because I am an out and proud gender-variant person who no longer buys into cissexist double standards. Or perhaps I have simply become desensitized to such comments, as I have had to deal with them far more than cisgender people typically do. To be clear, I am by no means claiming that trans people who are desensitized to cissexist comments are "more evolved than" trans people who are highly sensitive to such comments. I am merely pointing out that a foundational premise upon which the lack-of-history trope is based is not always true.

13. Accusations of appropriation often lie at the heart of the "slumming," "tourist," "dabbling," and "parodying" tropes. I have unpacked many of the underlying assumptions that fuel such claims in Chapter 44, "Considering Trans and Queer Appropriation."

14. Historically, the infiltrator trope has been used by cis feminists who oppose the existence of trans women in their communities, and by gay men and lesbians who oppose bisexual folks in their communities. Within trans communities, the infiltrator trope is most commonly evoked via accusations that the person in question is a "chaser" or "fetishist." While sometimes these labels are used to condemn those who sexually objectify or harass trans people, other times they are invoked to dismiss legitimate and respectful partners of trans folks (see Chapters 42 and 43). I have also been in trans spaces where people who I know to be crossdresser-identified (but who were not "dressed" on that particular occasion) were accused of being "chasers" (i.e., infiltrators) simply because their transness was not visible to others.

15. Self-identified "real transsexuals" (and their separatist ideology) are discussed in Chapter 37. Some people who take this position identify as suffering from "Harry Benjamin Syndrome" (described in Chapter 45, Note 28) rather than considering themselves to be "transsexual".

16. "I know it when I see it," *Wikipedia* (http://en.wikipedia.org/wiki/I_know_it_when_I_see_it).

17. bell hooks, *Feminist Theory: From Margin to Center* (Boston: South End Press, 1984), 26.

18. For the record, I believe that trans activism should not solely be concerned with "cissexist oppression," but rather challenge all forms of sexism and marginalization (for reasons I discuss throughout Serano, *Excluded*). And I believe that this broader intersectional approach to trans activism is consistent with the bell hooks quote that I am analogizing here.

19. Not all forms of "identity politics" constitute reverse discourses, as I discuss in Note 5 of this chapter.

20. I discuss this more in depth in the "stigma versus acceptance" section of Chapter 44.

21. I discuss this more in depth in the "integration versus separatism" section of Chapter 44.

22. All of these pieces are included in this book (Chapters 44, 45, 46, and 47) except for Julia Serano, "Regarding 'Generation Wars': some reflections upon reading the recent Jack Halberstam essay," July 13, 2014 (http://juliaserano.blogspot.com/2014/07/regarding-generation-wars-some.html).

There Is No Perfect Word (A Transgender Glossary of Sorts)
1. I introduced the concept of "word sabotage" (and differentiated it from the phenomenon of "word elimination") in Serano, "Regarding Trans* and Transgenderism."

Credits

Excerpts from "Issues of Psychiatric Diagnosis of Cross-Dressers" by Kelley Winters appear courtesy of the author.

Excerpts from "The New Yorker's Skewed History of Trans-Exclusionary Radical Feminism Ignores Actual Trans Women" by Mari Brighe appear courtesy of the author.

Excerpts from "Let's Talk About 'Tranny'" by Tobi Hill-Meyer appear courtesy of the author.

Acknowledgments

Most of the individuals who provided me with support and/or personally influenced my thinking and writing about gender, trans issues, and activism during the time period chronicled in this book are mentioned by name in the Acknowledgment sections of my two previous books, *Whipping Girl* and *Excluded*, so I will not reiterate them here, although I continue to appreciate the positive impact they have had on my life. Many chapters in this book were originally written for specific events or publications—I mention many of the relevant people, organizations, and media outlets in the chapter intros and in the Notes section, but here I'd like to thank them once again, plus extend my appreciation to any and all behind-the-scenes people I may have overlooked.

Over the last twenty-plus years, I have shared discussions (either in person or online) with a bajillion different activists and advocates, and have read more transgender-themed books, articles, etc., than I could ever possibly recount. All of them have helped shape my thinking about transgender people and issues. Even those with whom I continue to disagree have challenged me to more thoroughly consider and better articulate my own positions and perspective. Those writings that have had the most profound impact on me are all cited somewhere within the Notes section of this book and/or my previous books.

I want to thank lore m. dickey, PhD for taking and granting me permission to use the 2009 APA Protest photo that appears on the front cover. Many thanks to Amy Butcher, Jen Cross, Minna Dubin, Sinclair Sexsmith, and Katherine Mancuso for encouragement and feedback on book design, and to the following beta readers for their help with editing and proofing: Sheila Addison, Mari Brighe, Jeffry J. Iovannone, Jodie Peeler, Bailey Poland, and Erin Schultz.

About the Author

Julia Serano is an Oakland, California–based writer, performer, activist, and biologist. She is the author of two other books, 2007's *Whipping Girl: A Transsexual Woman on Sexism and the Scapegoating of Femininity* (which *Ms. Magazine* ranked #16 on their list of the 100 Best Non-Fiction Books of All Time) and 2013's *Excluded: Making Feminist and Queer Movements More Inclusive* (which was a finalist for the 2013 Judy Grahn Award for Lesbian Nonfiction). Julia's other writings have appeared in over a dozen anthologies, in magazines and news outlets such as *TIME, The Guardian, The Advocate, The Daily Beast, Bitch, AlterNet, Out, Ms.,* and *Salon,* and have been used as teaching materials in queer and gender studies, anthropology, sociology, psychology, and human sexuality courses across North America. As a scientist, Julia has a PhD in Biochemistry and Molecular Biophysics from Columbia University, and spent seventeen years as a researcher at the University of California, Berkeley in the fields of genetics and evolutionary-developmental biology. In addition to all this, Julia writes silly, surreal, sex-positive fiction under the pen name Kat Cataclysm, and creates and performs noise-pop music under the moniker *soft vowel sounds*. More information regarding all of Julia's creative endeavors can be found at *juliaserano.com.*

Made in the USA
Lexington, KY
08 July 2017